CSPFA

Daniel P. Newman

CERTIFICATION

CSPFA Exam Cram 2

Copyright © 2004 by Que Publishing

All rights reserved. No part of this book shall be reproduced, stored in a retrieval system, or transmitted by any means, electronic, mechanical, photocopying, recording, or otherwise, without written permission from the publisher. No patent liability is assumed with respect to the use of the information contained herein. Although every precaution has been taken in the preparation of this book, the publisher and author assume no responsibility for errors or omissions. Nor is any liability assumed for damages resulting from the use of the information contained herein.

International Standard Book Number: 0-7897-3023-5

Library of Congress Catalog Card Number: 2003109244

Printed in the United States of America

First Printing: November 2003

06   05   04   03   4   3   2   1

Trademarks

All terms mentioned in this book that are known to be trademarks or service marks have been appropriately capitalized. Que Publishing cannot attest to the accuracy of this information. Use of a term in this book should not be regarded as affecting the validity of any trademark or service mark.

Warning and Disclaimer

Every effort has been made to make this book as complete and as accurate as possible, but no warranty or fitness is implied. The information provided is on an "as is" basis. The author and the publisher shall have neither liability nor responsibility to any person or entity with respect to any loss or damages arising from the information contained in this book or from the use of the CD or programs accompanying it.

Bulk Sales

Que Publishing offers excellent discounts on this book when ordered in quantity for bulk purchases or special sales. For more information, please contact

U.S. Corporate and Government Sales

1-800-382-3419

corpsales@pearsontechgroup.com

For sales outside of the United States, please contact

International Sales

1-317-428-3341

international@pearsontechgroup.com

Publisher
Paul Boger

Executive Editor
Jeff Riley

Acquisitions Editor
Carol Ackerman

Development Editor
Michael Watson

Managing Editor
Charlotte Clapp

Project Editor
Dan Knott

Production Editor
Megan Wade

Indexer
Chris Barrick

Proofreader
Linda Seifert

Technical Editors
Kristina Fitzgerald
Ed Yanez

Publishing Coordinator
Pamalee Nelson

Multimedia Developer
Dan Scherf

Interior Designer
Gary Adair

Cover Designer
Anne Jones

Page Layout
Bronkella Publishing

CERTIFICATION

Que Certification • 800 East 96th Street • Indianapolis, Indiana 46240

A Note from Series Editor Ed Tittel

You know better than to trust your certification preparation to just anybody. That's why you, and more than two million others, have purchased an Exam Cram book. As Series Editor for the new and improved Exam Cram 2 series, I have worked with the staff at Que Certification to ensure you won't be disappointed. That's why we've taken the world's best-selling certification product—a finalist for "Best Study Guide" in a CertCities reader poll in 2002—and made it even better.

As a "Favorite Study Guide Author" finalist in a 2002 poll of CertCities readers, I know the value of good books. You'll be impressed with Que Certification's stringent review process, which ensures the books are high-quality, relevant, and technically accurate. Rest assured that at least a dozen industry experts—including the panel of certification experts at CramSession—have reviewed this material, helping us deliver an excellent solution to your exam preparation needs.

We've also added a preview edition of PrepLogic's powerful, full-featured test engine, which is trusted by certification students throughout the world.

As a 20-year-plus veteran of the computing industry and the original creator and editor of the Exam Cram series, I've brought my IT experience to bear on these books. During my tenure at Novell from 1989 to 1994, I worked with and around its excellent education and certification department. This experience helped push my writing and teaching activities heavily in the certification direction. Since then, I've worked on more than 70 certification-related books, and I write about certification topics for numerous Web sites and for *Certification* magazine.

In 1996, while studying for various MCP exams, I became frustrated with the huge, unwieldy study guides that were the only preparation tools available. As an experienced IT professional and former instructor, I wanted "nothing but the facts" necessary to prepare for the exams. From this impetus, Exam Cram emerged in 1997. It quickly became the best-selling computer book series since "...*For Dummies*," and the best-selling certification book series ever. By maintaining an intense focus on subject matter, tracking errata and updates quickly, and following the certification market closely, Exam Cram was able to establish the dominant position in cert prep books.

You will not be disappointed in your decision to purchase this book. If you are, please contact me at etittel@jump.net. All suggestions, ideas, input, or constructive criticism are welcome!

Ed Tittel

The Smartest Way To Study for Your CCSP Certification!

Exam Cram 2 offers the concise, focused coverage you need to pass your CCSP exams. These books are designed to be used as a refresher on important concepts, as well as a guide to exam topics and objectives.
Each book offers:

- CD that includes a PrepLogic Practice Exam
- Two text-based practice exams with detailed answers
- Tear-out Cram Sheet that condenses the important information into a handy two-page study aid
- Key terms and concepts, notes, exam alerts, and study tips

Check out these CCSP Exam Cram 2 titles:

**CCSP SECUR
Exam Cram 2,**
Exam 642-501
ISBN: 0789730251
$29.99

**CCSP CSVPN
Exam Cram 2,**
Exam 642-511
ISBN: 078973026x
$29.99

**CCSP CSPFA
Exam Cram 2,**
Exam 642-521
ISBN: 0789730235
$29.99

**CCSP CSIDS
Exam Cram 2,**
Exam 642-531
ISBN: 0789730227
$29.99

**CCSP CSI
Exam Cram 2,**
Exam 642-541
ISBN: 0789730243
$29.99

Buy
the pack and
SAVE!
Get all five CCSP
Exam Cram 2
titles with CDs
for just **$124.99!**
ISBN: 0789731118

Books are available online or at your favorite bookstore.

CERTIFICATION

www.examcram2.com

I dedicate this book to my dad and my daughter.

To my dad, who has made me independent, stubborn, and incredibly willful. You have given me the strength and ability to accomplish any task I put my mind to. Dad, I can't say it any other way—thank you from making me like you. Love, your son Daniel.

To my little Aranza, the most wonderful, amazing, and happy daughter a father could ever have. I am so proud of you and just want the whole world to know how special you are to me. All this hard work is for you. Love, your Papito.

❧

About the Author

Daniel P. Newman has been in the computer industry for more than ten years, working as a consultant, systems integrator, programmer, development manager, and technical trainer for projects all over the world. As a systems integrator, Daniel has implemented several computer and network solutions to a wide variety of industries ranging from titanium plants, diamond mines, robotic-control systems, and secure Internet banking. Exposure to countries such as Australia, Brazil, Canada, Chile, Malaysia, New Zealand, the United States, and the United Kingdom has given him expertise in presenting and implementing computer network solutions despite various cultural challenges and language barriers. Daniel is currently working as a senior technical trainer for Cisco and Microsoft products. He holds the following certifications: CCNP, CCDA, CSS1, CCSP, INFOSEC, MCSA, MCSE, MCDBA, MCT, A+, Network+, I-Net+, Server+, Security+, and Linux+. Daniel is currently pursuing a CCIE in security. In his free time, when he isn't trying to learn the details of computing, Daniel enjoys hiking and scuba diving with his wife and daughter. He can be reached at danielpaulnewman@yahoo.com.

About the Technical Editors

Ed Yanez has been in the computer industry for 14 years, working with Cisco products for 8 years. He trained on Novell, Windows, and Cisco and has worked for Zenith Data Systems; BCS/Tech Center; Cox Communications (high-speed Internet division); and KnowledgeNet, where he is currently a Cisco instructor teaching the advanced courses for DQoS, CSPFA, CSIDS, SECUR, CSVPN, CSI, CCIE R/S, CCIE Security, as well as others. Ed has also been a Cisco network troubleshooter and design consultant. He lives in Gilbert, Arizona, with his wife, Carolina, and two children, Jaycee and Stephanie.

Ed holds the following certifications: Security+, MCSE+I, CCNA, CCDA, CCDP, CCNP, CSS1, and CCIE #6784 (R/S and Security).

Kristina M. FitzGerald is a senior network engineer with Mitsui, one of the world's oldest companies with a network spanning 122 countries. She specializes in virtual private networks and multicast, integrating terrestrial and bi-directional satellite wide area networks. She has worked with Cisco technologies since 1996; has earned CCNA, CCDA, CCNP, and MCSA certifications; and is currently pursuing a CCSP.

Kristina earned a bachelor of science degree in molecular biology from the University of Wisconsin-Madison in 1991. Kristina is based in England, where she enjoys writing and traveling to Europe.

Acknowledgments

. . . .

I would first like to thank all the staff at Que Publishing for giving me the opportunity to create this book. To Carol Ackerman, thank you for your wonderful help and guidance, you are truly a gem! Thanks so much, Carol.

To my technical editors, Kristina Fitzgerald and Ed Yanez, thank you for your hard work in making this content accurate and producing a great book.

To Michael Watson, who can look at a page and magically reorder it into perfection. To Megan Wade, for being able to read and fix my sentences—now that is an amazing feat! And to Dan Knott who project edited all the changes and edits and helped us make those final deadlines even with those silly time zone issues. Thank you Dan!

I would also like to thank all my friends and family who supported me during this work. However, I would like to highlight four individuals; Ross Brunson, Matt Rawlinson, Joe Bates, and Dave Minutella. Ross, thank you for presenting me this opportunity—it has truly been an educational and growing experience! Thanks, Ross, and I hope you can get that keyboard driver working. Matt, you truly provided a huge help making this book happen by keeping me focused and on target when I needed a little push in the right direction—thank you, Matt. Joe, my long-time friend who I can always count on no matter how much time passes, thanks for your support and egging me on when I needed it. And finally, to Dave, who was there in the beginning and who was there in the eleventh hour. It has been great fun Dave, and keep up those obscure analogies—someone will understand them. Thanks, everyone!

Lastly, I would like to thank the most important person, my wife, who has always worked behind the scenes holding down the fort taking care of our precious daughter while I'm off traveling the world and working away on computer systems. You are truly amazing and wonderful, and I just want to say a special thank you for always being there. This book could not have been done without your wonderful love and dedication to us. Thank you.

Contents at a Glance

Table of Contents

. . . .

We Want to Hear from You!

. . . .

As the reader of this book, *you* are our most important critic and commentator. We value your opinion and want to know what we're doing right, what we could do better, what areas you'd like to see us publish in, and any other words of wisdom you're willing to pass our way.

As an executive editor for Que Publishing, I welcome your comments. You can email or write me directly to let me know what you did or didn't like about this book—as well as what we can do to make our books better.

Please note that I cannot help you with technical problems related to the topic of this book. We do have a User Services group, however, where I will forward specific technical questions related to the book.

When you write, please be sure to include this book's title and author as well as your name, email address, and phone number. I will carefully review your comments and share them with the author and editors who worked on the book.

Email: feedback@quepublishing.com

Mail: Jeff Riley
Executive Editor
Que Publishing
800 East 96th Street
Indianapolis, IN 46240 USA

For more information about this book or another Que Publishing title, visit our Web site at www.examcram2.com. Type the ISBN (excluding hyphens) or the title of a book in the Search field to find the page you're looking for.

Introduction

. . . .

Welcome to *CSPFA Exam Cram 2 (642-521)*! Whether this is your 1st or 15th *Exam Cram 2* series book, you'll find information here that will help ensure your success as you pursue knowledge, experience, and certification. This introduction explains Cisco's certification programs in general and talks about how the *Exam Cram 2* series can help you prepare for Cisco's Cisco Secure PIX Firewall Exam (CSPFA 642-521). Chapter 1, "Introduction to Cisco Certification," discusses the basics of Cisco certification exams, including a description of the testing environment and a discussion of test-taking strategies. Chapters 2–14 are designed to remind you of everything you'll need to know to take—and pass—the Cisco Secure PIX Firewall (CSPFA 642-521) exam. The two sample tests in Chapters 15 and 17 should give you a reasonably accurate assessment of your knowledge—and, yes, we've provided the answers and their explanations to the tests. Read the book and understand the material, and you'll stand a very good chance of passing the test.

Exam Cram 2 books help you understand and appreciate the subjects and materials you need to pass Cisco certification exams. *Exam Cram 2* books are aimed strictly at test preparation and review. They do not *teach* you everything you need to know about a topic. Instead, in this book I present and dissect the questions and problems you're likely to encounter on a test. I've worked to bring together as much information as possible about Cisco certification exams.

Nevertheless, to completely prepare yourself for any Cisco test, I recommend that you begin by taking the Self-Assessment included in this book, immediately following this Introduction. The Self-Assessment tool will help you evaluate your knowledge base against the requirements for the Cisco Secure PIX Firewall exam under both ideal and real circumstances.

Based on what you learn from the Self-Assessment, you might decide to begin your studies with some classroom training, practice with the hardware, or background reading. On the other hand, you might decide to pick up and read one of the many study guides available from Cisco or third-party vendors on certain topics. I also recommend that you supplement your study program with visits to www.examcram2.com to receive additional practice questions, get advice, and track the CCSP program.

I also strongly recommend that you install, configure, and play around with the software and hardware that you'll be tested on because nothing beats hands-on experience and familiarity when it comes to understanding the questions you're likely to encounter on a certification test. Book learning is essential, but without a doubt, hands-on experience is the best teacher of all!

Taking a Certification Exam

After you've prepared for your exam, you need to register with a testing center. Each computer based exam costs $125, and if you don't pass, you can retest for $125 for each additional try. In the United States and Canada, tests are administered by Prometric and VUE. Here's how you can contact them:

➤ *Prometric*—You can sign up for a test through the company's Web site at www.prometric.com. Within the United States and Canada, you can register by phone at 800-755-3926. If you live outside this region, you should check the Prometric Web site for the appropriate phone number.

➤ *VUE*—You can sign up for a test or get the phone numbers for local testing centers through the Web at www.vue.com/cisco.

To sign up for a test, you must possess a valid credit card or contact either Prometric or VUE for mailing instructions to send a check (in the United States). Only when payment is verified or your check has cleared can you actually register for the test.

To schedule an exam, you need to call the number or visit either of the Web pages at least one day in advance. To cancel or reschedule an exam, you must call before 7 p.m. Pacific standard time the day before the scheduled test time (otherwise, you might be charged, even if you don't show up to take the test). When you want to schedule a test, you should have the following information ready:

➤ Your name, organization, and mailing address.

➤ Your Cisco test ID. (Inside the United States, this usually means your Social Security number; citizens of other nations should call ahead to find out what type of identification number is required to register for a test.)

➤ The name and number of the exam you want to take.

➤ A method of payment. (As mentioned previously, a credit card is the most convenient method, but alternative means can be arranged in advance, if necessary.)

After you sign up for a test, you are told when and where the test is scheduled. You should try to arrive at least 15 minutes early. You must supply two forms of identification—one of which must be a photo ID—and sign a nondisclosure agreement to be admitted into the testing room.

All Cisco exams are completely closed book. In fact, you are not permitted to take anything with you into the testing area, but you are given a blank sheet of paper and a pen (or in some cases, an erasable plastic sheet and an erasable pen). You should immediately write down on that sheet of paper all the information you've memorized for the test. In *Exam Cram 2* books, this information appears on a tear-out sheet inside the front cover of each book. You are given some time to compose yourself, record this information, and take a sample orientation exam before you begin the real thing. I suggest that you take the orientation test before taking your first exam, but because all the certification exams are more or less identical in layout, behavior, and controls, you probably don't need to do this more than once.

When you complete a Cisco certification exam, the software tells you immediately whether you've passed or failed. If you need to retake an exam, you must schedule a new test with Prometric or VUE and pay another $125.

How to Prepare for an Exam

Preparing for any Cisco-related test (including exam CSPFA 642-521) requires that you obtain and study materials designed to provide comprehensive information about the product and its capabilities that will appear on the specific exam for which you are preparing. The following list of materials can help you study and prepare:

➤ The Cisco Secure PIX Firewall Advanced (CSPFA) v3.1 is a five-day, instructor-led training course provided by Cisco-certified trainers. More details can be found at http://www.cisco.com/pcgi-bin/front.x/wwtraining/CELC/index.cgi?action=CourseDesc&COURSE_ID=2617.

➤ The documents and material located on the Cisco Web site can help solidify complex topics! More details can be found at http://www.cisco.com/en/US/products/hw/vpndevc/ps2030/index.html.

➤The exam-preparation advice, practice tests, questions of the day, and discussion groups on the www.examcram2.com e-learning and certification destination Web site can be very helpful.

➤ Cisco Press can also provide a valuable list of books and resources for the Cisco product lines. For more details, see http://www.ciscopress.com.

What This Book Will Not Do

This book will *not* teach you everything you need to know about computers, or even about a given topic. Nor is this book an introduction to computer technology. If you're new to networking and looking for an initial preparation guide, check out www.quepublishing.com, where you will find a whole section dedicated to the CCSP certifications. This book will review what you need to know before you take the test, with the fundamental purpose dedicated to reviewing the information needed for the Cisco 642-521 certification exam.

This book uses a variety of teaching and memorization techniques to analyze the exam-related topics and provide you with ways to input, index, and retrieve everything you'll need to know to pass the test. Once again, it is *not* an introduction to Cisco PIX firewall devices or networking.

What This Book Is Designed To Do

This book is designed to be read as a pointer to the areas of knowledge on which you will be tested. In other words, you might want to read the book one time, just to get an insight into how comprehensive your knowledge of firewalls is. The book is also designed to be read shortly before you go for the actual test and to give you a distillation of the entire field of Cisco PIX firewall devices in as few pages as possible. I think you can use this book to get a sense of the underlying context of any topic in the chapters—or to skim-read for exam alerts, bulleted points, summaries, and topic headings.

I've drawn on material from Cisco's own listing of knowledge requirements, other preparation guides, and the exams themselves. I've also drawn from a battery of third-party test-preparation tools and technical Web sites, as well as from my own experience with the PIX firewall and the exam. My aim is to walk you through the knowledge you will need—looking over your shoulder, so to speak—and point out those things that are important for the exam (exam alerts, practice questions, and so on).

The 642-521 exam makes a basic assumption that you already have a strong background of experience with the Cisco PIX firewall device. I've tried to demystify the jargon, acronyms, terms, and concepts. Also, wherever I think you're likely to blur past an important concept, I've defined the assumptions and premises behind that concept.

About This Book

If you're preparing for the 642-521 certification exam for the first time, I've structured the topics in this book to build upon one another. Therefore, the topics covered in later chapters might refer to previous discussions in earlier chapters.

I suggest you read this book from front to back. You won't be wasting your time because nothing I've written is a guess about an unknown exam. I've had to explain certain underlying information on such a regular basis that I've included those explanations here.

After you've read the book, you can brush up on a certain area by using the Index or the Table of Contents to go straight to the topics and questions you want to reexamine. I've tried to use the headings and subheadings to provide outline information about each given topic. After you've been certified, I think you'll find this book useful as a tightly focused reference and an essential foundation of Cisco PIX firewall devices.

Chapter Formats

Each *Exam Cram 2* chapter follows a regular structure, along with graphical cues about especially important or useful material. The structure of a typical chapter is as follows:

➤ *Opening hotlists*—Each chapter begins with lists of the terms you'll need to understand and the concepts you'll need to master before you can be fully conversant with the chapter's subject matter. I follow the hotlists with a few introductory paragraphs, setting the stage for the rest of the chapter.

➤ *Topical coverage*—After the opening hotlists, each chapter covers the topics related to the chapter's subject.

➤ *Alerts*—Throughout the topical coverage section, I highlight material most likely to appear on the exam by using a special exam alert layout that looks like this:

This is what an exam alert looks like. An exam alert stresses concepts, terms, software, or activities that will most likely appear in one or more certification exam questions. For that reason, I think any information found offset in exam alert format is worthy of unusual attentiveness on your part.

Even if material isn't flagged as an exam alert, *all* the content in this book is associated in some way with test-related material. What appears in the chapter content is critical knowledge.

➤ *Notes*—This book is an overall examination of PIX. As such, I'll dip into many aspects of Cisco PIX firewall configurations. Where a body of knowledge is deeper than the scope of the book, I use notes to indicate areas of concern or specialty training.

Cramming for an exam will get you through a test, but it won't make you a competent IT professional. Although you can memorize just the facts you need to become certified, your daily work in the field will rapidly put you in water over your head if you don't know the underlying principles of Cisco PIX firewall features and configuration settings.

➤ *Tips*—I provide tips that will help you to build a better foundation of knowledge or to focus your attention on an important concept. Tips provide a helpful way to remind you of the context surrounding a particular area of a topic under discussion.

The PIX firewall has several features, and tips can provide information on settings or configuration items found in the real world.

➤ *Exam Prep Questions*—This section presents a short list of test questions related to the specific chapter topic. Each question has a following explanation of both correct and incorrect answers. The practice questions highlight the areas I found to be most important on the exam.

➤ *Need to Know More?*—Every chapter ends with a section titled "Need to Know More?" This section provides pointers to resources I found to be helpful in offering further details on the chapter's subject matter. If you find a resource you like in this collection, use it, but don't feel compelled to use all these resources. I use this section to recommend resources I have used on a regular basis, so none of the recommendations will be a waste of your time or money. These resources might go out of print or be taken down (in the case of Web sites), so I've tried to reference widely accepted resources.

The bulk of the book follows this chapter structure, but there are a few other elements I would like to point out, such as

➤ *Sample tests*—The sample tests, which appear in Chapters 15 and 17 (with answer keys in Chapters 16 and 18), are very close approximations of the types of questions you are likely to see on the current 642-521 exam.

➤ *Answer keys*—These provide the answers to the sample tests, complete with explanations of both the correct responses and the incorrect responses.

➤ *Glossary*—This is an extensive glossary of important terms used in this book.

➤ *Cram Sheet*—This appears as a tear-away sheet, inside the front cover of this *Exam Cram 2* book. It is a valuable tool that represents a collection of the most difficult-to-remember facts and numbers I think you should memorize before taking the test. Remember, you can dump this information out of your head onto a piece of paper as soon as you enter the testing room. These are usually facts that I've found require brute-force memorization. You need to remember this information only long enough to write it down when you walk into the test room. Be advised that you will be asked to surrender all personal belongings before you enter the exam room itself.

You might want to look at the Cram Sheet in your car or in the lobby of the testing center just before you walk in to the testing center. The Cram Sheet is divided by headings, so you can review the appropriate parts just before each test.

➤ *The CD*—The CD includes many helpful practice questions on topics covered on the exam. If you work through the questions on the CD, you'll understand the techniques that you're likely to be tested on.

Contacting the Author

I've tried to create a real-world tool you can use to prepare for and pass the 642-521 certification exam. I'm interested in any feedback you would care to share about the book, especially if you have ideas about how I can improve it for future test-takers. I'll consider everything you say carefully and will respond to all reasonable suggestions and comments. You can reach me via email at danielpaulnewman@yahoo.com.

Let me know if you found this book to be helpful in your preparation efforts. I'd also like to know how you felt about your chances of passing the exam *before* you read the book and then *after* you read the book. Of course, I'd love to hear that you passed the exam—and even if you just want to share your triumph, I'd be happy to hear from you.

Thanks for choosing me as your personal trainer, and enjoy the book. I would wish you luck on the exam, but I know that if you read through all the chapters and work with the product, you won't need luck—you'll pass the test on the strength of real knowledge!

Self-Assessment

The Self-Assessment in this *CSPFA Exam Cram 2* book will help you evaluate your readiness to take the Cisco Secure PIX Firewall Exam (CSPFA 642-521). It should also help you to understand what you need to know to master the topics necessary to become a Cisco PIX specialist. However, before you take the examination, you'll need to take a moment and assess your current skill level in this section.

PIX Certification in the Real World

Security is always an interesting and exciting field in the real world. Everyone seems to want more and more protection from hackers and other security threats, and firewalls help provide a small piece of the massive security puzzle required to protect a network.

Networking engineers are always taxed with the normal duties of maintaining a network solution for a company. The firewall configuration can be a tricky item to set up, configure, and maintain. Many companies might look outside to find a certified solution when installing a firewall system. Having a system set up by a specialist gives a company the assurance that everything is being done to help protect its network. Becoming certified on such a device and even becoming a specialist will increase your knowledge in security and your worth to a company and provide a better solution when you need to set up a firewall system.

As a Cisco PIX Firewall Specialist, you will have a better understanding of the threats facing a network and the countermeasures you can use to defend against them.

Choosing Cisco Systems Career Certification helps to expand your knowledge learned from the CCNA days into the next level of understanding security defense.

Putting Yourself to the Test

The following series of questions and observations is designed to help you figure out how much work you must do to pursue Cisco PIX Firewall Specialist certification and what resources to consult on your quest. Be absolutely honest in your answers; otherwise, you'll end up wasting money on exams you're not ready to take. You'll not find right or wrong answers, only steps along the path to certification. Only you can decide where you really belong in the broad spectrum of aspiring candidates.

The following two things should be clear from the outset, however:

➤ Even a modest background in computer science will be helpful.

➤ Hands-on experience with Cisco products and technologies is an essential ingredient to certification success.

Education Background

1. Have you ever taken any computer-related classes? [Yes or No]

   If yes, proceed to question 2. If no, proceed to question 3.

2. Have you taken any networking concepts or technologies classes? [Yes or No]

   If yes, you will probably be able to handle networking terminology, concepts, and technologies. If you are rusty, brush up on basic networking concepts and terminology, especially the OSI Reference Model, routing technologies, and TCP/IP.

   If no, you might want to read one or two books in this topic area. The two best books that I know are *Computer Networks, Fourth Edition*, by Andrew S. Tanbaum (Prentice-Hall, 2002, ISBN 0-130-66102-3) and *Computer Networks and Internets, Second Edition*, by Douglas E. Comer and Ralph E. Droms (Prentice-Hall, 2001, ISBN 0-130-9144-5). When it comes to TCP/IP, also consider Richard Steven's magnificent book *TCP/IP Illustrated, Volume 1: The Protocols* (Addison-Wesley, 1994, ISBN 0-201-63346-9).

3. Have you done any reading on general security concepts or information security? [Yes or No]

   If yes, review the recommendations stated in the first paragraph after question 2. If you meet those recommendations, move on to the next section.

If no, review the recommendations stated in the second paragraph in question 2 before you move forward to the next section.

Hands-on Experience

The most important key to success on the Cisco PIX firewall test is hands-on experience. If I leave you with only one realization after taking this self-assessment, it should be that you can't find any substitute for time spent installing, configuring, and using the various Cisco equipment on which you'll be tested repeatedly and in depth.

4. Have you installed, configured, and worked with Cisco PIX firewalls? [Yes or No]

   If yes, make sure that you understand ACL, VPN, fix-ups, and NAT.

   If no, I recommend you obtain access to at least one Cisco PIX firewall, so that you can exercise the concepts that you will be learning. I suggest a PIX 515 or at a minimum a PIX 506 model.

5. Have you installed, configured, and worked with Cisco Secure ACS and CiscoWorks? [Yes or No]

   If yes, I recommend brushing up on RADIUS, TACACS+, PIX MC, and downloadable access control lists.

   If no, I recommend you obtain access to at least one Cisco PIX firewall, Cisco Secure ACS software, and CiscoWorks before moving forward.

Before you even think about taking any Cisco exam, be sure that you've spent enough time with the related equipment and software to understand how to install, configure, monitor, and troubleshoot it. This will help you during the exam and in real life!

Testing Your Exam-readiness

Whether you attend a formal class on a specific topic to get ready for an exam or use written materials to study on your own, some preparation for the Cisco PIX firewall exam is essential. At $125 a try, pass or fail, you want to do everything you can to pass on your first try. That is where studying comes in.

I have included two practice exams in this book, so if you don't score well on the first test, you can study more and then take the second test. If you still don't get a score of at least 90% after these tests, you should investigate the practice test resources mentioned here (feel free to use your favorite search engine to look for more; this list is by no means exhaustive):

➤ *PrepLogic*—www.preplogic.com

➤ *MeasureUp*—www.measureup.com

➤ *Transcender*—www.transcender.com

For any given subject, consider taking a class if you have tackled self-study materials, taken the test, and failed anyway. The opportunity to interact with an instructor and fellow students can make all the difference in the world, if you can afford that privilege. For information about Cisco PIX firewall classes, use your favorite search engine with a string such as Cisco PIX Firewall Class or Cisco PIX Firewall training. Even if you can't afford to spend much money, you can still invest in some low-cost practice exams from commercial vendors.

   6. Have you taken a Cisco PIX firewall 642-521 practice exam? [Yes or No]

   If yes, and you scored 90% or better, you are probably ready to tackle the real thing. If your score isn't above that threshold, keep at it until you break that barrier.

   If no, obtain all the free and low-budget practice tests you can find (check for pointers at www.examcram2.com and www.cramsession.com or check out offerings from the for-a-fee practice test vendors listed earlier in this chapter) and get to work. Keep at it until you can break the passing threshold comfortably.

When it comes to assessing your test readiness, no better way exists than to take a good-quality practice exam and pass with a score of 90% or better. When I'm preparing, I shoot for 95%+, just to leave room for the weirdness factor questions that sometimes show up on Cisco exams.

Assessing Readiness for the CSPFA Exam

In addition to the general exam-readiness information in the previous section, there are several things you can do to prepare for the Cisco PIX firewall exam. As you're getting ready for the CSPFA 642-521 exam, visit the Cisco Web site at www.cisco.com. Its open forum and technical tips sections are great places to ask questions and get good answers or to watch for questions that others ask (along with the answers, of course). Also visit the www.examcram2.com and www.cramsession.com Web sites. You can sign up for question-of-the-day services for several exams, so watch for the PIX exam on these sites.

Onward, Through the Fog!

After you have assessed your readiness, undertaken the background studies, obtained the hands-on experience that will help you understand the products and technologies at work, and reviewed the many sources of information to help you prepare for a test, you'll be ready to take a round of practice tests. When your scores come back positive enough to get you through the exam, you're ready to go after the real thing. If you follow the assessment regime, you'll know not only what you need to study, but also when you're ready to make a test date. Good luck!

Introduction to Cisco Certification

. . . .

Terms you'll need to understand:

✓ Radio button
✓ Check box
✓ Careful reading
✓ Exhibits
✓ Multiple-choice question formats
✓ Process of elimination

Techniques you'll need to master:

✓ Preparing to take a certification exam
✓ Practicing to take a certification exam
✓ Making the best use of the testing software
✓ Budgeting your time
✓ Guessing (as a last resort)

No matter how well prepared you might be, exam taking is not something that most people look forward to. In most cases, familiarity helps relieve test anxiety. You probably won't be as nervous when you take your fourth or fifth Cisco exam as you'll be when you take your first one.

Whether it's your first exam or your tenth, understanding the finer points of exam-taking (how much time to spend on questions, the setting you will be in, and so on) and the exam software will help you concentrate on the questions at hand rather than on the surroundings. Likewise, mastering some basic exam-taking skills should help you recognize and perhaps even outfox some of the tricks and traps you are bound to find in several of the exam questions.

Besides explaining the Cisco PIX Firewall exam environment and software, this chapter describes some proven exam-taking strategies you should be able to use to your advantage.

The Exam Situation

When you arrive at the exam testing center, you must sign in with an exam coordinator and show two forms of identification—one of which mush be a photo ID. After you have signed in and your time slot arrives, you will be asked to deposit any books, bags, or other items you brought with you. Then, you will be escorted into a closed room. Typically, the room will be furnished with from one to six computers and each workstation will be separated from the others by dividers designed to keep you from seeing what is happening on someone else's computer.

You will be furnished with a pen or pencil and a blank sheet of paper—or, in some cases, an erasable plastic sheet and an erasable felt-tip pen. You are allowed to write any information you want on both sides of the sheet. Before the exam, memorize as much of the material that appears on the Cram Sheet (inside the front cover of this book) as you can and write that information on the blank sheet as soon as you are seated in front of the computer. You can refer to your rendition of the Cram Sheet anytime you like during the test, but you will have to surrender the sheet when you leave the room.

Most test rooms feature a wall with a large picture window. This permits the exam coordinator standing behind it to monitor the room, prevent exam takers from talking to one another, and observe anything out of the ordinary that might occur. The exam coordinator will preload the appropriate Cisco certification exam—for this book, that's exam 642-521—and you will be permitted to start as soon as you are seated in front of the computer.

All Cisco certification exams allow a certain maximum amount of time in which to complete the work (this time is indicated on the exam by an onscreen counter/clock, so you can check the time remaining whenever you want). Exam 642-521 consists of 65–70 randomly selected questions. You can take up to 75 minutes to complete the exam. To pass, you are required to achieve a score of 825 or better on a scale of 300–1,000.

All Cisco certification exams are computer-generated and use a multiple-choice format. From time to time, you might be prompted to enter actual configuration commands into boxes or into actual PIX simulations. It is important not to abbreviate the commands in any way when this type of question is posed. Although this might sound quite simple, the questions are constructed not only to check your mastery of basic facts and figures about Cisco PIX firewall configuration, but also to require you to evaluate one or more sets of circumstances or requirements. Often, you will be asked to give more than one answer to a question. Likewise, you might be asked to select the best or most effective solution to a problem from a range of choices, all of which are technically correct. Taking the exam is quite an adventure, and it involves real thinking. This book shows you what to expect and how to deal with the potential problems, puzzles, and predicaments you are likely to encounter.

Exam Layout and Design

Some exam questions require you to select a single answer, whereas others ask you to select multiple correct answers. The following multiple-choice question requires you to select a single correct answer. Following the question is a brief summary of each potential answer and why it is either right or wrong.

Question 1

What does AAA stand for?

- O A. Authentication, authorization, accounting
- O B. Authentication, authentication, accounting
- O C. Authentication, authorization, application
- O D. Authentication, accounting, access-control

Answer A is correct. AAA stands for authentication, authorization, and accounting. Therefore, answers B, C, and D are incorrect.

This sample question format corresponds closely to the Cisco PIX firewall exam format—the only difference on the exam is that answer keys do not follow questions. To select an answer, position the cursor over the radio button next to the answer and then click the mouse button to select the answer.

Let's examine a question that requires choosing multiple answers. This type of question provides check boxes rather than radio buttons for making all appropriate selections.

Question 2

Which licenses are supported on the PIX 515E model? (Select two.)

❑ A. Unlimited

❑ B. Restricted

❑ C. Limited

❑ D. Unrestricted

Answers B and D are correct. The PIX 515E can support three types of licenses: restricted, unrestricted, and failover. There is no such license called limited or unlimited. Therefore, answers A and C are incorrect.

For this type of question, more than one answer is required. As far as the author can tell, such questions are scored as wrong unless all the required selections are chosen. In other words, a partially correct answer does not result in partial credit when the test is scored. For question 2, you have to check the boxes next to answers B and D to obtain credit for a correct answer. Notice that picking the right answers also means knowing why the other answers are wrong!

These two basic types of questions can appear in many forms; they constitute the foundation on which all Cisco certification exam questions rest. More complex questions include drag-and-drop and Cisco device simulations. The drag-and-drop questions require you to drag and match question and answer pairs together. The Cisco device simulations asks you to configure a PIX firewall on a software simulation that behaves very similarly to the real firewall device.

Using Cisco's Exam Software Effectively

Unlike some exams by Cisco and other companies, the 642-521 exam software does not allow you to mark questions or review them later. You cannot skip questions or go back to them later. In fact, the test engine does not let you proceed if you have not selected an answer or have not chosen the correct number of answers.

With this in mind, time management is very important during the test. You cannot save difficult or lengthy questions to answer at the end of the exam. For this reason, it is helpful to monitor your progress by checking the clock periodically during the test. Be sure that you are one third of the way through the test when one third of your time is up. So, you must move through the test efficiently and not spend too much time on the simulation-style questions.

Exam-taking Basics

The most important advice about taking any exam is this: *Read each question carefully.* Some questions are deliberately ambiguous, some use double negatives, and others use terminology in incredibly precise ways. The author has taken numerous exams—both practical and live—and has missed at least one question in nearly every exam because he did not read the question closely or carefully enough.

Here are some suggestions for how to deal with the tendency to jump to an answer too quickly:

➤ *Be sure you read every word in the question*—If you find yourself impatiently skipping ahead, go back and start over.

➤ *As you read, try to reformulate the question in your own words*—If you can do this, you should be able to pick the correct answer(s) much more easily.

➤ *When returning to a question after your initial read-through, read every word again carefully.*

➤ *If you return to a question more than twice, ask yourself what you don't understand about the question, why the answers don't appear to make sense, or what appears to be missing*—If you think about the subject for a while, your subconscious might provide the details that are lacking or you might notice a trick that points to the correct answer.

Above all, try to deal with each question by thinking through what you know about the PIX firewall—the characteristics, behaviors, and facts involved. By reviewing what you know (and what you have written down on your information sheet), you will often recall or understand enough to be able to deduce the answer to the question.

Question-handling Strategies

Based on exams the author has taken, some interesting trends have become apparent. For questions that require a single answer, two or three of the answers will usually be obviously incorrect and two of the answers will plausible—of course, only one can be correct. Unless the answer leaps out at you (if it does, reread the question to look for a trick; sometimes those are the ones you are most likely to get wrong), begin the process of answering by eliminating those answers that are most obviously wrong.

Things to look for in obviously wrong answers include spurious menu choices or utility names, nonexistent software options, and terminology you have never seen. If you have done your homework for an exam, no valid information should be completely new to you. In that case, unfamiliar or bizarre terminology probably indicates a bogus answer.

Numerous questions assume that the default behavior of a particular device is in effect. If you know the defaults and understand what they mean, this knowledge will help you cut through many Gordian knots.

As you work you way through the exam, another counter that Cisco thankfully provides will come in handy—the number of questions completed versus the questions outstanding. Budget your time by making sure that you have completed one third of the questions one third of the way through the exam period and two thirds of them two thirds of the way through.

If you are not finished when 95% of the time has elapsed, use the last few minutes to guess your way through the remaining questions. Remember, guessing is potentially more valuable than not answering; blank answers are always wrong, but a guess might turn out to be right. If you do not have a clue about any of the remaining questions, pick answers at random. The important thing is to submit an exam for scoring that has an answer for every question.

Just remember that, as you select answers, you will not be able to return to them, so double-check your selection before moving to the next question.

Mastering the Inner Game

In the final analysis, knowledge breeds confidence and confidence breeds success. If you study the material in this book carefully and review all the exam prep question at the end of each chapter, you should become aware of those areas where additional learning and study are required.

Next, follow up by reading some or all of the materials recommended in the "Need to Know More?" section at the end of each chapter. The idea is to become familiar enough with the concepts and situations you find in the sample questions that you can reason your way through similar situations on a real exam. If you know the material, you have every right to be confident that you can pass the exam.

After you have worked your way through the book, take the practice exams in Chapters 15 and 17. This will provide a reality check and help you identify areas you need to study further. Be sure that you follow up and review materials related to questions you miss on the practice exams before scheduling a real exam. Take the real exam only when you have covered all of the ground and feel comfortable with the entire scope of the practice exam.

If you take the practice exam and do not score at least 95% correct, you need additional practice.

Armed with the information in this book and the determination to augment your knowledge, you should be able to pass the certification exam. You need to work at it, however; otherwise, you will spend the exam fee more than once before you finally pass. If you prepare seriously, you should do well. Good luck!

Additional Resources

A good source of information about Cisco certification exams comes from Cisco itself. Because its products and technologies (and the exams that go with them) change frequently, the best place to go for exam-related information is online.

Cisco's Web site is `http://www.cisco.com/warp/public/10/wwtraining/certprog/index.html`.

Introduction to Network Security Threats

Terms you'll need to understand:

✓ Denial of service (DoS)
✓ Distributed denial of service (DDoS)
✓ Reconnaissance attacks
✓ Access attacks
✓ Internal threats
✓ External threats
✓ Unstructured threats
✓ Structured threats
✓ Cisco Secure Access Control Server (CSACS)
✓ Cisco Secure Scanner

Techniques you'll need to master:

✓ Security policy
✓ Types of attacks
✓ Cisco security wheel

Introduction to security involves discussing the types of threats we face in our secure environments. Policies and processes help us protect our secure environments from threats in this ever-changing world of security. This chapter introduces a basic understanding of the types of threats we face and the policies and processes necessary for maintaining secure environments.

Network Security Threats

Data communications networks have served the academic, corporate, and government sectors for many years; however, the concept of security within these networks has only recently become a high priority. As data becomes readily available by connecting networks to public media or even other internal networks, the vulnerability of data to attacks and threats becomes apparent. Several distinct types of threats have emerged, and the network security community has developed new ways to protect us from these threats.

Types of Security Threats

Several types of threats exist in secure environments, but most of them can be classified into the following four main categories:

➤ Internal threats

➤ External threats

➤ Unstructured threats

➤ Structured threats

Internal Threats

Internal threats are more widespread than most people realize. These threats typically come from users who have legitimate access to the computers or networks they want to harm. Disgruntled or former employees whose privileged access has not been promptly terminated can cause a considerable amount of damage to a system. Lastly, these internal threats can be some of the most difficult to monitor and defend against.

 Results of surveys conducted by the Computer Security Institute (CSI) revealed that 70% of organizations polled admitted to security breaches, 60% of which came from within the organizations themselves (internal threats).

External Threats

External threats originate from individuals who are operating outside an organization's network. The individuals typically do not have authorized access to the network but use remote access channels such as dial-up or Internet connections to attempt security breaches. This threat is difficult to protect against and is always present when external access is provided by the company. If no Internet access or dial-up capabilities exist, you are safe from true external threats.

Unstructured Threats

Unstructured threats are caused by individuals commonly known as *script kiddies* who use prebuilt tools, programs, or scripts readily available on the Internet to launch their attacks. Script kiddies can be compared to kids joy riding in a car; their actions are motivated more by excitement than by any calculated thought or knowledge. If their tools fail to give them access to the networks they desire, they typically move on to another target, rapidly losing interest. Script kiddies might seem harmless, but the damage they can cause makes them potentially very dangerous. In most cases, unstructured threats are performed by individuals lacking an understanding of how their actions can impact themselves or the target network.

Structured Threats

By contrast, *structured* threats are performed by individuals who are fully aware of what they intend to do and who use programs and tools to attack networks or computers. The attackers have the ability to modify their tools as required and the skills to develop their own new methods of attack against unknown vendor vulnerabilities. Structured attackers can be driven by certain goals, including credit card number theft, software code theft, or intentional damage to a competitor's Web site and internal networks. In addition to their tools, these attackers also have the patience needed to penetrate the networks, using meticulously self-created programs or even social engineering tactics. Competitors, law enforcement, or other agencies might hire the services of structured attackers to acquire information, test security, or cause damage to specific networks.

Social engineering is a means of collecting information from people by fooling them; it's also known as *people hacking*. A typical example of this is calling or sending an email message to a corporate user, posing as a manager or an administrator, to extract information such as a user's password.

Three Types of Attacks

There are several types of attacks on networks. Some aim to gain information or access to restricted locations, whereas others focus on bringing down computers. These attacks are categorized into three main types:

➤ Reconnaissance attacks

➤ Access attacks

➤ Denial-of-service attacks

Reconnaissance Attacks

A *reconnaissance* attack is a form of information gathering from a network or computer system. Hackers might start mapping out a network using tools such as ping sweepers to locate active computers. Additional information, such as operating systems in use and available open ports, can be acquired through port scanners and Simple Network Management Protocol (SNMP). Reconnaissance attacks usually occur prior to a denial-of-service (DoS) or access attack.

Access Attacks

The *access* attacks involve collecting or obtaining access to data or networks that usually are not available to the individual. These attacks can come in several forms, including unauthorized data retrieval, unauthorized system access, and unauthorized privilege escalation. This form of attack can be accomplished in several ways; however, two common hacking tools used to gain access are password hacking programs and Trojan horses. The types of access attacks are described in the following list:

➤ *Unauthorized data retrieval*—The process of reading, writing, and possibly deleting normally inaccessible information

➤ *Unauthorized system access*—The process of gaining access to a system by exploiting a weakness in the operating system

➤ *Unauthorized privilege escalation*—The process in which a low-level user tries to gain a higher level of access such as administrator-level privileges

A *Trojan horse* is an impostor that hides inside an email message or another program. When the email is opened or the program launched, the Trojan horse is released, causing unlimited possible problems. This type of attacking mechanism (which Cisco might reference as a *virus*, on the exam) can delete files, steal passwords, give access to remote systems, or even download more Trojan horses and viruses.

Denial-of-Service Attacks

Hackers use *denial-of-service (DoS)* attacks when trying to disable, slow down, or corrupt a network, thus denying service to the network's intended users. Even though the hacker might not actually have a valid user account on the network computers, if network access is achieved, the hacker can launch an attack. This attack typically floods the targeted computer or network with traffic with the intention to disable it.

Distributed DoS (DDoS) attacks combine the power of multiple attacking computers, which focus their attacks on a single receiving computer or network. Because DDoS attacks can come from so many computers in different geographical areas, administrators have extreme difficulty repelling such attacks. For example, if a single computer pings a Web server, little stress is placed on the server. However, if 10,000 computers are pinging a Web server all at the same time, the server can be so busy responding to the ping requests that users accessing a Web page time out and never receive the page. These types of attacks are some of the most feared by network administrators because blocking all the attacking computers without blocking legitimate users is very difficult.

Denial-of-service and distributed DoS attacks send large amounts of useless traffic into a network to disable or cripple a server or network.

The Secure Network

Obtaining a secure network is not a destination, but a never-ending quest to provide the best protection while the environment is constantly changing. A secure system today could be a very insecure system tomorrow, as hackers discover new vulnerabilities and security holes. Security policies and processes help set rules and guidelines to assist in acquiring and maintaining the most secure network environment possible.

The Security Policy

The security policy is the core document or set of procedures used to describe how an organization's information, data, and services will be protected. The policy supports the organization's primary security objectives, as defined by who will be allowed access, who will be denied access, and what explicitly the policy aims to protect. Lastly, this document should define roles, responsibilities, and managed expectations and provide guidelines in the event of a security breach or noncompliance.

 RFC 2196, "Site Security Handbook," states, "A security policy is a formal statement of the rules by which people who are given access to an organization's technology and information assets must abide."

The Security Process

Security requires an ongoing process of evaluation and adaptation. What works today might not be secure enough tomorrow. Cisco has created the security wheel to represent graphically the continuously evolving process of security. This process entails securing, monitoring, testing, and improving the security policy and technical changes necessary to protect the environment. Figure 2.1 shows the Cisco security wheel.

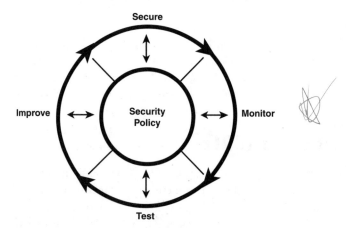

Figure 2.1   The Cisco security wheel.

The Cisco Security Wheel contains four basic steps to help visually display the process needed to maintain a secure environment. These steps are listed here:

- *global*—Creates a global list of addresses to be used by the NAT ID
- *route*—Creates any necessary static routes or defaults routes
- The show version command displays flash contents.
- The passwd command changes the Telnet password.
- The copy tftp flash command copies the images to the flash.

TRANSLATIONS AND CONNECTIONS

- The translation table contains layer 3 IP address mappings and is commonly known as the xlate table. Use the show xlate command to display the contents and the clear xlate command to clear the contents of the table.
- The connection table contains layer 4 TCP or UDP sessions. Use the show conn command to display the contents and the clear conn command to clear the contents of the table.
- To allow traffic inbound, you need to use an ACL or a conduit with a static mapping.
- NAT is dynamic inside to outside layer 3 IP address-to-IP address mapping. PAT is dynamic inside to outside layer 3 plus layer 4 IP address and port-to-IP and port mapping.
- The static command is used to create a one-to-one IP address mapping or a one-to-one port to address mapping.
- The nat 0 command tells the PIX not to perform translation on an IP address as it passes through the firewall. It is commonly used when public addresses are on the inside of a firewall and don't need translating.
- The static or NAT parameter called max_conns is used to define the maximum TCP connections permitted. *protecting internal hosts*
- The static or NAT em_limit parameter sets the maximum number of embryonic or half-open connections, which is used to prevent SYN attacks.

ACCESS CONTROL LISTS AND TRAFFIC CONTROL

- The conduit command always needs to be paired with a static command.
- Turbo ACLs are very simple to create and work on all models of the PIX except the 501. The 501 does not support Turbo ACLs. Turbo ACLs are typically not used on smaller firewall models because they require too much memory.
- conduit or ACL commands always need to be paired with a static command to permit traffic initiated from a lower security level interface to reach a higher security level interface.
- The order of the conduit and access-list commands is as follows:

- conduit permit tcp (DESTINATION)(SOURCE)
- access-list 101 permit tcp (SOURCE)(DESTINATION)
- Interfaces can have only one ACL attached to them in the inbound direction. Use the access-group command to attach the ACL to an interface. ACLs also take precedence over conduits.
- When working on large, complex access lists, object groups enable you to save on the number of entries needed to create the access list. The following are the object group types and commands:
- *object-group network*—Defines a group of hosts or subnets. The following commands create a network object-group:

  (config)# object-group network
  TheNetworkList
  (config-network)# network-object
  host 10.0.0.1

- *object-group services*—Defines a group of TCP and UDP port numbers. The following commands create a service object group:

  (config)# object-group service
  ThePortList tcp   *not service-object!*
  (config-service)# port-object eq
  telnet

- *object-group protocol*—Defines a group of IP protocols, such as IP, ICMP, TCP, and UDP. The following commands create a protocol object group:

  (config)# object-group protocol
  TheProtocolList
  (config-protocol)# protocol-object
  tcp *eg.*

- *object-group icmp-type*—Defines a group of ICMP messages. The following commands create an ICMP object group:

  (config)# object-group icmp-type
  TheICMPList
  (config-icmp-type)# icmp-object
  echo

SYSTEM MANAGEMENT

- The SSH uses the username of the PIX firewall and the current Telnet password.
- When you see the period symbol (.), the PIX is generating server keys to use for encryption.
- The PIX supports SSH version 1 with up to five connections.
- The ca zeroize rsa command clears all RSA-generated keys from flash.
- The ntp server command enables you to synchronize the PIX clock with an NTP server.
- The reload command is used to reboot the PIX.
- The logging host command *specifies* allows syslog servers to receive system messages.
- The logging trap command *specifies* enables the log levels for syslog traps *that will be forwarded to the syslog server.*

ADVANCED PROTOCOL HANDLING AND PIX FIREWALL FEATURES

- When in standard FTP mode, the inside client initiates the control connections to the FTP server and the server initiates the data connections. You use the `fixup protocol ftp 21` command to allow the PIX to create a dynamic return connection for the data returning from the server.

- When in passive FTP mode, the inside client initiates both the control and data connections, so the ASA will allow return traffic through the PIX without a need for the `fixup protocol ftp 21` command.

- The `show fixup` command displays the active fixup protocols on the PIX firewall.

- The PIX supports the SCCP, Skinny, SIP, and H.323 VoIP protocols.

- RTSP is a real-time audio and video protocol used by several multimedia applications, such as RealPlayer, Cisco IP/TV, Quicktime 4, Netshow, and VDO live. The `fixup protocol rstp` command enables RTSP support for NAT only.

- WebSense and N2H allow URL traffic filtering when fixup protocol HTTP 80 is enabled.

- The `filter URL` command is used to identify which traffic you want to forward to the URL servers.

- The PIX firewall can be a DHCP client and a DHCP server at the same time.

- The `dhcpd dns` command allows you to set only two DNS server IP addresses.

- When configured, PPPoE can connect to the service providers without user interaction.

ATTACK GUARDS AND INTRUSION DETECTION

- DNSGuard prevents DoS and UDP session hijacking by closing the UDP port after the first received DNS response.

- The SYN Floodguard protects hosts from TCP SYN attacks, which are half-open connections (called *embryonic* connections) from hackers. The embryonic limit is a parameter in the nat and static commands.

- Embryonic connections are half-open, three-way handshake connections that could be left open intentionally by a hacker. If the embryonic limit is reached, TCP intercept on the PIX handles any new handshakes until they are proven to be valid requests. This feature was introduced in version 5.2.

- The `fixup protocol smtp` command inspects SMTP traffic and allows only the following seven commands: DATA, HELO, MAIL, NOOP, QUIT, RCPT, and RSET.

- The shun command is used for IDS blocking of inbound source traffic.

- The PIX firewall contains a subset of the signatures of a full Cisco IDS system.

- By default, all IDS audit signatures are enabled. If you want to disable them, use the `ip audit signature <number> disable` command.

- The `ip audit interface <if_name> <name>` command applies an audit policy to an interface.

- False positives are alarms triggered by legitimate traffic that matches a pattern of a monitored signature.

- The embryonic parameter is used by the nat and static commands.

AAA CONFIGURATION

- The `privilege` command is used to assign a specific command to a specific privilege level.

- During the Cisco Secure ACS install, you are prompted for an NAS IP address called access server name. This is the IP address of the PIX firewall.

- The cut-through proxy enables you to control standard ports for HTTP, FTP, and Telnet services through the PIX firewall.

- Virtual HTTP is used to prevent caching problems with Web browsers.

- Virtual Telnet can be used when nonstandard port access is needed. HTTP, FTP, and Telnet are the standard ports.

- Named ACLs are shared among several users and are downloaded only once during authentication. Unnamed ACLs are not shared and are downloaded during authentication.

- Downloadable ACL can be performed only with RADIUS protocol, not TACACS+.

- AAA stands for authentication, authorization, and accounting. You cannot have authorization without successful authentication first.

- TACACS+ uses TCP for connections between AAA servers and clients, whereas RADIUS uses UDP connections.

- The AAA command parameter local specifies the use of the local database for usernames and passwords.

- The aaa-server command specifies the location of the AAA services: local, RADIUS, or TACACS+.

- When users fail authentication, their basic connections are dropped.

FAILOVER

- Non-stateful failover does not replicate xlate and connection table information.

- Stateful failover replicates xlate and connection table information.

- Stateful failover requires an extra LAN interface to interconnect the two firewalls.

- Cable-based configuration requires a special serial cable with one end labeled "primary" and the other end labeled "secondary."

- LAN-based configuration requires a dedicated switch or hub to interlink the two PIX firewalls. Do not use a crossover cable.
- LAN-based and cable-based failovers both support configuration on the primary firewall and stateful failover.
- When a primary interface fails, the secondary becomes active and inherits the primary's IP and MAC addresses. The primary moves into a fail or standby state and assumes the secondary firewall's IP and MAC addresses.
- Failover requires the hardware models, RAM sizes, flash memory sizes, and software versions to be the same.
- Failover is not supported on the 501 or 506 models.
- RAM configuration information is replicated automatically to the standby firewall.
- The write standby command can be used to force a replication of the RAM configuration in memory to the standby firewall.
- The failover active command is used to enable failover on the PIX firewall.
- Hello messages are sent across all the interfaces and, if two messages are missed, the failover process begins.
- The four failover tests are
  - NIC status
  - Network activity
  - ARP
  - Ping
- The network activity test monitors for traffic for 5 seconds. If no traffic is found, the PIX moves to the next test (the ARP test)—not standby mode.

IPSEC AND VIRTUAL PRIVATE

- Authentication headers (AHs) provide data integrity, anti-replay, and data origin authentication.
- Encapsulating Security Payload (ESP) provides data integrity, anti-replay, data origin authentication, and data confidentiality.
- The maximum number of transformations in the crypto ipsec transform-set command is three.
- The ip local pool command is used to create a pool of IP addresses used by remote access clients using PPTP or L2TP.
- Internet Key Exchange (IKE) is a hybrid protocol used to exchange keys.
- AH and ESP can both be used at the same time. ESP is performed first and then encapsulated inside the AH.
- The clear ipsec sa command is used to delete or clear all the current security associations.
- Security associations can be created using either IKE dynamically or a manual process.

THE PIX DEVICE MANAGER

- The Pix Device Manager (PDM) performs an interactive setup automatically when the PIX firewall has not been configured.
- The PDM is supported on Windows, Linux, and Sun Solaris operating systems.
- When unsupported PDM commands are found, the PIX firewall allows only the monitoring tab to be available.
- The five main configuration areas are Access Rules, Translation Rules, VPN, Host/Networks, and System Properties.
- The auto update configuration settings are configured on the System Properties tab under the Auto Update link.

ADVANCED MANAGEMENT

- Cisco Secure Access Control Server (CSACS) is used to manage AAA services.
- CiscoWorks is an enterprise tool used to monitor, manage, and configure Cisco devices. CiscoWorks' default port is 1741.
- The CiscoWorks Management Center for PIX Firewalls (PIX MC) uses a Web-based interface for configuring and managing multiple PIX firewalls and Firewall Services Modules (FWSMs).
- The PIX MC provides the capability to group devices with similar attributes. By using the Devices tab, you can create more groups. However, the default group is called Global Group.
- The PIX MC provides mandatory or default rules for groups or devices. Keep the following in mind:
  - *Mandatory rules*—These cannot be overridden, are applied at the group, and are ordered down to a device.
  - *Default rules*—These can be overridden and are ordered from the device up to the enclosing groups.
- The CiscoWorks Auto Update Server (AUS) is used to upgrade device software images and configuration files. The AUS's default port is 443.
- The Auto Update Server configuration tabs are as follows:
  - *Devices*—Provides summary information
  - *Images*—Displays information about images, PDM images, and configuration files and allows you to add and remove firewall and PDM images
  - *Assignments*—Enables you to change device-to-image and image-to-device assignments
  - *Reports*—Displays reports
  - *Admin*—Performs administrative tasks, such as changing passwords

The CSPFA Cram Sheet

This Cram Sheet contains distilled, key facts about Cisco PIX firewalls. Review this information as the last thing you do before you enter the testing center, paying special attention to those areas in which you feel you need the most review. You can transfer any of these facts from your head onto a blank sheet of paper immediately before you begin your exam.

INTRODUCTION TO NETWORK SECURITY THREATS

- The Security Wheel components are secure, monitor, test, and improve.
- Types of attacks include internal threats, external threats, unstructured threats, and structured threats.
- Types of attacks include reconnaissance attacks, access attacks, denial-of-service (DoS) attacks and distributed denial-of-service (DDoS) attacks.

BASICS OF THE PIX FIREWALL

- The types of firewalls include
  - *Packet filters*—These monitor source and destination layer 3 and 4 information with no session information and are based on ACL.
  - *Proxy servers*—These operate as middlemen, maintaining session connections between themselves and the client and between themselves and the destination systems. They typically run on other multipurpose operating systems.
  - *Stateful packet filters*—These monitor traffic as packet filters do; however, they record the traffic into connection and xlate tables to allow only requested traffic back into the system. The PIX uses stateful packet filters.
- The Adaptive Security Algorithm controls traffic flow through the PIX firewall, performing stateful inspection of packets.
- The PIX firewall supports WebSense and N2H2 content services.
- The security levels include
  - *Security Level 100*—This is the highest level and is set on the inside (trusted) interface.
  - *Security Level 0*—This is the lowest level and is set on the outside (untrusted) interface.
  - *Security Level 50*—This typically is set on the DMZ interface and can access lower security levels but not higher security levels.
- The PIX models are described in the following table.

VPN accelerator card

Model	501	506E	515E	525	535
Throughput	10Mbps	20Mbps	188Mbps	360Mbps	1Gbps+
Interfaces	2	2	6	8	10
Failover	No	No	Yes	Yes	Yes
VAC	No	No	Yes	Yes	Yes

- The PIX 535 interface slots are as follows:

Interface Slots	Bus Speed
Slots 0 and 1	64-bit/66MHz
Slots 2 and 3	64-bit/66MHz
Slots 4 to 8	32-bit/33MHz

- The PIX interface cards are as follows:

PIX-1FE	32-bit/33MHz
PIX-4FE	32-bit/33MHz
PIX-VPN-ACCEL	32-bit/33MHz
PIX-1GE-66	64-bit/66MHz

SETTING UP A PIX FIREWALL

- The firewall modes include
  - *Unprivileged*—Enables you to change the current setting to privileged mode or logout. Its prompt is `pixfirewall>`.
  - *Privileged*—Enables you to view restricted settings on the system. Its prompt is `pixfirewall#`. config t
  - *Configuration*—Enables you to change system configurations. Its prompt is `pixfirewall(config)#`.
  - *Monitor*—Enables you to upload images over the network. Its prompt is `monitor>`.
- The six basic commands include
  - `nameif`—Assigns a name and sets the security level to a hardware ID interface
  - `interface`—Sets the interface speed and enables the interface
  - `ip address`—Assigns an IP address to a named interface
  - `nat`—Creates a NAT ID that defines which local IP addresses will be translated on a specific named interface

1. Securing the environment

2. Monitoring the environment for violations and attacks

3. Testing the security of the environment

4. Improving the security policy

Step 1: Securing the Environment

Securing the environment involves the implementation of various tools addressing different points of vulnerability. Authentication systems, such as One-Time-Passwords (OTP) support and Cisco Secure Access Control Server (CSACS), aid protection by allowing only authenticated users into the environment. Encryption techniques can be used to disguise data traveling across insecure media; virtual private network (VPN) tunnels encrypted using Internet Protocol Security (IPSec) are a good example of this. Implementing firewalls, which filter incoming and outgoing traffic, can provide another layer of protection between a corporate inside network and outside intruders. Systems with known security holes should be kept up-to-date through the use of vulnerability patching. Physical security, which is often overlooked, involves keeping equipment secure behind locked doors. For example, if an intruder can physically access Cisco equipment, he can employ password-breaking procedures and have his way with your systems.

Step 2: Monitoring the Environment for Violations and Attacks

Monitoring for violations plays a critical role in determining how effective the secured environment is in supporting the security policy requirements. Using intrusion detection systems, such as Cisco Secure Intrusion Detection Systems (CSIDS), can provide an excellent solution for monitoring and blocking unwanted traffic. In addition, logging information such as user access and modifications to system settings can be recorded. Because the recording of log files can accumulate large amounts of raw data, you should store this data in a separate location, such as the Syslog server.

Step 3: Testing the Security of the Environment

After establishing your secure environment and security monitors, testing your environment is the only way you can ensure that your security measures are upholding your policy. Also, testing helps find new security holes in the environment before hackers find them. Cisco Secure Scanner is a tool you can use to test and identify such security holes.

Step 4: Improving the Security Policy

Improving the security policy within a varying and highly unpredictable external environment is an ongoing job. Continuously monitoring, testing, and identifying flaws and attacks against the network are imperative in refining and tuning the security policy. Vulnerability reports enable administrators to maintain an awareness of new potential attacks and should be considered during this step.

This chapter introduced the types of security threats that can be present against your networks. The security policy can be used to help you document what in your company needs protecting and how you will go about protecting that data. Cisco's security wheel demonstrates the ever-evolving enhancements you need to make to your security policy to keep you on the leading edge of protection and monitoring

Exam Prep Questions

Question 1

> The Computer Security Institute (CSI) conducted a survey showing that what percentage of the organizations polled admitted to security breaches?
>
> ○ A. 60%
>
> ○ B. 50%
>
> ○ C. 70%
>
> ○ D. 7%

Answer C is correct. The CSI conducted surveys that found that 70% of the organizations polled had security breaches and that 60% of them came from within the organizations themselves. Therefore, answers A, B, and D are incorrect.

Question 2

> What is the primary goal of a DDoS attack?
>
> ○ A. To gather secure information
>
> ○ B. To use many networks against a single computer
>
> ○ C. To stop a network from working
>
> ○ D. To collect information about possible active ports

Answer C is correct. DDoS attacks are intended to disable or slow a network or network services. DDoS attacks combine the power of multiple attacking computers and focus their attacks on a single receiving network. Therefore, answers A, B, and D are incorrect.

Question 3

> Using the Cisco security wheel, what are the four main steps?
>
> ○ A. Secure, security policy, monitor, test
>
> ○ B. Secure, monitor, test, improve
>
> ○ C. Security policy, monitor, test, improve
>
> ○ D. Secure, monitor, test, update

Answer B is correct. The security wheel contains four main steps: secure, monitor, test, and improve. These steps form a circle around the security policy and are used to maintain and update the policy as necessary. The security policy itself is not a step. Therefore, answers A, C, and D are incorrect.

Question 4

> Using the Cisco security wheel, which tool could be used to help test and validate your security policy?
>
> ○ A. Cisco Secure Intrusion Detection Systems
> ◉ B. Cisco Secure Scanner
> ○ C. Cisco Network Cniffor   ← does not exist
> ○ D. Cisco Secure Access Control Server

Answer B is correct. The Cisco Secure Scanner tool can be used to identify and test your security. Cisco Secure Intrusion Detection Systems is used to monitor traffic and possible attacks against the network, so answer A is incorrect. Answer C is incorrect because Cisco Network Sniffer does not exist. Answer D is incorrect because Cisco Secure Access Control Server (CSACS) is used as an authentication service.

Question 5

> What are the four security threat categories? (Select four.)
>
> ❑ A. Reconnaissance threats
> ☑ B. Structured threats
> ❑ C. Inexperienced threats
> ☑ D. Internal threats
> ☑ E. External threats
> ☑ F. Unstructured threats
> ❑ G. Experienced threats

Answers B, D, E, and F are correct. Experienced individuals perform structured threats, whereas inexperienced individuals known as script kiddies perform unstructured threats. Individuals working inside the corporation, such as disgruntled employees, execute internal threats. External threats are executed by individuals working outside the corporation. The other threats listed do not exist. Therefore, answers A, C, and G are incorrect.

Question 6

> What are the three categories of attacks? (Select three.)
>
> ☑ A. Reconnaissance attack
>
> ❑ B. Experienced attack
>
> ☑ C. Access attack
>
> ☑ D. Denial-of-service attack
>
> ❑ E. Unstructured attack

Answers A, C, and D are correct. Reconnaissance attacks employ tools such as ping sweepers and port scanners in an effort to discover active systems that could be targets in the future. Access attacks take advantage of authentication weaknesses to gain access to data and information. Finally, DoS attacks send large amounts of useless traffic into a network to disable or slow down that network. Answer B is incorrect because an experienced attack is not one of the main attacks, although it sounds like the structured threats performed by experienced hackers. Answer E is incorrect because an unstructured attack is not an actual attack, although it sounds like the unstructured security threat.

Question 7

> Against which type of attack would strong authentication be used as a first line of defense?
>
> ◉ A. Access attack
>
> ○ B. Password attack
>
> ○ C. Reconnaissance attack
>
> ○ D. Denial-of-service attack

Answer A is correct. There are several types of access attacks, including password guessing and the use of brute-force password programs. Brute-force and dictionary password cracking programs attempt to discover a password by either trying commonly used passwords or every possible combination of characters. The use of strong authentication can prevent the discovery of passwords during an access attack. Therefore, answers B, C, and D are incorrect.

Question 8

Which type of attack is a Trojan horse?

○ A. Access attack

○ B. Reconnaissance attack

○ C. Distributed denial-of-service attack

○ D. Denial-of-service attack

Answer A is correct. Trojan horses are one type of access attack. Trojan horses are typically programs hidden within other programs or email messages and can cause several problems, including sending an email message to everyone in the recipient's address book, deleting files, or collecting password information to be forwarded to a hacker. Therefore, answers B, C, and D are incorrect.

Question 9

Which tool would you use when using the security wheel monitoring step?

○ A. Access monitor

○ B. Cisco Secure Intrusion Detection Systems

○ C. Cisco Secure Access Control Server

○ D. Cisco Secure Scanner

Answer B is correct. During the monitoring step of the security wheel, Cisco Secure Intrusion Detection Systems can be used to monitor traffic signatures and help detect attacks. Access monitor does not exist, so answer A is incorrect. Cisco Secure Access Control Server is used to provide better security in the first (secure) step, so answer C is incorrect. Cisco Secure Scanner is used in the testing step, so answer D is incorrect.

Question 10

Network security is constantly changing. The security wheel consists of four mains steps to maintain effective network security. What do the four steps update?

- ○ A. Security personnel
- ○ B. The budget for the network
- ◉ C. The security policy
- ○ D. The resources needed to protect the network

Answer C is correct. The security wheel steps are secure, monitor, test, and improve. These steps are used to either apply or evaluate the security policy recommendations, and furthermore to update the policy where weaknesses exist. Therefore, answers A, B, and D are incorrect.

Need to Know More?

 Chapman, David and Andy Fox. *Cisco Secure PIX Firewalls.* Indianapolis, IN: Cisco Press, 2002.

 Visit the Computer Security Institute Web site at `http://www.gocsi.com`.

 See the Cisco Secure Encyclopedia at `http://www.cisco.com/pcgi-bin/front.x/csec/csecHome.pl`.

Basics of the PIX Firewall

Terms you'll need to understand:

- ✓ Inside (trusted)
- ✓ Outside (untrusted)
- ✓ DMZ
- ✓ Bastion hosts
- ✓ Packet filters
- ✓ Proxy filters
- ✓ Stateful packet filters
- ✓ Embedded operating system
- ✓ URL filtering
- ✓ Failover, hot standby
- ✓ Activation keys

Techniques you'll need to master:

- ✓ Security levels
- ✓ Software licensing
- ✓ Adaptive Security Algorithm (ASA)
- ✓ Cut-Through proxy
- ✓ Traffic flow
- ✓ Hardware differences between models

There are several areas of a network in a secure environment; the most common are the inside, the outside, and the DMZ firewalls that help divide and control traffic between them. Cisco has designed the PIX series of firewalls to be the primary devices for performing these functions. This chapter covers the basics of the PIX firewall areas that connect to the firewall—the trusted, untrusted, and DMZ.

Trusted, Untrusted, and DMZ Defined

The PIX firewall always contains trusted and untrusted areas that are used to identify the types of areas around the firewall. Firewalls with more than two interfaces can contain areas called DMZs. These areas are created to support servers that need to be accessed from an untrusted area without compromising the trusted locations. This section covers each in more detail.

Trusted

The term *trusted* is used to refer to users and computers that are in an area considered more secure or protected. This area is typically a private section of the network that needs to be protected against malicious hackers and other security threats. Security in the trusted area is established by blocking all traffic from less trusted sections of the firewall.

Untrusted

The term *untrusted* defines areas of the network that might contain malicious hackers or other security threats. One good example of an untrusted area is the Internet side of your firewall or even segments of your own internal network that are exposed to unknown access. Such an area could be a segment exposed to outside use—for example, kiosk computers on a storeroom floor.

DMZ

The *demilitarized zone (DMZ)* sits between both trusted and untrusted areas and usually hosts computers that need to be available to users from both of these areas. For example, a Web server in the DMZ can be accessed by people on the Internet, which is untrusted, as well as by users in the private trusted network. From the perspective of the inside, private, and trusted portion of your network, the DMZ area is considered untrusted, so traffic initiated from computers in the DMZ is blocked.

Areas of a Network

Areas of the network are defined by where the traffic is initiated from and where it is flowing to. For example, as traffic on the corporate side of a firewall flows toward the Internet, it is known as traffic flowing from the trusted inside (corporate) to the untrusted outside area of the network.

Firewalls help us divide the networks into the trusted, DMZ, and untrusted areas. The most basic firewall configuration contains only two interfaces—the inside (trusted) and the outside (untrusted)—and there is no official DMZ (see Figure 3.1). If two basic firewalls are stacked together, a DMZ area can be created between them, as shown in Figure 3.2. However, most high-end models of firewalls contain at least three interfaces and are correspondingly called *three-pronged* firewalls, as shown in Figure 3.3. The inside interface connects to the trusted area; the outside connects to the untrusted area; and the DMZ connects to the semi-trusted area. In all these types of setups, most environments contain a perimeter router used to provide Internet service provider (ISP) connection.

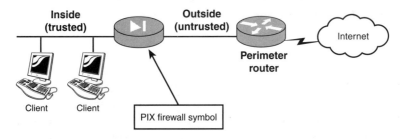

Figure 3.1   Standard firewall without a DMZ.

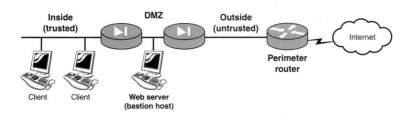

Figure 3.2   Stacked firewall with a DMZ.

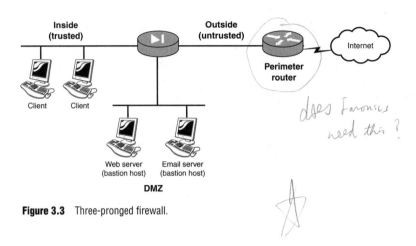

Figure 3.3 Three-pronged firewall.

Inside (Trusted)

The inside interface connects the trusted section of the network to untrusted areas such as the DMZ and Internet. It's worth keeping in mind that trusted areas might not always be made up of users needing protection only from the Internet; they might also require protection from other internal corporate users. For example, an engineering team might need to protect its secret widget network from the probing eyes of other users within the company; the computers hosting the top-secret widget data would then be attached to the inside interface of a PIX firewall.

Outside (Untrusted)

The outside interface connects the firewall to the most untrusted areas, such as the Internet. A firewall's primary function is to protect the DMZ and inside areas from undesired traffic originating from the outside interface. Traffic from the inside and DMZ can travel through the outside interface to the untrusted area, but traffic from the untrusted area is blocked from entering. Consider Jack, for example, a user on the inside interface who is allowed to connect to the Internet and check for the latest GPS software release dates. On the other hand, Jimmy the evil hacker cannot connect to Jack's computer because Jimmy's traffic is originating on the outside interface.

If necessary, a firewall can allow traffic initiated from the outside to connect to computers within the DMZ or inside area. However, you must manually configure the firewall to allow this traffic, and in doing so you effectively

allow a security hole. So, be careful. The more traffic you allow from the outside to inside or DMZ areas, the higher probability a hacker will find an open
IP address or port and send an attack toward it. So, typically a few holes are
created to allow only what is required through. For example, port 80 might
be opened to allow traffic to pass through the firewall to a Web server in a
DMZ area and all other traffic would be blocked.

Demilitarized Zone Details

The demilitarized zone is an isolated portion of the network that contains
computers called *bastion hosts*. Bastion hosts are systems that have been hardened by applying lock-down procedures, turning off unnecessary services,
and installing security patches. These hosts are placed in the DMZ when
access from the outside areas need to reach services on these computers.
Web, email, and FTP programs are a few of these types of services with
which you might be familiar. As an example, if Company B has a Web server that it needs to allow Internet users to access, Company B places the Web
server in the DMZ, hardens the system, and configures the firewall so that
outside users can have access to this single system. Because bastion hosts can
be accessed from the Internet or other untrusted areas, always remember
that Jimmy the evil hacker can potentially be attacking this system. So,
always have backups of your bastion hosts!

 Computers in the DMZ can be non-bastion hosts also, meaning they have not been
hardened with software patches and have had unused services and programs
removed or disabled. However, they are high-risk systems just looking for trouble
from hackers.

Perimeter Routers

Perimeter routers, also called *border routers*, provide the final connection to
the Internet or untrusted networks. Typically, these devices do not provide
many security features; their function is simply to provide an interface to an
ISP or a wide area network (WAN) connection. A perimeter router can, for
instance, connect an Ethernet local area network (LAN) to a digital subscriber line (DSL) modem—or, better yet, a high-speed, enterprise-grade
satellite link. They can provide a basic isolation from the ISP and also provide basic packet filtering to traffic before it reaches the firewall, adding to
your security suite.

Types of Firewall Filtering Technologies

Basic firewalls provide protection from untrusted traffic while still allowing trusted traffic to pass through. Packet filters, proxy filters, and stateful packet filters are some of the technologies used to accomplish this protection. Each one works in a different way to filter and control traffic.

In Table 3.1, the seven-layer Open System Interconnect (OSI) model is shown as a reference for the discussion of these three types of technologies.

Table 3.1	The OSI Model	
Layer	**Name**	**Examples**
7	Application	Telnet, HTTP, FTP, SSH, and so on
6	Presentation	ASCII, PDF, MP3, BMP, GIF, JPG and so on
5	Session	RPC, SQL, NetBIOS
4	Transport	TCP and UDP
3	Network	IP and ICMP
2	Data Link	Ethernet and Token Ring
1	Physical	Wireless, fiber, and copper wire

The next section describes in more detail the three methods of providing protection to a network. Each method works from the seven-layer OSI model to provide protection to a network or networks.

Packet Filter

Packet filters are the most basic traffic control mechanism of the three technologies. By inspecting layer 3 and layer 4 information, these filters allow traffic to pass through, provided that the source and destination information match the configured rule. The types of information in layers 3 and 4 that are used by packet filters include

➤ Source IP address

➤ Source port

➤ Destination IP address

➤ Destination port

➤ Protocol, such as TCP, UDP, IP, and ICMP

Packet filters can be implemented using access control lists (ACLs), which are commonly found on most Cisco IOS routers. Figure 3.4 shows a router between the private network and the Internet.

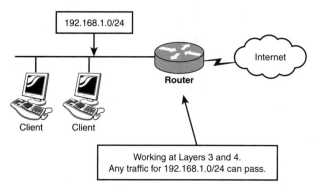

Figure 3.4 Basic packet filter.

The packet filter (Cisco IOS) examines every packet against the ACLs for matches. If a match is found, the packet is either permitted or denied passage through the interface. If a match is not found, the packet is implicitly denied passage. Packet filters process information only up to layer 4, making them very fast and efficient. However, packet filters don't track the TCP session information generated when two computers are communicating with one another. When computers first start to communicate using TCP, they perform a three-way handshake, which is used to establish the TCP session. Because these sessions aren't monitored by packet filters, the computers become vulnerable to spoofing.

Spoofing is the process by which a hacker modifies source information with the intention of bypassing a standard packet filter. The filter examines the packet, determines that the (modified) source is acceptable, and passes it. This enables a hacker to disguise *(spoof)* his attacks as legitimate traffic originating from a computer internal to the network.

Proxy Filter (Server)

Proxy filters, also known as *application proxy servers*, extend beyond the reach of packet filters by examining information from layers 4–7. A proxy server sits between the client and the destination working as a middleman between the two communicating parties (see Figure 3.5). It requires the client to establish a session with the proxy itself, which in turn creates a second session between itself and the destination. Consider, for instance, a client computer that requests information from a remote Web site. The client creates a session with the proxy server, which can then authenticate the user for valid access to the Internet before creating a second session between the Web site and itself. As the information comes back from the Web site, the proxy server examines layers 4–7 for a valid connection to the inside network.

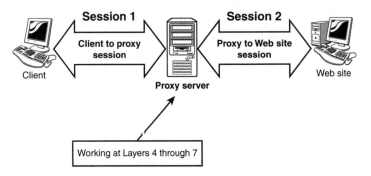

Figure 3.5 Proxy server sessions.

Although proxies can provide some of the most effective measures of protection, they can introduce speed and performance issues, particularly when a large number of sessions are being simultaneously negotiated. They are also built on general-purpose operating systems such as Unix, Linux, or Microsoft Windows, which can make them vulnerable to OS-related attacks.

Stateful Packet Filter—Stateful Inspection

This type of firewall combines the speed of packet filters with the enhanced security of stored session information typified by proxies. While traffic is being forwarded through the firewall, stateful inspections of the packets create slots in session flow tables. These tables contain source and destination IP addresses, port numbers, and TCP protocol information. Before traffic can travel back through the firewall, stateful inspections of the packets are cross-referenced to the session flow tables for an existing connection slot. If a match is found in the tables, the packets are forwarded; otherwise, the packets are dropped or rejected. The Cisco PIX firewall uses stateful inspection as its primary method to control traffic flow. Figure 3.6 shows the client and session flow tables being used.

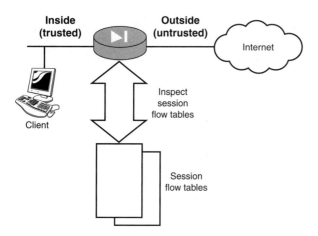

Figure 3.6   Stateful inspection.

Cisco PIX Firewall Features

Cisco PIX firewalls bring together a plethora of powerful features that make the PIX series one of the best choices in the appliance firewall market. Embedded operating system, Adaptive Security Algorithm, cut-through proxy, VPN support, URL filtering control, and hot standby failover capabilities are just some of the features that make it one of the best choices.

Embedded Operating System

The PIX firewall appliance is a dedicated system providing one main function, and that is to be a firewall. Unlike other firewalls that run on general-purpose operating systems such as Linux, Unix, or Microsoft Windows, the PIX series runs on a proprietary embedded operating system using a simplified kernel. This allows for both enhanced speed and protection against known operating system vulnerabilities.

Adaptive Security Algorithm

The adaptive security algorithm (ASA) is the heart of the PIX firewall. It controls all traffic flow through the PIX firewall, performs stateful inspection of packets, and creates remembered entries in connection and translations tables. These entries are referenced every time traffic tries to flow back through from lower security levels to higher security levels. If a match is found, the traffic is allowed through. Finally, the ASA provides an extra level of security by randomizing the TCP sequence numbers of outgoing packets in an effort to make them more difficult to predict by hackers.

Cut-Through Proxy

Cut-through proxy is the capability of the PIX firewall to control which users have access to the system. It does this by requiring a username and password authentication for users who want to use HTTP, Telnet, or FTP across the firewall. The authentication occurs only once, making the process extremely fast and efficient, especially when compared to the same type of technologies available on application proxies that authenticate every packet. If you need to support other protocols that fall out of the HTTP, Telnet, or FTP realm, you can use a technology named Virtual Telnet. This is covered in a later chapter.

Virtual Private Networks

Virtual private network (VPN) support by the PIX firewall is one of the core features that enables flexibility in a variety of environments. The PIX supports both site-to-site and remote-access VPNs encryption. This dual support provides the ability to connect two branch offices together using only PIX firewalls on each side (site-to-site), or to connect remote users to the office via a VPN across the Internet (remote-access). IPSec, PPTP, and L2TP are the main VPN technologies supported.

URL Filtering

In many situations, a set of valid and invalid Web site addresses might be an appropriate and effective way to filter network traffic. In response to this, Cisco PIX firewalls have integrated an advanced feature of URL filtering that enables the PIX firewall to work with content filtering services. These services allow the capturing of World Wide Web requests to support the enforcement of policies or monitor user traffic. For example, if Jack requests to go to www.JackGPS.com, the PIX forwards this request to a content server that references a database of valid or invalid Web sites. If the content server gives the PIX the okay, Jack is allowed to access this Web site. The PIX firewall supports only two content servers: WebSense and N2H2. These products enable administrators to create acceptable and unacceptable Web site lists for their users' Internet access.

Failover/Hot Standby

Today's applications are often mission critical, requiring the reliability of a resilient network infrastructure to support them. In response to this, Cisco PIX firewalls support hot standby failover features. *Failover* is the capability to link two PIX firewalls together, creating an active and a standby failover configuration. If the active firewall fails, the standby firewall assumes the IP and MAC addresses of the once-active, failed firewall. *Hot standby* means that this failover occurs without the need for a power reset that other systems can require. This failover capability helps provide a fault-tolerant firewall system with reduced human intervention.

ASA Security Rules

A PIX firewall has a very simple mechanism to control traffic between interfaces. The ASA uses a concept of security levels to determine whether traffic can pass between two interfaces. The higher the security level setting on an interface, the more trusted it is.

Security Levels

The ASA allows traffic to pass from trusted to untrusted, but not the reverse. Therefore, traffic can pass from interfaces with higher security levels to interfaces with lower security levels. Correspondingly, ASA blocks traffic from interfaces with lower settings from passing through to interfaces with higher settings. To illustrate, consider a common scenario where the inside interface has a security level number of 100 and the outside has a level of 0. The ASA allows traffic to pass from the inside to the outside; however, the ASA prevents traffic from flowing from the outside to the inside because the inside has a higher security level.

Figure 3.7 shows a three-pronged firewall with different security levels on each interface. Interface e0 has security a level of 0, which makes it the lowest security level of all the interfaces. Any traffic initiated on this side of the firewall will not be able to communicate with computers on the other side of the firewall.

The following are the primary security levels created and used on the PIX firewall:

➤ *Security level 100*—The highest possible level, it is used by the inside interface by default. Using the trusted-untrusted terminology, this level is considered the most trusted.

➤ *Security level 0*—The lowest possible level, it's used by the outside interface by default, making it the most untrusted interface. Traffic can pass from this interface to other interfaces only if manually configured to do so.

➤ *Security levels 1–99*—Can be assigned to any other interface on the PIX. On a three-pronged PIX firewall, the inside is typically 100, the outside is 0, and the third interface could be 50. Traffic from interfaces between 1 and 99 can pass through to the outside (0), but it is prevented from passing to the inside (100). This is because the interface has a lower security level setting than the inside.

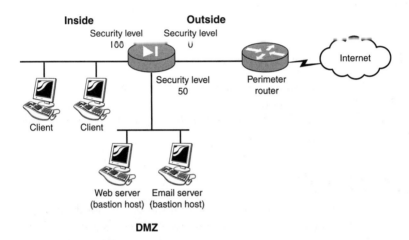

Figure 3.7 Security levels.

 Security levels are a very import concept with PIX configuration. Remember, only higher security-level traffic can pass to lower security-level interfaces by default. The default value for the inside interface is 100, and the outside value is 0.

Connection and Translation Tables

The ASA uses two tables to track traffic flowing through the PIX—the connection table and the translation (xlate) table. The *connection* table contains a reference to the session connection between the two computers that are talking. The *translation* table maintains a reference between the inside IP address and the translated global IP address. These topics are covered in further detail later.

PIX Firewall Models

The Cisco PIX firewall comes in several models. Unlike the Cisco router series that requires different software for each model, software on the PIX is the same for all models. The only differences across firewall models are size of the unit, power supply capabilities, number of interfaces supported, and failover capabilities.

The four main PIX models are listed here. Table 3.2 displays the firewall model specifications in detail.

The models are as follows:

➤ PIX 501

➤ PIX 506E

➤ PIX 515E

➤ PIX 525

➤ PIX 535

Table 3.2 displays the default capabilities found on the PIX firewall hardware models.

Table 3.2	PIX Firewall Models				
Model	501	506E	515E	525	535
Processor	133MHz	300MHz	433MHz	600MHz	1GHz
RAM	16MB	32MB	32MB, 64MB	256MB	1GB
Flash memory	8MB	8MB	16MB	16MB	16MB
Throughput	10Mbps	20Mbps	188Mbps	360Mbps	1Gbps
Connections	7,500	25,000	130,000	280,000	500,000
Max. number of interfaces	1, + 1 four-port switch	2	6	8	10
Failover	No	No	Yes	Yes	Yes
VAC available	No	No	Yes	Yes	Yes
Solution for	Small-office/home-office (SOHO)	Remote-office/branch-office (ROBO)	Medium-size office	Enterprise	Enterprise or solution provider

Make sure you know for which solution each firewall model is designed and the simultaneous connections each supports.

Cisco PIX 501 Firewall

The PIX 501 is the entry model into Cisco's firewall family and is intended for small-office/home-office (SOHO) locations. This model has a fixed physical configuration that supports two network interfaces and a single console port for configuration. The inside interface, Ethernet 1, contains a four-port 10/100Mbps Ethernet switch, and the outside interface, Ethernet 0, is a single 10Mbps Ethernet port. The model runs on a 133MHz AMD processor with 16MB of RAM and 8MB of flash memory. The 501, like all PIX firewalls, supports VPN capabilities. A free license for DES IPSec encryption can be acquired; alternatively, for a fee an upgrade to triple DES–level encryption can be obtained. The basic model comes with a 10-user license with VPN DES IPSec support out of the box and can be later upgraded to a 50-user license as required for enhanced scalability.

Figure 3.8 shows the interfaces and console port on the back of the PIX 501. Interfaces 1, 2, 3, and 4 are a four-port switch for the Ethernet 1 interface.

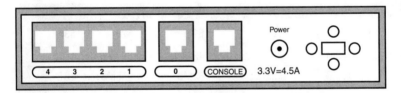

Figure 3.8   The PIX 501's back panel.

Cisco PIX 506E Firewall

The 506E is a newer, enhanced model of the earlier 506 versions and is intended for remote-office/branch-office (ROBO) locations. This model, similar to the 501, has a fixed physical configuration, supporting two 10/100MHz Ethernet interfaces and a single console port for configuration. The 506E, however, has a 300MHz Intel Celeron processor with 32MB of RAM and 8MB of flash memory. The throughput and processor speed are double that of the 501 model, resulting in a compact and efficient firewall package. Lastly, a USB port is reserved for future enhancements.

Figure 3.9 shows the interfaces on the back of a PIX 506. Notice it has only a single interface on Ethernet 1, unlike the PIX 501 that contains a four-port switch for Ethernet 1.

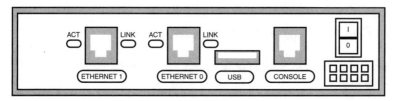

Figure 3.9   The PIX 506's back panel.

Cisco PIX 515E Firewall

The 515E is a newer, enhanced model of the earlier 515 versions and is intended for the small to medium-size enterprise market. The model comes in a 1U form factor and has expandable capability that allows for up to six interfaces, as well as failover features and a VPN accelerator card (VAC) available with additional licensing options. The 515E uses a 433MHz Intel Celeron processor with 32MB or 64MB of RAM and 16MB of flash memory.

Figure 3.10 shows an example to the PIX 515E back view. The 15-pin connection on the right is used for the failover cable that can be connected to another PIX 515E to provide failover capability. The USB port is used for future enhancements.

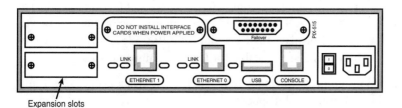

Expansion slots

Figure 3.10   The PIX 515E's back panel.

Cisco PIX 525 Firewall

The 525 is the replacement model for its predecessor, the PIX 520. The 520 actually contained a floppy drive, whereas the 525 does not. The model is extremely powerful and is designed for large enterprise environments in which speed and failover capabilities are a must. It ships in a 2U form factor with expandability that allows for up to eight interfaces, failover features, and a VAC. The PIX 525 uses a 600MHz Intel Pentium III processor with up to 256MB of RAM and 16MB of flash memory. The license schema on this model is based on the number of interfaces and failover support. Lastly, it contains a USB port reserved for future enhancements.

Figure 3.11 displays a typical 525 PIX firewall back view.

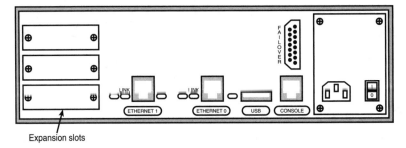

Expansion slots

Figure 3.11 The PIX 525's back panel.

Cisco PIX 535 Firewall

The 535 is Cisco's enterprise-class firewall. This model is a 3U form factor that is highly configurable, supporting up to 10 interfaces, some of which can be fiber interfaces. The specification sheet boasts 1Gbps throughput; 500,000 concurrent connections; and 2,000 VPN tunnels. The speed and power of this firewall come from the 1GHz Intel Pentium III with 1GB of RAM. The 535 can contain four 66MHz/64-bit PCI slots and five 33MHz/32-bit PCI slots. The PIX 535 also contains dual redundant power supplies. Figure 3.12 displays the back view of a PIX 535. As you can see in Figure 3.12, three buses are available for Cisco expansion cards.

The PIX 535 supports two main types of PCI interface slots: 32-bit and 64-bit. Table 3.3 displays slot speeds.

Table 3.3 PIX 535 Interface Slots	
Interface Slots	**Bus Speed**
Slots 0 and 1	64-bit/66MHz
Slots 2 and 3	64-bit/66MHz
Slots 4–8	32-bit/33MHz

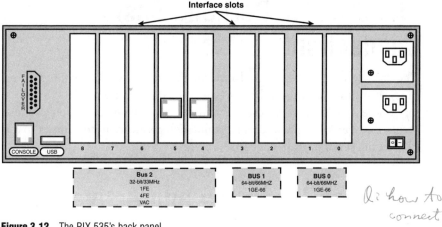

Figure 3.12   The PIX 535's back panel.

Q: how to connect 10 interfaces?

Cisco PIX Expansion Cards

Cisco provides several optional cards that can expand the PIX's capabilities and performance. The PIX-4FE card is a 33MHz/32-bit card that adds four Ethernet interfaces to your PIX. The PIX-VPN-ACCEL is designed to offload encryption and decryption from the main processor by using an onboard processor and hardware random number generator to increase VPN tunneling performance.

Table 3.4 displays several of the Cisco proprietary cards and their bus speeds.

Table 3.4 PIX Expansion Cards		
Interface Card	**Maximum Bus Speed**	**Description**
PIX-1FE	32-bit/33MHz	Single-port 10/100 Fast Ethernet PCI expansion card
PIX-4FE	32-bit/33MHz	Four-port 10/100 Fast Ethernet PCI expansion card
PIX-VPN-ACCEL	32-bit/33MHz	3DES IPSec hardware VAC
PIX-1GE-66	64-bit/66MHz	Single-port Gigabit Ethernet 64-bit/66MHz PCI expansion card

The PIX-4FE and PIX-VPN-ACCEL 32-bit/33MHz cards can be installed only in 32-bit/33MHz slots. Other 32-bit/33MHz cards can be installed in either 66MHz slots or 33MHz slots.

The Console Port and Basic Connection

The console port is a serial null-modem connection used to configure the PIX. Most models, such as the ones mentioned here, use an RJ-45 connector, whereas older models use a standard DB-9 connector. You can use HyperTerm or other ANSI terminal emulation applications to connect to the PIX via the serial port on your PC.

Software Licensing and Activation Keys

The PIX firewall licensing is unique compared to some of Cisco's other products. PIX licensing usually doesn't require the installation of new software, unlike licensing for Cisco routers. The PIX uses activation keys to enable extra features such as adding more RAM, failover, extra interface cards, and so on. Activation keys are acquired by sending Cisco your serial number and the feature you want enabled (oh, and don't forget the cash, too!). Cisco then sends you a unique activation key computed from both the hardware serial number and the required new feature. Because the activation key is unique to each feature, you must get a new activation key if you replace your flash.

Displaying activation key information is straightforward. By using the show version command, you can display information such as the software version, hardware platform, enabled licensed features, serial number, and running activation key. Listing 3.1 displays the show version command and its output.

Listing 3.1 The show version Command

```
Pixfirewall# show version

Cisco PIX Firewall Version 6.2(2)
Cisco PIX Device Manager Version 2.1(1)
Compiled on Fri 07-Jun-02 17:49 by morlee
pixfirewall up 16 days 21 hours
Hardware:   PIX-501, 16 MB RAM, CPU Am5x86 133 MHz
Flash E28F640J3 @ 0x3000000, 8MB
BIOS Flash E28F640J3 @ 0xfffd8000, 128KB
0: ethernet0: address is 000c.3085.5640, irq 9
1: ethernet1: address is 000c.3085.5641, irq 10
Licensed Features:
Failover:          Disabled
VPN-DES:           Enabled
VPN-3DES:          Disabled
```

Listing 3.1   The show version Command (continued)

```
Maximum Interfaces: 2
Cut-through Proxy:  Enabled
Guards:             Enabled
URL-filtering:      Enabled
Inside Hosts:       10
Throughput:         Limited
IKE peers:          5

Serial Number: 807082785 (0x301b1b21)
Running Activation Key: 0x2d284af1 0xd032aa26 0x38b7db1f 0x70cfa8ee
Configuration last modified by enable_15 at 09:57:56.047 UTC Sun Mar 30 2003
```

The show activation-key command shows information about the activation key. Listing 3.2 displays the output of this command.

Listing 3.2   The show activation-key Command

```
pixfirewall# show activation-key
Serial Number: 807082785 (0x301b1b21)
Running Activation Key: 0x2d284af1 0xd032aa26 0x38b7db1f 0x70cfa8ee
Licensed Features:
Failover:           Disabled
VPN-DES:            Enabled
VPN-3DES:           Disabled
Maximum Interfaces: 2
Cut-through Proxy:  Enabled
Guards:             Enabled
URL-filtering:      Enabled
Inside Hosts:       10
Throughput:         Limited
IKE peers:          5
```

Updating the activation keys on the latest software release is a simple process. After you have received your new activation key from Cisco, you can use the activation-key command, like so:

```
activation-key <activation-key-four-tuple>
```

Here's another example of the activation-key command in use:

```
Pixfirewall(config)# activation-key 2d284af1 d032aa26 38b7db1f 70cfa8ee
```

Licensing

Cisco has three main types of licenses: restricted, unrestricted, and failover. Based on the original purchase agreement, *restricted* licenses support only certain features and allow a fixed number of users. As you need more functionality, you can just bolt them on by ordering activation keys. An *unrestricted* license is exactly what it sounds like: You get all the features your PIX can provide. However, as expected, these licenses can be expensive. Lastly, *failover* licenses enable operation as an active or standby PIX firewall and are necessary only in failover scenarios. Additional licenses outside of the main three are available to address more advanced encryption features. For example, various licenses are available if you want to enable DES, triple DES (3DES), or AES encryption.

Exam Prep Questions

Question 1

What is the maximum number of interfaces the PIX 506E can support?

○ A. 2
○ B. 3
○ C. 8
○ D. 6

Answer A is correct. The PIX 506E can support two interfaces: the inside and the outside interfaces. Only the PIX 515 and above can support more than two interfaces. Therefore, answers B, C, and D are incorrect.

Question 2

Which two licenses are supported on the PIX 515E model?

❏ A. Unlimited
❏ B. Restricted
❏ C. Limited
❏ D. Unrestricted

Answers B and D are correct. The PIX 515E can support three types of licenses: restricted, unrestricted, and failover. There is no such license called limited or unlimited. Therefore, answers A and C are incorrect.

Question 3

Which of the following is true about the PIX 515E?

A. Supports 130,000 simultaneous connections

B. Supports 160,000 simultaneous connections

C. 64MB RAM

D. 128MB RAM

E. Supports 6 interfaces

F. Supports 8 interfaces

G. Supports 10 interfaces

H. Supports failover

I. Does not support failover

○ A. A, C, E, H

○ B. B, D, E, H

○ C. B, C, F, I

○ D. A, C, F, H

Answer A is correct. The PIX 515E supports 64MB of RAM; 130,000 concurrent connections; failover; and up to 6 interfaces with the appropriate licenses. Therefore, answers B, C, and D are incorrect.

Question 4

By default, how much flash and RAM memory does the PIX 506E have?

○ A. 6MB of flash, 16MB of RAM

○ B. 8MB of flash, 16MB of RAM

○ C. 8MB of flash, 32MB of RAM

○ D. 16MB of flash, 32MB of RAM

Answer C is correct. The PIX 506E supports 8MB of flash and 32MB of RAM. Therefore, answers A, B, and D are incorrect.

Question 5

Which is the primary filtering method that the Cisco PIX firewall uses?

○ A. Packet filtering

○ B. Stateful packet filtering

○ C. Proxy server

○ D. All of the above

Answer B is correct. The PIX firewall uses the stateful packet filtering method of inspecting inbound and outbound traffic. Packet filters use ACLs only to control traffic; no session information is recorded, so answer A is incorrect. Proxy servers run on general-purpose operating systems and make session connections between themselves and the client and the destinations they desire, so answer C is incorrect.

Question 6

If you install a new interface card in a PIX 515E, what else might you need to do?

○ A. Simply configure the card.

○ B. Obtain the appropriate license to enable the card.

○ C. Add more RAM to support the card.

○ D. Install the correct version of software to support card.

Answer B is correct. If you install a new interface card in a PIX 515E without an unrestricted license, you must obtain the activation key to enable the new card. More RAM or new software are not needed; therefore, answers A, C, and D are incorrect.

Question 7

What is the default security level of the inside interface for a PIX 506E?

○ A. 50

○ B. 0

○ C. 100

○ D. 110

Answer C is correct. The default security levels on a PIX 506E are 100 for the inside interface and 0 for the outside interface. Therefore, answers A, B, and D are incorrect.

Question 8

Which of the following statements is true about traffic passing from the DMZ interface to the inside interface?

○ A. Traffic passes by default.

○ B. Traffic is blocked by default.

○ C. Traffic passes if ACLs are set up between the outside and the DMZ.

○ D. Traffic passes if the inside security level is higher than the DMZ interface's level.

Answer B is correct. By default, most inside interfaces are set with a security level of 100 and the DMZ is set to something lower. The ASA allows traffic only from the higher security levels to pass to interfaces with lower security levels. This means that traffic passing from the DMZ to the inside interface is blocked by default. This functionality can be manually overridden. Therefore, answers A, C, and D are incorrect.

Question 9

> Which of the following statements is true about stateful packet filtering?
>
> ○ A. They are based on ACLs.
> ○ B. They request connections between client and destination computers.
> ○ C. They inspect inbound and outbound packets.
> ○ D. They process packets at layers 4–7.

Answer C is correct. Stateful packet filters inspect inbound and outbound packets for valid translations and connection entries. Standard packet filters use ACL, so answer A is incorrect. Proxy servers create two sessions: one between the client and itself and a second between itself and the destination. Therefore, answers B and D are incorrect.

Question 10

> What does the ASA do with TCP sequence numbers?
>
> ○ A. Nothing
> ○ B. Randomizes them
> ○ C. Adds 100 to each one of them
> ○ D. Converts them to characters

Answer B is correct. To provide an extra level of security, the ASA can randomize the TCP sequence numbers of outgoing packets. This helps prevent hackers from predicting what the TCP sequence numbers will be. Therefore, answers A, C, and D are incorrect.

Need to Know More?

 Chapman, David and Andy Fox. *Cisco Secure PIX Firewalls.* Indianapolis, IN: Cisco Press, 2002.

 Khan, Umer, Vitaly Osipov, Mike Sweeney, and Woody Weaver. *Cisco Security Specialist's Guide to PIX Firewall.* Rockland, MA: Syngress Media Inc., 2002.

 Read about the Cisco PIX 500 Series Firewalls at http://www.cisco.com/en/US/products/hw/vpndevc/ps2030/prod_models_home.html.

 Read the Cisco PIX 500 Series Firewalls Data Sheets at http://www.cisco.com/en/US/products/hw/vpndevc/ps2030/products_data_sheets_list.html.

Setting Up a PIX Firewall

Terms you'll need to understand:

✓ Privileged mode
✓ Unprivileged mode
✓ Configuration mode
✓ Monitor mode
✓ **show xlate**
✓ **clear xlate**
✓ **passwd**
✓ **reload**
✓ **write**
✓ **show version**

Techniques you'll need to master:

✓ Access modes
✓ Default interface names
✓ Setting a Telnet password
✓ Copying an image from a TFTP server
✓ Password recovery

Cisco's Command Line Interface (CLI) is the main tool used to configure the PIX firewall. The CLI is a text-based interface you can connect to using the console port or Telnet. The PIX does have a Web interface, called the PIX Device Manager, which is discussed further in Chapter 13, "IPSec and Virtual Private Networks." This chapter covers some important commands needed to execute, monitor, and back up your PIX configurations.

Factory Default Configurations

The default configuration of the PIX is dependent on the model of firewall you have. The PIX 501 and 506E both come with basic configurations designed for SOHO and RODO environments. The PIX 515E, 525, and 535 have no basic configuration settings; apparently Cisco figures that if you buy an expensive firewall then you had better know how to configure it!

Cisco PIX 501 and 506E Default Settings

Both models are ready right out of the box, with the following configurations set to their default settings. Tables 4.1 and 4.2 display the inside and outside default configuration settings.

Table 4.1 Ethernet 0 (Outside)	
Configuration	**Setting**
Interface name	outside
Security level	0
DHCP	client

Table 4.2 Ethernet 1 (Inside)	
Configuration	**Setting**
Interface name	inside
Security level	100
IP address/subnet mask	192.168.1.1 255.255.255.0
DHCP	Allows clients to automatically obtain an IP address from the PIX

The traffic flow is set to the default, which means that traffic is allowed to travel from the inside (100) to the outside (0) normally. Any traffic from the outside (0) to the inside (100) is not allowed, however. The enable password is blank, and the Telnet password is cisco, all lowercase.

CLI Administrative Access Modes

The CLI has several administrative access modes that are similar to other Cisco equipment. Similarly, the commands you're allowed to execute are defined by the current access mode. Unprivileged, privileged, configuration, and monitor are the access modes covered in this section.

Unprivileged Mode

Unprivileged mode, also known as user EXEC mode, contains a > symbol at the prompt. This is the first access mode you come to when entering the CLI, and it allows only a very small subset of the available commands. The question mark command displays the available commands in unprivileged mode:

```
pixfirewall> ?
enable     Turn on privileged commands
help       Help list
login      Log in as a particular user
logout     Exit from current user profile, and to unprivileged mode
pager      Control page length for pagination
quit       Quit from the current mode, end configuration or logout
pixfirewall>
```

The commands in unprivileged mode can't actually change any configuration settings, but they do allow you to move to the next level—privileged EXEC mode.

Privileged Mode

Privileged mode, also known as privileged EXEC mode, is symbolized by a pound sign (#) at the prompt. Privileged EXEC mode gives you the full set of available commands that enable you to configure your PIX firewall. To enter this mode, you need to type the word `enable` and enter the password at the user EXEC prompt. To move back to user EXEC mode, you must type the command `disable`. Listing 4.1 shows how to use the `enable` and `disable` commands to enter and exit privileged EXEC mode.

Listing 4.1   The enable and disable Commands

```
pixfirewall> enable
Password:
pixfirewall# disable
pixfirewall>
```

Configuration Mode

Configuration mode is represented by a `(config)#` prompt. This mode allows access to interfaces, virtual private networks (VPNs), DCHP servers, hostname settings, and so on. You can enter this mode by entering the command `config terminal` at the privileged EXEC prompt. To return to privileged EXEC mode, you must type `exit` (or `disable` to return even further back to unprivileged user EXEC mode). Listing 4.2 demonstrates the `config terminal` command.

Listing 4.2   The config terminal Command

```
pixfirewall> enable
Password:
pixfirewall# config terminal
pixfirewall(config)# exit
pixfirewall# config terminal
pixfirewall(config)# disable
pixfirewall>
```

Monitor Mode

Monitor mode is symbolized by the `monitor>` prompt. This special mode enables you to perform maintenance features that are sometimes unavailable during normal operation. New binary images and password breaking procedure files can be downloaded in this mode. To enter monitor mode, reload your PIX. During the bootup phase, you will be prompted with this message: `Use BREAK or ESC to interrupt flash boot..` Press either Break or ESC to enter monitor mode the 10-second timeout. Listing 4.3 is an example of the output displayed when entering monitor mode.

Listing 4.3   Monitor Mode

```
Cisco Secure PIX Firewall BIOS (4.2) #6: Mon Aug 27 15:09:54 PDT 2001
Platform PIX-501
Flash=E28F640J3 @ 0x3000000

Use BREAK or ESC to interrupt flash boot.
Use SPACE to begin flash boot immediately.
Flash boot interrupted.
0: i8255X @ PCI(bus:0 dev:17 irq:9 )
1: i8255X @ PCI(bus:0 dev:18 irq:10)

Using 1: i82557 @ PCI(bus:0 dev:18 irq:10), MAC: 000c.3085.5641
Use ? for help.
monitor>
```

Most CLI commands can be abbreviated, making your configuration tasks a little faster. For example, the command **enable** can be abbreviated to just **en** and the **config terminal** command can be just **con t**.

 Be sure know your administrative access modes, which are as follows:

➤ *Unprivileged mode*—**pixfirewall>**

➤ *Privileged mode*—**pixfirewall#**

➤ *Configuration mode*—**pixfirewall(config)#**

➤ *Monitor mode*—**monitor>**

Knowing the General Commands

Several commands are covered in this section. These commands will help you monitor, display, and save your configurations, and they are all within the privileged or configuration mode. Therefore, use the enable and config terminal commands to enter the necessary access mode.

Here's a preview of the commands:

```
clear arp              reload
clear xlate            show arp
                       show enable
enable                 show conn
enable password        show history
                       show telnet
hostname               show xlate
passwd  — for Telnet   telnet
          access
ping
```

vs

The **enable** Command

enable allows you to enter the privileged EXEC mode. Although this mode requires a password, the password is blank by default and simply pressing Enter when you see the password prompt lets you enter privileged EXEC mode.

The enable password command sets a privilege EXEC mode password. These passwords are case sensitive, so be careful. You can use the show enable command to display the encrypted version of the password stored in the configuration, like so:

not useful!!

```
pixfirewall(config)# enable password oregon
pixfirewall(config)# show enable
enable password W5TSthJO5zEtPi9F encrypted
pixfirewall(config)#
```

The **passwd** Command

The passwd command is used to set the password for Telnet access to the PIX. By default, this password is cisco; it must be in all lowercase because it's case sensitive. The following command sets the password to cisco:

```
pixfirewall(config)# passwd cisco
pixfirewall(config)#
```

The **telnet** Command

The telnet command specifies which hosts can connect to the PIX inside interface using Telnet. Telnet users can access the PIX on all interfaces except the outside interface. If users need access via the outside interface, an IPSec established connection is required before Telnet will connect. The Telnet syntax is as follows:

```
telnet <local_ip> [<mask>] [<if_name>]
```

Table 4.3	The telnet Command Options
Option	**Function**
local_ip	This is the IP address of the host you want to allow Telnet access.
mask	This is optional and can be used to define a whole subnet if necessary.
if_name	This is optional and is required only when you are using IPSec to connect to the outside interface.

The following example shows how to allow host 192.168.1.11 to Telnet into the PIX firewall on the inside interface:

```
pixfirewall(config)# telnet 192.168.1.11
pixfirewall(config)# show telnet
192.168.1.11 255.255.255.255 inside
pixfirewall(config)#
```

The **hostname** Command

The hostname command is used to change the command-line prompt as well as the fully qualified domain name used to generate RSA keys. The default hostname is `pixfirewall`. The following command sets the hostname to firewall2:

```
pixfirewall(config)# hostname firewall2
firewall2(config)#
```

The **show history** Command

The `show history` command displays a list of previously entered commands. The following command displays the history:

```
pixtraincenter# show history
  show history
  show interface
  enable
```

The **show conn** Command

The `show conn` command displays connection table information about TCP traffic traveling through the PIX. In this example, host 192.168.1.11 with port 11969 is going to 165.193.123.44 port 80:

```
pixfirewall# show conn
1 in use, 5 most used
TCP out 165.193.123.44:80 in 192.168.1.11:1969 idle 0:00:03 Bytes 334
pixfirewall#
```

The **show xlate** Command

Use the `show xlate` command to view the current translation slots made in the translation table (recall that a PIX uses a connection table and a translation table to track the flow of traffic through its interfaces). *Translation slots* is the term used to describe the translation mapping from an internal address to a global external address. In this example, a local user using IP address 192.168.1.11 with port 1969 has been translated to a global outside interface address of 169.254.8.31 port 1237:

```
pixfirewall# show xlate
1 in use, 53 most used
PAT Global 169.254.8.31(1237) Local 192.168.1.11(1969)
PAT Global 169.254.8.31(2346) Local 192.168.1.12(5671)
pixfirewall#
```

The **clear xlate** Command

The `clear xlate` command clears the current translation slot entries. This should be done every time you add, modify, or delete something using the following commands: aaa-server, access-lists, alias, conduits, global, nat, and routes type. This helps to reset the xlate table and make the previous command operate as expected. The following shows the command being executed from the privileged EXEC mode:

```
pixfirewall# clear xlate
```

The ping Command

The ping command enables you to test whether the PIX firewall can reach another IP address, and it results in a new mapping in the Address Resolution Protocol (ARP) table. The following example shows a ping command and a response:

```
pixfirewall# ping 192.168.1.11
    192.168.1.11 response received — 0ms
    192.168.1.11 response received — 0ms
    192.168.1.11 response received — 0ms
```

> The **ping** command can be used to show that an IP address is reachable, but it doesn't test whether traffic can flow through the PIX firewall.

The show arp Command

The show arp command displays the ARP table, which maps an IP address to a physical MAC address. The following command displays the ARP cache:

```
pixfirewall# show arp
    inside 192.168.1.11 0002.a599.aa96
    inside 255.255.255.255 0002.a599.aa96
```

The clear arp Command

The clear arp command flushes all the entries in the ARP cache from RAM. The following command clears the ARP cache:

```
pixfirewall# show arp
    inside 192.168.1.11 0002.a599.aa96
    inside 255.255.255.255 0002.a599.aa96
pixfirewall# clear arp
pixfirewall# show arp
pixfirewall#
```

The **reload** Command

The reload command reboots the PIX firewall and loads the flash memory configuration into RAM. Please note that there is no such thing as a reboot command. The reload command displays the reload command and the resulting output from the command:

```
pixfirewall# reload
Proceed with reload? [confirm] y

Rebooting....

CISCO SYSTEMS PIX-501
Embedded BIOS Version 4.3.200 07/31/01 15:58:22.08
```

Viewing and Saving the Configuration

The ability to view and save the PIX firewall configuration is a vital part of setup and troubleshooting. The following section covers several of the most common commands. Here's a preview of them:

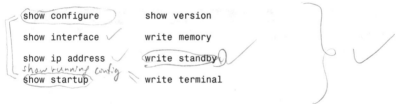

```
show configure        show version
show interface        write memory
show ip address       write standby
show startup          write terminal
```

The **show startup** Command

The show startup and show configure commands both display configurations saved in flash memory. These configurations are loaded into RAM during bootup. The following displays only the first eight lines of the output from the show startup command:

```
pixfirewall# show startup
: Saved
: Written by enable_15 at 04:55:12.917 UTC Wed Apr 2 2003
PIX Version 6.2(2)
nameif ethernet0 outside security0
nameif ethernet1 inside security100
enable password W5TSthJO5zEtPi9F encrypted
passwd 2KFQnbNIdI.2KYOU encrypted
hostname pixfirewall
```

≡ show running-config

The **write terminal** Command

You use the write terminal command to display the configuration currently running in RAM to the console. This configuration is also known as the *running config* and can be displayed using the (show running-config) command, as in other Cisco devices. This code displays the command's output:

```
pixfirewall# write terminal
: Saved
:
PIX Version 6.2(2)
nameif ethernet0 outside security0
nameif ethernet1 inside security100
enable password W5TSthJO5zEtPi9F encrypted
passwd 2KFQnbNIdI.2KYOU encrypted
hostname pixfirewall
```

The **show interface** Command

The show interface command displays information such as the IP address, line status, protocol status, and interface counter information. To display only one interface, add the hardware ID to the end of the command. Listing 4.4 displays the show interface output for interface Ethernet 1.

Listing 4.4   The show interface Output

```
pixfirewall(config)# show int e1
interface ethernet1 "inside" is up, line protocol is up
 Hardware is i82559 ethernet, address is 000c.3085.5641
 IP address 192.168.1.1, subnet mask 255.255.255.0
MTU 1500 bytes, BW 10000 Kbit full duplex
    261 packets input, 32294 bytes, 0 no buffer
    Received 249 broadcasts, 0 runts, 0 giants
    0 input errors, 0 CRC, 0 frame, 0 overrun, 0 ignored, 0 abort
    27 packets output, 3802 bytes, 0 underruns
    0 output errors, 0 collisions, 0 interface resets
    0 babbles, 0 late collisions, 0 deferred
    0 lost carrier, 0 no carrier
    input queue (curr/max blocks): hardware (128/128) software (0/1)
    output queue (curr/max blocks): hardware (0/2) software (0/1)
pixfirewall(config)#
```

The **show IP address** Command

You use the show IP address to display the address information assigned to each of the device's interfaces. The following command displays all the IP addresses assigned to the PIX firewall:

```
pixfirewall# show IP address
System IP Addresses:
    IP address outside 169.254.8.1 255.255.255.0
    IP address inside 192.168.1.1 255.255.255.0
```

```
Current IP Addresses:
    IP address outside 169.254.8.1 255.255.255.0
    IP address inside 192.168.1.1 255.255.255.0
pixfirewall#
```

The **show version** Command

The show version command enables you to view the firewall's software version, processor type, operating time since last reboot, flash memory type, interface boards, serial number, and activation keys. Listing 4.5 displays the output from the show version command.

Listing 4.5   The show version Command

```
pixfirewall# show version

Cisco PIX Firewall Version 6.2(2)
Cisco PIX Device Manager Version 2.1(1)

Compiled on Fri 07-Jun-02 17:49 by morlee

pixfirewall up 8 hours 31 mins

Hardware:  PIX-501, 16 MB RAM, CPU Am5x86 133 MHz
Flash E28F640J3 @ 0x3000000, 8MB
BIOS Flash E28F640J3 @ 0xfffd8000, 128KB

0: ethernet0: address is 000c.3085.5640, irq 9
1: ethernet1: address is 000c.3085.5641, irq 10
Licensed Features:
Failover:       Disabled
VPN-DES:        Enabled
VPN-3DES:       Disabled
Maximum Interfaces: 2
Cut-through Proxy: Enabled
Guards:         Enabled
URL-filtering:  Enabled
Inside Hosts:   10
Throughput:     Limited
IKE peers:      5

Serial Number: 807082785 (0x301b1b21)
Running Activation Key: 0x2d284af1 0xd032aa26 0x38b7db1f 0x70cfa8ee
Configuration last modified by enable_15 at 10:45:05.183 UTC Tue Apr 1 2003
pixfirewall#
```

The **write memory** Command

The write memory command saves the current running configuration to flash memory. When the system is reloaded, this configuration is loaded into RAM and executed as the running configuration. The following displays the command's syntax:

```
pixfirewall# write memory
Building configuration...
Cryptochecksum: 827c289b 6a6d8181 829b5b98 d3f1c82a
[OK]
pixfirewall#
```

Similarly, the write standby command saves the running configuration from the active PIX firewall to the standby PIX firewall when you are working with failover configurations. You can also think of this as writing from active RAM to standby RAM. Following is an example of the write standby command:

```
pixfirewall# write standby
```

The Six Basic Commands

The PIX firewall's basic setup is based on six primary commands. The commands shown in the following list provide the most basic configuration settings to allow traffic to flow through the firewall. This section covers each command in detail.

Here's a preview of the commands:

```
global        nameif
interface     nat
ip address    route
```

Naming Interfaces

Before we begin discussing these commands, a brief explanation is necessary to understand how interfaces are handled by the PIX. A name association needs to be designated for each hardware interface; it is this associated name rather than the hardware ID that is used in most of the configuration commands. For example, the interface e1 is by default named inside. This name of inside is used throughout the PIX command structure as a pointer to the real hardware ID of interface e1.

Network Address Translation

Network address translation (NAT) is the process of translating multiple internal addresses to multiple global addresses. Every packet leaving the NAT translator uses the next available global address, and a translation table entry is made to record a link between the internal address and the outgoing global address. As packets flow back, the translated global address is reverted to the original internal address. This is known as *dynamic mapping*, and the global addresses are only temporarily used. Table 4.4 displays the subnet of 192.168.1.0, which all share a global address pool of 169.254.8.31–169.254.8.35:

Table 4.4 NAT Mapping Table	
NAT Internal Addresses	**Global Address Pool**
192.168.1.0 255.255.255.0	169.254.8.31–169.254.8.35

Table 4.5 shows a temporary mapping of the internal address of 192.168.1.11 to 169.254.8.31. If the internal host closes the session or loses the session, or the connection times out, 169.254.8.31 is released so another internal address can use it.

Table 4.5 Internal-to-Global Address Mapping	
Internal Addresses	**Globally Mapped Addresses**
192.168.1.11	169.254.8.31 (temporary)
192.168.1.12	169.254.8.32 (temporary)
	169.254.8.33 (temporary)
	169.254.8.34 (temporary)
	169.254.8.35 (temporary)

For example, as Jack's computer talks to the Internet, his IP address of 192.168.1.11 is translated by the PIX using NAT to an address of 169.254.8.31 and subsequently passes the interface connected to the Internet. If another user, such as Timmy with an IP address of 192.168.1.12, is going through the PIX to the Internet, Timmy's IP address is translated to the next available global IP address, which is 169.254.8.32. This process continues to allocate the next available global IP address until none are left. At this point, a process of NAT *overloading*—also known as *PAT*—takes over. Figure 4.1 displays Jack's computer being translated to 169.254.8.31 as it travels through the PIX firewall.

Port Address Translation

Port address translation (PAT) is also called NAT overloading and is the process of translating multiple internal addresses to a single global address. Every packet leaving the PAT translator uses the same global address with a modified source port number. For example, as Jack's packet travels through the PIX, his IP address and port number are changed. An address of 192.168.1.11 port 1237 is modified to an address of 169.254.8.31 and the next available port, such as port 5001. When Timmy requests information from the Internet, his address of 192.168.1.12 port 2403 is modified to the same 169.254.8.31 address but the port number is the next available port, such as 5002. When a request comes back from the Internet with 169.254.8.31 port 5001, this is referenced in the translation table to show that the packet should be changed back to 192.168.1.11 port 1237, and the packet is delivered to Jack.

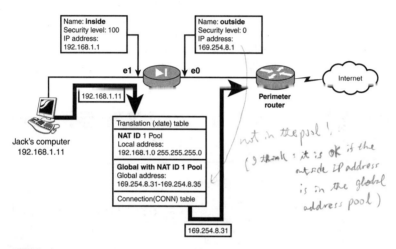

Figure 4.1 A NAT diagram.

Table 4.6 PAT Address Table

Nat Internal Address	Global Address Pool
192.168.1.0 255.255.255.0	169.254.8.31

Table 4.7 PAT IP Address and Port Mapping Table

Internal Addresses	Globally Mapped Addresses
192.168.1.11:**1237**	169.254.8.31:**5001** (temporary)
192.168.1.12:**1937** 2403	169.254.8.31:**5002** (temporary)

Steps to Setting Up the PIX with the Six Basic Commands

1. nameif—Assign a name to a hardware ID interface and set the security level.

2. interface—Set the interface speed and enable the interface.

3. ip address—Assign an IP address to a named interface.

4. nat—Create a NAT ID that defines which local IP addresses will be translated on a specific named interface.

5. global—Create a global list of addresses to be used by the NAT ID in step 4.

6. route—Create any necessary static routes or default routes.

The **nameif** Command

The nameif command creates a name that is associated with a hardware interface and that is used throughout several other commands. Some examples of good names to use are inside, outside, and DMZ. The syntax of the nameif command is as follows:

```
nameif <hardware_id> <if_name> <security_lvl>
```

Table 4.8	nameif Options
Option	**Function**
hardware_id	The hardware ID is the name of the physical hardware, such as **e0** or **Ethernet0**.
if_name	This is the name you want to call the interface.
security_lvl	The security level setting is between 0 and 100. 0 is reserved for the outside interface, and 100 is used for the most secure inside interface.

The following example shows that hardware interface Ethernet 1 is being set to inside:

```
pixfirewall(config)# nameif e1 inside security100
pixfirewall(config)#
```

The **interface** Command

The interface command sets the hardware speed and enables or disables an interface. Here's the syntax of the interface command:

```
interface <hardware_id> [<hw_speed> [<shutdown>]]
```

Table 4.9	interface Options
Option	**Function**
hardware_id	The hardware ID is the name of the physical hardware, such as **e0** or **Ethernet0**.
hw_speed	This determines the connection speed used by this interface.
	The options are as follows:
	Auto—Autodetects the network speed
	10BASE-T—10Mbp Ethernet half-duplex
	10full—10Mbp Ethernet full-duplex
	100BASE-TX—100Mbp Ethernet half-duplex
	100full—100Mbp Ethernet full-duplex
shutdown	Defines whether the interface is administratively shut down.

The first command in the example enables the interface with 10BASE-T, and the second command disables the interface:

```
pixfirewall(config)# interface e1 10baseT
pixfirewall(config)# interface e1 10baseT shutdown
```

The **ip address** Command

The `ip address` command defines the layer 3 IP address on the interface and uses the name of the interface, as opposed to the hardware address. Its syntax is shown here:

```
ip address <if_name> <ip_address> [<mask>]
```

Table 4.10	ip adddress Options
Option	**Function**
if_name	This is the name given to the hardware ID using the **nameif** command.
ip_address	This is the IP address you want to have on the address.
mask	This is the network mask.

In the following example, the inside interface (e1) is being set to an IP address of 192.168.1.1 and a subnet mask of 255.255.255.0:

```
pixfirewall(config)# ip address inside 192.168.1.1 255.255.255.0
```

Syntax may not be correct !!

The **nat** and **global** Commands

The nat and global commands work together to determine which addresses need translating and to what those addresses will be translated. NAT defines which addresses need to be translated. The ID field in the nat command corresponds to a global command that contains a pool of addresses used for translation. The nat command's syntax is shown here:

for access-list version
see ★ on p.97

```
nat [(<if_name>)] <nat_id> <local_ip> [<mask> [dns] [outside]
                  [<max_conns> [emb_limit] [<norandomseq>]]]]
```

Can have access-list version note : *no keyword "netmask" is required (for global command: keyword "netmask" is required)*

Table 4.11   The nat Command's Options

Option	Function
if_name	This is the name of the internal interface to which this command is linked.
nat_id	This is the ID number that groups the **nat** command with the **global** command
local_ip	This defines which IP addresses are within this **nat_id** group.
mask	This defines the local_IP network mask.
dns	This specifies that the DNS replies that match xlate tables are translated.
outside	This specifies that the **nat** command applies to the outside interface.
max_cons	This defines the maximum number of TCP connections allowed.
emb_limit	This specifies the embryonic limit. The default is **0**, which is unlimited embryonic connections.
norandomseq	This states not to randomize the normal TCP packet sequence numbering.

The global command is used to allocate the address to which the internal address will be assigned. The syntax shown here details the global command:

```
global [(<ext_if_name>)] <nat_id> {<global_ip>[-<global_ip>]
[netmask <global_mask>]} | interface
```
see p.94 ★

Keyword

Table 4.12   The global Command's Options

Option	Function
ext_if_name	Defines the external interface on which these global addresses will be used.
nat_id	The ID number that links the **nat** command with the **global** address pool command. *for translated from a pool of inside addresses*
global_ip	Assigns a single address or a pool of addresses to which the **nat** command will translate its internal address.
interface	If you use this option, the interface is to set up to use PAT or NAT overloading on the same IP address assigned to the interface.

netmask   Reserved word that prefaces the network global_mask variable.
global_mask   The network mask for global_ip.

In Listing 4.6, the address 192.168.1.20 on the inside interface is translated
to an IP address of 169.254.8.5 on the outside interface. These two commands are linked by the nat_id of 12.

netmask

Listing 4.6   The nat and global Commands for a Single Host

```
pixfirewall(config)# nat (inside) 12 192.168.1.20 255.255.255.255
pixfirewall(config)# global (outside) 12 169.254.8.5 255.255.255.0
```

In Listing 4.7, the network of 192.168.1.0 255.255.255.0 on the inside interface is translated to a global pool of addresses 169.254.8.10–169.254.8.20 on
the outside interface. These two commands are linked by the nat_id of 5.

Listing 4.7   The nat and global Commands for a Subnet

```
pixfirewall(config)# nat (inside) 5 192.168.1.0 255.255.255.0
pixfirewall(config)# global (outside) 5 169.254.8.10-169.254.8.20 netmask 255.255.255.0
```

In Listing 4.8, all the addresses on the inside interface are translated to the
global address that is defined as the outside interface IP address. This many-
to-one solution uses PAT.

Listing 4.8   nat and global Commands

```
pixfirewall(config)# nat (inside) 1 0.0.0.0 0.0.0.0
pixfirewall(config)# global (outside) 1 interface
```

In Listing 4.9, three networks on different interfaces are all part of the nat_id
3 group. The global command linked to nat_id 3 defines an address range of
168.254.8.5–168.254.8.10 to be used.

Listing 4.9   The nat and global Commands for Multiple Interfaces

```
pixfirewall(config)# nat (inside) 3 192.168.1.0 255.255.255.0
pixfirewall(config)# nat (dmz) 3 192.168.2.0 255.255.255.0
pixfirewall(config)# nat (dmz2) 3 192.168.3.0 255.255.255.0
pixfirewall(config)# global (outside) 3
                168.254.8.5-168.254.8.10 netmask 255.255.255.0
```

You can use the show nat and show global commands to display the list of NAT
and global entries made, and you can use the no nat and no global commands
to disable the entries made.

The route Command

The route command is used to add a static or default route to an interface.
This syntax shows the command:

```
route <if_name> <foreign_ip> <mask> <gateway> [<metric>]
```

Table 4.13	route Command Options
Option	Function
if_name	This is the internal or external interface name the traffic will use to exit from the PIX.
foreign_ip	The foreign IP is the destination network address. To define a default route, you can use 0.0.0.0 as the address and 0.0.0.0 as the mask.
gateway	This is the gateway, which is also known as the *next hop router*.
metric	This is the metric value used to define the number of hops away the destination network is.

In this example a default route has been created that will forward traffic to a router at 169.254.8.100 with a metric of 1:

```
pixfirewall(config)# route outside 0.0.0.0 0.0.0.0 169.254.8.100 1
```

Using the Six Commands

For the exam, be sure you cover this section and know these commands to configure a PIX firewall. Listing 4.10 shows the commands needed to configure your PIX firewall according to Figure 4.2.

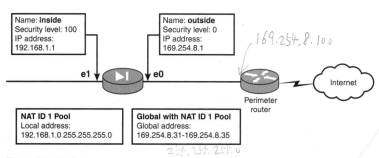

Figure 4.2   NAT diagram.

Listing 4.10	Sample Code

```
pixfirewall# config t
pixfirewall(config)# nameif e0 outside security0
pixfirewall(config)# nameif e1 inside security100

pixfirewall(config)# interface e0 10baseT
pixfirewall(config)# interface e1 10full

pixfirewall(config)# ip address outside 169
pixfirewall(config)# ip address inside 192.
```

Listing 4.10 Sample Code *(continued)*

```
pixfirewall(config)# nat (inside) 1 192.168.1.0 255.255.255.0
pixfirewall(config)# global (outside) 1 169.254.8.31-169.254.8.35 netmask 255.255.255.0

pixfirewall(config)# route outside 0.0.0.0 0.0.0.0 169.254.8.100 1
```

Working with the Trivial File Transfer Protocol

PIX firewalls can save, restore, and install new images from Trivial File Transfer Protocol (TFTP) servers. TFTP servers enable clients such as the PIX firewall to save and read files, similar to the way in which normal FTP functionality allows clients to download and upload files on the Internet. Several TFTP programs are available on the market, and Cisco provides a simple TFTP server for free with the PIX firewall. Alternatively, the TFTP server can be downloaded from the Cisco Web site.

NOTE Images are typically operating system upgrades or PDM images needing to be uploaded to the PIX.

TIP A general TFTP command can be used to help make the other commands a little shorter.

The command is **tftp-server [if_name] ip_address path** and it enables you to enter the default TFTP server parameters used on other commands.

Upgrading OS Images

There are two methods of upgrading a new OS image to the PIX firewall. The first method uses the copy command or booting to monitor> mode.

e copy Command

command is available on IOS versions 5.1 and 5.3 and above, and it is
download images from a TFTP server to the firewall. The TFTP
of the command is for the location and path of the image, whereas the
tion determines whether it's an image or PDM software. The copy
's syntax is as follows:

```
[[//location] [/pathname]]] flash[:[image ¦ pdm]]
```

Table 4.14	copy Command Options
Option	Function
tftp	This option allows for the location and path of the image you want to download.
flash	This option enables you to specify which type of image you are downloading: an image for a new IOS or a PDM for Cisco's graphical user interface.

Most Cisco IOSes use the **copy** command in one form or another. One of the most common problems when remembering the **copy** command syntax is the order of the parameters. An easy way to remember the order is the phrase, *copy from to*, or just CFT, which is alphabetical. This means copy from some location to some destination.

The following is the step-by-step process you would use to copy an image from a TFTP server to a PIX firewall. Figure 4.3 displays the networking layout, and Listing 4.11 shows the necessary commands. Follow these steps:

1. Start the TFTP program on your server; this example uses 192.168.1.11 as the server.

2. Enter the `copy tftp flash` command.

3. At the prompt, enter the TFTP server IP address—for example, enter `192.168.1.11`.

4. At the prompt, enter the source filename—for example, enter `pix622.bin`.

5. Enter `yes` to continue. This starts the download of the image to the PIX firewall.

6. Reload the PIX and enjoy your new OS!

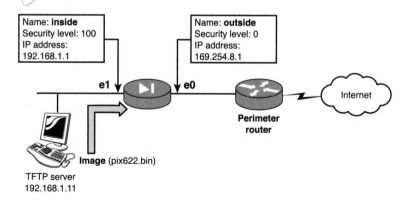

Figure 4.3 TFTP diagram.

Listing 4.11   Copying from a TFTP Server

```
Pixfirewall# copy tftp flash
Address or name of remote host []? 192.168.1.11
Source file name []? pix622.bin
copying tftp://192.168.1.11/pix622.bin to flash:image
[yes¦no¦again]? yes
!!!!!!!!!!!!!!!!!!!!!!!!!!!!!!!!!!!!!!!!!!!!!!!!!!!!!!
Received 1658880 bytes
Erasing current image
Writing 1540152 bytes of image
!!!!!!!!!!!!!!!!!!!!!!!!!!!!!!!!!!!!!!!!!!!!!!!!!!!!!!
Image installed
pixfirewall#
```

tedious, can't remember (similiar steps for pass word recovery)

Using Monitor Mode to Upgrade Images

In the past, using monitor mode was the only way you could upgrade your
OS images. However, this process has now been replaced by the copy command. Follow these step-by-step instructions on how to upload an image in
monitor mode:

not PIX !!

1. Start the TFTP program on your server; this example uses 192.168.1.11
   as the server

2. Restart your PIX by cycling power or using the reload command.

3. Press Break or ESC to interrupt the flash boot and enter into monitor
   mode.

4. Enter the interface you want to use—for example, enter monitor>
   interface 1.

5. Enter the interface IP address—for example, enter monitor> address
   192.168.1.1.

6. Enter the default gateway, if required—for example, enter monitor>
   gateway <IP address>. *listing 4.12 does not mention this !*

7. Test communication with the TFTP server using the ping command—
   for example, enter monitor> ping 192.168.1.11.

8. Enter the TFTP server IP address—for example, enter monitor> server
   192.168.1.11.

9. Enter the image's filename—for example, enter monitor> file pix622.bin.

10. Begin the TFTP process by entering the keyword tftp.

11. When the upload is done, enter y to copy the image to flash.

12. Reload the PIX.

Listing 4.12 displays the monitor mode and TFTP steps needed to upload an image to your PIX.

Listing 4.12   Monitor Mode's tftp Command

```
monitor> interface 1
monitor> address 192.168.1.1
address 192.168.1.1
monitor> ping 192.168.1.11
monitor> server 192.168.1.11
server 192.168.1.11
monitor> file pix622.bin
file pix622.bin
monitor> tftp
..................................................................
Received 1658880 bytes

Cisco Secure PIX Firewall admin loader (3.0) #0:
Fri Jun 7 17:35:02 PDT 2002
Flash=E28F640J3 @ 0x3000000
BIOS Flash=E28F640J3 @ 0xD8000
Flash version 6.2.2, Install version 6.2.2
Do you wish to copy the install image into flash? [n] y

Installing to flash

Serial Number: 807082785 (0x301b1b21)
Activation Key: 2d284af1 d032aa26 38b7db1f 70cfa8ee

Do you want to enter a new activation key? [n]n
Writing 1540152 bytes image into flash...
```

Configuration Files

Saving, erasing, and restoring your configurations are all basic functions you will need to master. All the following examples assume you already have a TFTP server running.

The **write net** Command

Making a backup of your configuration is always a good idea because it makes recovery easy. You can save your configuration to a TFTP server using the write net command, like so:

```
write net [[server_ip]:[filename]]
```

Table 4.15	The write net Command Options
Option	**Function**
server_ip	This is the IP address of the TFTP server.
filename	This is the path and name you want to save the configuration as.

Here is an example of the write net command:

```
pixfirewall# write net 192.168.1.11:backup1
Building configuration...
TFTP write 'backup1' at 192.168.1.11 on interface 1
[OK]
```

The write erase Command

The write erase command erases your configuration from flash, giving you an empty configuration on the next reload. Here's a command example:

```
pixfirewall(config)# write erase
Erase PIX configuration in flash memory? [confirm]
```

The configure net Command

Finally, the configure net command enables you to merge your configuration back into the PIX from a TFTP server. Make a note that you must configure at least one interface with an IP address and enable it before you can reload your configuration. Here's its syntax:

```
configure net [<location>]:[<pathname>]
```

Table 4.16	configure net Command Options
Option	**Function**
location	The location option is the IP address of the TFTP server.
pathname	This is the path and filename of the configuration.

The write net command's syntax is as follows:

```
pixfirewall# write net 192.168.1.11:backup1
Building configuration...
TFTP write 'backup1' at 192.168.1.11 on interface 1
[OK]
```

Password Recovery

If you forget your enable password, the PIX firewall requires you to upload a file to the flash. This special file nullifies the current password without erasing your configuration. The process is virtually identical to loading a new image using the `monitor>` prompt and a TFTP server. You can download the password file for your specific version of OS image at www.cisco.com/warp/public/110/34.shtml.

The password file for 6.2 release, for instance, is `np62.bin`. This utility resets the enable and Telnet passwords to their default settings, which ~~is cisco for both of them.~~ *are blanks for* *enable password and cisco for Telnet password*

Listing 4.13 shows the steps for uploading a password recovery file.

Listing 4.13   Password Recovery Example

```
monitor> interface 1
monitor> address 192.168.1.1
address 192.168.1.1
monitor> server 192.168.1.11
server 192.168.1.11
monitor> file np62.bin
file np62.bin
monitor> tftp
tftp np62.bin@192.168.1.11..........................
Received 73728 bytes

Cisco Secure PIX Firewall password tool (3.0) #0:
Wed Mar 27 11:02:16 PST 2002
Flash=E28F640J3 @ 0x3000000
BIOS Flash=E28F640J3 @ 0xD8000

Do you wish to erase the passwords? [yn] y
The following lines will be removed from the configuration:
    enable password ZFatiF0MarNtVoTD encrypted
    passwd 2KFQnbNIdI.2KYOU encrypted

Do you want to remove the commands listed above
from the configuration? [yn] y
```

Password recovery on older PIX firewalls such as the PIX 510 and 520 is done using a floppy disk: A password lockout utility is loaded from a floppy, and the PIX firewall is rebooted.

Exam Prep Questions

Question 1

> On the PIX, what are the main access modes? (Select three.)
>
> ☐ A. Enable
> ☐ B. User
> ☑ C. Privileged
> ☐ D. Common
> ☑ E. Configuration
> ☑ F. Unprivileged

Answers C, E, and F are correct. The three main access modes are privileged, configuration, and unprivileged. Therefore, answers A, B, and D are incorrect.

Question 2

> Which command associates a name security level to a hardware interface?
>
> ○ A. ifname e2 dmz1 security100
> ◉ B. nameif e2 dmz1 security100
> ○ C. interface e2 dmz1 security100
> ○ D. interface e2 dmz1 security 100

Answer B is correct. nameif is the command used to assign a name and the security level to an interface. The ifname command does not exist, so answer A is incorrect. The interface command is used to set the speed and enable the interface, so answers C and D are incorrect.

Question 3

> Which command clears all the active translations in the translation table?
>
> ○ A. clear translations
> ○ B. stop translations
> ○ C. delete translations *
> ◉ D. clear xlate
> ○ E. delete xlate

Answers D is correct. The `clear xlate` command removes all active translations. `clear translations`, `stop translations`, `delete translations`, and `delete xlate` do not exist. Therefore, answers A, B, C, and E are incorrect.

Question 4

> What does the **nameif** command do?
>
> O A. It enables an interface.
>
> O B. It sets an IP address on an interface.
>
> O C. It sets a name and security level to an interface.
>
> O D. The **nameif** command is not a valid command.

Answer C is correct. The `nameif` command is used to configure a name and security level to an interface. Answer A is done by the `interface` command, so it's incorrect. Answer B is done by the `ip address` command, so it's incorrect. Answer D is incorrect because the `nameif` command is a valid command used to set an interface name and security level of an interface.

Question 5

> Which command reboots the PIX?
>
> O A. **reboot**
>
> O B. **reload**   do not exict !!
>
> O C. **restart**
>
> O D. **exit**

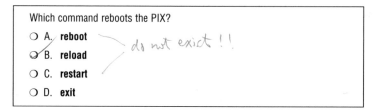

Answer B is correct. The `reload` command reboots the PIX firewall. Answers A and C do not exist, so they are incorrect. Answer D does not reboot the PIX, so it is incorrect.

Question 6

> How do you save a running configuration to a startup configuration in flash?
>
> O A. **copy running-config startup-config**   ← really ??
>
> O B. **copy running-config flash**
>
> O C. **save memory**
>
> O D. **write memory**

Answer D is correct. The `write memory` command is used to save the RAM configuration to flash. Answers A and B are not used in this way on the PIX firewall, so they are incorrect. Answer C does not exist, so it is incorrect.

Question 7

> What are the default interface names on a PIX firewall? (Select two.)
> ☐ A. Network
> ☑ B. Inside
> ☐ C. DMZ
> ☐ D. Outside
> ☐ E. Console

Answers B and D are correct. By default, interface `e0` is called outside and interface `e1` is called inside. Therefore, answers A, C, and E are incorrect.

Question 8

> Which command is used to configure an IP address to an interface?
> ○ A. **interface inside 192.168.1.11 255.255.255.0**
> ○ B. **global inside 192.168.1.11 255.255.255.0**
> ○ C. **ip address inside 192.168.1.11 255.255.255.0**
> ○ D. **ip address e1 192.168.1.11 255.255.255.0**

Answer C is correct. The `ip address` command is used to configure the IP address. Answers A and B do not configure the IP address, so they are incorrect. Answer D does use the `ip address` command; however, the `ip address` command uses the name rather than the hardware ID designation. Therefore, answer D is incorrect.

Question 9

> What is needed to perform a password recovery on a PIX 520? (Select two.)
> ☑ A. Use a PIX password lockout utility.
> ☐ B. Reboot into `rommon` mode. *no such thing !!*
> ☐ C. Change the configuration register.
> ☐ D. Execute the **passwd** command.
> ☑ E. Reboot the PIX.

Answers A and E are correct. On the PIX 510 and 520, password recoveries are done from a floppy disk. A password lockout utility file is placed on a floppy disk, and then the PIX firewall is rebooted. Answer B is incorrect because there is no such thing as rommon mode on the PIX; this term could be confused with the monitor mode. Answer C is incorrect because there is no configuration register. Answer D is incorrect because the passwd command sets the Telnet password.

Question 10

> Which command is used to set the Telnet password?
>
> ○ A. **telnet passwd**
> ○ B. **telnet password**
> ○ C. **password**
> ○ D. **passwd**

Answer D is correct. The passwd command is used to set the Telnet password. The default password is the word cisco in lowercase. Answers A, B, and C are not commands on the PIX firewall, so they are incorrect.

Question 11

> Which command would you use to upgrade the PIX IOS?
>
> ○ A. **write tftp flash**
> ○ B. **upgrade flash**
> ○ C. **copy tftp flash**
> ○ D. **copy flash tftp**
> ○ E. **write net tftp flash**

Answer C is correct. The copy tftp flash command is used to copy a new OS image from a TFTP server to the flash memory. Answers A, B, D, and E have invalid commands, so they are incorrect.

Question 12

Which command displays the flash installed and the amount of memory on the PIX firewall?

○ A. **show memory**

○ B. **show version**

○ C. **show flash**

○ D. **write memory**

Answer B is correct. The show version command displays the amount of memory installed and displays the licensing features available. Answer A is incorrect because the show memory command displays the memory used. Answer C is incorrect because it displays the images install in the flash memory. Answer D is incorrect because write memory saves the configuration file to flash.

Need to Know More?

 Chapman, David and Andy Fox. *Cisco Secure PIX Firewalls.* Indianapolis, IN: Cisco Press, 2002.

 See the Cisco PIX Firewall Command Reference, Version 6.2 at `http://www.cisco.com/univercd/cc/td/doc/product/iaabu/pix/pix_sw/ v_62/cmdref/index.htm.`

 See the Password Recovery and AAA Configuration Recovery Procedure   for   the   PIX   at   `http://www.cisco.com/warp/ public/110/34.shtml.`

Translations and Connections

Terms you'll need to understand:

✓ Translation table
✓ Connection table
✓ TCP
✓ Embryonic connection
✓ UDP
✓ Static mapping
✓ Dynamic mapping
✓ Port redirection

Techniques you'll need to master:

✓ The **clear xlate** command
✓ The **show xlate** command
✓ The **show conn** command
✓ The **static** command
✓ NAT and PAT
✓ **nat 0**
✓ Port redirection

The PIX firewall allows traffic to flow from higher security levels to lower security levels using features such as network address translation (NAT), port address translation (PAT), and static mappings. Traffic originating from lower security level interfaces destined to higher security level interfaces must be manually configured using the static and conduit commands before the traffic can pass. This chapter covers how to use the PIX firewall features to allow traffic to flow between interfaces.

Transport Protocols (Layer 4)

When programmers create applications that need to communicate across a network, they typically choose the Transmission Control Protocol (TCP), the User Datagram Protocol (UDP), or both protocols. These protocols help applications deliver data in either a reliable, connection-oriented (TCP) fashion or an unreliable, fast, connectionless-oriented (UDP) fashion. The PIX firewall tracks the TCP or UDP traffic traversing the firewall in slightly different ways, but both are monitored to provide users with stateful sessions across the firewall.

TCP Overview

TCP is a connection-oriented protocol. Connection-oriented protocols provide reliability that guarantees the delivery of data to its destination and that has enough know-how to retransmit missing data. TCP contains a defined state machine mechanism similar to a modem calling another computer. The following are the three states of TCP:

1. Set up the connection.

2. Send the data.

3. Disconnect the connection.

During the connection setup state, a process known as the *three-way hand-shake* takes place. This handshake helps the two communicating computers establish connection parameters that will be used during the transmission of data. The first step of the handshake opens a connection by sending a synchronization (SYN) request. This is sent to the destination computer, which in step two sends its own SYN request back with an acknowledgement (ACK) for the SYN it has received. In step three, the original computer responds to the SYN and ACK received with the last and final ACK. At this point the two computers are ready to send data. After the data transfer is finished, a FIN message is sent to disconnect the session.

For example, in Figure 5.1 Jack wants to communicate with Peter's computer. The following steps take place:

1. Jack sends a synchronization message to open a connection.

2. Peter's computer responds with its own SYN to Jack and an acknowledgement to Jack's SYN.

3. Jack receives Peter's SYN and ACK and responds with a final ACK back to Peter.

4. Data transmission begins.

5. The computers are disconnected by the FIN message being sent.

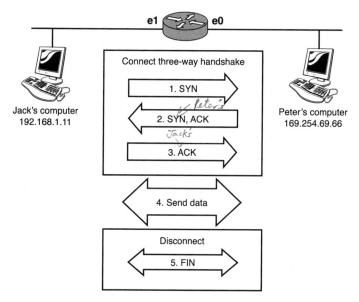

Figure 5.1   A three-way handshake.

How the PIX Works with TCP

The PIX is a stateful firewall that monitors the traffic flowing through it. The TCP protocol is very predictable, and the PIX system uses this to its advantage. Using the previous example, when Jack first communicates with Peter, the PIX records the connection information into its connection table. It then allows the SYN and ACK messages from Peter to pass back through the firewall to Jack—and only Jack. After Jack sends the final ACK, the TCP session is established and a connection slot is established in the PIX that allows Jack and Peter to send data back and forth. If you were to view the connection table, you would see that a connection is being made between Jack and Peter. As they disconnect from each other, a FIN message is sent that closes each TCP session. The PIX monitors the traffic for this FIN message and uses it as a flag to remove the connection table entry created for the two. If Peter were to send more information to Jack after the FIN message has been sent, no entry would be found in the table and Peter's data would be discarded, thus protecting Jack from uninitiated traffic.

By default, the PIX firewall drops all initiated traffic from lower-level interfaces (Peter) to higher-level interfaces (Jack). A manual static entry can be added to override this, though.

Embryonic Connections

The process TCP uses is very predictable; hackers can use this to their advantage when trying to hack a system. For example a *SYN attack* occurs when a hacker sends hundreds or even thousands of SYN open connection requests to a computer, with the intention of never acknowledging those requests with an ACK. This leaves the victim computer wasting resources for each of those half-open connections. If too much of the victim's resources are wasted, the computer can fail, causing a denial of service. These half-open connections can be limited by using *embryonic connection values* on several of the PIX commands. Limiting the number of half-open connections helps guarantee that the computer won't be overloaded with false open requests.

UDP Overview

The User Datagram Protocol is a connectionless protocol. Connectionless protocols do not guarantee that data will be delivered to the destination through the use of SYN, ACK, or FIN messages, thus they're faster than TCP. If reliability is necessary, however, the application layer needs to monitor for missing data. UDP causes the PIX several problems. Because UDP does not use a three-way handshake or FIN messages, the PIX never really knows when to remove the connection slot entry between two computers. As a result, the PIX uses an idle timer to monitor whether traffic is passing between the two computers. If the timer expires before any traffic has passed, the connection is assumed ended and the connection slot entry is removed.

Private Addresses

Private address are IP addresses that are available for everyone to use inside a private company, home, or office. RFC 1918, "Address Allocation for

Private Internets," designates IP address ranges that have been blocked by IANA from use on the Internet.

Although you might think that private addresses are nonroutable, this is technically not true. These addresses work just fine in routing tables; they just do not exist—or should not exist—in routing tables on the Internet and thus cannot be routed anywhere. In the field, you will see these ranges used repeatedly because companies typically don't like to use real public Internet addresses inside their building or private networks. Instead, they prefer to use NAT to translate these nonroutable, private addresses to real public addresses that can be routed on the Internet. The list shown here displays the private IP address ranges that can be used:

➤ *Class A*—10.0.0.0–10.255.255.255 mask 255.0.0.0

➤ *Class B*—172.16.0.0–172.31.255.255 mask 255.240.0.0

➤ *Class C*—192.168.0.0–192.168.255.255 mask 255.255.0.0

Address Translation

The PIX firewall creates IP address-to-IP address mappings of traffic flowing through the firewall. Typically, the inside interface uses private addressing (RFC 1918) that cannot be used on the Internet. So, as the traffic is funneled out of the outside interface, NAT or PAT translation occurs. NAT replaces the source's private address with an available global public address on the outside interface, allowing traffic to travel on the public network while hiding the real (private) user IP address.

Translation (xlate) and Connection (conn) Tables

The PIX uses two main tables to track the traffic flowing through the system: the translation (xlate) table and the connection (conn) table. The translation table is used for IP address-to-IP address mapping and is commonly known as the xlate table. For example, as data from Jack travels across the firewall, his source address of 192.168.1.11 is changed to 169.254.8.1. These entries are sometimes called *slots*.

ie. 3 hours

xlate table entries remain in the table for 180 minutes by default. You can use the **timeout xlate** command to change this setting.

vs

connection?

The connection table contains layer 4 TCP or UDP sessions and is used to track with whom Jack has a current session. For example, as Jack sends data to Peter, a connection is made in the xlate table that represents the session generated between the two. After the two have finished sending data, the connection entry is automatically removed. Listing 5.1 shows the xlate and conn commands.

Listing 5.1   The show xlate and show conn Commands

```
Pixfirewall# show xlate
1 in use, 53 most used
PAT Global 169.254.8.1(1237) Local 192.168.1.11(1969)
Pixfirewall#
Pixfirewall# show conn
1 in use, 5 most used
TCP out 169.254.69.66:80 in 192.168.1.11:1969 idle 0:00:03 Bytes 334
Pixfirewall#
```

Listing 5.1 shows that the local address 192.168.1.11 (Jack) is being translated to 169.254.8.1. The show conn command shows that a TCP session exists between 192.168.1.11 (Jack) and IP address 169.254.69.66.

Step-by-Step Flow

The following demonstrates the step-by-step flow that occurs as Jack's computer connects to Peter's computer through the PIX firewall:

1. Jack wants to connect to Peter's computer, and the xlate slot is made for Jack to travel through the PIX. His IP address of 192.168.1.11 is translated to 169.254.8.1.

2. Jack opens a connection (SYN) with Peter (IP address 169.254.69.66).

3. The session between Jack and Peter is recorded in the conn table and the data is ready to be sent.

4. Jack and Peter send data back and forth.

5. The conn table entry is removed when either the TCP FIN message is seen or the conn timer expires.

Note that the xlate slot is not removed yet; if Jack wants to communicate with Peter or another computer, the xlate slot for 192.168.1.11 to 169.254.8.1 is reused. In Figure 5.2 Jack's computer is connecting to four Web servers on the Internet and the PIX is using NAT to translate addresses. The xlate table shows a single entry for the translation, and the conn table displays the four TCP sessions created to each Web site. Figure 5.2 displays Jack's xlate and connection information.

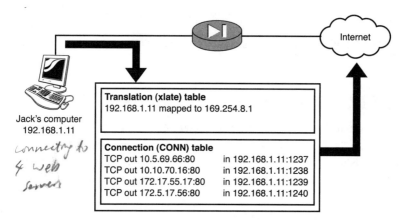

Figure 5.2   xlate and conn tables.

 Whenever you make changes using the **access-lists**, **alias**, **global**, **interface**, **ip address**, **nameif**, **nat**, **outbound**, or **static** command, you should clear the xlate table using the **clear xlate** command.

The **show** and **clear xlate** Table Commands

The xlate command has several parameters that can be used with it. When using the xlate by itself, you display or clear the entire table. The parameters give you the granularity to work with only a few entries or groups of entries. The following is the xlate command's syntax:

```
show¦clear xlate [global¦local <ip1[-ip2]> [netmask <mask>]]
            [gport ¦lport <port1[-port2]>]
            [interface <if1[,if2]>]
            [state <static[,portmap][,norandomseq][,identity]>]
            [debug]
            [count]
            [detail]
```

Table 5.1 displays several xlate commands and their descriptions.

Table 5.1 xlate Commands

Command	Description
show xlate	Displays the contents of the xlate table
show xlate detail	Displays more detail about the entries in the table
show xlate state static	Displays only the static entries in the xlate table
show xlate count	Displays the current entries being used and the most frequently used ones
clear xlate	Clears the entire table
clear xlate state static	Clears only the static mappings in the table

The show conn Table Commands

The conn command is very similar to the xlate command; you can view or affect the entire table or just a subset of its entries. Remember that the connection table is used to monitor and control the sessions between two computers. Therefore, the parameters for the conn command include things such as FIN, TCP, and UDP. The command syntax is as follows:

```
show conn [count] ¦ [protocol <tcp¦udp>]
        [foreign¦local <ip1[-ip2]> [netmask <mask>]]
        [lport¦fport <port1[-port2>]
        [state <up[,finin][,finout][,http_get][,smtp_data]
                [,data_in][,data_out][,...]>]
```

[detail]

Table 5.2 conn Commands

Command	Description
show conn	Displays the entire contents of the connection table
show conn detail	Displays detailed information about each connection entry
show conn protocol udp	Displays only the UDP traffic connection table entries

Outbound Traffic

The PIX firewall, by default, allows traffic from higher security level interfaces to traverse to interfaces with lower security level interfaces. This means that traffic initiated on the inside interface is allowed to pass to the outside interface. Setting up outbound traffic is a fairly easy task. You can use the nat, global, and static commands to help control which IP address translations you want to occur. You can also use commands such as access-list to control

dynomic translation   static translation

who can and cannot traverse your firewall. Also, you can use various methods, such as static and dynamic translation, to translate inside IP addresses to outside IP addresses.

To set up a basic scenario, use Figure 5.3 as the network diagram. Subnets 192.168.1.0/24 are the inside addresses that need to be translated to outside addresses.

Contradicts with # in P.88 !

No traffic is allowed to pass through the PIX until a **nat-global** or **static** command has been issued.

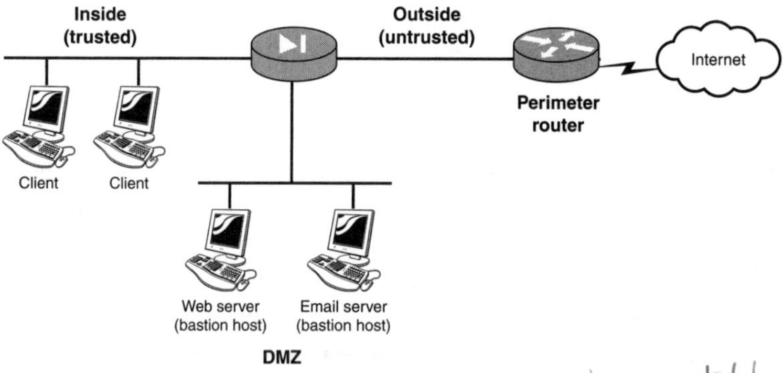

Figure 5.3 — labeled diagram:

Inside (trusted) — Outside (untrusted) — Perimeter router — Internet

Client   Client

Web server (bastion host)   Email server (bastion host)

DMZ

Figure 5.3   Network diagram.

Syntax may not be current !!

use static command

Static Address Translations

ver 6.2 & higher

To configure static NAT, you can use the `static` command, as shown here:

```
Pixfirewall(config)# [no] static [(internal_if_name, external_if_name)]
               {<global_ip>|interface}<local_ip> [dns] [netmask <mask>]
               [<max_conns> [<emb_limit> [<norandomseq>]]]
```

access-list <acl-id>} [dns] [<max_conns> [<emb_limit>)
[norandomseq] [<max-conns>] [<emb-limit>)

oh, but is the default if not specify, this?

Although the **static** command lists the interface names in internal-external sequence, the sequence of the IP addresses that follow is reversed! Figure 5.4 shows how the internal inside interface address of 192.168.1.11 is mapped to the outside address of 169.254.8.1.

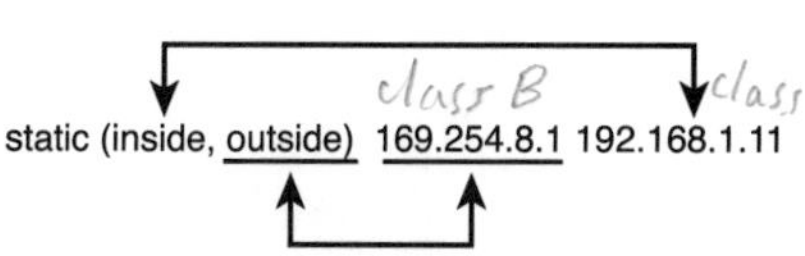

A: default mask for the IP address class is used.

class B   class C

static (inside, outside) 169.254.8.1 192.168.1.11   *netmask 255.255.255.255*

Q: what if global ip & local ip are in diff. address class & netmask is not specified?

Figure 5.4   The **static** command syntax.

acl_id ... ... Specifies the access list to use with policy-based static address translation

Table 5.3 static Command Options

Option	Function
internal_if_name	This defines the internal interface name that has a higher security level.
external_if_name	This defines the external interface name that has a lower security level.
global_IP	This is the global IP address you want your internal user to always use.
local_IP	This is the internal IP address you want statically assigned.
network_mask	The mask is used for both the internal and the external IP addresses. By using 255.255.255.255, you can define a specific host; by using 255.255.255.0, you can define an entire subnet.
max_conns	This defines the maximum number of connections an IP address can use at the same time.
em_limit	This defines the embryonic connection limit. The default is **0**, which means unlimited connections are allowed.
norandomseq	This allows you to turn off randomizing the TCP/IP packet sequence numbers. This is not recommended, but the parameter is available if necessary.

used to specify global ip and local ip

dns   Specifies that DNS replies which match the xlate are translated.

The static command enables you to bind an internal inside IP address to an outside global address, making a one-to-one mapping. Every time a specific inside user travels across the PIX, that user is assigned the same global address. For example, if Jack's internal IP address is 192.168.1.11, you can use the static command shown here to bind Jack's address to a specific global address, such as 169.254.8.1. The following command creates this one-to-one mapping:

```
Pixfirewall(config)# static (inside, outside) 169.254.8.1 192.168.1.11
```

netmask 255.255.255.255

Now, when Jack is traveling across the firewall, he will always use 169.254.8.1 on the public side and the PIX xlate table will show the following:

```
Pixfirewall# show xlate
1 in use, 1237 most used
Global 169.254.8.1 Local 192.168.1.11
```

Listing 5.2 creates a static one-to-one mapping from the three internal addresses to three global addresses. Figure 5.5 display the one-to-one mapping graphically.

Listing 5.2   Static One-to-One Mapping

```
Pixfirewall(config)# static (inside, outside) 169.254.8.1 192.168.1.11
Pixfirewall(config)# static (inside, outside) 169.254.8.2 192.168.1.12
Pixfirewall(config)# static (inside, outside) 169.254.8.3 192.168.1.13
Pixfirewall(config)#
Pixfirewall(config)# exit
Pixfirewall# clear xlate
```

netmask 255. 255. 255. 255

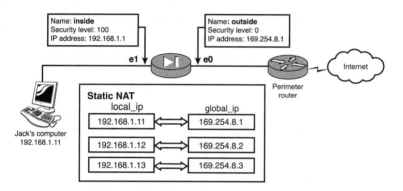

Figure 5.5   The **static** command.

Dynamic Address Translations

use {nat, global} commands

By using the static command, you can specify a global address for each host. However, this manual binding can be too tedious to set up, or you might not have enough global addresses for every internal user. Dynamic address translation enables you to set up groups of internal addresses that can be assigned to a single global address or a pool of global addresses. The two main forms of dynamic address translations are NAT and PAT.

Network Address Translation

NAT enables you to dynamically assign groups of internal addresses to a pool of global addresses. This configuration takes a minimum of two commands: nat and global. Listing 5.3 demonstrates these commands.

Listing 5.3   The nat and global Commands Used for Dynamic Mappings

```
Pixfirewall(config)# IP address outside 169.254.8.1 255.255.255.0
Pixfirewall(config)# IP address inside 192.168.1.1 255.255.255.0
Pixfirewall(config)#
Pixfirewall(config)# route outside 0.0.0.0 0.0.0.0 169.254.8.254 1
Pixfirewall(config)#
Pixfirewall(config)# nat(inside) 1 0.0.0.0 0.0.0.0
```

everything

Listing 5.3   The nat and global Commands Used for Dynamic Mappings *(continued)*

```
Pixfirewall(config)# global (outside) 1 169.254.8.2-169.254.8.6
                netmask 255.255.255.0
Pixfirewall(config)#
Pixfirewall(config)# exit
Pixfirewall# clear xlate
```

The nat and global commands work together to allow all traffic on the inside interface to exit the outside interface within the range of 169.254.8.2–169.254.8.6.

The 0.0.0.0 0.0.0.0 in the nat command is similar to a default route command; all IP addresses will use the global address range using a NAT ID of 1. The first address will consume the IP address of 169.254.8.2, and the next will use 169.254.8.3, and so on. If a computer stops passing traffic through the firewall, the PIX will release the xlate slot and allow another computer to reuse the global address.

 Use the **no nat** and **no global** commands to delete all **nat** and **global** configuration entries.

In the example in Figure 5.6, computers coming from network 192.168.1.0 use the global range of 169.254.8.2–169.254.8.6 and computers from network 10.0.0.0 use the range of 169.254.8.7–169.254.8.11. The NAT ID portion of the nat and global commands helps to bind which inside NAT pool and which global pools go together.

Listing 5.4 demonstrates the commands necessary to create the mappings in Figure 5.6.

Listing 5.4   nat and global Commands for Two Dynamic Mappings

```
Pixfirewall(config)# IP address outside 169.254.8.1 255.255.255.0
Pixfirewall(config)# IP address inside 192.168.1.1 255.255.255.0
Pixfirewall(config)#
Pixfirewall(config)# route outside 0.0.0.0 0.0.0.0 169.254.8.254 1
Pixfirewall(config)#
Pixfirewall(config)# nat (inside) 2 192.168.1.0 255.255.255.0
Pixfirewall(config)# nat (inside) 3 10.0.0.0 255.0.0.0
Pixfirewall(config)# global (outside) 2 169.254.8.2-169.254.8.6
                netmask 255.255.255.0
Pixfirewall(config)# global (outside) 3 169.254.8.7-169.254.8.11
                netmask 255.255.255.0
Pixfirewall(config)#
Pixfirewall(config)# exit
Pixfirewall# clear xlate
```

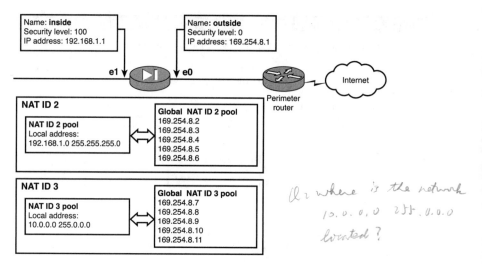

Figure 5.6 Using **nat** with two pools.

Port Address Translation

PAT enables you to use a single address for many internal addresses. For example, if your ISP assigns you only one address, you can have all your internal users share the same global IP address by implementing PAT. PAT modifies the port numbers of the source address to provide the tracking capability necessary on the return requests. For example, as Jack travels across the PIX, his address is changed from 192.168.1.11 port 1939 to the global address of 169.254.8.1 port number 5000. As Kristina travels across the PIX at the same time, her address of 192.168.1.25 port 1970 is changed to the same IP address Jack received—169.254.8.1—but with a different port number, such as 5001. The PIX tracks these IP address-to-port translations in the xlate table.

In Figure 5.7 all the inside addresses coming into the PIX will use the single address of 169.254.8.1 as their global source address. Because all the internal addresses use the same global address, PAT will also modify the source port to provide a specific mapping back to the internal source.

Listing 5.5 displays the PAT being set up with the global command using the option called interface. This option sets the outside interface IP address of 169.254.8.1 as the global address.

Listing 5.5   PAT and global Command for Dynamic Mappings

```
Pixfirewall(config)# IP address outside 169.254.8.1 255.255.255.0
Pixfirewall(config)# IP address inside 192.168.1.1 255.255.255.0
Pixfirewall(config)#
```

Listing 5.5   PAT and global Command for Dynamic Mappings *(continued)*

```
Pixfirewall(config)# route outside 0.0.0.0 0.0.0.0 169.254.8.254 1
Pixfirewall(config)#
Pixfirewall(config)# nat (inside) 1 0.0.0.0 0.0.0.0
Pixfirewall(config)# global (outside) 1 interface
Pixfirewall(config)#
Pixfirewall(config)# exit
Pixfirewall# clear xlate
```

set the outside interface
IP address as the
global address

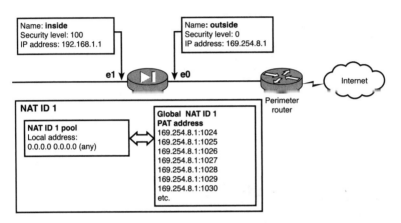

Figure 5.7   PAT example.

NAT and PAT Together

You've learned how to use NAT to translate internal addresses to a global address creating a one-to-one mapping. You have also seen how to use a single address and use PAT to change the source port numbers to create a mapping back to the internal source. Now, let's see how to use both at the same time.

Figure 5.8 and Listing 5.6 demonstrate the use of NAT and PAT together. Users from the inside first use the NAT address in the range of 169.254.8.1–169.254.8.5 until all the entries have been allocated. Then they begin to share the PAT address and use different port numbers.

Listing 5.6   NAT, PAT, and the global Command

```
Pixfirewall(config)# IP address outside 169.254.8.1 255.255.255.0
Pixfirewall(config)# IP address inside 192.168.1.1 255.255.255.0
Pixfirewall(config)#
Pixfirewall(config)# route outside 0.0.0.0 0.0.0.0 169.254.8.254 1
Pixfirewall(config)#
Pixfirewall(config)# nat (inside) 1 0.0.0.0 0.0.0.0
Pixfirewall(config)# global (outside) 1 169.254.8.2-169.254.8.6
                netmask 255.255.255.0
```

Listing 5.6   NAT, PAT, and the global Command (continued)

```
Pixfirewall(config)# global (outside) 1 169.254.8.11
                 netmask 255.255.255.255
Pixfirewall(config)#
Pixfirewall(config)# exit
Pixfirewall# clear xlate
```

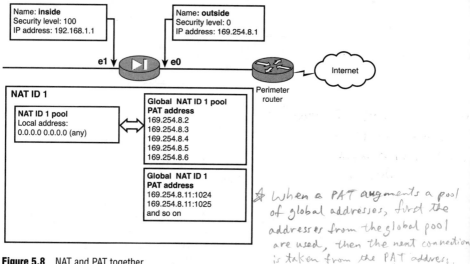

Figure 5.8   NAT and PAT together.

When a PAT augments a pool of global addresses, first the addresses from the global pool are used, then the next connection is taken from the PAT address.

ALERT

PAT has several problems when working with H.323, caching name servers, multi-media applications, and PPTP. So, if you are working with these technologies, use NAT instead of PAT.

Working Without NAT or PAT

You might encounter a situation in which addresses in the inside interface are just fine the way they are and don't need translating. If this is the case, you can use the nat 0 command. For example, if your address is 192.168.1.11 and it doesn't need to be translated on the other side of the PIX, the nat 0 command simply passes the traffic through without changing the source address.

without using access list

b) **nat 0**   *Syntax : nat (inside) 0 192.168.1.0 255.255.255.0*

The nat 0 command stands by itself. It doesn't need the use of a global command because it doesn't change the source address; it only passes it through the firewall like a router would.

Q: How to configure if the rest of the addresses need translation?

Nat0 — identity NAT
you can accept the inbound traffic only when the traffic is initiated from the inside and after the xlate is created.

In Figure 5.9 the nat 0 command does not translate the three networks; it just passes them on.

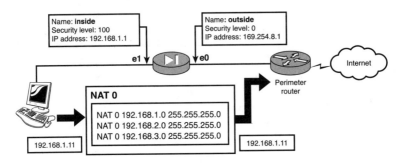

Figure 5.9 The nat 0 command.

Listing 5.7 shows that three nat 0 commands are used to allow the three sub-nets of 192.168.1.0, 192.168.2.0, and 192.168.3.0 to pass through the PIX firewall without translating their addresses.

Listing 5.7 Using the nat 0 Command

```
Pixfirewall(config)# nat (inside) 0 192.168.1.0 255.255.255.0
Pixfirewall(config)# nat (inside) 0 192.168.2.0 255.255.255.0
Pixfirewall(config)# nat (inside) 0 192.168.3.0 255.255.255.0
Pixfirewall(config)#
Pixfirewall(config)# exit
Pixfirewall# clear xlate
```

nat 0 access-list — NAT Exemption *Allows traffic whenever it matches the referenced ACL, regardless of*

b) **Using nat 0 with an Access Control List** *whether or not there is already an*

not true !! *xlate*

You can accomplish the same nat 0 task as in Listing 5.8 by using an access control list to point to a list of address you want to use. Listing 5.8 uses the access-list option in the nat 0 command to point to an access list named cool-no-nat. The three access-list commands create the pool of addresses that will not be translated.

Beware that the mask on **access-list** commands on the PIX firewall are similar to normal subnet masks, not wildcard masks as on a Cisco IOS router. For example, to define a subnet for 192.168.1.0, the PIX would use a mask of 255.255.255.0, whereas IOS routers would use 0.0.0.255 for the same subnet.

A PIX firewall would use the following command:

`access-list 1 permit IP 192.168.1.0 `**`255.255.255.0`**

An IOS router, on the other hand, would use this command:

`access-list 1 permit IP 192.168.1.0 `**`0.0.0.255`**

Listing 5.8   Using the nat 0 Command with an Access List

```
Pixfirewall(config)# nat (inside) 0 access-list cool-no-nat
Pixfirewall(config)#
Pixfirewall(config)#access-list cool-no-nat permit IP 192.168.1.0
            255.255.255.0
Pixfirewall(config)#access-list cool-no-nat permit IP 192.168.2.0
            255.255.255.0
Pixfirewall(config)#access-list cool-no-nat permit IP 192.168.3.0
            255.255.255.0
Pixfirewall(config)# access-group cool-no-nat in interface inside
Pixfirewall(config)# exit
Pixfirewall# clear xlate
```

Inbound Traffic

By default, the PIX prevents any traffic initiated on the lower security levels from accessing higher security level interfaces. However, when computers such as Web servers are located in a DMZ, you might need to open the firewall and allow external users to access the Web server. By using the static and conduit command, you can allow traffic initiated from the outside in to the DMZ or inside interfaces. Access lists can also be used to allow traffic in (they are covered in Chapter 6, "Access Control Lists and Traffic Control").

For example, to allow Peter access to your Web server located in the DMZ, you first need to create a static mapping of the Web server to a global IP or port address. Then, you must use either the conduit command or an access list to allow traffic to pass from the lower security level interface to the DMZ.

You've seen the static command in action, and you know how to create a one-to-one mapping of IP addresses. But the conduit command is a special case because it is currently being replaced by the introduction of the access control list commands into the PIX IOS. Cisco doesn't recommend using the conduit command, but you do need to be familiar with it. Using conduits enables you to control inbound access to the PIX. In Figure 5.10, any traffic from the outside is allowed to access the Web server.

Listing 5.9 demonstrates the conduit command.

Listing 5.9   The conduit Command

```
Pixfirewall(config)# static (dmz, outside) 169.254.8.2 172.16.0.5
Pixfirewall(config)# conduit permit tcp host 169.254.8.2 eq www any
Pixfirewall(config)#
Pixfirewall(config)# exit
Pixfirewall# clear xlate
```

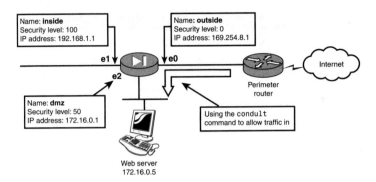

Figure 5.10 The **static** and **conduit** commands.

The static command in Listing 5.9 maps the Web server's internal address to the global address of 169.254.8.2. The conduit command permits any traffic destined to global address 169.254.8.2 with port 80 (www) to enter the PIX. Once inside, the PIX translates the destination of the global address of 169.254.8.2 to the mapped internal address of 172.16.0.5 and passes the traffic.

This setup works well when you have several NAT-able addresses. Figure 5.11 displays three servers in the DMZ that need to be accessed via the outside interface. The static commands map global addresses to DMZ addresses, and the conduits create exceptions to the ASA for certain protocols using the static mappings.

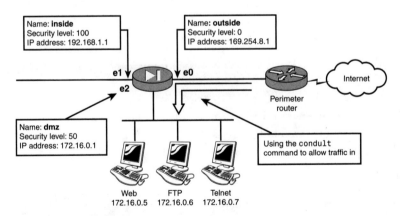

Figure 5.11 Static and conduit to multiple DMZ servers.

Listing 5.10 shows the static and conduit commands allowing traffic from any host to any of the three servers.

Listing 5.10   Conduit Commands for Multiple DMZ Servers

```
Pixfirewall(config)# static (dmz, outside) 169.254.8.2 172.16.0.5
Pixfirewall(config)# static (dmz, outside) 169.254.8.3 172.16.0.6
Pixfirewall(config)# static (dmz, outside) 169.254.8.4 172.16.0.7
Pixfirewall(config)#
Pixfirewall(config)# conduit permit tcp host 169.254.8.2 eq www any
Pixfirewall(config)# conduit permit tcp host 169.254.8.3 eq ftp any
Pixfirewall(config)# conduit permit tcp host 169.254.8.4 eq telnet any
Pixfirewall(config)#
Pixfirewall(config)# exit
Pixfirewall# clear xlate
```

The **static** command is used to create binding and permanent mapping from an internal address to a global address. The **conduit** command is used to allow lower security level interfaces to access higher security level interfaces.

Cisco doesn't recommend using this command

→ *Can use access-list instead*

Port Redirection

Using NAT is great for creating one-to-one mappings of internal and global external addresses. However, if your ISP gives you only a single address to work with and you still want internal computers to be accessed via the Internet, port redirection is your solution. By using a single IP address on the outside, you can direct the traffic to the desired internal server by mapping the port numbers. For example, if Jack has only one outside address (169.254.8.1) but needs to access three servers via the Internet, he could create a mapping as shown in Table 5.4. Table 5.4 shows that external global addresses and ports are mapped to internal addresses and ports.

Table 5.4   Port Redirection Example

Internal Address: Port	External Global Address: Port
172.16.0.1:80	169.254.8.1:80 *www*
172.16.0.2:21	169.254.8.1:21 *ftp*
172.16.0.3:23	169.254.8.1:23 *telnet*

Whenever traffic comes in entering 169.254.8.1:80, it is redirected to the internal server at 172.16.0.1:80. This enables Jack to use a single IP address and still access several services hosted behind the firewall. Listing 5.11 is an example of using the `static` command with the `port` option to make one-to-one mappings using a single address and a specific port.

tcp ? *can use the keyword "interface" instead*

Listing 5.11 Port Redirection

```
Pixfirewall(config)# static (dmz, outside) 169.254.8.1 80 172.16.0.1 80    port #
Pixfirewall(config)# static (dmz, outside) 169.254.8.1 21 172.16.0.2 21
Pixfirewall(config)# static (dmz, outside) 169.254.8.1 23 172.16.0.3 23
Pixfirewall(config)#
Pixfirewall(config)# conduit permit tcp host 169.254.8.1 eq www any
Pixfirewall(config)# conduit permit tcp host 169.254.8.1 eq ftp any
Pixfirewall(config)# conduit permit tcp host 169.254.8.1 eq telnet any
Pixfirewall(config)#
Pixfirewall(config)# exit
Pixfirewall# clear xlate
```

???

In PIX OS version 6.0, the **static** command has been modified to allow port redirection without the need for a **conduit** command (see Cisco's site for more information: **http://www.cisco.com/en/US/products/hw/vpndevc/ps2030/products_tech_note09186a00800094aad.shtml#topic9**)

Q: what is the syntax?

A: static [(internal-if-name, external-if-name)] tcp|udp
global-ip | interface global-port local-ip local-port
[netmask mask]

Exam Prep Questions

Question 1

What are two methods of address translation?

- ❏ A. PATH
- ☑ B. Dynamic
- ☑ C. Static
- ❏ D. Manual

Answers B and C are correct. Two types of translations are dynamic and static. Dynamic translation uses NAT or PAT to translate internal addresses to global external addresses. Static translation is the process of creating a permanent, one-to-one mapping of an internal address to a global address. Answer D manual is wrong. Although static mappings are a manual process, the most correct answer between static and manual is static. Answer A, PATH, has nothing to do with PIX firewall translations. Therefore, answer A is incorrect.

Question 2

Which command would you use to display only active static translations?

- ○ A. **show xlate**
- ○ B. **show xlate state static**
- ○ C. **show static**
- ○ D. **show static active**

Answers B is correct. The `show xlate state static` command displays only the active static entries in the xlate table. `show xlate` displays both static and dynamic entries in the table; the question asks for only active static translations, so answer A is incorrect. The `show static` command displays the manual static mappings you have created, not the actual active connections, so answer C is incorrect. The `show static active` command does not exist, so answer D is incorrect.

Question 3

> What is the default xlate table entry timeout?
>
> O A. 5 minutes
> O B. 30 minutes
> O C. 60 minutes
> ⊘ D. 180 minutes

Answers D is correct. The default xlate table entry timeout is 180 minutes. If no traffic is using the xlate slot after 180 minutes, the entry is removed. Therefore, answers A, B, and C are incorrect.

Question 4

> Packets travel through the PIX firewall if no connection or xlate entries exist.
>
> O A. True
> ⊘ B. False

Answer B is correct. Without a connection state or xlate slot, traffic will not flow through the PIX firewall. Normally, traffic from high security level interfaces can freely traverse the firewall, but in doing so a connection slot is created. Therefore, answer A is incorrect.

Question 5

> What does the **xlate** keyword do?
>
> ⊘ A. It views and clears translations.
> O B. It sets timeout values.
> O C. It configures static mappings.
> O D. It creates translations.

Answer A is correct. The xlate command can be used to view and clear xlate translations. The timeout command is used to set timeout values, so answer B is incorrect. To configure static mappings, the static command is used, so answer C is incorrect. The xlate command does not create translations, so answer D is incorrect.

Question 6

What function does the **NAT** command perform? (Select two.)

☑ A. It enables address translations.

☑ B. It disables address translations.

❑ C. It creates active address translations.

❑ D. It removes active address translations.

Answers A and B are correct. The nat command is used to create address pools that will be translated with the corresponding global command. The no nat command removes NAT configuration statements. The nat 0 command stops translations from occurring. This command does not create active address translations, so answer C is incorrect. It also does not remove active address translations, so answer D is incorrect.

Question 7   tricky !!

If you have addresses that don't need network address translation, which command would you use?

○ A. **no nat**

○ B. **nat 0**

○ C. **no nat 0**

○ D. **global 0**

Answer B is correct. The nat 0 command enables you to specify addresses that you don't want the PIX firewall to translate. This works well when you have computers in a DMZ that already have Internet public addresses but are protected by a firewall. The no nat command turns off NAT altogether, so answer A is incorrect. no nat 0 removes the NAT bypassing command, so answer C is incorrect. The global 0 command doesn't exist, so answer D is incorrect.

Question 8   see answer key

Why would you choose not to use PAT?

○ A. PAT works only when you have few users.

○ B. PAT doesn't work with Telnet.

○ C. PAT doesn't work with most multimedia protocols.

○ D. It's not available on the PIX firewall.

Answer C is correct. Some multimedia protocols do not work across PAT because they use specific port numbers that PAT might have allocated to other users. If you need to support these protocols, use NAT because it translates only IP addresses and not ports. PAT can support 64,000 ports for users, so answer A is incorrect. Answer B is incorrect because PAT does work well with Telnet. PAT is available on the PIX firewall; therefore, answer D is incorrect.

Question 9

Why would you choose to use PAT over NAT?

○ A. You have enough IP address for all your internal users.

○ B. You have only a single IP address for all your internal users.

○ C. You have a small PIX firewall.

○ D. You want to save on memory allocations on your firewall.

Answer B is correct. PAT is a good choice when you have only a single IP address from your ISP. By using PAT, all your internal users can share a single IP address, and PAT uses port numbers for resolution. If you have enough IP addresses for all your internal users, you can use NAT, so answer A is incorrect. PAT is available on all sizes of PIX firewall and will not save you any memory by using it; therefore, answers C and D are incorrect.

Question 10

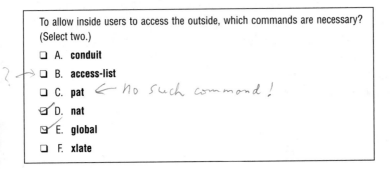

To allow inside users to access the outside, which commands are necessary? (Select two.)

❑ A. **conduit**

❑ B. **access-list**

❑ C. **pat**   ← No such command!

❑ D. **nat**

❑ E. **global**

❑ F. **xlate**

Answers D and E are correct. The two commands necessary to allow access outside the PIX are nat and the corresponding global command. conduit commands allow inbound access and must be used in conjunction with a static command, so answer A is incorrect. The access-list command enables you to control who can enter an interface, so answer B is incorrect. The pat command does not exist, making answer C incorrect. `xlate` is used to view or clear translations, so answer F is incorrect.

Question 11   ○

Select two reasons to use NAT.

- ☑ A. To hide internal computers' real IP addresses from external users
- ❑ B. To allow traffic to flow between interfaces   *Vague.*
- ❑ C. To create routing tables
- ☑ D. To conserve non-RFC 1918 for Internet users

Answers A and D are correct. NAT enables you to hide internal addresses from external users. NAT can also prolong the life of IPv4 by allowing private users to share addresses as they travel across the Internet. Answer B is incorrect because, when NAT helps translate internal addresses to external global addresses from the inside to the outside, `static` and `conduit` commands or access lists are needed to allow traffic from the outside interface to the inside interface. So, answer B is not totally correct; NAT alone does not allow all traffic to flow between interfaces. Answer C is incorrect because the `route` command is used to create routing table entries.

Need to Know More?

 Chapman, David and Andy Fox. *Cisco Secure PIX Firewalls*. Indianapolis, IN: Cisco Press, 2002.

 Deal, Richard A. *Cisco PIX Firewalls*. Berkeley, CA: McGraw-Hill/Osborne, 2002.

Access Control Lists and Traffic Control

. . . .

Terms you'll need to understand:

✓ Access list

✓ Access group

✓ Turbo ACLs

✓ Object grouping

✓ Allowing traffic in

✓ Controlling traffic out

✓ Conduits

Techniques you'll need to master:

✓ Access lists

✓ Turbo ACLs

✓ Network object groups

✓ Protocol object groups

✓ Nesting object groups

✓ ICMP through the PIX

The Cisco PIX firewall has several commands in its arsenal to control traffic flow: conduit commands to control traffic from lower security level interfaces to higher security level interfaces; outbound filter commands to control traffic from higher security level interfaces to lower level interfaces; and Cisco Access Control List (ACL) commands. The ACL commands can do everything conduit and outbound filter commands do, but they do them better and even come with powerful features such as turbo ACLs and object grouping. This chapter talks about the uses of conduits, outbound filters, ACLs, turbo ACLs, and object grouping.

Controlling Traffic Coming In

The previous chapter introduced the use of the conduit command, which allows you to enable traffic initiated from lower security level interfaces to pass through to higher security level interfaces. Originally, the PIX firewall started with the conduit command, but Cisco has introduced the IOS-style ACL into newer PIX images. Cisco recommends doing away with the older conduit commands and prefers the newer ACL commands in their place. Before we jump into the recommended ACL commands for letting traffic in, however, let's explore the conduit command and some of its features.

The conduit Command

The conduit command makes an exception in the ASA to permit or deny specific traffic from lower security level interfaces to pass to higher security level interfaces. Figure 6.1 displays the traffic flow from the outside to the inside interface. The traffic first enters the PIX via the global IP address assigned to the outside interface. Then the conduit entries are checked to verify whether a permit match exists. If a permit match is found, the packet is forwarded to the static mapping statements where the global address is changed to the mapped inside address. Otherwise, if a deny match entry exists, or no match at all exists, the packet is dropped.

Be aware that the **conduit** command always needs to be paired with a **static** command. Otherwise, traffic will not be translated through the PIX.

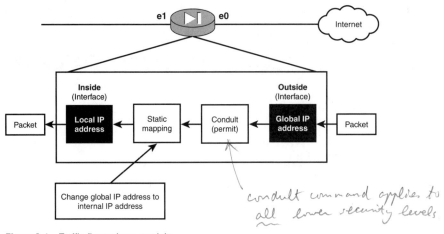

Figure 6.1 Traffic flow using a conduit.

As an example, if Peter, who is on the outside, wants to connect to Jack's computer on the inside using Telnet, the following steps must be taken:

1. Set up a `static` command to create a one-to-one mapping for Jack's computer to a global outside address.

2. Enter a `conduit` command to allow traffic from Peter's outside computer to connect to the global address that maps to Jack's inside computer.

Figure 6.2 shows Jack's and Peter's computers for the following command example.

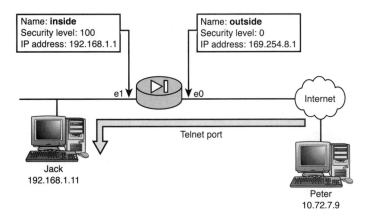

Figure 6.2 Outside traffic connecting to an inside computer.

The following Listing 6.1 allows Peter's computer to connect to Jack's computer:

Listing 6.1   static and conduit Commands

```
Pixfirewall(config)# static (inside, outside) 169.254.8.11 192.168.1.11
Pixfirewall(config)#
Pixfirewall(config)# conduit permit tcp
            ↪host 169.254.8.11 eq telnet host 10.72.7.9
Pixfirewall(config)#
Pixfirewall(config)# exit
Pixfirewall# clear xlate
```

(handwritten in margin: V.S. Listing 6.2)

(handwritten annotation: not "any")

Notice that the conduit command uses the global outside address instead of Jack's real internal address. All filters use the global address because, as traffic enters the PIX firewall, the filters take effect before the static command translates the global address to the real internal address.

> The order of the source and destination parameters for the **conduit** command are in reverse compared to the standard **access-list** command. To illustrate, the commands are ordered as follows:
>
> **conduit:**
>
> ```
> conduit permit tcp (DESTINATION) (SOURCE)
> ```
>
> **access-list:**
>
> ```
> access-list 101 permit tcp (SOURCE) (DESTINATION)
> ```

The conduit command is very easy to use, but it does have some flaws. You might not have noticed that we didn't attach this command to the outside interface—or any interface, for that matter. This command is not defined against any single interface; it's applied to all interfaces with lower security levels. The conduit entries are also processed in the order in which you entered them into the system. So, if you entered a permit conduit command and then a deny command below it, the deny entry would never be processed; you would have to drop all the conduit entries and reenter them in the correct order.

A Basic conduit Command

Table 6.1 displays the field descriptions for the following conduit command syntax:

```
Pixfirewall(config)# [no] conduit permit ¦ deny protocol global_ip
            ↪global_mask [operator port [port]]
            ↪foreign_ip foreign_mask[operator port [port]]
```

Table 6.1 conduit Command Options	
Option	**Function**
permit I deny	This defines whether to allow or disallow the matching traffic.
protocol	This defines the transport protocol, such as IP, TCP, UDP, or ICMP. (You use **ip** to specify all the protocols.)
global_ip global_mask	This is the global address you specified in the **static** command that eventually maps back to the internal address.
operator port	This is a comparison operand that lets you define single or multiple ports.
port	This enables you to specify the service you want to permit or deny. For example, you can use port 80 or the text **www** to allow HTTP traffic.
foreign_ip foreign_mask	This is the address of the outside computer trying to go through the PIX, sometimes known as the foreign address.

Access Control Lists

The access control list commands are used in just about every Cisco product to provide controlled access across a device or to define groups of addresses. We will talk here about access lists as named or numbered sets of entries that either permit or deny access across the PIX. A single access list can contain several, if not hundreds, of entries using permit or deny statements. These entries test traffic for source and destination address and ports matches. Access lists are created in the global area and can be attached to the desired interface needing control. Because they are created in the global area, a single access list can be attached (also known as *grouped*) to several interfaces simultaneously. If a change is made to the access list, all the interfaces using it are affected by that change. Figure 6.3 shows how ACLs filter the flow of traffic.

The ACL commands are similar to the commands on the Cisco IOS-based routers. They were introduced to the PIX firewall to provide more control, flexibility, and granularity and to support the standardization of Cisco commands across products. The ACL commands can perform the same functions as the conduit commands for traffic initiated on the outside needing to connect to inside computers. You can also use these commands to deny traffic you want to ensure is never allowed to enter a particular interface.

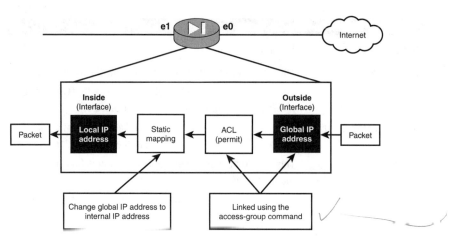

Figure 6.3 Traffic flow using access lists.

If you are using both the **access-list** command and the **conduit** command at the same time, the **access-list** command is processed first. Remember: Cisco has a large preference to the ACL commands, so use them instead of **conduit** commands when you can.

Access list commands also are slightly different from the normal IOS commands. PIX uses a normal mask and not a wildcard mask, as IOS routers do.

Configuring the access-list command to allow traffic inside involves three main steps:

1. Create a static mapping.

2. Set up the access list.

3. Attach it to the interface using the access-group command.

Working with the example in Figure 6.2, in which Peter wants to Telnet into Jack's computer, let's look at the syntax involved, only this time using an access list. The syntax to accomplish this task is similar to that of the conduit command, but the access-list (SOURCE) (DESTINATION) parameter ordering is different.

Listing 6.2 enables Peter to access Jack's computer using Telnet.

Listing 6.2   static and access-list Commands

```
Pixfirewall(config)# static (inside, outside) 169.254.8.11 192.168.1.11
Pixfirewall(config)# access-list Let-Peter-In permit tcp host 10.72.9.7
        ↪host 169.254.8.11 eq telnet
Pixfirewall(config)# access-group Let-Peter-In in interface outside
Pixfirewall(config)#
Pixfirewall(config)# exit
Pixfirewall# clear xlate
```

The `access-list` command in Listing 6.2 creates an access list called `Let-Peter-In`. The entry made in the list permits Telnet traffic coming from Peter (the source) to Jack's statically mapped global address (the destination). The `access-group` command attaches the list to the outside interface for all inbound traffic. The `access-group` command on the PIX can attach access lists only to the incoming traffic, not outgoing traffic as well as with IOS-based routers.

If you want to add more entries to an access list—for instance, to allow three computers access to the inside—just create the entries with the same name. The list will be processed in a top-down order. These commands create a list with three entries:

```
access-list 100 permit ip host 192.168.1.11 host 1.1.1.1
access-list 100 permit ip host 192.168.1.11 host 1.1.1.2
access-list 100 permit ip host 192.168.1.11 host 1.1.1.3
```

Access Control List Commands

Before we show you any more examples of access lists, a review of the details of the basic commands is necessary. Table 6.2 displays a list of several commands used to view, create, and delete access lists or access groups.

Table 6.2 ACL-related Commands	
Command	**Description**
show access-list	Displays either all the access lists or a single access list
show access-group	Displays access groups
access-list	Used to create, append, or delete an access list
access-group	Used to attach an access list to or remove it from an interface
clear access-list	Used to delete either all the access lists or a single list
clear access-group	Used to delete either all the access groups or a single group

The show access-list Command

The `show` commands enable you to display access list entries and their respective hit counts. The hit count feature is quite useful. As traffic that matches an access list entry travels through an interface, this small counter increments and gives you an indication of how frequently your access list entry is being used. For example, the `show access-list` command in Listing 6.3 displays access list 100 and reveals that the first entry has been hit seven times, the second entry has been hit only four times, and the third has never been hit.

Listing 6.3 The show access-list Command

```
pixfirewall# show access-list 100
access-list 100; 3 elements
access-list 100 permit ip host 192.168.1.11 host 1.1.1.1 (hitcnt=7)
access-list 100 permit ip host 192.168.1.11 host 1.1.1.2 (hitcnt=4)
access-list 100 permit ip host 192.168.1.11 host 1.1.1.3 (hitcnt=0)
```

 If you place a **deny IP any** any command as the last line of an access list, it will provide a hit count for all the traffic not matching the previous entries.

The show access-group Command

The show access-group command enables you to display all the access lists that are attached in an inward direction on all interfaces.

Listing 6.4 shows that access list 100 is attached to the inbound traffic on the outside interface and access list 1 is attached to the inside interface.

Listing 6.4 The show access-group Command

```
pixfirewall# show access-group
access-group 100 in interface outside
access-group 1 in interface inside
```

 Access lists are bound to the inbound direction of an interface, not the outbound direction. If you want to control traffic leaving the outside interface, you must bind an ACL to the inbound traffic on the inside interface.

The access-list Command

The access-list command creates and deletes access lists and access list entries. An access list can have a single entry or several entries that are processed in the order in which you added them to the list; sometimes the hardest part about working with access lists is ensuring that the entries are in the order you need to provide the desired result. If you put the entries in the wrong order, you'll need to delete the entire list and start again. Note that you can delete single entries from an access list, so this feature can be a little helpful.

When access lists are created, they exist in a global area of the PIX firewall, meaning they can be attached to several interfaces simultaneously if you want. The command format for access-list commands is shown in Listing 6.5, and the access-list options are listed in Table 6.3.

Listing 6.5   access-list Command Syntax

```
Pixfirewall(config)# [no] access-list id permit|deny protocol
                     ➥source_ip_address
                     ➥source_subnet_mask [operator port]
                     ➥destination_ip_address
                     ➥destination_subnet_mask [operator port]
```

could be protocol group

Could be source network group

could be destination network group

could be service group

it could be icmp promoter (see table 6.16)

Table 6.3   access-list Command Options

Option	Function
id	This is the number or name of the access list you are creating or appending to.
**permit	deny**	This defines whether to allow or disallow the matching traffic.
protocol	This defines the transport protocol, such as IP, TCP, UDP, or ICMP.
source_ip_address	This specifies the source IP address to detect. The keyword **any** can be used to specify all the source addresses, and the keyword **host** can be used to specify an exact address match.
operator port	This is a comparison operand that lets you define which ports will pass the acceptance criteria: **eq** is equals; **lt** is less than; and **gt** is greater than.
port	This allows you to specify the service you want to permit or deny. For example, you can use port 80 or the text **www** to allow HTTP traffic. Other keywords include **http**, **ident**, **nttp**, **ntp**, **pop2**, **pop3**, **rpc**, **smtp**, **snmp**, **snmptrap**, **sqlnet**, **telnet**, **tftp**, and **www**.
destination_ip_address	This is the destination address you are checking for. Be sure you are using the global address and not the real internal address—unless, of course, you are using the NAT 0 and bypassing translation.

syntax?
80 ?
port 80 ?

In Listing 6.6, the access list named 101 is created with three entries.

Listing 6.6   Creating Three Entries in an Access List

```
Pixfirewall(config)# access-list 101 permit tcp host 10.10.12.37
                     ➥host 169.254.8.1 eq telnet
Pixfirewall(config)# access-list 101 permit tcp host 10.10.12.27
                     ➥host 169.254.8.1 eq www
Pixfirewall(config)# access-list 101 deny ip any any
```

10.10.12.37
255.255.255.255

means all the protocols

Listing 6.6 creates an access list with three entries. The first entry states that traffic from source 10.10.12.37 to the destination (global) address of 169.254.8.1 port 23 (telnet) is permitted. The second command permits traffic from source 10.10.10.27 to the destination address of 169.254.8.1 port 80 (www). The last entry denies any source to any destination.

This example removes only a single entry from the access list named 101:

```
Pixfirewall(config)# no access-list 101 deny ip any any
```

Using the no statement in front of the access-list command without specifying an individual entry allows you to remove the entire list from the system. The following command removes the access list named 101:

```
Pixfirewall(config)# no access-list 101      ≡  clear access-list 101
```

The access-group Command

for inbound direction of the interface applied only

The access-group command enables you to attach and remove an access list from an interface. Access groups allow you to attach only a single ACL to the inbound direction of the interface. Attaching an ACL to the outbound direction is not an option on the PIX firewalls yet. The command format is as follows, and the command options are shown in Table 6.4:

```
Pixfirewall(config)# [no] access-group <access-list> in interface <if_name>
```

vs. clear access-group ?

Table 6.4	access-group Command Options
Option	**Function**
access-list	This is the name or number of the access list you created, sometimes known as the ID.
in	Although this defines the direction of inbound traffic, *in* is in fact the only direction you can control.
interface	This is a required word that is used to specify to which interface you want the access list to be attached.
if_name	This defines the interface to which you want to attach the access list. For example, you can specify **outside**, **inside**, **dmz**, or whatever you've called your interface.

Here's how you use the access-group command:

```
Pixfirewall(config)# Access-group Let-Peter-In in interface outside
```

In the previous example, the access list named Let-Peter-In is bound to the inbound direction of the outside interface.

The following command deletes an access group binding:

```
Pixfirewall(config)# No Access-group Let-Peter-In in interface outside
```

The previous command removes the access list named Let-Peter-In from the outside interface. The access list itself is not deleted; only the link between the interface and the list is removed.

(for single or for all)   *vs no access-list (for single)*

The clear access-list Command

The `clear access-list` can apply to either a single ACL or all the ACLs in your PIX. So be careful with this command! You might find yourself deleting all your ACLs and looking for that TFTP backup of your configuration you made last year (or hopefully more recently!). You can also use the `no access-list` command to delete a single access list. The `clear access-list` command's option is listed in Table 6.5, and its command format is as follows:

```
Pixfirewall(config)# Clear access-list [access-list]
```

Not specifying which access-list to be applied will remove all the access lists from the PIX firewall

i. for single or for all

Table 6.5 The clear access-list Command Option	
Option	**Function**
[access-list]	This is the name or number of the access list you created, sometimes known as the ID.

Here's how you use the `clear access-list` and `no access-list` commands:

```
Pixfirewall(config)# Clear access-list Let-Peter-In
```

or

```
Pixfirewall(config)# no access-list Let-Peter-In
```

In the previous example, the `clear` command deletes the access list named `Let-Peter-In`. The alternative command to delete `Let-Peter-In` is the `no access-list` command.

The following demonstrates the `clear access-lists` command:

```
Pixfirewall(config)# clear access-list
```

This command removes all the access lists from the PIX firewall, so use this command with caution.

(for all)   *v.s. no access-group (for single)*

The clear access-group Command

The `clear access-group` command allows you to remove all access groups from your PIX firewall. If you want to delete only a single access group entry, you need to use the `no access-group` command. The command format is as follows:

— unlike clear access-list

```
Pixfirewall(config)# Clear access-group [access-group]
```

An Access List Example

Now that you have learned about access lists, let's build a larger system using a three-pronged firewall such as the one in Figure 6.4. In this example, you will configure the entire firewall from the beginning to review the basic six commands. Then you will loosen up the firewall to allow traffic from the outside to access internal Web servers. Lastly, you'll allow Peter and Kristina to access Jack's computer via Telnet.

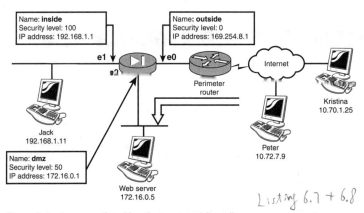

$Listing\ 6.7 + 6.8$

Figure 6.4   An access list with a three-pronged firewall.

Table 6.6 displays the basic commands needed to configure the firewall.

Table 6.6	The Six Basic Commands
Command	Description
nameif	Names the interface and sets the security levels.
interface	Defines the interface speed and duplex setting.
ip address	Sets the interface's IP address.
nat	Sets the NAT address ranges.
global	Sets the global range of addresses the NAT ID will use.
route	Sets the default route.

Listing 6.7 uses these six commands to configure the firewall shown previously in Figure 6.4.

Listing 6.7   Using the Six Basic Commands

```
Pixfirewall(config)#
Pixfirewall(config)# name-if e0 outside security0
Pixfirewall(config)# name-if e1 inside security100
Pixfirewall(config)# name-if e2 dmz security50
```

Listing 6.7   **Using the Six Basic Commands** *(continued)*

```
Pixfirewall(config)#
Pixfirewall(config)# interface e0 10baseT
Pixfirewall(config)# interface e1 10baseT
Pixfirewall(config)# interface e2 10baseT
Pixfirewall(config)#
Pixfirewall(config)# ip address outside 169.254.8.1 255.255.255.0
Pixfirewall(config)# ip address inside 192.168.1.1 255.255.255.0
Pixfirewall(config)# ip address dmz 172.16.0.1 255.255.0.0
Pixfirewall(config)#
Pixfirewall(config)# nat (inside) 1 192.168.1.0 255.255.255.0
Pixfirewall(config)# nat (dmz) 1 172.16.0.0 255.255.0.0
Pixfirewall(config)#
Pixfirewall(config)# global (outside) 1 169.254.8.10-169.254.8.253
                ➡255.255.255.0
Pixfirewall(config)#
Pixfirewall(config)# route outside 0.0.0.0 0.0.0.0 169.254.8.254 1
Pixfirewall(config)#
```

The sequence of commands in Listing 6.7 performs the following functions:

➤ The name-if command defines the interface name and security levels needed for the setup.

➤ The interface command sets all the interfaces to 10BASE-T.

➤ The ip address command sets the interface IP addresses.

➤ The first nat command allows the subnet 192.168.1.0 to be translated to an IP address in the global pool ID or 1.

➤ The second nat command allows the DMZ subnet 172.16.0.0 to be translated.

➤ The global command defines a range of global addresses that will be used by the nat id 1 commands.

➤ The last command creates a default route to the perimeter router.

At this point, your firewall will allow traffic to pass in a single direction from higher security levels to lower security levels and the ASA will allow return traffic back through the PIX.

Now, let's allow traffic initiated from the outside to access the Web server located in the DMZ. We'll also need to allow Peter and Kristina to access Jack's computer using Telnet. The following are the three main steps you need to perform:

1. Create a static map of the global address 169.254.8.1 to map to the internal address of the Web server, 172.16.0.5. Then, you must map the global address of 169.254.8.2 to Jack's computer.

wordble 3

2. Next, you must create an access list that allows Web traffic from the outside to access the global address of 169.254.8.1. This address is mapped to the Web server. Then, you append to the access list Peter's and Kristina's addresses to allow Telnet access.

3. Finally, you use the access group to bind the ACL to the outside interface.

Listing 6.8 displays the code used in these three steps.

could be?

Listing 6.8   Configuring Traffic to Come In

```
Pixfirewall(config)# static (dmz, outside) 169.254.8.1 172.16.0.5
Pixfirewall(config)# static (inside, outside) 169.254.8.2 192.168.1.11
Pixfirewall(config)#
Pixfirewall(config)# access-list Let-Traffic-In permit tcp any
               ➥host 169.254.8.1 eq www
Pixfirewall(config)# access-list Let-Traffic-In permit tcp
               ➥host 10.70.1.25 host 169.254.8.2 eq telnet
Pixfirewall(config)# access-list Let-Traffic-In permit tcp
               ➥host 10.72.7.9 host 169.254.8.2 eq telnet
Pixfirewall(config)#
Pixfirewall(config)# access-group Let-Traffic-In in interface outside
Pixfirewall(config)#
Pixfirewall(config)#clear xlate
Pixfirewall(config)#
Pixfirewall(config)# exit
Pixfirewall# write memory
Pixfirewall(config)#
```

Listing 6.8 gives you the ability to allow traffic to the Web server and traffic to Jack's computer if it's from Peter or Kristina. The ACL must be bound to the outside interface, and a static address is used to translate the traffic coming in.

Interfaces can have only one ACL attached to them in the inbound direction.

Controlling Traffic Going Out

We have been talking about controlling traffic coming into the firewall initiated from the outside. But the PIX can also control traffic heading toward the outside interface. To accomplish this, ACLs or outbound filter commands need to be placed on the higher security interfaces to permit or deny outbound traffic through that interface.

Using ACLs Going Out

use of access-list *command*
access-group

Access control lists are the preferred method used by Cisco to control traffic flowing into the PIX. However, you cannot use ACLs on interfaces in the outbound direction as you can on IOS routers. Therefore, if you need to control traffic leaving the outside interface, you must attach the access list to the inside inbound interface, thus blocking the traffic before it gets to the outbound interface.

For example, if you wanted to prevent Jack's computer from reaching the Web site of 169.254.39.39, you would use the commands shown in Listing 6.9.

Listing 6.9   Blocking a Single Destination

```
Pixfirewall(config)# Access-list stop-jack deny IP host 192.168.1.11
              ➥host 169.254.39.39
Pixfirewall(config)# Access-list stop-jack permit IP any any
Pixfirewall(config)#
Pixfirewall(config)# Access-group stop-jack in interface inside
Pixfirewall(config)#
Pixfirewall(config)# Clear xlate
```

To prevent a whole subnet of 192.168.8.0 from accessing the PIX, the commands is Listing 6.10 could be used.

Listing 6.10   Blocking a Subnet

```
Pixfirewall(config)# Access-list stop-Sub deny IP 192.168.8.0
              ➥255.255.255.0 any
Pixfirewall(config)# Access-list stop-Sub permit IP any any
Pixfirewall(config)#
Pixfirewall(config)# Access-group stop-Sub in interface inside
Pixfirewall(config)#
Pixfirewall(config)# Clear xlate
```

Use access lists on the inside interface to prevent traffic from traveling across the PIX in the outbound direction.

using outbound *command*   *old method!*

Filtering Outbound Traffic   *Skipped!*

The outbound command is an older command that can be used to control traffic from higher security level interfaces to lower security level interfaces. The command is similar to the conduit command, but in the opposite direction. Also similar to the conduit command, it's being replaced by the access-list command. We will list the command only once here just to cover its basics. More information about this old command can be found at Cisco's Web site (www.cisco.com).

These two steps are required to set up an outbound command:

1. Create the outbound filter.

2. Attach the outbound filter to an interface.

The outbound Command

The command used to create these filters is explained in Table 6.7. Its syntax is as follows:

```
Pixfirewall(config)# [no] outbound <outbound_id> permit¦deny¦except
    IP_address [<mask> [port[-port]] [<protocol>]]
```

Table 6.7 outbound Command Options	
Option	**Function**
outbound_id	Lists the number for the outbound filter
permit|deny|except	Permits, denies, or makes an exception
ip_address	The IP address of the internal address or the destination address that you want to block
port protocol	The port and the protocol

The apply Command

The second part of the outbound filter is the apply command, which attaches it to an interface. The following is the apply command's syntax:

```
Pixfirewall(config)# [no] apply [(<if_name>)] <outbound_id>
              ➥outgoing_src¦outgoing_dest
```

The Table 6.8 displays all the options for the apply command.

Table 6.8 apply Command Options	
Option	**Function**
if_name	Name of the interface to which you want to attach the outbound ID
outbound_id	The ID number used to identify an outbound list
outgoing_src	States that the addresses in the **outbound** command are the internal source addresses that will be denied or permitted
outgoing_dest	States that the addresses in the **outbound** command are destination addresses that will be denied or permitted

Outbound Filter Example

In Listing 6.11, address 192.168.1.11 and address 192.168.1.12 are allowed to pass but all other outbound traffic is denied.

Listing 6.11   apply and outbound Example

```
Pixfirewall(config)# outbound 1 deny 0.0.0.0 0.0.0.0 0 0
Pixfirewall(config)# outbound 1 permit 192.168.1.11 255.255.255.255 0 0
Pixfirewall(config)# outbound 1 permit 192.168.1.12 255.255.255.255 0 0
apply (inside) 1 outgoing_src   ← what should be here?
```

Pixfirewall(config)#

Note the `outbound` command doesn't follow the order in which you entered the commands as the ACL does; it actually reorders the entries. This makes it very difficult to get used to and takes proper planning before you use it.

Turbo ACLs

Software release 6.2 introduced a new feature called *turbo ACLs.* Turbo ACLs decrease the time it takes to scan through large access lists. Large access lists take longer to process because every entry might need to be scanned for a possible match. The longer it takes to scan the access list, the slower your traffic will be.

Turbo ACLs create a compiled index against large access lists that contain 19 or more entries. This index is similar to a database index or an index in a book. The PIX scans the index for a match instead of the list itself. This reduces the time it takes to search for possible matches in an ACL, making your throughput faster.

Some of the requirements needed for turbo ACLs are as follows:

➤ Software release 6.2 and above

➤ Minimum of 2.1MB of available flash   *free memory*   *check this with Cisco web site*

➤ A PIX firewall that has 16MB or more flash memory

➤ Access lists with 19 or more entries

Turbo ACLs speed things up but are very memory intensive, requiring 2.1MB of free memory. Therefore, smaller PIX firewalls such as the 501 cannot use turbo ACLs because they don't have enough free memory in flash.

Turbo ACLs are simple to create and work on all models of the PIX except the 501. The 501 does not support turbo ACLs—turbo ACLs are typically not used on smaller firewall models because they use too much memory.

The turbo ACLs command is `access-list compile`, and the following is an example of compiling all your access lists:

```
Pixfirewall(config)# access-list compiled
```
for all access lists

You can also be selective on which access lists you compile by placing the name of the ACL in the command, as shown here:

```
Pixfirewall(config)# access-list Let-Peter-In compiled
```
for a specific access list

To view turbo ACLs, you use the `show access-list` command; to delete a compiled access list, you use the `no access-list compiled`.

Note: the usage of no here is diff. from the one used in access-list and access-group commands

Turbo ACLs work best on access lists with 19 or more entries. If a list has fewer than 19 entries, you really don't get any speed increase by reading the index instead of the list itself.

Not familiar!!

The Basics of Object Grouping

Another new feature introduced in version 6.2 is object grouping for access control lists and `conduit` commands. *Object grouping* creates groups of networks, services, ICMP, and protocols that allow themselves to be joined together in access lists, conduits, or members of other object groups.

Object groups enable you to save the amount of access list entries needed to create large ACLs by allowing you to reference object groups. For example, a typical access list that needs 5 IP addresses and 3 services (such as Telnet, WWW, and FTP) for each would require 15 ACL entries. If you used object grouping, you would need only 1 object group for the 5 IP addresses (`network`) and 1 object group for the 3 ports (Telnet, WWW, and FTP [`services`]). Then, you could join these 2 groups with a single access list. The result of the 2 groups would produce a large list of 15 entries that contains every combination of IP address and services.

When working on large, complex access lists, object groups enable you to save on the number of entries needed to create the access list.

Figure 6.5 displays an access list joining two object groups into one access list entry that contains every combination of the two object groups.

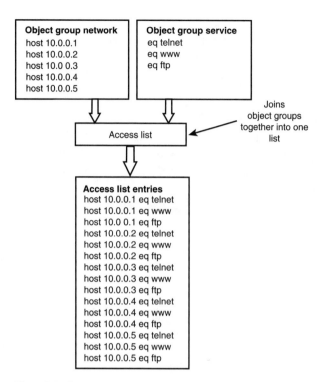

Figure 6.5   Object groups joined with an access lists.

Types of Object Groups

The four types of object group commands that can be used are network, service, protocols, and icmp-types. Table 6.9 displays the object group commands.

Command	Description
Table 6.9 Types of object-group Commands	
Command	**Description**
object-group network X	Defines a group of hosts or subnets
object-group services X y	Defines a group of TCP and UDP port numbers *such as Telnet, www, FTP*
object-group protocol X	Defines a group of IP protocols, such as IP, ICMP, TCP, and UDP
object-group icmp-type X	Defines a group of ICMP messages

$X = obj\text{-}grp\text{-}id$ $y = tcp$ or udp or $tcp\text{-}udp$

The object group commands listed in Table 6.9 place you into a subconfiguration mode. To leave this mode, just type exit to return to the normal configuration mode prompt.

> Know the four types of object groups: **network**, **service**, **protocol**, and **icmp-type**.
> Also, be sure you know the commands needed to create them.

Object Group Networks

Network groups are used to create large lists of hosts or networks that can be used in access list commands. The command sequence is shown in Listing 6.12, and the options are listed in Table 6.10.

Listing 6.12   object-group Network Commands

```
Pixfirewall(config)# object-group network obj_grp_id
Pixfirewall(config-network)# description dor
Pixfirewall(config-network)# network-object host host_address
Pixfirewall(config-network)# network-object network_address subnet_mask
Pixfirewall(config-network)# group-object ref_obj_grp_id
```

Table 6.10   object-group network Command Options

Option	Function
obj_grp_id	Defines the name of the object group you are creating or editing
description	Sets a description to the object group
network-object	Specifies the host or network you are listing
group-object	Allows you to reference another network object group

Listing 6.13 displays a network object group called TheNetworkList being created. The description is set, and four host addresses and one subnet entry are added to the group.

Listing 6.13   Example of the object-group network Command

```
pixfirewall(config)# object-group network TheNetworkList
pixfirewall(config-network)# description This is my great network list
pixfirewall(config-network)# network-object host 10.0.0.1
pixfirewall(config-network)# network-object host 10.0.0.2
pixfirewall(config-network)# network-object host 10.0.0.3
pixfirewall(config-network)# network-object host 10.0.0.4
pixfirewall(config-network)# network-object 11.0.0.0 255.0.0.0
pixfirewall(config-network)# exit
pixfirewall(config)# show object-group id TheNetworkList     ← see table 6.14
object-group network TheNetworkList
  description: This is my great network list
  network-object host 10.0.0.1
  network-object host 10.0.0.2
  network-object host 10.0.0.3
  network-object host 10.0.0.4
  network-object 11.0.0.0 255.0.0.0
pixfirewall(config)#
```

Object Group Services

Service groups are used to create lists of TCP and UDP port number services, such as Telnet, WWW, and FTP. The command sequence is shown in Listing 6.14.

Listing 6.14 object-group Services Commands

```
Pixfirewall(config)# object-group service obj_grp_id tcp|udp|tcp-udp
Pixfirewall(config-service)# description des
Pixfirewall(config-service)# port-object eq|range
Pixfirewall(config-service)# group-object ref_obj_grp_id
```

Table 6.11 displays the commands and syntax needed to support the object-group service command.

Table 6.11 object-group services Command Options

Option	Function
obj_grp_id	Defines the name of the object group you are creating or editing
tcp|udp|tcp-udp	Defines the service protocol to create
description	Sets a description to the object group
port-object	Specifies the exact port using the **eq** operator or a range of port numbers with the **range** operator
group-object	Allows you to reference another service object group

Listing 6.15 displays a service object group called ThePortList being created. This group sets the description and creates matching entries for Telnet, WWW, and FTP ports. Lastly, a range of ports from 1433 to 1435 is set.

Listing 6.15 Example of the object-group service Command

```
pixfirewall(config)# object-group service ThePortList tcp
pixfirewall(config-service)# description This is my great port list
pixfirewall(config-service)# port-object eq telnet
pixfirewall(config-service)# port-object eq www
pixfirewall(config-service)# port-object eq ftp
pixfirewall(config-service)# port-object range 1433 1435
pixfirewall(config-service)# exit
pixfirewall(config)# show object-group id ThePortList
object-group service ThePortList tcp
  description: This is my great port list
  port-object eq telnet
  port-object eq www
  port-object eq ftp
  port-object range 1433 1435
pixfirewall(config)#
```

(handwritten: Is service group, protocol is specified as well!)

Object Group Protocols

Protocol groups enable you to create a group of protocols such as IP, TCP, UDP, or ICMP. This object group can be used in the protocol portion of an access list command. The command sequence is shown in Listing 6.16.

Listing 6.16 object-group protocol Commands

```
Pixfirewall(config)# object-group protocol obj_grp_id
Pixfirewall(config-protocol)# description   des
Pixfirewall(config-protocol)# protocol-object protocol
Pixfirewall(config-protocol)# group-object  ref-object-group-id
```

Table 6.12 displays the command options for the `object-group protocol` command.

Table 6.12 object-group protocol Command Options

Option	Function
obj_grp_id	Defines the name of the object group you are creating or editing.
description	Sets a description to the object group.
protocol-object	Specifies the protocol either by name or number. Sample protocols are IP, TCP, UDP, and ICMP. *(handwritten: To include all IP protocols, use the keyword IP.)*
group-object	Allows you to reference another protocol object group.

(handwritten left margin: subconfiguration mode)

Listing 6.17 displays a protocol object group called `TheProtocolList` being created. This group sets the description and creates three entries for TCP, UDP, and GRE protocols.

Listing 6.17 Example of the object-group protocol Command

```
pixfirewall(config)# object-group protocol TheProtocolList
pixfirewall(config-protocol)# description This is my great protocol list
pixfirewall(config-protocol)# protocol-object tcp
pixfirewall(config-protocol)# protocol-object udp
pixfirewall(config-protocol)# protocol-object gre
pixfirewall(config-protocol)# exit
pixfirewall(config)# show object-group id TheProtocolList
object-group protocol TheProtocolList
  description: This is my great protocol list
  protocol-object tcp
  protocol-object udp
  protocol-object gre
pixfirewall(config)#
```

After the **object-group protocol FastStuff** command, the next line takes you into the configuration for that object group (**FastStuff**). The command prompt displays **pixfirewall(config-protocol)#**.

ICMP Groups

Q: How to use it in access-list command ??
A: probably, it looks like Listing 6.22

ICMP groups enable you to create groups based on ICMP messages. Listing 6.18 shows the syntax for this command.

Listing 6.18   object-group icmp Commands

```
Pixfirewall(config)# object-group icmp-type obj_grp_id
Pixfirewall(config-icmp-type)# description    des
Pixfirewall(config-icmp-type)# icmp-object type — numeric value or name
Pixfirewall(config-icmp-type)# group-object  ref_object_group_id
```

Table 6.13 displays the options for the `object-group icmp` command.

Table 6.13   object-group icmp Command Options

Option	Function
obj_grp_id	Defines the name of the object group you are creating or editing
description	Sets a description to the object group
icmp-object	Specifies the type of ICMP message—for example, **echo** and **echo-reply**
group-object	Allows you to reference another ICMP object group

not icmp-type-object !

Listing 6.19 displays an ICMP object group called TheICMPList being created. This group sets the description and creates two ICMP entries: echo and echo-reply.

Listing 6.19   Example of the object-group icmp-type Command

```
pixfirewall(config)# object-group icmp-type TheICMPList
pixfirewall(config-icmp-type)# description This is my great icmp list
pixfirewall(config-icmp-type)# icmp-object echo
pixfirewall(config-icmp-type)# icmp-object echo-reply
pixfirewall(config-icmp-type)# exit
pixfirewall(config)# show object-group id TheICMPList
object-group icmp-type TheICMPList
  description: This is my great icmp list
  icmp-object echo
  icmp-object echo-reply
pixfirewall(config)#
```

Displaying Object Groups

To display existing object groups, you can use the show object-group commands, which are explained in Table 6.14.

Table 6.14	show object-group Commands
Command	**Description**
show object-group	Displays all the object groups
show object-group [protocol | service | icmp-type | network]	Displays the object group based on the type, such as network, service, protocol, or ICMP type
show object-group id <obj_grp_id>	Displays the object group ID with the matching name

Deleting Object Groups

To delete an object group, you must first remove it from any other reference that might be using it. For example, if the object group TheICMPList is being used by an access list, you must remove it from the access list before you can delete it. Table 6.15 displays the commands used to delete object groups.

Table 6.15	clear object-group Commands
Command	**Description**
clear object-group	Deletes all the object groups
clear object-group [protocol | service | icmp-type | network]	Deletes all the object groups of a specific type, such as network, service, protocol, or ICMP type
no object-group [protocol | service | icmp-type | network] name	Removes a single object group by name and type

The command shown here deletes the object group called TheICMPList:

```
pixfirewall(config)# no object-group icmp-type TheICMPList
```

Nesting Object Groups

Object groups can also be nested inside other object groups. In Figure 6.6, two network groups are referenced in a third network object group. This new group could then be used by an access list or conduit command to produce the result of all the addresses.

One restriction is that you can only nest groups of the same type. For example, network groups can be nested only into other network groups.

To demonstrate, Listing 6.20 shows how two groups can be nested into a third group.

The max. no. of allowed levels of a hierarchical object group is 10.

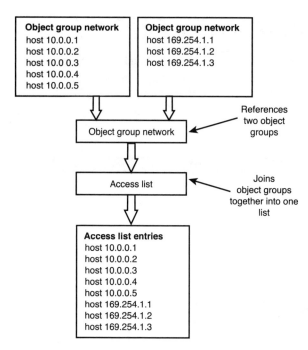

Figure 6.6 Object groups nested within an object group.

Listing 6.20   Nesting object-group Commands Example

```
pixfirewall(config)# object-group network TheIPList1
pixfirewall(config-network)# description This is my great list 1
pixfirewall(config-network)# network-object host 10.0.0.1
pixfirewall(config-network)# network-object host 10.0.0.2
pixfirewall(config-network)# network-object host 10.0.0.3
pixfirewall(config-network)# network-object host 10.0.0.4
pixfirewall(config-network)# network-object host 10.0.0.5
pixfirewall(config-network)# exit
pixfirewall(config)#
pixfirewall(config)# object-group network TheIPList2
pixfirewall(config-network)# description This is my great list 2
pixfirewall(config-network)# network-object host 169.254.1.1
pixfirewall(config-network)# network-object host 169.254.1.2
pixfirewall(config-network)# network-object host 169.254.1.3
pixfirewall(config-network)# exit
pixfirewall(config)#
pixfirewall(config)# object-group network TheIPList3
pixfirewall(config-network)# description This is my great list 3
pixfirewall(config-network)# group-object TheIPList1
pixfirewall(config-network)# group-object TheIPList2
pixfirewall(config-network)# exit
pixfirewall(config)#
```

Listing 6.20 shows that the object group TheIPList3 contains references to both the TheIPList1 and TheIPList2 object groups.

ICMP Through the PIX Firewall

lower security levels to higher security levels

passing through or directly

By default, the PIX firewall blocks all ICMP traffic such as trace routes and pings. The two points at which ICMP traffic is directed are when passing through the PIX and when directed at the PIX. The PIX blocks both. Table 6.16 displays some of the ICMP message numbers that can be used on the PIX.

Table 6.16 ICMP Message Numbers	
Message Number	**Cisco Parameter**
0	echo-reply
3	unreachable
4	source-quench
5	redirect
8	echo
11	time-exceeded
12	parameter-problem
13	timestamp-request
14	timestamp-reply
15	information-request
16	information-reply

Outbound ICMP Traffic

In

By default:

The PIX allows ICMP traffic to pass from higher security levels to lower security levels but blocks ICMP traffic from lower security level interfaces to higher security level interfaces. To allow ICMP traffic to flow both ways, you need to configure a static translation and use a conduit or ACL command.

The following two steps are needed to permit returning ICMP ping traffic to pass back to the source:

1. Create a static mapping.

2. Use an access-list or conduit command to allow ICMP traffic to pass. If you use the access-list command, you also must use the access-group command to link it to an interface.

Listing 6.21 demonstrates how to permit return traffic from the outside interface to ping traffic on the inside.

Listing 6.21 Using the conduit Command to Allow ICMP Traffic In

```
Pixfirewall(config)# static (inside,outside) 169.254.8.1 192.168.1.11
            ➥netmask 255.255.255.255 0 0
Pixfirewall(config)#
Pixfirewall(config)# conduit permit icmp 169.254.8.1 255.255.255.255
            ➥0.0.0.0 0.0.0.0 echo-reply
Pixfirewall(config)# conduit permit icmp 169.254.8.1 255.255.255.255
            ➥0.0.0.0 0.0.0.0 source-quench
Pixfirewall(config)# conduit permit icmp 169.254.8.1 255.255.255.255
            ➥0.0.0.0 0.0.0.0 unreachable
Pixfirewall(config)# conduit permit icmp 169.254.8.1 255.255.255.255
            ➥0.0.0.0 0.0.0.0 time-exceeded
```

Listing 6.22 demonstrates how to permit return traffic from the outside interface to ping traffic on the inside using the access-list command.

Listing 6.22 Using the access-list Command to Allow ICMP Traffic In

```
Pixfirewall(config)# static (inside,outside) 169.254.8.1 192.168.1.11
            ➥netmask 255.255.255.255 0 0
Pixfirewall(config)#
Pixfirewall(config)# access-list 100 permit icmp any host 169.254.8.1
            ➥echo-reply
Pixfirewall(config)# access-list 100 permit icmp any host 169.254.8.1
            ➥source-quench
Pixfirewall(config)# access-list 100 permit icmp any host 169.254.8.1
            ➥unreachable
Pixfirewall(config)# access-list 100 permit icmp any host 169.254.8.1
            ➥time-exceeded
Pixfirewall(config)# access-group 100 in interface outside
```

ICMP Directed at the PIX

The PIX firewall can be set to block ICMP traffic directed at it. This allows the PIX to reject responses to ICMP requests; as a result it is more difficult for hackers to discover the firewall. To allow the firewall to respond to ICMP traffic requests, you must use the icmp command instead of an ACL command. The following is the syntax for the icmp command:

```
pixfirewall(config)# [no] icmp permit¦deny <ip-address> <net-mask>
            ➥ [<icmp-type>] <if-name>
pixfirewall(config)# [clear¦show] icmp
```

Table 6.17 displays the options available for the icmp command.

Table 6.17	icmp Command Options
Option	**Function**
permit|deny	This permits or denies ICMP traffic.
ip-address	This is the source IP address of the ICMP traffic.
net-mask	This is the mask of the allowed traffic. 255.255.255.255 would allow only a specific IP address.
icmp-type	This is the type of ICMP traffic, such as **echo-reply** or **unreachable**.
if-name	This is the name of the interface to which the ICMP entry is applied.

The following command allows the outside interface to respond to ping requests on the outside interface:

```
icmp permit any echo outside
```

or echo-reply

To deny ICMP traffic on the outside interface, the following command is necessary:

```
icmp deny any echo outside
```

Exam Prep Questions

Question 1 ⊘ ⊘

> When you need inbound access through the PIX firewall, which commands are required? (Select two.)
>
> ❑ A. **pat** *Is there such a command? A: No*
> ☑ B. **access-list**
> ❑ C. **pass-through** *Note: Acess Group command is also required*
> ❑ D. **nat**
> ☑ E. **static**

Answers B and E are correct. To allow inbound access to the PIX firewall, the static command is needed to create a static NAT entry to direct the traffic inbound. Also, the access-list command is needed to allow traffic into the interface. Answers A and D are incorrect because the pat and nat commands are used for traffic exiting the PIX firewall. Answer C is incorrect because the pass-through command does not exist.

Question 2

> When creating turbo ACLs, why would you not use them on the smaller PIX firewall models?
>
> ○ A. They are not supported on the PIX 506.
> ○ B. They consume too much CPU power.
> ○ C. They are too complicated to set up.
> ◉ D. They require a large amount of memory.
> ○ E. They are supported only on PIX 525 and PIX 535.

Answer D is correct. Turbo ACLs require a minimum of 2MB of free memory and 16MB of flash to operate. Smaller firewalls such as the 506 can use them, but turbo ACLs typically consume too much flash memory and should therefore be used only when large numbers of access list entries exist. Large firewalls have more memory and can be configured with several turbo ACLs. Answer A is incorrect because turbo ACLs are supported on the 506; however, they are not supported on the 501. Answer B is incorrect because turbo ACLs consume a lot of CPU power only when you compile them.

Otherwise, they run faster than normal ACLs. Answer C is incorrect because turbo ACLs are very easy to set up; you only need to add the parameter `compiled` on the access list. Answer E is incorrect because turbo ACLs are supported on all new PIX firewalls except the 501.

Question 3

Which command is used to bind an ACL to an interface?
- ○ A. **access-group**
- ○ B. **object-group**
- ○ C. **access-list**
- ○ D. **bind-interface**

Answer A is correct. The `access-group` command is used to bind an access list to an interface. Answer B is incorrect because the `object-group` command is used to create new object groups. Answer C is incorrect because the `access-list` command creates entries for ACLs and doesn't bind them to an interface. Answer D is incorrect because the `bind-interface` command does not exist.

Question 4

Why would you bind an access list to the inside interface?
- ○ A. To control which traffic can enter the PIX firewall from the outside interface
- ○ B. To control outbound traffic
- ○ C. To allow outside interface traffic to the inside internal users
- ○ D. Because access lists can be set only on the outside interface

Answer B is correct. Access lists set on the inside interface enable you to control which traffic can enter the firewall. This can be used to block internal addresses from entering the PIX firewall and traveling to specific outside IP addresses. Answers A and C are incorrect because binding to the outside interface would control traffic coming in from the outside. Answer D is incorrect because an ACL can be placed on any interface.

Question 5

Which object group types can be created on the PIX firewall? (Select four.)

- ☑ A. Service
- ☐ B. Port
- ☑ C. ICMP type
- ☐ D. DNS
- ☑ E. Protocol
- ☐ F. Host
- ☑ G. Network

Answers A, C, E, and G are correct. The four types of object groups are service, protocol, ICMP type, and network. Therefore, answers B, D, and F are incorrect.

Question 6

Object groups can be members of other object groups.

- ◉ A. True
- ○ B. False

Answer A is correct. Object groups can be members of other object groups as long as all the groups are the same type. Therefore, answer B is incorrect.

Question 7

Which command allows you to delete object groups? (Select two.)

- ☑ A. **no object-group**
- ☐ B. **delete object-group**
- ☐ C. **remove object-group**
- ☑ D. **clear object-group**

Answers A and D are correct. To delete object groups, you use the `no object-group` or `clear object-group` command. The `no object-group` command deletes a single group, whereas the `clear object-group` command can delete all object groups. Answers B and C do not exist; therefore, they are incorrect.

Question 8

> What must be done to allow traffic to pass from the outside interface to a Web server behind the interface named **dmz**? (Select two.)
>
> ❑ A. Create a static mapping entry to the outside interface.
> ❑ B. Create a static mapping entry to the **dmz** interface.
> ☑ C. Create a static mapping entry to the Web server.
> ❑ D. Remove the ACL on the outside interface.
> ☑ E. Link an ACL to the outside interface. — *by access group command*

Answers C and E are correct. To allow traffic initiated on the outside to pass into the DMZ, a static mapping of a global address to the Web server must be created. Secondly, a conduit command or ACL must be used to permit traffic to come in from the outside interface. Answer A would not allow access to the Web server and is therefore incorrect. Answer B would only map a global address to the firewall address and *dmz interface's IP* is therefore also incorrect. Answer D is incorrect because you must have an ACL binding to the outside interface to allow traffic in.

Question 9

> What is the difference between **access-list** and **conduit** commands?
>
> ○ A. **access-list** commands can only have deny statements.
> ○ B. **conduit** command can only have permit statements.
> ○ C. **conduit** commands are applied directly to an interface.
> ⊙ D. **access-list** commands list the source and then destination, whereas **conduit** commands list the destination and then source.

Answer D is correct. access-list commands list the source and then the destination, whereas conduit commands are reversed, listing the destination followed by the source. Here are two examples: access-list (SOURCE)(DESTINATION) and conduit (DESTINATION)(SOURCE). Answers A and B are incorrect because both the access-list and conduit commands support permit and deny statements. Answer C is incorrect because the conduit command is not linked or assigned to a specific interface.

v.s. access-list command

it applies to all interfaces with lower security levels. (p.110)*

Question 10

> When setting up complex access lists, what could you use to minimize the number of access list entries to be entered?
>
> ○ A. Use a **conduit** command instead.
> ○ B. Use object grouping.
> ○ C. Use turbo ACLs.
> ○ D. Use static mappings.

Answer B is correct. By using object grouping, you can create small object groups of entries and reference them in other groups or the ACL. This would minimize the number of access list entries needed to be typed in. Answer A is incorrect because conduit commands would not minimize the number of entries. Answer C is incorrect because turbo ACLs speed up the processing of ACLs but do not minimize the number of entries. Answer D is incorrect because static mappings are used to transform a global address to an internal address.

see p. 50#

Need to Know More?

 Chapman, David and Andy Fox. *Cisco Secure PIX Firewalls.* Indianapolis, IN: Cisco Press, 2002.

 Deal, Richard A. *Cisco PIX Firewalls.* Berkeley, CA: McGraw-Hill/Osborne, 2002.

 See the Cisco PIX Firewall Command Reference, Version 6.2 at http://www.cisco.com/univercd/cc/td/doc/product/iaabu/pix/pix_sw/v_62/cmdref/index.htm.

 See Using and Configuring PIX Object Groups at http://www.cisco.com/en/US/products/hw/vpndevc/ps2030/products_tech_note09186a00800d641d.shtml.

 Read the commands reference, M through R, at http://www.cisco.com/en/US/products/sw/secursw/ps2120/products_command_reference_chapter09186a008010423e.html#1038172.

 Read "Handling ICMP Pings with the PIX Firewall" at http://www.cisco.com/en/US/products/hw/vpndevc/ps2030/products_tech_note09186a0080094e8a.shtml.

 Find out about the turbo ACL Commands, A through B, at http://www.cisco.com/en/US/products/sw/secursw/ps2120/products_command_reference_chapter09186a0080104239.html#1054473.

System Management

Terms you'll need to understand:

✓ Network Time Protocol (NTP)

✓ Secure Shell (SSH)

✓ Telnet

✓ Simple Network Management Protocol (SNMP)

✓ Syslog server

Techniques you'll need to master:

✓ Setting the clock

✓ Configuring NTP

✓ Using Telnet

✓ Configuring for SSH

✓ Logging to a syslog server

✓ Setting syslog timestamps

This chapter covers the ways of remotely accessing the PIX firewall, how to set up time servers, SNMP traps, and the capabilities of logging system messages to remote syslog servers.

The Importance of the Date and Time

The PIX firewall has the capability of logging system messages locally or remotely. This capability helps you to track what is happening across the PIX firewall. As with any tracking, you need the ability to display the correct date and time to know when the event took place. The date and time can be set using the local commands, or they can be acquired from a time server using the Network Time Protocol (NTP).

Setting the Date and Time

Manually setting the time requires three main steps:

➤ Setting the date and time

➤ Setting the time zone

➤ Setting whether to use daylight saving time (DST)

The clock set Command

The clock set command is used to manually set the date and time. Use of the clock set command is as follows:

```
pixfirewall(config)# clock set <hh:mm:ss> {<day> <month> |
                <month> <day>} <year>
```

Table 7.1	clock set Command Options
Option	Function
hh:mm:ss	The hour, minute, and second expressed in 24-hour format. For example, **13:10:11** is used for 1:10 p.m.
name_of_month	Using the first three characters of the month. For example, you'd use **aug** for August.

Table 7.1	clock set Command Options *(continued)*
Option	Function
day	The number of the day of the month. For example, **31** would be used for the 31st day.
year	The year expressed with four characters. For example, **2003** would be used.

The following example sets the clock:

```
pixfirewall(config)# clock set 13:01:11 31 aug 2003
pixfirewall(config)#
pixfirewall(config)# show clock
13:01:16.920 UTC Sun Aug 31 2003
pixfirewall(config)#
```

The clock timezone Command

The `clock timezone` command sets the time zone of your PIX firewall. The command syntax is as follows:

```
pixfirewall(config)# [no] clock timezone <zone> <hours> [<minutes>]
```

Table 7.2	clock timezone Command Options
Option	Function
zone	The name of the time zone, such as PST or EST. The default time zone, UTC, is also know as Greenwich Mean Time (GMT).
hours	This allows you to manually offset the hours from UTC.
minutes	This allows you to manually offset the minutes from UTC.

The following example sets the clock time zone:

```
pixfirewall(config)# clock timezone PST -8 0
pixfirewall(config)#
pixfirewall(config)# show clock
05:15:16.107 PST Sun Aug 31 2003
pixfirewall(config)#
```

The previous example sets the time zone name to PST, with a –8 hours and 0 minutes offset from UTC time. The `timezone` command is used for display purposes only; the actual time in the PIX firewall is UTC time.

The clock summer-time Command

The clock timezone command set supports the DST feature, which is turned off by default. The following is the command syntax:

```
pixfirewall(config)# [no] clock summer-time <zone> recurring
                [<week> <weekday> <month> <hh:mm>
                <week> <weekday> <month> <hh:mm>] [<offset>]

pixfirewall(config)# [no] clock summer-time <zone> date {<day>
                <month> ¦ <month> <day>} <year>
                <hh:mm> {<day> <month> ¦ <month> <day>}
                <year> <hh:mm> [<offset>]
```

The summer-time command enables you to offset the time once by using the clock summer-time date command or to perform the offset every year with the clock summer-time recurring command.

The show clock Command

The show clock command displays the current date and time on the firewall. By using the detail option, you can display the method used to set the clock, like so:

```
pixfirewall(config)# show clock [detail]
```

Table 7.3	show clock Command Option
Option	**Function**
detail	This option displays the source of the time, either user configured or NTP.

Listing 7.1 sets the clock and then displays the clock details:

Listing 7.1 Using the clock set Command

```
pixfirewall(config)# clock set 13:01:11 31 aug 2003
pixfirewall(config)#
pixfirewall(config)# clock timezone PST -8 0
pixfirewall(config)#
pixfirewall(config)# show clock
05:01:53.671 PST Sun Aug 31 2003
pixfirewall(config)#
pixfirewall(config)# show clock detail
05:01:59.941 PST Sun Aug 31 2003
Time source is user configuration
pixfirewall(config)#
```

The **clear clock** Command

The clear clock command removes user configuration from the clock to set the display time back to UTC time zone, and it also removes any DST settings.

Network Time Protocol

Network Time Protocol (NTP) servers enable computers and devices such as the PIX firewall to synchronize their internal clocks with a centralized timing server. NTP works off a hierarchy in which one master clock server dictates the time settings and sends them down to several NTP servers, which synchronize with the master server. These lower NTP servers help to balance the load for hundreds or thousands of possible NTP clients looking to synchronize their clocks. The PIX firewall can become an NTP client, allowing NTP to set the clock instead of manually configuring it with the clock command. Figure 7.1 displays a simple NTP hierarchy.

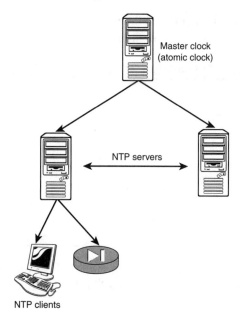

Figure 7.1   An NTP hierarchy.

Configuring NTP Clients on the PIX

To configure the PIX firewall as an NTP client, the use of several commands might be necessary. The basic NTP command set designates the NTP server itself. If security is needed, a second set of commands is required to configure authentication keys. ⟩

The **ntp server** Command

The ntp server command enables you to designate the NTP server; its syntax is as follows:

```
pixfirewall(config)# [no] ntp server <ip_address> [key <number>]
                 source <if_name> [prefer]
```

optional if this command is used alone, but is compulsory when authentication commands used

Table 7.4	**ntp server Command Options**
Option	**Function**
ip_address	The IP address of the NTP server
key number	A number, between 1 and 4,294,967,295, used to authenticate with the NTP server
if_name	The name of the interface on which the NTP server resides
prefer	Allows you to define a preference for a specific time server

Listing 7.2 configures the PIX to use three possible time servers and to give preference to the last time server for synchronizing time.

Listing 7.2	**NTP Server Configuration Example**

```
pixfirewall(config)# ntp server 192.168.1.100 source inside
pixfirewall(config)# ntp server 192.168.1.101 source inside
pixfirewall(config)# ntp server 192.168.1.102 source inside prefer
pixfirewall(config)#
pixfirewall(config)# show ntp
ntp server 192.168.1.100 source inside
ntp server 192.168.1.101 source inside
ntp server 192.168.1.102 source inside prefer
pixfirewall(config)#
pixfirewall(config)# show clock detail
14:17:31.014 UTC Sun Aug 31 2003
Time source is NTP
pixfirewall(config)#
```

In Listing 7.2, the show ntp command displays the configured NTP servers and the show clock detail displays the time source as being NTP rather than user configured.

NTP Authentication Commands

In secure environments, the NTP data can be sent using authentication between the NTP server and the PIX, allowing an MD5 hash against the time information passed. To do so, the following commands are required:

➤ ntp authenticate

➤ ntp trusted-key <number>

➤ ntp authentication-key <number> md5 <value>

The ntp authenticate Command

The ntp authenticate command enables authentication for NTP communications. When this command is used, the PIX and the NTP server must authenticate to allow the PIX firewall to accept the NTP information.

The ntp trusted-key Command

The ntp trusted-key command sets a number that must match in the ntp server command's key option. This same value must be sent by the NTP server in every packet for the PIX to accept the NTP information.

The ntp authentication-key Command

The ntp authentication-key command enables you to match an MD5 string with an NTP server. This match is made with the number option that corresponds to an ntp trusted-key command with the name number. In Listing 7.3, the NTP server is using 123 as its key and timebandits as the MD5 algorithm string. Listing 7.3 displays the commands used to create a secure connection.

Listing 7.3   Example of Configuring Secure NTP

```
pixfirewall(config)# ntp server 192.168.1.100 key 123 source inside
pixfirewall(config)# ntp authenticate
pixfirewall(config)# ntp trusted-key 123
pixfirewall(config)# ntp authentication-key 123 md5 timebandits
pixfirewall(config)#
```

MD5 is used to hash the NTP information and allow secure NTP traffic to be passed between the PIX and the NTP server.

Displaying NTP Information

Now that the PIX firewall is configured for NTP, the following three commands will enable you to verify its operational status:

➤ show ntp

➤ show ntp status

➤ show ntp associations [detail]

The **show ntp** Command

The show ntp command displays the current NTP configurations. The following example displays the NTP configuration created in Listing 7.3:

```
pixfirewall(config)# show ntp
ntp authentication-key 123 md5 ********
ntp authenticate
ntp trusted-key 123
ntp server 192.168.1.100 key 123 source inside
pixfirewall(config)#
```

The **show ntp status** Command

The show ntp status command displays the current clock status, like so:

```
pixfirewall(config)# show ntp status

Clock is synchronized, stratum 5, reference is 192.168.1.100
nominal freq is 99.9967 Hz, actual freq is 99.9967 Hz, precision is 2**6
reference time is a13124b9.46c2936b (06:28:16.000 UTC Thu Feb 7 2036)
clock offset is 0.3213 msec, root delay is 52.32 msec
root dispersion is 32.1 msec, peer dispersion is 4.4 msec
pixfirewall(config)#
```

The previous status shows the IP address of the NTP server as 192.168.1.100.

The **show ntp associations** Command

The show ntp associations command displays information about the servers you have configured. Here is an example of the command:

```
pixfirewall(config)# show ntp associations

address          ref clock      st  when  poll reach  delay  offset     disp
*~192.168.1.100 0.0.0.0          5   30    64   377    5.0    -3.00      4.2.
* master (synced), # master (unsynced), + selected, - candidate,
~ configured
```

Notice the ledger that is displayed with the command. The asterisk symbol (*) designates that the master has synced.

Accessing the PIX

You can access the PIX firewall in several ways, such as using console ports, Telnet, Secure Shell (SSH), and HTTP. All these ways enable you to configure and manage the firewall, but by default only console port access is permitted. Figure 7.2 displays the preferred methods of access and shows that console access from the outside is allowed only when using SSH.

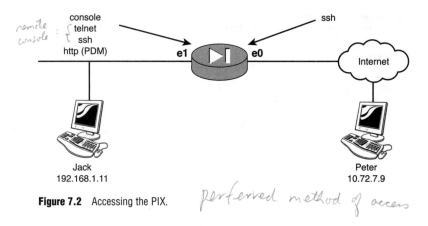

remote console : { console, telnet, ssh, http (PDM) }

Jack
192.168.1.11

Peter
10.72.7.9

Figure 7.2   Accessing the PIX.   _preferred method of access_

The Console Port

The console port allows access for a local serial connection connected direct-ly into the PIX firewall. Procedures such as password breaking and loading new images are recommended via this connection point, but the physical dis-tance a technician can be from the firewall is limited. Chapter 3, "Basics of the PIX Firewall," describes how to connect to the PIX via the console cable.

Telnet

Telnet enables you to remotely connect to the firewall using TCP/IP to cre-ate a remote console. With TCP/IP, physical distance is no longer a concern, making Telnet a convenient way to configure and manage your firewall with-out ever getting up from your chair.

 Telnet communications are carried out in clear text. So, if hackers are sniffing the network, they could intercept passwords or configuration information about your PIX. Telnet access is therefore not recommended from the outside interface.

To enable Telnet access to the PIX, you must first use the `telnet` command to specify which IP addresses are allowed access. The following is the `telnet` command syntax:

```
pixfirewall(config)# [no] telnet <local_ip> [<mask>] [<if_name>]
```

Table 7.5	telnet Command Options
Option	**Function**
local_ip	The subnet or IP address allowed to Telnet into the PIX.
mask	The optional mask allows you to specify an exact host with 255.255.255.255 or a subnet with a mask such as 255.255.255.0.
if_name	The name of the interface to accept the Telnet access.

default: the one with the highest security level (I believe)

The following three examples all allow 192.168.1.11 Telnet access on the inside interface to the PIX firewall:

```
pixfirewall(config)# telnet 192.168.1.11
```

Cann't confirm this from Cisco web site !!

or

```
pixfirewall(config)# telnet 192.168.1.11 255.255.255.255
```

or

```
pixfirewall(config)# telnet 192.168.1.11 255.255.255.255 inside
```

The following command allows all addresses on the inside interface Telnet access:

```
pixfirewall(config)# telnet 0.0.0.0 0.0.0.0 inside
```

> Telnet also has the **who** command, which displays the current active Telnet sessions, and the **kill** command, which forces a Telnet session to disconnect.

Syntax ?

Secure Shell

Secure Shell, like Telnet, allows remote console connections; however, with SSH, the connections are secure. SSH provides encryption of traffic from the PIX to the client, creating a secure environment in which to manage your PIX. To create this secure environment, you must create a public key and private RSA keys. Four main steps are required to configure SSH:

five

1. Configure a hostname. *hostname <hostname>*

2. Configure a domain name. *domain-name <domain.name>*

3. Create a public and private RSA key pair. *ca generate rsa key <modulus size>*

4. Specify which IP addresses are allowed SSH access. *see # on p.152*

5. Save the key to flash memory   ca save all

When connecting to the PIX using SSH, you are prompted to enter a username and password. Cisco uses the username **pix**, which can't be changed, and the current Telnet password for these prompts. The default Telnet password is **cisco**, in all lowercase.

Q: how to set the Telnet password?

A: passwd <password> see p.54

The **hostname** Command

SSH requires a hostname to be configured; the command shown here configures a hostname for the PIX:

```
Cisco(config)# hostname pixfirewall
pixfirewall(config)#
```

The **domain-name** Command   *not domainname!*

The PIX firewall needs a domain name that will be used inside the RSA key pairs. After you generate the keys, be sure you never change the domain name of the PIX; otherwise, you will have to regenerate the RSA keys. The following command sets the domain name to `newman.cla`:

```
pixfirewall(config)# domain-name newman.cla
pixfirewall(config)#
pixfirewall(config)# show domain-name
domain-name newman.cla
pixfirewall(config)#
```

The hostname and domain name are combined to form a fully qualified domain name (FQDN) that is used during key generation. For example, the FQDN in the previous example would be **pixfirewall.newman.cla**.

The **ca generate rsa key** Command

The `ca generate rsa key` command creates a pair of keys that are used to help create a secure connection between the client and the PIX. The values you used for the hostname and domain name are used inside the keys and should not be changed after the keys are generated. You can create modulus sizes for 512, 768, 1024, or 2048 bits. Also note that this command can take quite some time to execute.

Use the **ca zeroize rsa** command to remove any current RSA key pairs from the PIX.

The following commands are needed to create a pair of keys:

```
pixfirewall(config)# ca zeroize rsa
pixfirewall(config)#                              modular size
pixfirewall(config)# ca generate rsa key 1024
For <key_modulus_size> >= 1024, key generation could
  take up to several minutes. Please wait.
..
pixfirewall(config)#
```

The ssh Command

The ssh command is used to define which IP addresses are allowed access to the Secure Shell console on the PIX firewall. The ssh command also defines the idle timeout of an SSH connection, like so:

```
pixfirewall(config)# [no] ssh <local_ip> [<mask>] [<if name>]
```

Table 7.6	ssh Command Options
Option	**Function**
local_ip	The subnet or IP address allowed to SSH into the PIX.
mask	The optional **mask** allows you to specify an exact host with 255.255.255.255 or a subnet with a mask such as 255.255.255.0.
if_name	The name of the interface to accept the Telnet access.

The following example allows SSH secure access to 10.72.7.9 on the outside interface:

```
pixfirewall(config)# ssh 10.72.7.9 255.255.255.255 outside
pixfirewall(config)#
pixfirewall(config)# show ssh
10.72.7.9 255.255.255.255 outside
pixfirewall(config)#
```

The ssh timeout command can be used to limit the idle timeout for SSH sessions. The command example shown here sets the timeout to 10 minutes:

```
pixfirewall(config)# ssh timeout 10
pixfirewall(config)#
pixfirewall(config)# show ssh timeout
ssh timeout 10 minutes
pixfirewall(config)#
```

When you first connect to the PIX firewall, you might see a prompt with periods (.). This means the firewall is busy generating server keys and it could take several seconds before you are prompted for username and password.

Displaying and Saving SSH Information

After you have configured SSH, four more commands are available that you can use to verify its operation and disconnect users. They are

➤ `show ca mypubkey rsa`

➤ `ca save all`   ⬠

➤ `show ssh sessions` ✓

➤ ~~disconnect ssh session~~ ✓
  ssh disconnect

The **show ca mypubkey rsa** Command

The `show ca mypubkey rsa` command enables you to view the public key that was generated with your hostname and domain name. The command syntax is shown here:

```
pixfirewall(config)# show ca mypubkey rsa
% Key pair was generated at: 09:05:34 UTC Aug 31 2003
Key name: pixfirewall.newman.cla
 Usage: General Purpose Key
 Key Data:
  30819f30 0d06092a 864886f7 0d010101 05000381 8d003081 89028181 00c5af11
  97e073ae ece530d1 cfea4649 84521282 768557e3 c1bb1315 8f6627cc 50224607
  14b1b9cd bf7a9c61 3e28d997 ea92b816 c04c63fd 0751748e 588cbcd2 0659675b
  ece86f2b 6592bc39 f707de5e b040e889 cc350b03 ab1a8582 ca329402 31ce17a3
  26a4c8be 3c72cd25 a80612d6 19e7419f afa68301 6c2c7682 d26a39c7 6b020301
  0001
pixfirewall(config)#
```

The **ca save all** Command

After you have generated your key, you must execute the `ca save all` command to save the key to flash memory. The following displays the command:

```
pixfirewall(config)# ca save all
```

The `ca save all` command might take several seconds to save, so be patient.

The **show ssh sessions** Command

The `show ssh sessions` command can be used to show who is currently connected to the PIX. Following is an example of this command:

```
pixfirewall(config)# show ssh sessions
```

Session ID	Client IP	Version	Encryption	State	Username
0	192.168.1.11	1.5	DES	6	pix

```
pixfirewall(config)#
```

The **ssh disconnect session** Command

After you have viewed who has an active SSH session using the show ssh sessions command, you can use the ssh disconnect session command to drop a specific session. The following is an example of this command:

```
pixfirewall(config)# show ssh sessions

Session ID     Client IP        Version Encryption     State     Username
      0         192.168.1.11      1.5     DES             6         pix
pixfirewall(config)#
pixfirewall(config)# ssh disconnect session 0
pixfirewall(config)# show ssh sessions
pixfirewall(config)#
```

HTTP PDM Access

The PIX firewall allows several methods of console access, but it also has a Web browser interface that can be used to monitor and configure the firewall. This interface is called PIX Device Manager (PDM). The PDM interface Web pages are hosted from PIX firewalls and downloaded to client browsers that support HTTPS (secure socket layer). The PIX firewall must have the HTTP server feature enabled to host the PDM Web pages. The following two steps are needed to configure HTTP access:

1. Turn on the HTTP server capability.

2. Specify which hosts can connect using HTTP.

The **http server** Command

To allow the clients to access the system using HTTP browsers you first must use the http server enable command to turn on the service. Here's an example of the command:

```
pixfirewall(config)# http server enable
```

The **http** Command

Now that the PIX is enabled to host the PDM interface, the next step, as in Telnet, is to specify which hosts can connect to the PIX using HTTP. The http command's syntax is as follows:

```
pixfirewall(config)# [no] http <local_ip> [<mask>] [<if_name>]
```

Table 7.7	http Command Options
Option	**Function**
local_ip	The subnet or IP address allowed to use HTTP to access the PIX.
mask	The optional mask allows you to specify an exact host with 255.255.255.255 or a subnet with a mask such as 255.255.255.0.
if_name	The name of the interface on which to accept the HTTP access.

The first example shown here allows 192.168.1.11 HTTP access on the inside interface, whereas the second example allows HTTP access to the PIX for all addresses on the 192.168.1.0 subnet:

```
pixfirewall(config)# http 192.168.1.11 255.255.255.255 inside
```

and

```
pixfirewall(config)# http 192.168.1.0 0.0.0.0 inside
```

You can use the show http command to display what has been configured, like so:

```
pixfirewall(config)# show http
http server enabled
192.168.1.11 255.255.255.255 inside
0.0.0.0 0.0.0.0 inside
pixfirewall(config)#
```

The PIX Device Manager is covered in more detail in later chapters.

Simple Network Management Protocol

The Simple Network Management Protocol (SNMP) was designed to help centrally manage devices using network management stations (NMSs). These stations can poll information, accept events from devices known as *traps*, and even configure the devices remotely. Devices such as hubs, routers, printers, firewalls, and even Microsoft computers can allow an NMS to collect information about them.

SNMP on the PIX

The three main versions of SNMP are 1, 2, and 3. The PIX firewall supports only versions 1 and 2. The PIX also supports only the reading of information, meaning you cannot remotely configure the PIX firewall using NMS as you can with other devices.

By default, SNMP is enabled on the PIX with a community name of public. Any NMS can read information about the PIX. Therefore, to provide some basic security, you should change the default community name to something other than public.

Configuring SNMP

Listing 7.4 is an example of configuring SNMP on the PIX firewall. The community setting should be the same as on the NMS, so that information can be polled from the PIX firewall. The location and contact settings provide basic information about where and who to contact about this device. The enable traps allow messages to be sent from the PIXs to the NMS. Finally, the host setting defines where to send the SNMP traps (which is the IP address of the NMS server).

Listing 7.4   Configuring SNMP

```
pixfirewall(config)# snmp-server community myarea
pixfirewall(config)# snmp-server location oregon
pixfirewall(config)# snmp-server contact Mr. Newman
pixfirewall(config)# snmp-server enable traps
pixfirewall(config)# snmp-server host inside 192.168.1.11
pixfirewall(config)# show snmp
snmp-server host inside 192.168.1.11
snmp-server location oregon
snmp-server contact Mr. Newman
snmp-server community myarea
snmp-server enable traps
pixfirewall(config)#
```

IP address of the NMS server

Or syntax of snmp-server?

Logging PIX Firewall Information

The PIX firewall enables you to log just about every type of event that takes place on the device. Events such as changing passwords, ACL hits, debug events, or even when someone just views the log itself can all be recorded.

Most of the logging commands in the following sections contain a severity level setting. The severity level setting enables you to specify how much detail you want to log.

Severity Levels

The PIX contains several logging security levels that help determine how much information should be logged. The higher the security level number, the more detail that is logged. Table 7.8 displays the eight severity level settings.

Table 7.8	PIX Logging Severity Levels	
Number	Name	Description
0	Emergencies	The system is becoming unstable.
1	Alerts	Take immediate action.
2	Critical	Critical conditions.
3	Errors	Error messages.
4	Warnings	Warning messages.
5	Notifications	Normal but significant conditions.
6	Informational	Information messages.
7	Debugging	Log debug messages, FTP commands, and WWW URLs.

the higher the number, the more detail is logged

 If you select severity level 3 in the logging command, level 3 and all the levels below it, including levels 2, 1, and 0, will be logged.

Similar to most Cisco products, the PIX can log information to several locations simultaneously. Figure 7.3 shows some of the locations where information can be logged:

➤ Internal buffer

➤ Console port

➤ SNMP management stations   *i.e. NMS server*

➤ Syslog servers

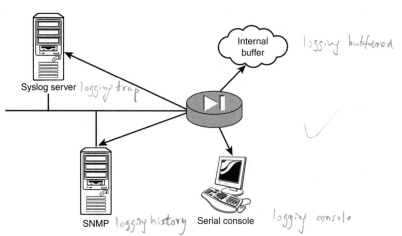

Syslog server logging trap

Internal buffer logging buffered

SNMP logging history   Serial console logging console

Figure 7.3 Places to log information.

Internal Buffers

You can log information to internal buffers maintained in RAM. The following commands enable this location for logging:

```
pixfirewall(config)# logging on
pixfirewall(config)# logging buffered 4
pixfirewall(config)#
```

The `logging on` command enables logging, and the `logging buffered 4` command enables logging severity level 4 messages to the internal buffer. Severity levels were described previously in Table 7.8.

The **show logging** command displays the internal buffer messages, whereas the **clear logging** command flushes the local logging buffer.

Console Port Logging

Logging to the console port enables your serial connection to display the messages being generated. Although this is fun to watch, it usually shouldn't be left on for too long. The following commands enable console logging:

```
pixfirewall(config)# logging on
pixfirewall(config)# logging console 4
pixfirewall(config)#
```

SNMP Management Station

By using the `logging history` command, you can send syslog traps to an SNMP management station, like so:

```
pixfirewall(config)# logging on
pixfirewall(config)# logging history 4
pixfirewall(config)#
```

I believe that it requires all the commands with ☆ in listing 7.4

Syslog Servers

Syslog servers are typically the primary location to log data. These are remote servers that can store your log messages to disk or other methods of storage. Syslog server software is freely available from several vendors, including Cisco. After the software is installed on a remote computer, you'll need to configure your PIX.

To enable messages to be sent to a syslog server, the `logging host` command needs to be executed. The following is the command syntax:

```
pixfirewall(config)# [no] logging host [<in_if>] <l_ip> [tcp¦udp/port#]
```

Table 7.9	logging host Command Options
Option	Function
in_if	This is the interface name the messages will exit.
l_ip	This is the IP address of the host.
tcpludp	You can specify TCP or UDP. TCP helps to guarantee your messages are delivered. This option also requires a port number.

The following example enables logging to a remote syslog server with an IP address of 192.168.1.15 and specifies that each message sent should have a timestamp value appended to it:

```
pixfirewall(config)# logging host inside 192.168.1.15
pixfirewall(config)# logging on
pixfirewall(config)# logging timestamp
pixfirewall(config)# logging trap 4
```

Use the **logging host** command to direct log messages to a remote syslog server.

General Logging Commands

Several other logging commands are available. Table 7.9 displays a few of the most common commands.

Table 7.10	Logging Command Options
Command	Description
logging on	Enables logging
logging timestamp	Works with syslog servers and adds a timestamp to each message to make them unique
logging monitor	Used to set which messages are sent to Telnet sessions
logging trap	Sets log levels for syslog traps e.g. logging trap 4
logging standby	Allows the standby PIX to send messages to the syslog server
clear logging	Clears all the log messages in the internal buffers
show logging	Displays the current logging settings and the messages located in the internal buffers

requires logging host command as shown in * above

The **logging timestamp** command places a timestamp on messages before they are sent to a syslog server.

Exam Prep Questions

Question 1

> Which command will clear the logging buffer?
> ○ A. **clear logging**
> ○ B. **flush log**
> ○ C. **delete log**
> ○ D. **clear buffer**

Answer A is correct. The `clear logging` command clears all the log entries in
the logging bugger. Answers B, C, and D do not exist and are therefore
incorrect.

Question 2

> Which command will ensure a specific timestamp is attached to a message
> before it is sent to a syslog server?
> ○ A. **logging timestamp**
> ○ B. **signed message log**
> ○ C. **unique log**
> ○ D. **flagged entry**

Answer A is correct. The `logging timestamp` command attaches a timestamp
to messages destined to a syslog server. Answer B does not exist and is therefore incorrect. Answer C does not exist and is therefore incorrect, and
answer D does not exist and is therefore incorrect.

Question 3

> Which command enables syslog traps?
> ○ A. **enable smtp**
> ○ B. **set trap syslog**
> ○ C. **logging trap**
> ○ D. **enable trap**

Answer C is correct. The `logging trap` command enables the log levels for syslog traps. Answer A does not exist and is therefore incorrect. Answers B and D also do not exist, so they are incorrect.

Question 4

Which command is used to specify a syslog server?

○ A. **syslog-server 192.168.1.11**

○ B. **logging host 192.168.1.11**

○ C. **host 192.168.1.11**

○ D. **logging 192.168.1.11**

Answer B is correct. The `logging host` command specifies the location of the syslog server. Answer A does not exist and is therefore incorrect. Answer C is incorrect because the `host` command changes the prompt hostname to 192.168.1.11. Answer D is an incomplete command and is therefore incorrect.

Question 5

What are syslog servers used for?

○ A. To collect SNMP traps

○ B. To host PDM files

○ C. To host configurations files

○ D. To collect system messages

Answer D is correct. Syslog servers are used to collect system messages. Answer A is incorrect because NMSs are used to collect SNMP traps. Answer B is incorrect because PDM files are located on the PIX and are used for HTTP interfaces to the PIX. Answer C is incorrect because host configuration files are located on TFTP servers.

Question 6

When connecting to the PIX firewall using SSH, what are the username and
password?

- ○ A. The username is **pix**, and the password is **pix**.
- ○ B. The username is **pix**, and the password is the enable password.
- ○ C. The username is **pix**, and the password is the Telnet password.
- ○ D. The username is **pix**, and the password is **CISCO**.

Answer C is correct. When connecting to the PIX firewall, the username is
always pix and the password is the current Telnet password. Answer D is
incorrect because the password cisco is not the default Telnet password; cisco
in all lowercase is. Answer A is incorrect because the password might not
necessarily be the word pix. The password is whatever the Telnet password
is, making answer C more correct. Answer B is incorrect also because the
password used is the Telnet password and not the enable password.

Question 7

Which command is used to collect time from an NTP server?

- ○ A. **ntp-server**
- ○ B. **ntp server**
- ○ C. **server-ntp**
- ○ D. **sync-server**

Answer B is correct. The ntp server command enables you to synchronize
the PIX clock with an NTP server. Multiple servers can be used at the same
time by entering the command multiple times. Answer A is incorrect because
the ntp-server command does not exist. Answers C and D are also incorrect
because these commands do not exist.

Question 8

Which command clears all existing RSA keys?

- ○ A. **clear rsa-keys**
- ○ B. **clear ca zeroize rsa**
- ○ C. **zeroize rsa**
- ○ D. **ca zeroize rsa**

Answer D is correct. The `ca zeroize rsa` command clears all RSA-generated keys from flash. Answer A is incorrect because the `clear rsa-key` command does not exist. Answer B is incorrect because the `clear ca zeroize rsa` command does not exist. Answer C is incorrect because the `zeroize rsa` command is missing the `ca` part.

Question 9

What does the **telnet** command do?

- ○ A. Allows you to Telnet from the PIX to another device
- ○ B. Allows specific computers to Telnet into the PIX
- ○ C. Enables Telnet traffic to pass through the PIX
- ○ D. Blocks Telnet traffic on the outside interface

Answer B is correct. The `telnet` command allows you to specify who can Telnet into the PIX firewall. By entering an IP address and mask, you can enable a specific host or a whole subnet to have Telnet access. Answer A is incorrect because the command is used to define who can Telnet into the PIX, not who can Telnet out of it. Answer C is incorrect because the Telnet traffic is automatically allowed through the PIX firewall in the outbound direction. The `telnet` command does not control who can Telnet across the PIX. Answer D is incorrect because `access-list` commands can be used to prevent Telnet access across the PIX firewall.

Question 10

When connecting to the PIX using SSH, you see a period (.). What does this mean?

- ○ A. The SSH connection has failed.
- ○ B. The SSH is generating server keys.
- ○ C. The SSH connection has timed out.
- ○ D. SSH has not been configured.

Answer B is correct. The . is displayed when the PIX is generating server keys to use for encryption. Answer A is incorrect because a text message displays stating that the connection has failed, and not the . symbol. Answer C is incorrect because a text message stating that a timeout has occurred appears—not the . symbol. Answer D is incorrect because, if the SSH has not been configured, you get a connection failure message and not the . symbol.

Need to Know More?

 Chapman, David and Andy Fox. *Cisco Secure PIX Firewalls.* Indianapolis, IN: Cisco Press, 2002.

 Deal, Richard A. *Cisco PIX Firewalls.* Berkeley, CA: McGraw-Hill/Osborne, 2002.

 See the Cisco PIX Firewall Command Reference, Version 6.2 at http://www.cisco.com/univercd/cc/td/doc/product/iaabu/pix/pix_sw/ v_62/cmdref/.

8

Advanced Protocol Handling and PIX Firewall Features

. . . .

Terms you'll need to understand:

✓ Fixups
✓ Standard and passive FTP
✓ SCCP
✓ Skinny
✓ SIP
✓ H.323
✓ URL filtering
✓ PPPoE
✓ Default route

Techniques you'll need to master:

✓ Using the Fixup protocol
✓ Configuring URL filtering
✓ Monitoring URL filtering
✓ Using DCHP servers and clients
✓ Configuring PPPoE
✓ Setting default routes

Firewalls today have to be very sophisticated about how to control traffic. Basic traffic can flow through a firewall effortlessly, but complex protocols need to have extra help. Cisco provides the PIX firewall with fixup support to assist these complex protocols. This chapter explains what they do, when they are required, and how to configure them. In addition, it covers the advanced topics of content filtering, DHCP settings, PPPoE configuration, and Routing Information Protocol (RIP) support.

Problems with Advanced Protocols and ASA

Several advanced protocols, including FTP, cause problems when trying to traverse across the PIX firewall. The problems arise when traffic on the outside client or server wants to send traffic to the inside, higher-security interfaces; this traffic is often unsolicited from the perspective of standard ASA. Normally, traffic flow is in response to a client's request and returns on the same source port on which the client request was sent. The ASA sees this normal request and opens a connection slot for the return traffic. Some advanced protocols respond or send data to the client on port numbers other than the ports in the source header, and this causes a problem for the normal ASA engine.

For example, if Jack is trying to download information from an FTP site using standard mode, he notifies the FTP server that his port—for example, 3002—is available to receive the data. The requested port 3002 is not in the normal source port header location but in the data portion of the packet. Because the ASA normally monitors the source port header and not the data portion, the connection slot is not made. As the FTP server starts to send data to Jack's port (3002), the PIX drops the packets because ASA never created a connection slot for the returning traffic.

The Function of Fixups

The PIX firewall implements fixup protocol features to help overcome the difficulties with advanced protocols. The fixup protocols perform what is known as *application inspection* on a limited number of advanced protocols. The inspection monitors the traffic across the PIX and dynamically opens and closes connection slots between the inside and outside interfaces. Fixups try to make the connections as secure as possible by dynamically opening only the necessary ports.

If fixup protocols did not exist, you would have to open large numbers of ports with ACLs or the established commands to allow traffic to pass, effectively compromising the granularity and overall value of your security solution. Table 8.1 displays some of the available fixup protocols with their respective ports and functions.

Table 8.1	Available Fixup Protocols	
Protocol	**Default Port**	**Function**
FTP	21	The FTP fixup works to help correct standard and passive FTP problems.
H323 h225	1720	The H323 monitors and helps correct the multimedia applications that use H323 back through the PIX firewall.
H323 RAS	1718 and 1719	This works with the H323 protocol suite.
HTTP	80	Helps monitor HTTP and is required for WebSense or N2H2 URL filtering services.
ILS	389	The ILS fixup works to help correct LDAP transactions across the PIX firewall.
RSH	514	Remote Shell.
RTSP	554	Real-Time Streaming Protocol.
SMTP	25	Simple Mail Transport Protocol.
SQL*Net	1521	Oracle communications.
SIP	5060	Session Initiation Protocol.
SCCP	2000	Skinny Client Control Protocol.

The show fixup Command

You can use the show fixup command to display the active fixup protocols on the PIX firewall. Listing 8.1 displays the output of the show fixup command.

Listing 8.1	show fixup Command Example

```
pixfirewall(config)# show fixup
fixup protocol ftp 21
fixup protocol http 80
fixup protocol h323 h225 1720
fixup protocol h323 ras 1718-1719
fixup protocol ils 389
fixup protocol rsh 514
fixup protocol rtsp 554
fixup protocol smtp 25
fixup protocol sqlnet 1521
fixup protocol sip 5060
fixup protocol skinny 2000
pixfirewall(config)#
```

The **fixup protocol** Command

The standard `fixup` command is similar for all the protocols listed in Table 8.1. Most protocols can have additional ports assigned to them that will enable application inspection monitoring of nonstandard ports for that protocol. This is the standard `fixup protocol` command's syntax:

```
pixfirewall(config)# [no] fixup protocol <prot> [<option>] <port>[-<port>]
```

Table 8.2 displays the `fixup protocol` options.

Table 8.2	**fixup protocol** Command Options
Option	Function
prot	Protocol setting, such as HTTP, SIP, RTSP, and so on.
port-port	A single port or a range or ports can be used to enable application inspections on traffic defined for the protocol option.

The following example adds a single port and a range of nonstandard ports for RTSP:

```
pixfirewall(config)# fixup protocol rtsp 1501
pixfirewall(config)# fixup protocol rtsp 1700-1710
pixfirewall(config)# show fixup protocol rtsp
fixup protocol rtsp 554
fixup protocol rtsp 1501
fixup protocol rtsp 1700-1710
pixfirewall(config)#
```

The **clear fixup** Command

The `clear fixup` command resets the fixup protocol to the default values, like so:

```
pixfirewall(config)# clear fixup
```

The File Transfer Protocol

File Transfer Protocol (FTP) enables two computers to upload and download data across a network. Although it has been around for a long time, as has Telnet and email, it is considered an advanced protocol because it operates a little differently in the way it uses ports.

FTP uses two main ports—20 and 21. Port 21 is used for a control connection that is used to transmit commands to and from the FTP server. For example, as a user enters FTP commands, the commands are transmitted on port 21. When data must be downloaded, port 20 provides this basic function. FTP comes in two main modes: standard and passive.

If you want to prevent FTP traffic, you need to block only one port. By blocking port 21, you prevent FTP commands from being sent to the normal default FTP servers. Port 20 doesn't need to be blocked because, without the commands, data can't be transferred.

Standard Mode *standard & passive*

FTP operates in a couple of modes. In *standard* mode, the FTP client and the server send commands across a command connection on port 21. In this command connection, the client requests to use a port for uploading or downloading. This request is embedded inside the data portion of a packet sent to the server. Because the ASA monitors source port and destination port headers, this request is missed by ASA. Additionally, as the server initiates the data connection back to the client, the firewall drops the packets because no connection slot is created for this traffic.

Figure 8.1 show a basic example of a client requesting traffic from an FTP server. In step 1 the client requests to use 3002 as its data port; in step 2 the server starts to make a connection to that port. No connection slot for port 3002 exists, so the packets are dropped.

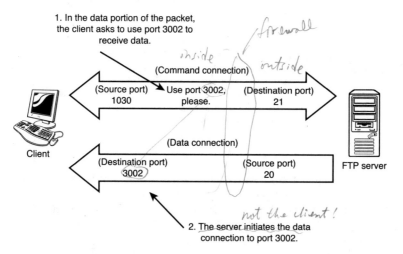

Figure 8.1 Standard mode FTP.

Passive Mode

The second FTP mode is *passive* mode, which operates a little differently from standard mode. The command connection still exists using port 21 on the server. However, the data connection on the server doesn't have to use port 20. When data needs to be transmitted, the client requests asks the server which port it should use. Again, this request is embedded in the data portion of a packet within the command connection traffic. The server sends the port number it wants the client to use, and then the client initiates the data connection to the server. This is the exact opposite from standard mode, in which the server initiates the data connection.

Figure 8.2 is a basic example of passive mode FTP. In step 1 the client and server negotiate which server port will be used to transfer data; then in step 2 the client initiates the data connection to the server. Because the client makes this connection, the ASA creates a connection slot and has no problems allowing traffic to pass back and forth.

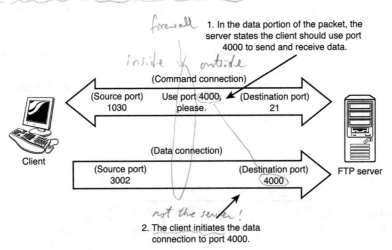

firewall 1. In the data portion of the packet, the server states the client should use port 4000 to send and receive data.

inside | *outside*

(Command connection)

(Source port) 1030 — Use port 4000, please. — (Destination port) 21

(Data connection)

Client

(Source port) 3002 — (Destination port) 4000 — FTP server

not the server!

2. The client initiates the data connection to port 4000.

Figure 8.2 Passive mode FTP.

For outbound connection (i.e., client inside, FTP server outside the firewall)

> **ALERT**
>
> It is important that you understand the difference between standard and passive mode. A good way to remember the difference is as follows:
>
> In *standard* mode the server calls the shots and initiates the data connection. This means clients on the inside have trouble connecting in standard mode.
>
> In *passive* mode, the server is passive and the client initiates the data connections. This means that passive mode works very well for clients on the inside of the PIX firewall.

without the need of using fixup protocol

In inbound connection (i.e. FTP server inside, client outside the firewall) different stories. See p.340 (Cisco press, for details)

The **fixup protocol ftp** Command

With the possible problems of FTP data connections and the ASA dropping uninitiated traffic, the PIX has a fixup protocol option for FTP that compensates for the FTP traffic. This fixup monitors the embedded data portions of the command connection traffic. When embedded port requests are detected, the PIX dynamically creates connection slots for the necessary ports, allowing the uninitiated traffic to flow. The following is the syntax for the ftp command:

```
pixfirewall(config)# fixup protocol ftp <port> [<strict>]
```

Table 8.3	**fixup protocol ftp** Command Options
Option	**Function**
port	This is the port number to monitor for FTP traffic. Typically, this is port 21.
strict	The strict option prevents any embedded FTP commands in HTTP connections. By default, this is allowed.

The following is the command to enable the FTP fixup protocol:

```
pixfirewall(config)# fixup protocol ftp 21
```

The Hypertext Transfer Protocol

The Hypertext Transfer Protocol (HTTP) fixup protocol allows application inspection of traffic using the default port 80. When HTTP fixups are enabled, three main functions become available:

➤ Filtering of URL features using WebSense or N2H2 servers

➤ Logging of HTTP GET requests

➤ Filtering of Java and ActiveX content.

You can create additional ports for the HTTP fixup protocol command. For example, the following command enables HTTP fixups on port 8080:

```
pixfirewall(config)# fixup protocol http 8080
```

With the previous command, application inspection for HTTP takes place on the both the default port 80 and on additional port 8080.

To turn off HTTP fixups, you use the following command:

```
pixfirewall(config)# no fixup protocol http 8080
pixfirewall(config)# no fixup protocol http 80
```

NOTE If you turn off all HTTP fixups, you will not able to perform URL filtering.

Remote Shell

Remote Shell (RSH) was originally created for Unix systems as an easy-to-use remote console that doesn't need a login as its brother Telnet does. RSH is very insecure and should be replaced at all costs with more secure connections, such as SSH.

RSH is similar to standard mode in the FTP protocol. Two connections are required for complete communication—one connection for commands and a second for standard error outputs. The client embeds the port number to which the server should send standard errors. The server then initiates the second connection that will not be in the connection table. If the `fixup protocol rsh` command is not enabled, the ASA rejects the server's request.

The `fixup protocol rsh` command inspects the RSH traffic for the embedded port requests needed on port 514. When a request for a port is sent, the ASA dynamically creates a connection slot to allow the server to send traffic back to the client. The following is the command syntax for RSH:

```
pixfirewall(config)# [no] fixup protocol rsh <port-[port]>
```

The following example enables RSH inspection on a range of additional ports:

```
pixfirewall(config)# fixup protocol rsh 2000-2003
```

SQL*Net Protocol

The SQL*Net protocol is used by Oracle clients and servers to query SQL databases. This advanced protocol mainly uses a single port for communication and should therefore not be an issue for the ASA engine. However, that port can be redirected to a different port or a different server during the connection lifetime. To allow traffic to pass securely, the `fixup protocol sqlnet` command is used to help monitor SQL*Net protocol connections. The following is the syntax for this command:

```
pixfirewall(config)# [no] fixup protocol sqlnet <port-[port]>
```

The following example enables SQL*Net inspection of port 1521:

```
pixfirewall(config)# fixup protocol sqlnet 1521
```

The Real Time Streaming Protocol

The Real Time Streaming Protocol (RTSP) is a real-time audio and video protocol used by several multimedia applications, such as RealPlayer, Cisco IP/TV, Quicktime 4, Netshow, and VDO live, to name a few. Similar to FTP, this protocol can operate in different modes depending on the application used. Each mode uses three different connections to function properly.

Real-Time Protocol (RTP) mode uses the following three connections:

➤ TCP control channel

➤ UDP RTP data channel

➤ UDP RTCP reports

RealNetworks' Real Data Transport (RDT) mode uses the following three connections:

➤ TCP control channel

➤ UDP data channel

➤ UDP resend

By default, no fixup protocols are set for RTSP applications; they must be manually set if such applications are needed. The default port used by RTSP is port 554. The following command enables fixups for RTSP:

```
pixfirewall(config)# fixup protocol rtsp 554
```

 RTSP is not supported using PAT. Most RTSP applications are also incompatible with NAT.

Voice Over IP

Voice over IP (VoIP) is not one protocol but a term used for several types of protocols that provide telephone call–like connections across IP networks. Protocols such as SCCP, SIP, and H.323 are covered here.

The Skinny Client Control Protocol

Skinny Client Control Protocol (SCCP) is typically just called *Skinny*. Cisco uses this simplified protocol for its VoIP phones and CallManager servers.

The basis of Skinny is its interoperability with another protocol called H.323, which is discussed later.

When an IP phone first boots, it requests an IP address from a DHCP server. Then, the phone downloads its configuration from a TFTP server and is ready for use.

When a call is made, the client's phone sends a signal connection to a CallManager server, which then contacts the destination phone and acquires the UDP port the phone needs for audio communication. Next, the server passes this information back to the calling phone so that the source and destination phones can connect. Figure 8.3 shows that basic high-level flow for a connection.

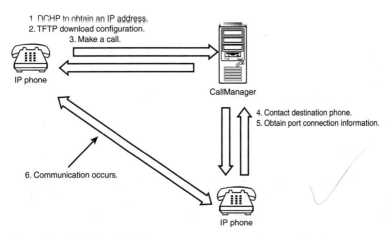

Figure 8.3 Basic Skinny VoIP flow.

Some of the application inspection problems with Skinny include the use of inside addresses and the dynamic destination port numbers. If the clients are behind NAT, the embedded IP information must be changed to reflect the external Internet addresses. The fixup protocol for Skinny monitors and changes the internal address used by NAT to an external address. It also dynamically creates connection slots to allow traffic to pass as needed.

 Skinny is supported on NAT but not PAT.

The following command enables the SCCP protocol to function across the PIX firewall:

```
pixfirewall(config)# fixup protocol skinny 2000
```

The Session Initiation Protocol

Session Initiation Protocol (SIP) is another VoIP protocol that allows connections between audio devices using IP. This protocol is similar to Skinny; at a high level, the process of making a call is the same. The caller contacts what is known as a VoIP *gateway*. This gateway locates the destination phone for the caller and helps the two get connected.

The default port for VoIP gateways is UDP port 5060. The following command enables SIP fixups:

```
pixfirewall(config)# fixup protocol sip 5060
```

H.323

H.323 is a complicated hybrid protocol that can be used for VoIP, video, and data. Like other multimedia protocols, but unlike VoIP, H.323 requires several ports to connect two devices. The protocol is actually a suite of other protocols put together to make the connections desired.

The following lists standards used between two H.323 devices:

➤ H.225 Registration, Admission, and Status (RAS)

➤ H.235 Call Signaling

➤ H.245 Control Signaling

➤ TPKT Header

➤ Q.931 Messages

➤ ASN.1 Encoding Packets

Several vendors use H.323 for their products; however, each vender implements this protocol in a slightly different way. So, not all H.323 applications are supported on the PIX firewall. The following is list of supported H.323 applications:

➤ Cisco Multimedia Conference Manager

➤ Microsoft NetMeeting

➤ CUseeMe Meeting Point and Pro

➤ Intel Video Phone

➤ VocalTec Internet Phone and Gatekeeper

Each of these applications needs its own special adjustments for available ports. See Cisco's Web site for detailed configurations needed for each application. Here are variations of the basic command to enable H.323:

```
pixfirewall(config)# fixup protocol h323 1720
pixfirewall(config)# fixup protocol h323 1718-1719
```

syntax: fixup protocol h323 [h225|ras] [port [-port]]

Web Traffic Filtering

requires HTTP fixup protocol

Although the firewall's main purpose is to protect inside users from outside threats, the PIX firewall can also help control which Web sites internal users can access. The PIX firewall can be linked to a URL filtering server such as WebSense or N2H2, which provide Internet monitoring and URL Web site blocking if necessary.

Figure 8.4 displays the basic Web filter process, which includes these steps:

1. The client opens a connection to a Web server and sends an HTTP GET message to access a Web page.

2. The PIX intercepts the call and forwards the request to the URL filtering server and the Web site at the same time.

3. The filtering server searches its database of Web sites to see whether the user has permission to access the Web site. In the meantime, the Web site is attempting to respond to the user's request.

4. If the URL server's response is yes, the PIX allows the Web site response to be forwarded to the requesting client. Otherwise, the Web site's response is dropped.

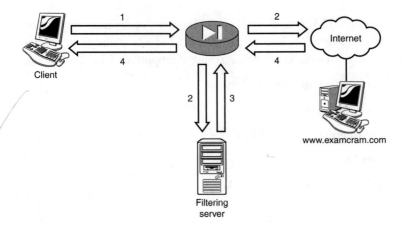

Figure 8.4 URL filtering process.

Configuring WebSense and N2H2

The PIX firewall can be configured to use WebSense or N2H2 URL filtering servers for HTTP traffic. The basic steps are the same for each vendor's configuration on the PIX firewall. They are as follows: *see # on p.180 for e.s.*

1. Identify the URL filtering server.

2. Specify which traffic needs to be forwarded to the filtering server.

3. Optionally, configure the URL cache.

 HTTP fixup protocols must be configured to allow URL filtering.

---

step 1:

The url-server Command

The first step is to identify the URL server you want to use. You use two different commands, based on which vendors you are actually using. However, their basic structures are the same: Identify the interface, identify the host, and set the timeout durations. The command syntax is as follows:

```
pixfirewall(config)# [no] url-server [<(if_name)>] {vendor websense}
                host <local_ip> [timeout <seconds>]        UDP cannot
                [protocol TCP¦UDP [version 1¦4]]          have this version!
pixfirewall(config)#[no] url-server [<(if_name)>] vendor n2h2     Cannot
                host <local_ip> [port <number>]                  run
                [timeout <seconds>] [protocol TCP¦UDP]          both
                                                            simultaneously
```

step 2:

The filter url Command

After the servers have been configured, you need to specify which traffic will be forwarded to them. The `filter URL` command is used to identify which local users' Web traffic will be forwarded to the URL servers. The following displays the syntax needed:

```
pixfirewall(config)# [no] filter url <port>[-<port>]¦except
                <lcl_ip> <mask> <frgn_ip> <mask> [allow]
```

The `filter url` command allows you to be granular enough to select specific inside (`lcl_ip`) to outside (`frgn_ip`) ranges to filter. The `except` option enables you to exclude certain IP addresses from the filter. The `allow` option defines what the PIX firewall will do when WebSense or N2H2 servers are offline. If `allow` is stated, Web traffic is allowed to pass through the firewall. Conversely, if `allow` is not stated, all Web traffic is blocked.

step 3 :

The **url-cache** Command

Web filtering does come at a cost to performance. The delays introduced by querying an external URL filtering server can be an issue. By using the url-cache command, the PIX can cache a request locally on the firewall and reuse this cache the next time a user goes to the same destination. This decreases the impact of delays and increases the users' throughput. However, you do lose some tracking information about users' Web activity that would have been recorded on the URL server. The command syntax for the url-cache command is shown here: *Cache entries based on the URL destination address*

```
pixfirewall(config)# [no] url-cache <dst¦src_dst> size <Kbytes>
```

Cache entries based on the source address initiating the URL request as well as the URL destination address.

A URL Filtering Example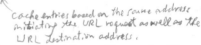

The following sequence of commands configures a WebSense filter as the filtering server. It then specifies that all traffic is to be forwarded to the WebSense filter, except traffic initiated by 192.168.1.11:

```
pixfirewall(config)# url-server (inside) vendor websense
               host 192.168.1.101 timeout 5 protocol TCP version 4
pixfirewall(config)# filter url http 0 0 0 0
pixfirewall(config)# filter url except 192.168.1.11 255.255.255.255
               0 0 allow
pixfirewall(config)# url-cache dst 128
```

means : for all users to all web site IP addresses

Monitoring URL Filtering

Several commands allow you to view your configuration and monitor your URL filtering traffic. Table 8.4 lists several of these.

Table 8.4 URL Filtering Commands	
Command	**Function**
show url-cache stat	Displays URL cache details *URL statistics*
show url-server	Displays the list of URL servers configured
show filter	Displays the URL filters configured
show perfmon	Displays performance monitor statistics, including URL access information *general firewall statistics including URL statistics*

To view URL filtering statistics, you use the **show perfmon** and show **url-cache stat** commands.

Filtering Java Applets and ActiveX Scripts

requires HTTP fixup protocol.

Web pages can use powerful features such as Java applets and ActiveX scripts. The scripts enable Web developers to provide dynamic content on Web pages. In the wrong hands, however, these scripts can be created to cause harm or collect considerable information about your computer's Internet browsing history. Most browsers enable you to control your security setting for scripts. But in a very secure environment, you might need to ensure that none of these scripts can be executed after traveling across the firewall to the inside users. Cisco has two commands that enable you to comment out the scripts in the HTTP Web pages before they reach clients' computers.

The filter java Command

The `filter java` command is a new command that allows you to specify which internal and external traffic should be filtered for Java code. The filtering adds comment tags around the Java code in the Web page. These comment tags prevent the scripts from being executed. The following is the command syntax:

```
pixfirewall(config)# [no] filter Java <port>[-<port>] <lcl_ip> <mask>
            <frgn_ip> <mask>
```

`lcl_ip` specifies the internal IP address (local), and `frgn_ip` specifies the external IP address (foreign) you want to filter. The following example filters Java code for all users to all Web site IP addresses:

```
pixfirewall(config)# filter Java http 0 0 0 0
```

e.g.

The filter activex Command

ActiveX scripts can also be filtered in the same way that Java scripts can. The command is basically the same:

```
pixfirewall(config)# [no] filter ActiveX <port>[-<port>]
            <lcl_ip> <mask> <frgn_ip> <mask>
```

The following command filters ActiveX content:

```
pixfirewall(config)# filter ActiveX http 0 0 0 0
```

e.g.

The Dynamic Host Configuration Protocol

Dynamic Host Configuration Protocol (DHCP) allows computers to obtain IP addresses and network configurations automatically from a DHCP server. The PIX firewall can be both a DHCP client on the outside interface and at the same time provide DHCP server functionality on the inside interface.

 The PIX firewall can be a DHCP client and a DHCP server at the same time.

DHCP Clients

The PIX firewall can be a DHCP client on the outside interface, enabling you to receive IP address and configuration information dynamically from another source such as an Internet service provider (ISP). The following is the command syntax:

```
pixfirewall(config)# ip address <if_name> dhcp [setroute]
```
?? not an option !!

The dhcp option is used with the ip address command to enable the interface to dynamically receive an IP address from a DHCP server source. The following example defines the outside to be a DHCP client rather than to use a fixed address:

```
pixfirewall(config)# ip address outside dhcp setroute retry 4
```

The setroute option enables you to receive the default route from the DHCP server, whereas the retry option enables the PIX to retry contacting the DHCP server a number of times before giving up. To renew your lease, you type the IP address command again.

After you have received an address, you can use the show IP address outside dhcp command to display the configuration information received.

DHCP Servers

how many?

The PIX can also perform the functions of a small DHCP server. The number of clients it can support is limited, and performing this function is really intended only for small SOHO environments. To configure the PIX to be a DHCP server, the commands in Table 8.5 are available.

Table 8.5 DHCP Server Commands

Command	Function
dhcpd address <ip1>[-<ip2>] inside	This sets the pool of addresses the server will hand out to clients.
dhcpd ping_timeout <timeout>	This command is the response delay the PIX uses as it tests for any other clients that might be using the address it currently wants to give a client.
dhcpd auto_config [<clnt_ifc_name>]	This command forwards all the options learned from the outside interface to the inside users.
dhcpd domain <domain_name>	This specifies the domain option.
dhcpd dns <dnsip1> [<dnsip2>]	This allows you to enter two DNS server IP addresses.
dhcpd wins <winsip1> [<winsip2>]	This allows you to enter two WINS server IP addresses.
dhcpd lease <lease_length>	This is the duration of the lease that clients will keep addresses before returning to the server for a new one.
dchpd option	This allows you to specify any additional options that might be needed.

Listings 8.2 and 8.3 show examples that configure the PIX to hand out IP addresses in the range of 192.168.1.2–192.168.1.33 with options manually configured or with options automatically configured. Automatic configuration allows the options learned from the outside DHCP server to be used as the default options for the inside clients.

Listing 8.2 demonstrates how to configure the PIX as a DHCP server with manually configured options to give to DHCP clients.

Listing 8.2 Configuring a DHCP Server with Manual Options

```
pixfirewall(config)# dhcpd address 192.168.1.2-192.168.1.33 inside
pixfirewall(config)# dhcpd lease 3000
pixfirewall(config)# dhcpd dns 192.168.1.100 192.168.1.101
pixfirewall(config)# dhcpd wins 192.168.1.99
pixfirewall(config)# dhcpd domain examcram.com
pixfirewall(config)# dhcpd enable inside
```

The **dhcpd dns** command allows you to set only two DNS server IP addresses.

Listing 8.3 demonstrates how to configure the PIX as a DHCP server with automatically configured options that are originally received from the ISP and are passed on to the PIX DHCP clients.

Listing 8.3   Configuring a DHCP Server with Automatic Options

```
pixfirewall(config)# dhcpd address 192.168.1.2-192.168.1.33 inside
pixfirewall(config)# dhcpd lease 3000
pixfirewall(config)# dhcpd auto_config
pixfirewall(config)# dhcpd enable inside
```

To display DHCP settings and bindings, the commands in Table 8.6 can be used.

Table 8.6   show dhcp Commands

Command	Function
show dhcpd	Displays current DHCP server settings
show dhcpd binding	Displays the MAC address-to-IP address bindings the PIX has assigned
show dhcpd statistics	Shows the active IP address leases, expired bindings, and several other extensive DHCP server details

TIP   The PIX firewall automatically issues the inside interfaces IP address as the default gateway option to the DHCP clients. *really?*

The Point-to-Point Protocol over Ethernet

The Point-to-Point Protocol over Ethernet (PPPoE) is an ethernet encapsulation of the Point-to-Point Protocol used most commonly for serial or dial-up connections. PPPoE's main purpose is similar to that of a DHCP client/server scenario. PPPoE clients receive IP address information from an ISP acting as a PPPoE server. The advantage of PPPoE over DHCP is that it can require a username and password authentication before giving out connection information. Typical areas where this might be used are cable modems or DSL line configuration.

Configuring PPPoE on the PIX

The PIX firewall can support client PPPoE configurations only on the outside interface. To configure PPPoE, the vpdn command is needed. This command is a versatile command that is also used for creating VPN tunnels into the PIX. The steps to creating a PPPoE client configuration are as follows:

1. Define a VPDN group.

2. Define the VPDN group authentication.

3. Set the VPDN group ISP username.

4. Configure a VPDN username and password.

5. Enable PPPoE on the outside interface.

The **vpdn group** Command

The vpdn group command creates a group with which all parameters for the PPPoE connection will be associated. The following displays the syntax of the vpdn group command for PPPoE:

```
pixfirewall(config)# vpdn group <group_name> request dialout pppoe
```

Table 8.7 displays the command options for the vpdn command for PPPoE.

Table 8.7 vpdn group command options	
Option	Function
group_name	This is the unique name you want to use for all the parameters you will send for the VPDN connection.
request dialout pppoe	This specifies that the group will be using a PPPoE connection for dial-out capabilities.

The following command demonstrates configuring a VPDN group named ExamCram that is using PPPoE as the requested dial-out connection:

```
pixfirewall(config)# vpdn group ExamCram request dialout pppoe
```

The **vpdn group authentication** Command

Just like PPP, PPPoE can use authentication. The PIX currently supports three types of authentication: PAP, CHAP, and MSCHAP. Its command syntax is shown here:

```
pixfirewall(config)# vpdn group <group_name>
            ppp authentication <pap¦chap¦mschap>
```

This command demonstrates setting a VPDN group named ExamCram to use PAP for authentication:

```
pixfirewall(config)# vpdn group ExamCram ppp authentication pap
```

Step 3:

The vpdn group localname Command

When connecting to an ISP, a username is given to the account, and this username must be linked to the VPDN group you are using for the PPPoE connection. The localname command links the username to the VPDN group. The command syntax is

```
pixfirewall(config)# vpdn group <group_name> localname <username>
```

The command shown here demonstrates setting a VPDN group named ExamCram with a local name of danny that will be sent to the ISP during the authentication phase:

```
pixfirewall(config)# vpdn group ExamCram localname danny
```

Step 4:

The vpdn username and password Command

The vpdn group localname command specifies only the username needed to connect to the ISP. However, the ISP also needs a password. This password is created separately from the vpdn group commands, but it is associated back to the group by using the same name as in the vpdn group localname command. For example, if you created a localname called danny, you would also create a username and password entry with danny. Here is the command syntax:

```
pixfirewall(config)# vpdn username <name> password <pwd>
```
user

This command demonstrates setting a VPDN username and password that will be sent to the ISP during the authentication phase. After it's configured, the PIX firewall will not require user interaction during the connection phase:

```
pixfirewall(config)# vpdn username danny password 123
```

After the username and password are configured for PPPoE, no user interaction is needed when the PIX acquires the IP address information from the ISP.

Step 5:

The ip address Command

The last step is to enable PPPoE on the outside interface. The ip address command is used to enable PPPoE on the interface, and its command syntax is as follows:

```
pixfirewall(config)# ip address <if_name> <ip_address> <mask>
                     pppoe [setroute]
```

The `setroute` option enables you to receive the default route from the ISP PPPoE server. The following is an example of setting the outside interface to use PPPoE with the `setroute` option:

```
pixfirewall(config)# ip address outside pppoe setroute
```

A PPPoE Example *hard to memorize!!*

Listing 8.4 displays the five commands needed to create a PPPoE client configuration on the PIX firewall.

Listing 8.4   Example Using PPPoE

```
pixfirewall(config)# vpdn group ExamCram request dialout pppoe        _ = keyword
pixfirewall(config)# vpdn group ExamCram ppp authentication pap
pixfirewall(config)# vpdn group ExamCram localname danny
pixfirewall(config)# vpdn username danny password 123
pixfirewall(config)# ip address outside pppoe setroute
```

Routing - Version 6.3 supports OSPF routing protocol
- 501 model does not support OSPF

The PIX firewall supports only two methods of routing—static and passive RIP. *Static* routing is the process of manually configuring a route, whereas *passive RIP* is the process of dynamically learning routes via the Routing Information Protocol (RIP) from other RIP-enabled routers. The PIX firewall does not share its routing information with other routers; it only passively listens to RIP advertisements.

After you assign an IP address to an interface, the PIX firewall creates a directly connected entry in the routing table. But any routes not directly connected need to be configured. Listing 8.5 uses the `show route` command to display the directly connected routes shown in Figure 8.5.

Listing 8.5   Connected Routes

```
pixfirewall(config)# show route
        outside 169.254.0.0 255.255.0.0 169.254.8.1 1 CONNECT static
        inside 192.168.1.0 255.255.255.0 192.168.1.1 1 CONNECT static
pixfirewall(config)#
```

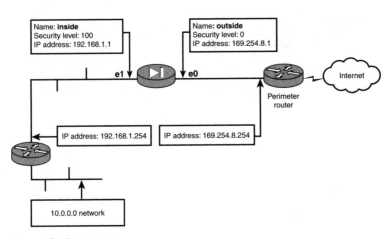

Figure 8.5 PIX network.

Static Routes

Manually configuring static routes enables the PIX firewall to direct traffic out the appropriate interface and off to the next hop. The route command is used to create a manual static route; its command syntax is shown here:

```
pixfirewall(config)# [no] route <if_name> <foreign_ip> <mask>
                     <gateway> [<metric>]
```

 # clear route

Table 8.8 displays the command options for the route command.

Table 8.8	route Command Options
Option	**Function**
if_name	This is the interface name where the route exists.
foreign_ip	This is the network address to be routed. Use 0.0.0.0 for the default route.
mask	This specifies a mask to use with the **foreign_ip** option.
gateway	This is the next hop IP address to get to the network defined in the **foreign_ip** option.
metric	This specifies the hops to the network.

default = 1

In Listing 8.6, two static routes are created. The first is a default route to the Internet, and the second is a static route to the 10.0.0.0 network.

Listing 8.6   Static Routes

```
pixfirewall(config)# clear route                = 0, 0
pixfirewall(config)# route outside 0.0.0.0 0.0.0.0 169.254.8.254 ⟵ a default route
pixfirewall(config)# route inside 10.0.0.0 255.0.0.0 192.168.1.254
pixfirewall(config)# show route
         outside 0.0.0.0 0.0.0.0 169.254.8.254 1 OTHER static
         inside 10.0.0.0 255.0.0.0 192.168.1.254 1 OTHER static
         outside 169.254.0.0 255.255.0.0 169.254.8.1 1 CONNECT static
         inside 192.168.1.0 255.255.255.0 192.168.1.1 1 CONNECT static
pixfirewall(config)#
```

In Listing 8.6, the first line clears all the existing routes, and the second line displays the route command needed to configure a static default route to the Internet according to Figure 8.5. The third line configures a static route to the 10.0.0.0 network going through the gateway of 192.168.1.254.

The Routing Information Protocol

The PIX firewall can learn routes dynamically using the routing protocols RIP v1 or RIP v2. The routing protocol RIP advertises the routes a device knows to other RIP-enabled devices. Although the PIX supports RIP, it listens to RIP advertisements only in a passive configuration. This enables the PIX to learn routes for other devices without advertising them to others. The exception to this is that the PIX can advertise a default route to another device, but it won't advertise any learned routes. The following is the rip command's syntax:

```
pixfirewall(config)# [no] rip <if_name> default¦passive [version <1¦2>]
                [authentication <text ¦md5> <key> <key id>]
```

Table 8.9 displays the rip command's options.

Table 8.9   rip Command Options

Option	Function
if_name	This is the interface name to perform RIP.
default	This broadcasts the default route on the interface.
passive	This enables passive RIP, which allows the PIX to learn RIP routes.
version 1¦2	This enables version 1 or 2 RIP.
authentication	This works with RIP v2 to provide secure routing updates.

Here is an example of the using the rip command:

```
pixfirewall(config)# rip inside passive version 1
```

Table 8.10 lists four other helpful routing and RIP commands.

Table 8.10	General Routing Commands
Command	**Function**
show route	Displays a routing table
clear route	Clears a single route or the whole routing table
show rip	Displays only RIP-learned routes
debug rip	Used to display RIP traffic

To create a default route, you use the route outside **0.0.0.0 0.0.0.0 <gateway ip address>** command. This command can also be written as **route outside 0 0 <gateway ip address>**.

Exam Prep Questions

Question 1

may not be correct ?!

> Why does passive mode FTP work with clients on the inside of the PIX firewall without the aid of the fixup protocol?
>
> ○ A. ACLs have been manually created. — *Is this important? Also true for standard mode ??*
>
> ○ B. The client initiates the command and data connections. *OK*
>
> ○ C. The outside server initiates the command and data connections.
>
> ○ D. The client initiates the command, and the server initiates the data.

Answer B is correct. When in passive FTP mode, the client initiates both the command and data connections, so the ASA allows traffic to pass as normal. Answer A is incorrect because ACLs do not need to be configured if fixup FTP is set. Answer C is incorrect because the server does not initiate connections in passive mode. Answer D is incorrect because the client initiates connections.

Question 2   *not covered in this chapter !!*

> Which method does the PIX use to allow secure connections for multimedia applications such as CUseeME?
>
> ○ A. It statically opens UDP ports.
>
> ○ B. It dynamically opens and closes UDP ports.
>
> ○ C. It creates ACL entries. *?*
>
> ○ D. It opens and closes static UDP ports.

Answer B is correct. Multimedia applications can be supported by using fixup functions. These fixups dynamically open and close the UDP ports needed for the application to work and provide the best possible secure connections. Answer A is incorrect because fixups open and close ports dynamically and not statically. Answer C is incorrect because ACLs are not needed. Answer D is incorrect because static ports are not needed.

Question 3

> What does the PIX firewall use WebSense for?
>
> ○ A. To filter outside traffic coming into the PIX
>
> ○ B. To control and monitor email traffic
>
> ○ C. To monitor Internet traffic
>
> ◉ D. To control and monitor Internet traffic

Answer D is correct. WebSense, when integrated with the PIX firewall, allows you to control and monitor Internet traffic. Answer A is incorrect because WebSense is not intended for outside traffic coming in. Answer B is incorrect because its primary function is for Web sites and not email. Answer C is an incomplete answer because WebSense can monitor but it can also control traffic. So answer D is more correct.

Question 4

> Which command enables URL filtering?
>
> ○ A. **filter url**
>
> ○ B. **filter-url**
>
> ○ C. **enable filter-url**
>
> ○ D. **enable url-filter**

Answer A is correct. The command to enable URL filtering is `filter url`. Answers B, C, and D are incorrect because they are not valid commands.

Question 5

> Which command allows you to view URL filtering statistics? (Select all that apply.)
>
> ❏ A. **show www**
>
> ❏ B. **show url-cache stats**
>
> ❏ C. **show perfmon**
>
> ❏ D. **show filter-url**

Answers B and C are correct. The `show url-cache stats` command displays URL statistics, and the `show perfmon` command displays general statistics about the PIX firewall, including information about WebSense statistics.

Answer A is incorrect because show www does not exist. Answer D is incorrect because the command is invalid.

Question 6

The command **fixup protocol rtsp** is supported when using PAT.

○ A. True

◉ B. False

Answer B is correct. RTSP is not supported using PAT, and only some RTSP applications are supported using NAT. Therefore, answer A is incorrect.

Question 7

What is the maximum number of default routes allowed on the PIX firewall?

◉ A. One

○ B. One per interface

○ C. One per IP address assigned to an interface

○ D. A maximum of three

Answer A is correct. The PIX supports only a single default gateway. Therefore, answers B, C, and D are incorrect.

Question 8

What does the **fixup protocol** command do?

◉ A. It is used to change a PIX firewall application protocol feature.

○ B. It displays all the fixup protocol settings.

○ C. It maps ports to interfaces.

○ D. It identifies active fixup protocols.

Answer A is correct. The fixup protocol command enables, disables fixup protocols. These commands enable the PIX to work with certain protocols by dynamically opening ports or looking inside packets above layer 4. Answer B is incorrect because the show fixup command displays fixup protocol settings. Answer C is incorrect because no command maps a port to an interface. Answer D is incorrect because the show fixup command performs this function.

Question 9

Which command will disable the default RTSP fixup protocol?

- ○ A. **no rtsp fixup**
- ○ B. **no fixup protocol rtsp**
- ○ C. **no fixup rtsp**
- ○ D. **disable fixup protocol rtsp**

Answer B is correct. The no fixup protocol command disables fixup protocols. Several fixup protocols are enabled by default but can be turned off if they are causing problems. Answers A, C, and D are all invalid commands and are therefore incorrect.

Question 10

How do you specify a WebSense server?

- ○ A. **host 192.168.8.31**
- ○ B. **node 192.168.8.31**
- ○ C. **websense 192.168.8.31**
- ○ D. **url-server 192.168.8.31**   *does not comply with the syntax mentioned in p.179 !!*

Answer D is correct. The command to configure a WebSense server is url-server <IP_address>. Answer A is incorrect because it renames the PIX prompt to 192.168.8.31. Answers B and C are not valid commands and are therefore incorrect.

Question 11

Which statement is true about the PIX firewall? (Select all that apply.)

- ☐ A. The PIX can be a DHCP client.
- ☐ B. The PIX cannot be a DHCP client.
- ☐ C. The PIX can be a DHCP server.
- ☐ D. The PIX cannot be a DHCP server.
- ☐ E. The PIX cannot be a DHCP server and client at the same time.
- ☐ F. The PIX can be a DHCP server and DHCP client at the same time.
- ☐ G. The PIX DHCP server hands out a maximum of two DNS server addresses.
- ☐ H. The PIX DHCP server hands out a maximum of one DNS server address.

Answers A, C, F, and G are correct. The PIX firewall can be a DHCP server and client, and it can be both at the same time. The PIX `dhcpd dns` command supports two DNS addresses. Therefore, answers B, D, E, and H are incorrect.

Question 12

> Why is H.323 more complicated to track than other protocols?
>
> ○ A. It does not use port numbers.
> ○ B. It is complicated to configure.
> ○ C. It uses more than one TCP port.
> ○ D. The bandwidth is too high.

Answer C is correct. The H.323 protocol requires several ports to function correctly, whereas other protocols need only a single port. Answer A is incorrect because H.323 does use port numbers. Answer B is incorrect because, on the PIX, you only need to enable the `fixup protocol h323` command for H.323 to function correctly. Answer D is incorrect because the H.323 might need a lot of bandwidth at times but doesn't cause tracking problems. Therefore, answers A, B, and D are incorrect.

Question 13

> Which command helps to configure PPPoE on the PIX? (Select three.)
>
> ☐ A. **vpdn group**
> ☐ B. **ip address pppoe**
> ☐ C. **vpdn pppoe group**
> ☐ D. **vpdn pppoe**
> ☐ E. **vpdn username**
> ☐ F. **pppoe interface**

Answers A, B, and E are correct. To configure the PIX as a PPPoE client, the `vpdn group`, `ip address pppoe`, and `vpdn username` commands are needed. Answers C, D, and F are invalid commands and are therefore incorrect.

Question 14 *tricky*

Which VoIP protocol does the PIX support? (Select four.)

☑ A. SCCP
☐ B. FastVoIP
☑ C. H.323
☐ D. VoIPv2
☑ E. Skinny
☐ F. SIP

Answers A, C, E, and F are correct. The PIX supports Skinny Client Control Protocol (SCCP), H.323, Skinny, and SIP. Answers B and D do not exist as VoIP protocols and are therefore incorrect.

Question 15 *where does the info come from?*

Which statement is true about the PIX firewall and multimedia applications? (Select two.)

☐ A. Multimedia is supported on PAT and NAT. *may not be correct!!*
☐ B. Multimedia is supported only on PAT.
☐ C. Multimedia is supported only on NAT.
☐ D. It dynamically opens and closes ports.
☐ E. You need to statically open ports.

Answers A and D are correct. The PIX firewall dynamically opens and closes ports to provide secure traffic control. The PIX also can support both PAT and NAT for most multimedia applications. Therefore, answers B, C, and E are incorrect.

Need to Know More?

 Chapman, David and Andy Fox. *Cisco Secure PIX Firewalls.* Indianapolis, IN: Cisco Press, 2002.

 Deal, Richard A. *Cisco PIX Firewalls.* Berkeley, CA: McGraw-Hill/Osborne, 2002.

 See the Cisco PIX Firewall Command Reference, Version 6.2 at http://www.cisco.com/univercd/cc/td/doc/product/iaabu/pix/pix_sw/v_62/cmdref/index.htm.

ok.

Attack Guards and Intrusion Detection

. . . .

Terms you'll need to understand:

✓ Attack guards
✓ Fragmentation guard
✓ Mail Guard
✓ Embryonic connections
✓ TCP intercept
✓ Signatures
✓ False positives
✓ Shunning

Techniques you'll need to master:

✓ Setting embryonic connections
✓ Setting IP audits to an interface
✓ Configuring the Mail Guard feature
✓ Disabling signatures

In addition to ACL filtering and application inspection, the PIX firewall has attack guards and intrusion detection built in to protect against access and denial-of-service (DoS) attacks. *Attack guards* help prevent penetration and DoS attacks from taking advantage of basic security threats such as weaknesses and security holes found in commonly used applications. Intrusion detection techniques are used by the PIX firewall to monitor and shun possible attacks by reviewing the IP signatures that pass through the device. This chapter reviews these features within the PIX firewall products.

Attack Guards

Attack guards enable the PIX firewall to monitor and reject requests or messages sent to commonly used applications or protocols. These requests and messages have been discovered and identified by hackers as a potential means to cause some form of harm to a computer or network. Over the life of the Internet, hackers have tended to focus on applications and protocols that have been readily accepted by the public; if a hacker can find a security hole or possible weakness in a widely used protocol or application, he could have the power to compromise several other systems across the Internet. For example, if a hacker found a security hole in a basic email request, he could exploit that hole on not one but thousands of servers.

Several attack guards are provided on the PIX firewall that help prevent hackers from taking advantage of known security holes. Although the guards use different commands to enable and disable them, they all help protect your environment from malicious attacks.

Table 9.1 lists the attack guards covered in this chapter and the commands that enable them.

Table 9.1 Attack Guards and Commands	
Guard	**Command**
DNS Guard	None; it's enabled by default and cannot be turned off.
Mail Guard	Use the **fixup protocol smtp 25** command. *enabled by default*
Fragmentation Guard	Use the **sysopt security fragguard** command. *disabled by default*
Syn Guard	Use the **max connections** and **embryonic connections** parameters of the **static** and **nat** commands.
AAA Floodguard	Use the **floodguard enable** command. *enabled by default*

hard to memorize!!

DNS Guard

Clients send UDP requests to resolve names, such as www.examcram.com, to an IP address before actually traveling to the Web site. This is called *domain name resolution* and is performed on domain name service (DNS) servers. These DNS servers maintain zones of name spaces that contain the actual name-to-IP-address mappings for the computers the client is looking for. A client might send out several UDP requests to resolve one name. Recall that with UDP traffic, the PIX uses an idle timer to monitor whether there is traffic passing between two computers. If the timer expires before any traffic has passed, the connection is assumed to be ended and the connection slot entry is removed from the connection table. Because DNS requests use UDP, a dynamic opening is created in the PIX firewall for 2 minutes to allow the return UDP traffic. If a response from a DNS server is received in 1 second, the opening created normally doesn't close until the 2-minute idle timer has expired. This leaves an open hole through which hackers can send attacks using a method called *hijacking*.

DNS Guard prevents DoS and UDP session hijacking by closing the UDP port after the first received DNS response.

The DNS Guard feature in the PIX firewall helps prevent hijacking by closing the dynamically opened port immediately after the first DNS response.

The DNS Guard feature is enabled by default and cannot be disabled.

Mail Guard

The Mail Guard feature is used to protect Simple Mail Transfer Protocol (SMTP) servers from known potentially harmful security problems. The guard performs application inspection using fixup protocols as discussed in Chapter 8, "Advanced Protocol Handling and PIX Firewall Features."

The fixup protocol smtp command provides a function known as Mail Guard which inspects SMTP traffic and allows only the seven commands defined in RFC 821 section 4.5.1 to pass. These commands are DATA, HELO, MAIL, NOOP,

QUIT, RCPT, and RSET. All other commands result in a `500 command unrecognized` response to the client and a discarding of the packet before the SMTP server ever receives it.

By default, `fixup protocol smtp` command is enabled for port 25. The commands shown here display how to enable and disable this guard using the `fixup protocol` commands:

```
pixfirewall(config)# fixup protocol smtp 25
```

or

```
pixfirewall(config)# no fixup protocol smtp 25
```

If the SMTP Mail Guard is turned off or disabled, hackers can send attachments to your email servers with unsecure email commands.

Fragmentation Guard

One form of attack committed by hackers uses packets that are broken down into hundreds and thousands of IP fragments. These fragments, when assembled, can amount to absolutely nothing or be harmless. More seriously, they can reassemble into a packet that causes another attack. The fragmented packets require resources to assemble back together and can cause a DoS if too many of them are allowed to reach the targeted devices.

The PIX firewall provides a guard against receiving too many fragmented packets by following the RFC 1858 recommendation. The guard allows only 100 fragments per internal destination host per second. Also, the guard expects to receive the first fragment before receiving other fragments. For example, if the middle fragment is received first, the packets are dropped.

To configure the Frag Guard, a system option command, `sysopt`, is necessary. This guard is disabled by default but can be enabled by using the following command:

```
pixfirewall(config)#sysopt security fragguard
```

The `show sysopt` command displays a list of all the system options configured. The following example displays an output of the default system options on a PIX with the Frag Guard enabled:

```
pixfirewall(config)# show sysopt
sysopt security fragguard
no sysopt connection timewait
sysopt connection tcpmss 1380
```

```
sysopt connection tcpmss minimum 0
no sysopt nodnsalias inbound
no sysopt nodnsalias outbound
no sysopt radius ignore-secret
no sysopt uauth allow-http-cache
no sysopt connection permit-ipsec
no sysopt connection permit-pptp
no sysopt connection permit-l2tp
no sysopt ipsec pl-compatible
no sysopt route dnat
```

SYN Floodguard

The SYN Floodguard protects hosts from TCP SYN attacks. TCP requires a three-way handshake to make a connection; therefore, hackers can exploit this technology by sending hundreds or thousands of SYN requests with no intention of ever responding to them. For example, when a host receives a SYN request, it responds with a SYN/ACK. Then, the host waits for a final acknowledgement from the initiating host. If that initiating host (the hacker) never responds with the final ACK, the internal host is left tied up waiting for the return ACK. In the end, the internal host could be left hanging with thousands of half-open connections—commonly called *embryonic* connections—which could cause a DoS attack on the host by consuming all available memory resources for each connection.

The PIX firewall implements protection against TCP SYN attacks with two main parameters at the end of the `static` and `nat` commands. These parameters are `max connections` and `embryonic limit`. The following are the `static` and `nat` commands with these parameters:

```
Pixfirewall(config)# [no] static [(internal_if_name, external_if_name)]
                     {<global_ip>|interface} <local_ip> [dns] [netmask <mask>]
                     [<max_conns> [<emb_limit> [<norandomseq>]]]

Pixfirewall(config)# [no] nat [(<if_name>)] <nat_id> <local_ip> [<mask>
                     [dns] [outside] [<max_conns> [emb_limit>
                     [<norandomseq>]]]]
```

The maximum number of connections defines the number of connections allowed to a host. If the number is exceeded, all future connections above this number are dropped. A value of `0` states that an unlimited number of connections is allowed.

The `embryonic connections` parameter dictates not the number of connections, but the number of half-open connections allowed to an internal host. If a host reaches this embryonic limit, the PIX performs a function called TCP intercept.

TCP intercept doesn't actually send the three-way handshake to the internal host, nor does it absolutely block the request. Instead, it performs a special trick on behalf of the internal host. The PIX performs the three-way handshake with the external host in an attempt to determine whether the external host's intentions are genuine. If the three-way handshake turns out to be successful and not a dead embryonic connection, the PIX contacts the internal host to bind it with the external host, thus establishing a valid connection. If the connection turns out to be a dead embryonic connection, nothing is lost; the PIX drops it and the internal host was never actually bothered with the request.

Embryonic connections are half-open three-way handshake connections that could be left open intentionally by a hacker. If the embryonic limit is reached, TCP intercept on the PIX handles any new handshakes until they are proven to be valid requests.

The following is an example of setting the maximum number of connections to 500 and the maximum number of embryonic connections to 400. This would enable the host to receive only 400 embryonic connections before TCP intercept would start to be performed by the PIX:

```
Pixfirewall(config)# static (inside, outside) 169.254.8.1 192.168.1.11
          netmask 255.255.255.255 500 400
```

The embryonic limit should be set a little lower than what the internal server can actually handle so you never overload the internal servers.

AAA floodguard

The PIX can use triple-A services known as AAA to authenticate, authorize, and accounting. AAA is discussed in more detail in later chapters. AAA is a way to authenticate and authorize user access across the firewall. However, it provides an avenue for hackers to attack a system. If a hacker tries to overwhelm the system with too many authentication requests, a DoS attack on the PIX could occur.

The `floodguard` command is used to automatically reclaim PIX resources from other services to prevent DoS attacks on user authentications. The PIX monitors the uauth connections. If there are too many for it to handle, it drops other resources in an attempt to maintain all the uauth connections. This list displays the order in which the PIX drops or shuts down the four resources:

1. Timewait

2. FinWait

3. Embryonic

4. Idle

By default, the `floodguard` command is enabled. This example displays the `floodguard enable` and `show` commands:

```
pixfirewall(config)#floodguard enable
pixfirewall(config)#
pixfirewall(config)#show flood
floodguard enable
```

The AAA **floodguard** is sometimes called **flood defender** by Cisco.

Intrusion Detection System

The intrusion detection system (IDS) provides the functionality to monitor IP traffic passing across a network and listen for potentially malicious traffic. The system monitors this traffic similar to the way a network sniffer does, except that intrusion detection compares the flowing traffic to known signatures of attacks. If a match is found, one or a combination of several things can be done: An alarm can be set; the packet can be dropped; and the TCP reset flags can be set to cease the connection.

Intrusion detection on the PIX firewall is a small engine that monitors more than 50 types of attacks, whereas a full IDS system can monitor more than 600 types of attacks. This makes the PIX IDS suitable only for basic IDS monitoring.

Signatures

Signatures are patterns found inside packets that have been known to result in some form of attack. The two general classes of signatures on the PIX are informational and attack. The detection of *informational* signatures does not necessarily indicate an attack on the network, but it can indicate the passing of traffic that is typically turned off, such as ICMP requests. *Attack* signatures are matches to traffic that produces some type of harmful danger, such as fragmented ICMPs, ping-of-death attacks, and other DoS attacks. The PIX firewall contains a subset of the possible instruction detection signatures that exists. The syslog error messages can be found in the range from 400000 to 407002. See "Cisco PIX Firewall System Log Messages" on the Cisco Web site for the current list.

 The PIX firewall only contains a subset of signatures compared to a full IDS system.

Configuring Audit Policies

The PIX firewall enables you to configure specific and general global audit policies. These audit policies define what action the PIX should perform if an attack or informational signature match is found. Table 9.2 displays the three types of actions the PIX can take.

Table 9.2	IDS Actions
Action	**Description**
Alarm	Creates a syslog message and sends it to the syslog server configured
Drop	Drops the packet(s)
Reset	Drops the packet and closes the connection

Global Audit Policies

 As stated previously, the PIX can have a global audit policy that defines what the PIX will do globally to any signature matches when a specific audit policy is not assigned to the offending interface. For example, if attack signatures are detected on the outside interface and no specific policy is set on that interface, the global policy defines what to do with those packets. The following is the command syntax for the global informational and attack audit policies:

```
pixfirewall(config)# [no] ip audit info [action [alarm] [drop] [reset]]
pixfirewall(config)# [no] ip audit attack [action [alarm] [drop] [reset]]
```

The show ip audit {info | attack} command can be used to display the global settings. The example shown here sets attack and informational global policies to alarm and drop matching signatures:

```
pixfirewall(config)# ip audit info action alarm drop
pixfirewall(config)# ip audit attack action alarm drop
pixfirewall(config)# show ip audit info
```

```
ip audit info action alarm drop
pixfirewall(config)# show ip audit attack
ip audit attack action alarm drop
```

read this section *hard to memorize*

Specific Audit Policies

The PIX can create specific audit policies to define what action to take when signature matches are found on an interface. Typically, only one policy is created and assigned to all the external interfaces. However, the PIX is capable of supporting a different policy for each interface if so desired.

Two steps are involved when working with specific audit policies. Step one creates the named policies, and step two links the policies to the designated interfaces. The following example displays creating and linking two separate policies named audit-info and audit-attack on the outside interface:

```
pixfirewall(config)# ip audit name Audit-Info info action alarm
pixfirewall(config)# ip audit name Audit-Attack attack action
                     alarm drop reset
pixfirewall(config)# ip audit interface outside Audit-Info
pixfirewall(config)# ip audit interface outside Audit-Attack
pixfirewall(config)# show ip audit interface
ip audit interface outside Audit-Info
ip audit interface outside Audit-Attack
```

syntax *e.g.* *why do we need drop as well??* *syntax* *syntax* *= keywords*

In IDS language, a false positive is an alarm or a signature match against legitimate traffic.

Disabling Signatures from Policies   *MCC*

This section covers how to exclude individual signatures from being audited. By default, all signatures are enabled, which can *why?* cause several false alarms (called *false positives*). To prevent false positives, the ip audit signature command can be used to disable individual signatures. One thing to note is that, when disabling a signature, the signature becomes disabled for the entire PIX, not just an interface or a specific policy. This example demonstrates how to globally disable several audit signatures: *??*

```
pixfirewall(config)# ip audit signature 2001 disable
pixfirewall(config)# ip audit signature 2002 disable
pixfirewall(config)# ip audit signature 2150 disable
pixfirewall(config)# show ip audit signature
ip audit signature 2001 disable
ip audit signature 2002 disable
ip audit signature 2150 disable
```

syntax *why*

syntax : ip audit signature <signature-number> disable

By default, all audit signatures are enabled. If you want to disable one, then the **ip audit signature <number> disable** command can be used.

The **shun** Command

When IDSs block traffic, they use a technique called *shunning*. The PIX can perform dynamic shunning, meaning it can block traffic if the traffic violates a signature. The shun command is used to manually block or unblock traffic. In the following, the shun command blocks traffic from source 169.254.70.1:

```
pixfirewall(config)# shun 169.254.70.1
pixfirewall(config)# show shun
Shun 169.254.70.1 0.0.0.0 0 0
```

The shun command is a powerful command that takes precedence over the conduits and ACLs. However, it's only a temporary command and is not actually shown or saved in the configuration: it is deleted when the device is restarted. To view active shunned addresses, use the show shun command. To clear all active shuns, use the clear shun command, and use the no shun for a specific entry.

The **shun** command is used to block traffic for instruction detection system (IDS).

[no] shun src-ip [dst-ip sport dport [protocol]]

Exam Prep Questions

Question 1

> When receiving an attack, which command provides a blocking function?
>
> ○ A. **access-list**
> ⊘ B. **shun**
> ○ C. **conduit**
> ○ D. **shutdown**

Answer B is correct. When an attack occurs, the shun command provides blocking for the PIX firewall. Answers A and C are incorrect because access-list and conduit commands are not used to block when attacks occur; they are manually set ahead of time. Answer D is incorrect because the shutdown command disables an interface permanently.

Question 2 ○

> Which function does the DNS Guard perform? (Select two.)
>
> ❏ A. It prevents denial -of-service attacks and UDP session hijacking.
> ❏ B. It blocks DNS transfers.
> ❏ C. It tears down the connection after the first DNS response is received.
> ❏ D. It allows DNS requests to enter the PIX only from the inside interface.

Answers A and C are correct. The DNS Guard prevents DoS attacks and UDP session hijacking by closing down the connection after the first DNS response is received. Answer B is incorrect because it does not block DNS transfers. Answer D is incorrect because it doesn't allow DNS requests from the inside. This can only be controlled by using access lists.

Question 3 ○

> Which command applies an IP audit policy to an interface?
>
> ○ A. **interface ip policy enable**
> ⊘ B. **ip audit interface**
> ○ C. **ip policy interface**
> ○ D. **audit interface**

Answer B is correct. The ip audit interface <if_name> <name> command applies an audit policy to an interface. Audits are used to define what to do with traffic that matches informational or attack signature types. Answers A, C, and D are incorrect because these commands do not exist.

Question 4

> What is the default action of an audit policy when it is first created and applied to an interface?
>
> ○ A. All signature classes are enabled.
> ○ B. Only informational signature classes are enabled.
> ○ C. Only attack signature classes are enabled.
> ○ D. All signature classes are disabled.

Answer A is correct. By default, when a policy is created, all signature classes are enabled. They must be manually disabled if required. Therefore, answers B, C, and D are incorrect.

Question 5

> What are false positive alarms in an IDS?
>
> ○ A. Alarms caused by legitimate traffic
> ○ B. Alarms caused by direct information or attacks on the system
> ○ C. Alarms that can be ignored
> ○ D. Alarms that need to be set by the administrator

Answer A is correct. False positives are alarms triggered by legitimate traffic that matches a pattern of a monitored signature. Answer B is incorrect because it indicates what should happen when malicious traffic matching an audited signature, not a false positive, is detected. Answer C is incorrect because not all false positives should be ignored; therefore answer A is more correct. Answer D is incorrect because the administrator can only disable alarms, not set them.

Question 6

> Which command uses the **embryonic** parameter? (Select two.)
>
> ❏ A. **access-list**
>
> ☑ B. **nat**
>
> ❏ C. **conduit**
>
> ☑ D. **static**

Answers B and D are correct. The embryonic parameter is used by the nat and static commands. The PIX monitors half-open connections and allows up to the value set by the embryonic parameter. Then TCP intercept is performed on behalf of the client, ensuring that only good, valid TCP connections are made with the client. Answers A and C do not use the embryonic connection parameter and are therefore incorrect.

Question 7

> Which function does Mail Guard perform?
>
> ○ A. It blocks POP3 mail requests.
>
> ○ B. It prevents illegal mail commands from passing.
>
> ○ C. It blocks all SMTP traffic.
>
> ○ D. It allows all SMTP mail commands except the seven insecure commands.

Answer B is correct. Mail Guard is implemented using a fixup protocol command and allows only seven safe email commands through the PIX: DATA, HELO, MAIL, NOOP, QUIT, RCPT, and RSET. All other commands are considered illegal. Therefore, answers A, C, and D are incorrect.

Question 8

> After the embryonic connection limit is reached, what does the PIX do?
>
> ○ A. It blocks all traffic to the specific internal host.
>
> ○ B. It drops all new connections to the host.
>
> ○ C. It sends TCP FIN requests to the incoming request.
>
> ○ D. It performs TCP intercept for the host.

Answer D is correct. The embryonic limit setting is used to calculate the number of half-open connections to a host. When this limit is reached, the PIX performs a function called TCP intercept, in which the PIX attempts to complete the three-way handshake for any new requests to that host. If the handshake is valid, the connection is passed on to the host; otherwise, it is dropped. Therefore, answers A, B, and C are incorrect.

Question 9

Which command enables fragmented packet protection?

- ○ A. **fragguard enable**
- ○ B. **onable fragguard**
- ○ C. **sysopt security fragguard**
- ○ D. **sysopt fragguard**

Answer C is correct. The `sysopt security fragguard` command enables protection against receiving too many fragmented packets. Answers A, B, and D contain invalid commands and are therefore incorrect.

Question 10

What does the Floodguard feature do?

- ○ A. It prevents fragments from entering the PIX.
- ○ B. It reclaims resources to handle more requests.
- ○ C. It drops port flood requests.
- ○ D. It prevents traffic from going too fast.

Answer B is correct. The AAA Floodguard reclaims resources from other services when too many requests are coming in for AAA services. Therefore, answers A, C, and D are incorrect.

Need to Know More?

 Chapman, David and Andy Fox. *Cisco Secure PIX Firewalls.* Indianapolis, IN: Cisco Press, 2002.

 See the Cisco PIX Firewall Command Reference, Version 6.2 at `http://www.cisco.com/univercd/cc/td/doc/product/iaabu/ pix/pix_sw/v_62/cmdref/index.htm`.

 See Security Considerations for IP Fragment Filtering at `http://www.ietf.org/rfc/rfc1858.txt`.

 See Cisco PIX Firewall System Log Messages, Version 6.2 at `http://www.cisco.com/en/US/products/sw/secursw/ps2120/ products_system_message_guide_book09186a008014638a.html`.

AAA Configuration

Terms you'll need to understand:

✓ AAA

✓ Cisco Secure Access Control Server (CSACS)

✓ TACACS+

✓ RADIUS

✓ Downloadable access control lists

✓ Cut-through proxy

✓ Virtual Telnet

✓ Virtual HTTP

Techniques you'll need to master:

✓ Configuring AAA services on the PIX

✓ Using the **group** tag

✓ Authenticating with RADIUS and TACACS+

✓ Using the **privilege** command

✓ Using named and unnamed downloadable ACLs

This chapter covers the powerful *triple A (AAA)* features the PIX firewall supports. Authentication, authorization, and accounting provide powerful control over who can access the network or the PIX and the capability to record when it happens. The capability to have downloadable access control lists (ACLs) gives PIX administrators limitless flexibility and granular control over users by restricting what they can and cannot do.

Introduction to AAA Services

In any Cisco environment, several features can provide administration overhead issues on your devices. The first administration feature your devices have is the enable or privilege exec password. This provides access to all the configuration commands on a device; however, managing this password could become an issue. For example, if Jack supports 300 Cisco routers and firewalls, trying to keep the enable password the same or changing it on all the devices could be an overwhelming task.

A second feature of Cisco devices is the capability to create several levels of access on the device. For example, if you have several different network engineers, each engineer can be restricted to a subset of commands and not the entire privilege exec list. However, if Jack had to create the same users on each of his 300 devices, it could take several days to configure and maintain the systems.

A third feature is providing access through devices. The PIX supports several features, such as cut-through proxy, that can require a user to authenticate before Internet access is granted. Again, if Jack had to manage 1,000 employee usernames and passwords on multiple PIX firewalls, he would have to spend all of his time managing and changing passwords.

AAA services help administrators manage Cisco devices by offloading authentication, authorization, and accounting tasks from local devices to centrally located servers. These servers can contain databases of users, passwords, dynamic ACLs, authorization settings, and account tracking features, just to name a few. Using central servers in the example with Jack, he could manage the central server username list in one location and just point all 300 devices to that location for AAA services.

Figure 10.1 displays two of these locations for usernames and passwords. One is called local and resides within the PIX configuration file; the other is called Cisco Secure ACS and is a user database located on a AAA server. The third place where users can exist, though not shown in Figure 10.1, is in external user databases such as Microsoft Windows.

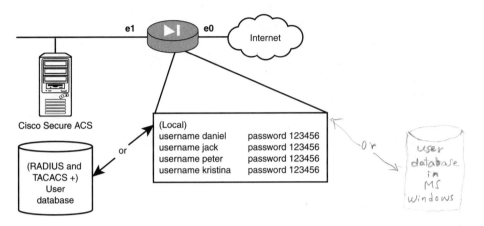

Figure 10.1   Username locations.

Authentication

Authentication is the process of validating a username and password. The PIX can check the local database or a remote AAA server database for valid usernames and passwords. After the user establishes positive authentication, authorization is the next step.

Authorization

Successful authentication is required before authorization can occur. *Authorization* defines what a user can and cannot do. For example, a dynamic ACL can be downloaded to the PIX, restricting a user to or from particular networks.

Accounting

Accounting is the feature that enables administrators to keep track of what their users do. For example, when a user logs in to the system, a log entry can be made.

AAA Server Protocols

When using AAA services, requests can be sent to remote AAA servers for authentication, authorization, and accounting. Cisco supports two main protocols for these requests: RADIUS and TACACS+. The request is sent to the servers, and the responses are used to allow the users into or out of the device. For example, in Figure 10.2 the PIX is configured to authenticate users before entering a privileged exec mode. The request is sent to the AAA server using RADIUS or TACACS+. Next, the AAA server authenticates the user either with its own database or, as shown in Figure 10.2, another database. After authentication is approved, authorization is checked and the responses are sent back to the PIX. Throughout all these transactions, accounting is working in the background logging and tracking user actions.

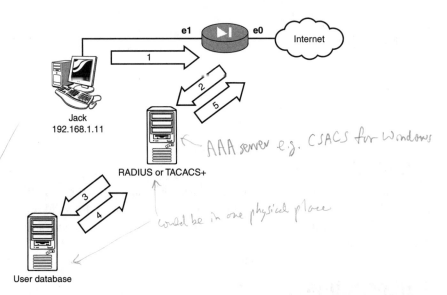

Figure 10.2 AAA services transaction.

AAA stands for authentication, authorization, and accounting. You cannot have authorization without successful authentication first.

Remote Access Dial-in User Service

The Remote Access Dial-in User Service (RADIUS) protocol was originally developed by Livingston Enterprises, Inc., as an access protocol. This protocol provides authentication and accounting services and can be used by just about any size network or vendor. The protocol is a client/server configuration, and the PIX devices are the clients and the AAA server would be the RADIUS server itself. The protocol uses a UDP connection and encrypts only the password and leaves the username in clear text.

Terminal Access Controller Access Control System Plus   *TACACS+*

Terminal Access Controller Access Control System (TACACS) was originally created by the U.S. government and is an open standard security protocol. Cisco uses a modified version of TACACS called Terminal Access Controller Access Control System Plus (TACACS+). In contrast to RADIUS, which uses UDP, the TACACS+ protocol provides a reliable TCP connection between the client and the server for AAA service requests. These requests are more secure than RADIUS because the body of the transaction is always encrypted.

For a detailed comparison of RADIUS and TACACS+, see Cisco's Web site at **www.cisco.com/warp/public/480/10.html**.

TACACS+ uses TCP port 49 for connections between AAA servers and clients, whereas RADIUS uses UDP port 1812 for authentication and UDP port 1813 for accounting.

Supported AAA Servers

The Cisco PIX firewall can support several AAA servers. Most third-party AAA servers support the RADIUS protocol, making installations in multivendor environments very flexible. The following is a list of some supported AAA servers: *Access Control Server*

➤ Cisco Secure ACS for Windows   *i.e. CSACS for Windows*

➤ Cisco Secure ACS for Unix   *i.e. CSACS for Unix*

➤ Livingston

➤ Merit

(is a software)

Cisco Secure Access Control Server

The Cisco Secure Access Control Server (CSACS) is Cisco's AAA server that supports both the RADIUS and TACACS+ protocols. The software provides centralized AAA services for AAA clients such as the PIX firewall. It is also very scalable, with the option to use its own user database or connect to an external user database, such as one of these: *external user database*

➤ Axent token server

➤ Generic LDAP

➤ Novell NDS

➤ SafeWord token server

➤ Windows NT/2000 local or domain controller

Installing CSACS

The CSACS can be installed onto Unix or Microsoft Windows Server. Cisco uses a Web page front-end to configure the system. The following are some of the Windows requirements:

➤ Pentium III processor with 550MHz or better

➤ 256MB of RAM

➤ 250MB of available disk space

➤ Windows 2000 with SP1 or Windows NT with SP6a

During the installation, the software asks for at least one network access server (NAS) to be set up. A NAS is an AAA client, and in this case it's the PIX firewall (see Figure 10.3). CSACS can support up to 2,000 AAA clients.

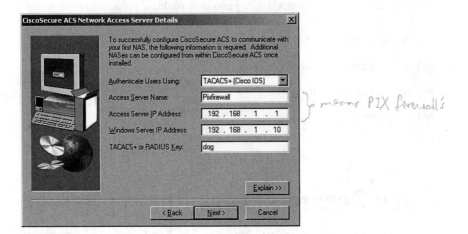

means PIX firewall's

Figure 10.3 The CSACS NAS dialog box.

During installation, the NAS's details dialog box has a prompt that states **Access Server IP Address**. This is the address of the PIX firewall or other network access server that will be using the CSACS server.

Cisco supports several solutions for CSACS. The latest version is CSACS for Windows 3.2 and v2.3 for Unix. CSACS may also be purchased in a 1 RU hardware solution called the CSCAS Solution Engine. More information can be found in the "Need to Know More?" at the end of the chapter.

Configuring AAA Services

see p.555 - 606
Cisco press fn more

Several steps are involved in configuring a system for AAA services. The next *details* section walks you through some of the steps needed to configure a system for AAA services, but here is an overview of the basic steps: *!)*

1. Configure AAA usernames and passwords. *username: p.221 ✕*
2. Configure AAA server locations. *aaa server — p.223 ✕*
3. Configure authentication. *aaa authentication — p.22✕✕ & p.228✕*
4. Configure authorization (optional). *privileage* / *aaa authorization* — *p.225✕ & ✕✕ & p.228 ✕✕*
5. Configure accounting (optional). *accounting — p.229 ✕*

Configuring AAA Usernames

The first step when configuring AAA services is to create usernames and passwords. As stated previously, three main locations exist for usernames and passwords—local, an AAA server, or an external database. However, in this *i.e. my Windows local or domain controller* chapter we discuss only local and CSACS.

Local Username and Password Commands *for database in the PIX*

The PIX enables you to create a username and password list inside the configuration file. This list can be referenced by the AAA commands when users log in. The syntax used to accomplish this is shown here:

```
pixfirewall(config)# username <username> {nopassword¦password
                <password>}[privilege <level>]
```

1 - 15, 15 is the highest test, default is 2

Table 10.1 displays the possible options for the username command.

? Command Authorization with Enable-Level Passwords : → enable
Q: how to set the previleged mode password ? privileage
A: enable password <pw> [level <priv-level>] [encrypted]. aaa authorization
Q: how to enter into the "enable" mode? enable
A: enable [priv-level] default is 15
see p 599 to 601 Cisco press

Table 10.1	username Command Options
Option	**Function**
username	The name of the user.
nopassword|password	The **nopassword** option specifies that no password is necessary. The **password** option specifies the password for the username.
privilege	This is the level of access you want to give the user. The default is **2**, and level 15 is for the privileged exec access level.

Listing 10.1 clears all users from the PIX, creates four users, and shows all the users that exist inside the PIX configuration file.

Listing 10.1	Configuring Username and Passwords

```
pixfirewall(config)# clear user
pixfirewall(config)# username daniel password 1234 privilege 15
pixfirewall(config)# username kristina password 1234 privilege 15
pixfirewall(config)# username jack password 1234
pixfirewall(config)# username peter password 1234
pixfirewall(config)# show user
username daniel password fOpmsyD0svtnnlr/ encrypted privilege 15
username peter password GCbahPTC/hAylaFE encrypted privilege 2
username kristina password wTsW2QC6pRXaJrTT encrypted privilege 15
username jack password 5zVJhD5YUb6zO7VH encrypted privilege 2
```

Adding Users with CSACS

To add a user to the CSACS database, you must open the user Web interface. First, you turn on the TACACS+ advanced features so you can configure privileged exec access on your user accounts. The steps to enable these advanced features are as follows:

1. On the left menu, click the Interface Configuration button.

2. Click the TACACS+ (Cisco IOS) link.

3. Scroll down until you find the Advanced Configuration Options section and place a check in the box labeled Advanced TACACS+ Features.

4. Click the Submit button at the bottom of the screen to enable the features.

The following are the steps to create a user account in Cisco Secure ACS:

1. Click the User Setup button from the menu list on the left side.

2. Enter the username **daniel** into the User: box and click the Add/Edit button.

3. Scroll down to the User Setup section and enter a password of **123456789.**

4. Now scroll down to the Advanced TACACS+ Settings section and select the Max Privilege for Any AAA Client radio button option. Then use the pull-down menu to select level 15. This will provide privilege-level access to the user named daniel.

5. Just below the advanced TACACS+ settings is a section called TACACS+ Enable Password. Select Use CiscoSecure PAP Password. This will use the password you previously set; alternatively, you could set a separate enable password if you wanted.

6. Click the Submit button to save the user.

Now that the usernames have been created, you are ready to configure AAA services on the PIX firewall.

Configuring the **aaa-server** Command

The aaa-server command is used to configure group tags that define where the AAA server is located. If the AAA server is remote, either RADIUS or TACACS+ security protocols can be used to request the remotely located AAA services. However, if the AAA server is local, no security protocol is required to communicate with the internal PIX configuration file. Table 10.2 describes the three possible locations and protocol used to acquire AAA services.

Table 10.2 aaa-server Locations	
Locations	**Description**
Local	This tells the PIX to look locally in the PIX configuration file for the usernames and passwords.
RADIUS	This configures the PIX to use a RADIUS security protocol and to request remotely located AAA services.
TACACS+	This configures the PIX to use a TACACS+ security protocol and to request remotely located AAA services.

The following is the syntax of the aaa-server command:

```
pixfirewall(config)# [no] aaa-server <group_tag> protocol tacacs+|radius
pixfirewall(config)# [no] aaa-server <group_tag> [<(if_name)>]
          host <ip_address> [<key>]
```

Table 10.3 displays the possible options for the aaa-server command.

Table 10.3   aaa-server Command Options

Option	Function
group_tag	This option is a grouping of server settings that can be referenced by all the AAA commands. You can create up to 14 group tags.
if_name	This is the interface where the AAA server is located.
ip_address	This is the IP address of the AAA server.
key	This is the key value used on the TACACS+ server to encrypt the data between the client and server.
protocol	This option defines one of the three protocol locations: local, RADIUS, or TACACS+.

The following example displays the current aaa-server group tags and then creates a new group tag called PIXAuth. This new group tag configures TACACS+ as the security protocol and 192.168.1.10 as the AAA server:

```
pixfirewall(config)# show aaa-server
aaa-server TACACS+ protocol tacacs+
aaa-server RADIUS protocol radius
aaa-server LOCAL protocol local

pixfirewall(config)# aaa-server PIXAuth protocol tacacs+
pixfirewall(config)# aaa-server PIXAuth (inside) host 192.168.1.10 dog
```

Configuring Authentication

AAA authentication can be used to control access into the PIX console, privileged exec mode, and access through the PIX. This section covers console access and access technologies used to control traffic through the PIX.

Authentication and Console Access

Console access requires a username and password. Access methods for AAA authentication to the PIX can be via serial, Telnet, SSH, HTTP, and privileged exec mode. The aaa authentication command syntax is as follows:

```
pixfirewall(config)# [no] aaa authentication serial|telnet|ssh|http|enable
        console <group_tag>
```

Table 10.4 displays the possible options for the aaa-authentication command.

Table 10.4 aaa authentication Options

Option	Description
serial	This causes the user to be prompted to enter a username and password when connecting using the serial port.
telnet	This requires Telnet connections to enter a username and password before entering the PIX console.
ssh	When users SSH into the PIX, AAA authentication is required.
http	This option is used when connecting to the PIX using the PDM Web interface, requiring AAA logon.
enable	Before a user can enter the privileged exec mode, a username and password must be supplied.
group_tag	The tag option defines the group name to associate the command with.

The following example displays the commands needed to configure the PIX firewall to use a TACACS+ server (192.168.1.10) for console authentication. As users connect via Telnet or enter privileged exec mode, they will be prompted to enter a username and password before allowing them to proceed:

```
pixfirewall(config)# aaa-server PIXAuth protocol tacacs+
pixfirewall(config)# aaa-server PIXAuth (inside) host 192.168.1.10 dog
pixfirewall(config)# aaa authentication enable console PIXAuth
pixfirewall(config)# aaa authentication telnet console PIXAuth
```

Authorization and Console Access Commands

Console access can be controlled by the AAA authentication, whereas console commands can be controlled by using AAA authorization. Controlling command access enables the PIX to contain several levels of users, some with full command access (level 15) and others with specifically allocated commands.

The privilege command is used to associate a specific command with a level of access. The command syntax is shown here:

```
pixfirewall(config)# [no] privilege [{show | clear | configure}]
          level <level> [mode {enable|configure}] command <command>
```

Table 10.5 displays the possible options for the privilege command.

Table 10.5	privilege command Options
Option	**Function**
show|clear|configure	These options enable you to specify the type of command you want to put in the list.
level	This option is used for the level of the list.
mode	This defines the area where the command is being restricted: enable mode or configure mode. This defines the command related to the first **show|clear|configure** option.

[handwritten: This option is for commands that are available in multiple modes. Do not use this option for commands that are not mode-specific.]

The privilege command shown in Listing 10.2 creates two users with different levels of access. Commands designated to access levels 11 and 12 are then assigned.

Listing 10.2	Creating Users and Setting Privilege Mode Commands

```
pixfirewall(config)# username jimmy password 123456 privilege 11
pixfirewall(config)# username richard password 123456 privilege 12

pixfirewall(config)# privilege show level 11 command access-list
pixfirewall(config)# privilege show level 11 command running-config
pixfirewall(config)# privilege show level 12 command interface

pixfirewall(config)# aaa authorization command LOCAL
```

[handwritten: mode ??]

In Listing 10.2, because Jimmy has privilege level 11, he will be able to execute any command assigned to level 11 and below. Richard, on the other hand, has a level that is higher and will therefore be able to execute any command associated with level 12 and below. The last aaa authorization command LOCAL designates the local username and password list for command authorization.

Authorization for commands can also be set up using the CSACS Web interface by clicking the Group Setup button, selecting the group options, and setting the commands.

The **privilege** command enables you to associate a command with an access level.

Authentication for Cut-through Proxy

Using cut-through proxy enables you to control HTTP, FTP, and Telnet services through the PIX firewall. Access lists provide general packet filtering, whereas cut-through proxy requires a username and password before allow-ing access. For example, if Jack wants to control which users can use HTTP through the PIX, he could implement cut-through proxy and prompt HTTP traffic with a username and password dialog box, as shown in Figure 10.4. This username and password would be forwarded to the AAA server for authentication and authorization using TACACS+ or RADIUS security pro-tocols.

Figure 10.4   The cut-through proxy HTTP dialog box.

 | Cut-through proxy works with FTP, HTTP, and Telnet.

The following shows two `aaa authentication` commands that can be used to implement cut-through proxy:

```
pixfirewall(config)# [no] authentication include|exclude <service>
                      inbound|outbound <if_name>
                      <internal_ip> <internal_mask>
                      [<external_ip> <external_mask>] <group_tag>

pixfirewall(config)# [no] aaa authentication match <access_list_name>
                      inbound|outbound <if_name> <if_name> <group_tag>
```

Table 10.6 displays the possible options for the `aaa authentication` command.

any supported IP protocol value or name, e.g. ip or igmp

Table 10.6 Cut-through Proxy aaa authentication Command Options

Option	Function
include|exclude	The **include** option is used to create a new rule, whereas the **exclude** option is used to create an exception to an include statement.
service	This option states the type of service to include or exclude. The following options are valid: **any**, **ftp**, **http**, and **telnet**.
if_name	This is the interface where the AAA server is located.
internal_ip internal_mask	This defines what internal traffic IP addresses are included. Using **0 0** defines all IP addresses.
external_ip external_mask	This defines what external traffic IP addresses are included. Using **0 0** defines all IP addresses.
group_tag	The tag option defines the group name to associate the command with.
match	This command works in conjunction with an access list. This allows you to use an access-list to define traffic.

(handwritten annotations:) echo request e.g. 8 — other options: https, icmp/<type>, <proto>, tcp/<port>, udp/<port> — tcp/443 — all TCP traffic — =tcp/80 — tcp/23 — tcp/21 — =tcp/6 & udp/0

Note: Only Telnet, FTP, HTTP, HTTPs traffic triggers interactive user authentication.

The example shown here enables cut-through proxy authentication on the inside interface:

```
pixfirewall(config)# aaa-server PIXAuth protocol tacacs+
pixfirewall(config)# aaa-server PIXAuth (inside) host 192.168.1.10 dog
pixfirewall(config)# aaa authentication include http
                     outbound 0 0 0 0 PIXAuth
```

(handwritten: syntax? details? =0 0??)

> **NOTE**
>
> Cut-through proxy can be used to authenticate both users in the inside interface going out and users coming in on the outside interface.

(handwritten: when do we need this? Difference %- this & regular authorization purpose?)

Authorization for Cut-through Proxy

After cut-through proxy authentication is configured, users are automatically allowed to pass through the firewall. However, authorization can be added to further control where your users are allowed to go. The commands used are similar to the authentication commands; the command syntax for authorization is as follows:

```
pixfirewall(config)# [no] aaa authorization include|exclude <service>
                     inbound|outbound <if_name>
                     <internal_ip> <internal_mask>
                     [<external_ip> <external_mask>] <group_tag>

pixfirewall(config)# [no] aaa authorization match <access_list_name>
                     inbound|outbound <if_name> <if_name> <group_tag>
```

Configuring Accounting

After authentication and authorization have been configured, configuration of accounting is often the next step. Accounting information enables you to track users who have logged on and accessed the device and the amount of time they're logged on. These two commands enable the accounting process:

```
pixfirewall(config)# [no] accounting include|exclude <service>
                        inbound|outbound <if_name>
                        <internal_ip> <internal_mask>
                        [<external_ip> <external_mask>] <group_tag>

pixfirewall(config)# [no] aaa accounting match <access_list_name>
                        inbound|outbound|<if_name> <if_name> <group_tag>
```

The format of the commands is similar to the authorization and authentication commands. The `include|exclude` parameters define the connections that need accounting, whereas the `match` parameter uses an ACL to define who needs accounting. The `service` parameter specifies the connection, such as `any`, `ftp`, `http`, `telnet`, or a protocol/port number.

The following is an example of enabling accounting for all internal traffic:

```
pixfirewall(config)# aaa accounting include any inbound 0 0 0 0 PIXAuth
pixfirewall(config)# aaa accounting include any outbound 0 0 0 0 PIXAuth
```

You do not need to configure any settings on the CSACS server itself; accounting requests should automatically be accepted. However, you should verify that traffic is being accounted by clicking the Reports and Activity button and the TACACS+ Accounting link.

Downloadable Access Control Lists

The PIX and CSACS support the capability to use downloadable ACLs, allowing you to create ACLs that are downloaded for a specific user or groups of users. The ACL can be downloaded during the authentication phase of a RADIUS connection, but TACACS+ does not support this feature. There are two types of downloadable access lists; named and unnamed.

 Downloadable ACLs are supported only on RADIUS and not TACACS+.

Named ACL

Named ACL gives you the ability to name an ACL that is downloaded once to the PIX and shared between many users. If a newer ACL is on the server, the newer version is downloaded and shared among the users assigned to the named ACL. Named ACLs work best for several users who all need the same ACL control and when several PIX access servers need that same ACL list.

The following is an example of a downloaded named ACL:

```
pixfirewall(config)# show access-list
access-list #ACSACL#-PIX-MySharedACL-3ef2957b; 3 elements
access-list #ACSACL#-PIX-MySharedACL-3ef2957b deny tcp any
            host 10.0.0.2 eq ftp (hitcnt=0)
access-list #ACSACL#-PIX-MySharedACL-3ef2957b deny tcp any
            host 10.0.0.3 eq www (hitcnt=0)
access-list #ACSACL#-PIX-MySharedACL-3ef2957b deny tcp any
            host 10.0.0.4 eq telnet (hitcnt=0)
```

The name of the list in the previous example is MySharedACL, and this list will be shared for all users who have been assigned the MySharedACL on the CSACS. The two tasks to configure named downloadable ACL within CSACS should be included here:

1. From Shared Profile Components in CSACS, define the named downloadable ACL.

2. From User Setup, apply the downloadable ACL to the corresponding users.

Unnamed ACLs

Unnamed ACLs are used to specify ACLs for individual users. The list created is used only by a single user, as opposed to a named ACL, which is shared. These lists are recommended only if each user requires an individual list.

An example of a downloaded unnamed ACL is shown here:

```
pixfirewall(config)# show access-list
access-list  AAA-user-daniel; 1 elements
access-list  AAA-user-daniel deny tcp any any eq www (hitcnt=0)
```

In the previous unnamed ACL example, an ACL is downloaded for a user named daniel and is used only by daniel.

a.wrell as several PIX

Named ACLs are shared among several users and are downloaded only once during authentication. Unnamed ACLs are not shared and are downloaded during authentication.

Authentication of Other Services and Authentication Issues

HTTPS

Normally, services such as HTTP, FTP, and Telnet can be authenticated using cut-through proxy. However, other services might need access through the PIX firewall. For example, if Jack's users need to access TFTP servers or Microsoft servers using NetBIOS, ports 69 and 139 would be used. Cut-through proxy does not work in these cases. You do have can use virtual telnet to allow users through. Also cut-through proxy may have some authentication issues with HTTP and Web browsers. If this is a problem the another service called Virtual HTTP can be used. This and Virtual Telnet are covered in the next section.

Virtual Telnet

It provides pre-authentication of users who require connections through the PIX Firewall using services or protocols that do not support authentication.

Virtual Telnet enables users to preauthenticate using a virtual Telnet session before executing the application that needs to pass through the PIX. For example, when Jack needs TFTP access, he must first open a Telnet session with PIX to a virtual Telnet IP address and then enter his username and password. The PIX caches the successful user logon and allows TFTP traffic through.

To use virtual Telnet, the `virtual telnet` command is needed. Its syntax is as follows:

```
pixfirewall(config)# [no] virtual telnet <ip>
```

The `ip` option is the IP address of the virtual Telnet server running on the PIX firewall. This address is the IP address clients use to enter their usernames and passwords. After authentication takes place, the user is allowed to pass traffic through the PIX. To log out, the user only has to connect using Telnet again and reenter her username and password.

The example shown here requires TFTP traffic to be authenticated before TFTP traffic is allowed through the PIX firewall. The user will create a Telnet session with 192.168.1.252:

```
pixfirewall(config)# aaa-server PIXAuth protocol tacacs+
pixfirewall(config)# aaa-server PIXAuth host 192.168.1.10 dog
pixfirewall(config)# aaa authentication include tcp/69
```
= *TFTP*

```
                outbound 0 0 0 0 PIXAuth
pixfirewall(config)# virtual telnet 192.168.1.252
```

 Virtual Telnet allows support for applications that don't use the typical HTTP, Telnet, and FTP ports.

Virtual HTTP

Virtual HTTP enables browser and Web server authentication to work correctly with the PIX when authentication with cut-through proxy is problematic. Web browsers can cache authentication requests, potentially causing future authentication problems. The Virtual HTTP works by redirecting the user's initial internal Web server request to a virtual HTTP server on the PIX. The user then authenticates his username and password and is redirected back to the original URL.

This example creates a virtual HTTP server that is used to catch HTTP traffic:

```
pixfirewall(config)# aaa-server PIXAuth protocol tacacs+
pixfirewall(config)# aaa-server PIXAuth host 192.168.1.10 dog
pixfirewall(config)# aaa authentication include any inbound 0 0 0 0 PIXAuth
pixfirewall(config)# virtual http 192.168.1.251
```

 Virtual HTTP helps to correct Web browser problems with HTTP authentication.

General AAA Commands

Several useful commands can help you view and confirm that your AAA services are configured correctly. Table 10.7 displays some of these.

Table 10.7	General AAA Commands
Command	**Description**
show aaa	This command displays all the currently configured AAA authentication, authorization, and accounting commands.
clear aaa	This deletes all the configured AAA authentication, authorization, and accounting commands.
show aaa-server	This command displays all the configured AAA servers.
show uauth	The output of this command displays the usernames and IP addresses of users who are currently logged in.

Table 10.7	General AAA Commands *(continued)*
Command	**Description**
clear uauth	This can remove a single user or all authentication users currently logged in.

Authentication Prompts

The authentication prompt command enables you to modify login prompts during AAA authentication. This command configures text for accepted, rejected, and basic prompts, and its syntax is as follows:

```
pixfirewall(config)# [no | clear] auth-prompt [prompt | accept | reject]
          "<prompt text>"
```

Table 10.8 displays the possible options for the auth-prompt command.

Table 10.8	auth-prompt Command Options
Option	**Function**
prompt	After this option, use quotes around the text you want to display to the user during general AAA logon attempts.
accept	This defines the accepted text after authentication is successful.
reject	This defines the text displayed after failed authentication attempts.

Here are some basic examples of setting the prompts:

```
pixfirewall(config)# auth-prompt prompt "AUTHORIZED PERSONNEL ONLY"
pixfirewall(config)# auth-prompt reject "WRONG"
pixfirewall(config)# auth-prompt accept "Welcome to the PIX firewall"
```

Authentication Timeouts

AAA authentication connections support two timeouts: inactivity and absolute. The *inactivity* timeout is used to disconnect the connection when the user is idle or inactive. The *absolute* timeout sets the total duration that the user is allowed to be logged in. Here is the command syntax:

```
pixfirewall(config)# timeout uauth hh:mm:ss [absolute|inactivity]
```

After timeouts are set, the show timeout command can be used to display all the values for the timeout command. The output of the command is shown here:

```
pixfirewall(config)# show timeout
timeout uauth 0:05:00 absolute
```

Exam Prep Questions

Question 1

> What does AAA stand for?
>
> ○ A. Authentication, authorization, accounting
> ○ B. Authentication, authentication, accounting
> ○ C. Authentication, authorization, application
> ○ D. Authentication, accounting, access control

Answer A is correct. AAA stands for authentication, authorization, and accounting. Therefore, answers B, C, and D are incorrect.

Question 2

> When using AAA commands what does the **local** parameter mean?
>
> ○ A. AAA local requests are sent to a server.
> ○ B. Only local logins are performed on the remote database.
> ○ C. Authenticate using a remote local server.
> ○ D. Authenticate using the local database.

Answer D is correct. The local parameter is used to define that the local database of usernames and passwords should be used, rather than a remote database. Answer A is incorrect because requests are not sent to a server. Answers B and C are incorrect because a local database is used and not a remote server.

Question 3

> By default, the PIX supports providing logon credentials for which basic protocols? (Select three.)
>
> ❑ A. SSL
> ❑ B. Telnet
> ❑ C. HTTP
> ❑ D. IPX
> ❑ E. TFTP
> ❑ F. FTP

Answers B, C, and F are correct. The PIX supports three basic protocols with cut-through proxy authentication: HTTP, FTP, and Telnet. Therefore, answers A, D, and E are incorrect.

Question 4

When talking about AAA services, what does the acronym ACS stand for?

- ○ A. Access control server
- ○ B. Authentication control server
- ○ C. Accounting Cisco Server
- ○ D. Authorization Cisco server

Answer A is correct. ACS stands for Access control server, and it can be used for RADIUS and TACACS+ AAA services. Therefore, answers B, C, and D are incorrect.

Question 5

Which command is used to direct authentication and accounting?

- ○ A. **aaa-server**
- ○ B. **aaa authentication**
- ○ C. **aaa remote-server**
- ○ D. **aaa authorization**

Answer A is correct. The aaa-server command, combined with the group tag, is used to define where to direct AAA services. Answers B and D are incorrect because the aaa authentication and aaa authorization commands are used to define which features need checking against the AAA services. Answer C is incorrect because this is an invalid command.

Question 6

If a user fails to authenticate on the PIX with an AAA server, what happens?

- ○ A. The user gains access.
- ○ B. The connection is dropped.
- ○ C. The user is forwarded to the Cisco Web site.
- ○ D. The user account is disabled.

Answer B is correct. If a user authentication has failed, the connection is dropped. Answer A is incorrect because the user does not gain access. Answer C incorrect, the user connection is dropped, not forwarded to Cisco's Web site. Answer D is incorrect because the user account is not disabled, only prevented from connecting.

Question 7

> Which AAA part denies a person the ability to Telnet?
>
> ○ A. Accounting
> ○ B. Authentication
> ○ C. Access control
> ○ D. Authorization

Answer D is correct. The authorization denies the ability to Telnet. Answer A is incorrect because accounting only tracks what a user does. Answer B is incorrect because authentication prevents a user from logging in—it does not just restrict Telnet. Answer C is not part of the AAA services, so it is incorrect.

Question 8

> What is virtual HTTP used for?
>
> ○ A. It's a replacement for Linux Web servers.
> ○ B. It enables Web browsers to work correctly with HTTP authentication.
> ○ C. It provides authentication for Telnet users.
> ○ D. It provides a Web interface to configure the PIX firewall.

Answer B is correct. Virtual HTTP is used to help overcome problematic issues with browsers and internal Web server issues. Answer A is incorrect because it is not a Web server replacement feature. Answer C is incorrect because Virtual HTTP is for HTTP connections. Answer D is incorrect because the PDM is the Web interface for the PIX firewall.

Question 9

What do RADIUS and TACACS+ use for a transport layer protocol?

○ A. TACACS+ uses TCP, and RADIUS uses TCP.

○ B. TACACS+ uses UDP, and RADIUS uses TCP.

○ C. TACACS+ uses TCP, and RADIUS uses UDP.

○ D. TACACS+ uses UDP, and RADIUS uses UDP.

Answer C is correct. The RADIUS protocol uses UDP, and the TACACS+ protocol uses TCP. The TACACS+ is considered to be more secure than RADIUS because all the payload is encrypted. Therefore, answers A, B, and D are incorrect.

Question 10

Which statement is true about the PIX firewall?

○ A. The PIX supports only local AAA services.

○ B. The PIX supports local, RADIUS, and TACACS+.

○ C. The PIX supports only local and RADIUS.

○ D. The PIX supports only TACACS+ and RADIUS.

Answer B is correct. The PIX firewall supports local, RADIUS, and TACACS+. Separate groups can be created for different types of traffic, and each group can point to a different RADIUS or TACACS+ server. Therefore, answers A, C, and D are incorrect because the PIX supports local, RADIUS, and TACACS+.

Question 11

Which statement is true about downloadable ACLs?

○ A. They're supported on RADIUS and not TACACS+.

○ B. They're supported on TACACS+ and not RADIUS.

○ C. They're supported on both RADIUS and TACACS+.

○ D. They're not supported on RADIUS or TACACS+.

Answer A is correct. Cisco supports downloadable ACLs on RADIUS and not TACACS+. Therefore, answers B, C, and D are incorrect.

Question 12 ✓   ?

> Which statements are true about named downloadable ACLs? (Select two.)
>
> ❏   A.   They are supported on TACACS+.
>
> ☑   B.   They are shared among PIX firewalls and users. ← *exact meaning* ?
>
> ❏   C.   They are shared among PIX firewalls but not users.
>
> ☑   D.   They are supported on RADIUS.

Answers B and D are correct. Named ACLs are shared between users and PIX firewalls, and Cisco supports downloadable ACLs on RADIUS and not TACACS+. Answer A is incorrect because downloadable ACLs are only supported on RADIUS not TACACS+. Answer C is incorrect because named access lists can be shared among users. Unnamed access lists are not shared among users.

Need to Know More?

 Chapman, David and Andy Fox. *Cisco Secure PIX Firewalls.* Indianapolis, IN: Cisco Press, 2002.

 See the Cisco PIX Firewall Command Reference, Version 6.2 at http://www.cisco.com/univercd/cc/td/doc/product/iaabu/pix/pix_sw/ v_62/cmdref/index.htm.

 See the Cisco Secure Access Control Server for Windows at http:// www.cisco.com/en/US/products/sw/secursw/ps2086/index.html.

 See the Cisco Secure Access Control Server for Windows at http:// www.cisco.com/en/US/products/sw/secursw/ps2086/index.html.

 See the Cisco Secure Access Control Server for Unix at http://www. cisco.com/en/US/products/sw/secursw/ps4911/index.html.

 See the Cisco Secure Access Control Server Solution Engine at http://www.cisco.com/en/US/products/sw/secursw/ps5338/index.html.

Failover

Detail/concept Not clear !!

Terms you'll need to understand:

✓ Primary firewall
✓ Secondary firewall
✓ Serial cable failover
✓ LAN-based failover
✓ Non-stateful failover
✓ Stateful failover
✓ Replication
✓ Primary firewall

Techniques you'll need to master:

✓ Configuring stateful firewalls
✓ Failing back

Previous chapters have talked about several features the PIX firewall can provide. These features can protect systems from access and reconnaissance attacks and enable you to control user access with AAA services. These features are excellent at what they do; however, they rely on one firewall connection. Therefore, that firewall must be functioning and online to allow traffic to flow. If that one firewall were to fail, all traffic would cease.

The PIX firewall addresses this single point of failure with a technology called *failover*. Failover enables two firewalls to work together to provide basic fault tolerance in the event the primary firewall fails. This chapter provides an overview of the failover feature offered by the PIX firewall.

Introduction to Failover

The PIX firewall provides the capability to support a backup-generator-style of fault tolerance. If the primary unit goes down, the secondary unit comes online to take its place. However, the secondary does not provide load-balancing capabilities, but rather a hot standby approach if the primary fails.

To support failover, firewalls are interconnected with a cable to provide a means of monitoring and configuring each other. This interconnection is provided by special serial cables or via a dedicated Ethernet interface cable called a *LAN-based* cable. Figure 11.1 displays a typical configuration of a primary and secondary firewall configuration.

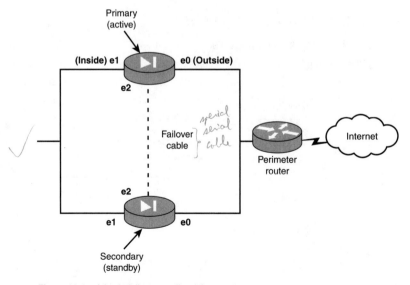

Figure 11.1 A basic failover configuration.

Non-stateful Failover

Non-stateful failover is the most basic solution of the failover options. When two firewalls are interconnected with either a serial cable or dedicated Ethernet interface, they send only RAM configuration information and session information across. If the primary (active) firewall cannot be detected across any interface, the secondary (standby) firewall assumes the active role, subsequently inheriting the primary's IP addresses and MAC address, and effectively become the operating firewall.

The primary, on the other hand, assumes the IP address and MAC address of the secondary firewall and stops passing traffic. When this happens, all xlate and connection table entries are lost and will have to be reestablished. For example, if Jack had an FTP connection through the firewall, when failover occurred Jack would have to reestablish a connection through the firewall to make his FTP operational. Figure 11.1 is a non-stateful failover configuration.

 When a primary interface fails (unplugged or broken cable), the secondary becomes the active firewall and inherits the primary's IP addresses. The primary moves into a fail or standby state and assumes the secondary firewall's IP addresses.

Stateful Failover

Stateful failover behaves in a similar way to non-stateful when a failover occurs. However, xlate and connection table information is maintained continually across a second dedicated Ethernet connection between the firewalls. When failover occurs, the secondary already contains the xlate and connection table information, providing users with a seamless failover. For example, if Jack had an FTP connection before the failover, that connection would still be maintained in the xlate and connection tables when the secondary took over. Figure 11.2 shows a stateful failover configuration.

The second Ethernet connection used for stateful failover must be a dedicated link between the two firewalls. The link can be FDDI, 100Mbps Fast Ethernet, or Gigabit Ethernet. When using 100Mbps Fast Ethernet, the connection is made using either a CAT 5 crossover cable or a dedicated full-duplex VLAN switch connection. Figure 11.2 shows the stateful connection using Ethernet 2 interfaces.

Note: ✗

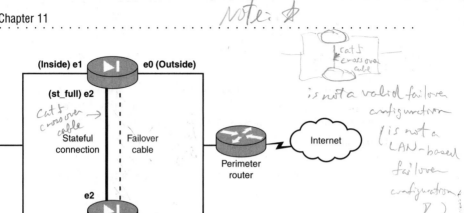

is not a valid failover configuration

(is not a LAN-based failover configuration)

Figure 11.2 A stateful failover configuration.

for cable-based configuration

Stateful failover requires an extra interface to connect the two firewalls. This interface carries stateful information to keep the firewall's xlate and connection tables in sync.

Standard failover = Cable-based failover
LAN-based failover

one special serial failover cable / two firewalls

(standard) Cable-based and LAN-based Configurations

Cable-based (serial) and LAN-based configurations dictate how the primary and secondary firewalls are linked together to provide failover support. The following provides an overview of each.

Both cable-based and LAN-based configurations support stateful failover solutions.

Cable-based Configurations

A cable-based configuration—also known as serial-based—requires a special serial cable from Cisco to connect the firewalls. The cable can be up to 6 feet in length and connects the dedicated failover port on the PIX models 515 and above. Before software version 5.2, the maximum speed that software provided across the serial cable was only 9.6Kbps; however, it's now 115Kbps.

This connection provides a means to replicate RAM information from the active to the standby firewall and provides detection of power loss on the other side. However, the limiting factor for this setup is that the distance between the firewalls can be only 6 feet.

 The special Cisco serial cable allows the detection of power on the other firewall. The cable is also labeled with the words "primary" and "secondary" to make installation easy.

LAN-based Configurations

A LAN-based configuration has been introduced in version 6.2 of the PIX firewall software. This enables the use of a dedicated Ethernet interface to perform the same functions as the serial cable-based configuration does. However, you are no longer restricted by the 6-foot distance limitation.

Some restrictions do exist when using LAN-based configurations. The two interfaces dedicated for LAN-based failover must be on the same subnet, so the two firewalls can't travel through a router. Another limitation is that the interface is completely dedicated to the failover monitoring and configuration and therefore should not be on the same LAN/broadcast domain as any other device. When linking the two firewalls, you must use a dedicated hub, switch, or VLAN. Please note that you cannot use a CAT 5 crossover cable for this connection. Figure 11.3 shows a typical LAN-based failover configuration.

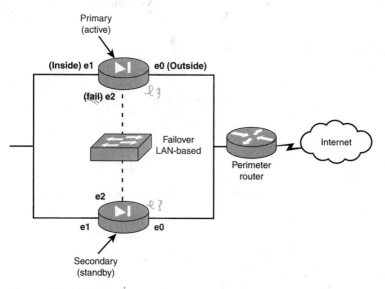

Figure 11.3   A LAN-based configuration.

The LAN-based connection must be through a dedicated hub, switch, or VLAN on a switch—do not use a crossover cable.

to connect the two PIX firewalls directly why?

Hardware and Software Requirements

Providing firewall failover capabilities involves several basic hardware and software requirements. The firewalls must have the following:

➤ Same PIX firewall hardware models *not even 515 & 515E !*

➤ Same amount of RAM memory

➤ Same amount of flash memory

➤ Same type and number of interfaces

➤ Special serial cable (optional)

➤ Same version of software

➤ Same activation keys for DES or 3DES *certain combination of* *or AES* *licensing (UR, FO)*

When configuring for failover, firewall models need to be exactly the same all the way down to their memory sizes.

Hardware

The PIX firewalls need to have the same hardware models for failover to work properly, but failover support is not available on all models. The 501, 506, and 506E do not support failover functionality; only the 515 and above models do. *515E, 525, 535* *515, 520*

Software

Software on the two firewalls also needs to be the same version number; otherwise, failover might not work properly.

Every model of the PIX firewall, including the 501, uses the same software—activation keys just enable extra features within the software. However, you still cannot use failover on the lower models.

Licensing

Activations keys also need to be installed to enable the failover functionality of the software. Cisco has several licensing features for failover, as listed in Table 11.1.

Table 11.1 Licenses	
License	Description
UR	The unrestricted license must be used on the primary (active) firewall and can optionally be used on the secondary (standby) firewall.
FO	The failover license is used for secondary standby modes only.
R	The restricted license cannot be used for either the primary or secondary firewall.

Now that you have seen the various licenses available, Table 11.2 displays the possible primary and secondary licensing combinations.

Table 11.2 Licensing Combinations		
	Primary (Active)	Secondary (Standby)
Combination 1	UR	UR
Combination 2	UR	FO

The PIX does not have separate software for failover protection. Only activation keys are necessary to enable the features.

Replication

When two firewalls are interconnected for failover, replication of the RAM configuration file (running config) occurs, keeping the standby firewall in sync with the primary firewall.

The following lists the methods by which the primary replicates its running configuration file across to the secondary firewall:

➤ When the standby starts, it obtains the latest configuration from the active firewall.

➤ When commands are entered into the active firewall, they are automatically replicated to the secondary firewall's RAM (the running configuration).

➤ The write standby command can be used to force a replication of the entire configuration in memory to the standby firewall.

One important item to note is that replication sends only the running configuration to the standby's RAM; the startup configuration is not sent to flash. Therefore, to save configuration on the standby to flash, you must issue the write memory command.

Replication of Stateful Failover

see p. 443
cisco press

In non-stateful failover configuration, only one cable is used to replicate the running configuration file. Conversely, in stateful failover, two cables are necessary—one for the normal running configuration file replication and another for the xlate table and other such stateful information. The following is a list of what is replicated across in a stateful failover configuration:

➤ The translation xlate table

➤ The connection table

➤ The negotiated fixup protocol ports

However, not all stateful information is sent across. This list of items is not replicated and, as such, is lost when failover occurs:

➤ The user authentication (uauth) table used by AAA services

➤ The ARP table

➤ Routing information

➤ ISAKMP and IPSec security association (SA) tables

Lastly, the following list shows what is sent across the serial or LAN-based failover cables:

➤ The running configuration replication

➤ MAC address exchanges

➤ The status (active or standby)

➤ The network interface status

➤ Hello keepalive messages

Together both cables help keep the firewall in sync to provide failover fault tolerance.

Failover Detection

Q: what are others?

The PIX can detect several types of failovers. One mechanism it uses is the hello message. This message is sent every 3–15 seconds out every interface to test communication. The default is 15 seconds, but it can be changed with the `firewall poll` command.

If a firewall unit doesn't see a hello message in two updates (30 seconds), both firewalls start to initiate failover tests to determine and confirm which of the firewalls has failed. If the primary is confirmed down, the standby moves into the active role; if the secondary firewall has failed, the primary continues to operate with no failover.

Q: the primary goes into standby mode? A: yes

Q: including stateful connection table?

Make sure you understand that Hello messages are sent across all interfaces, including the serial or LAN-based cable. By default, hello messages are sent every 15 seconds, and if two messages are missed, the failover process begins.

A: I guess, yes if the primary firewall does not have a full state.

Causes for Failovers

Failovers occur for many reasons. When a failover does occur, both firewalls work together to promote the standby firewall to the active state if possible. If the primary firewall detects an interface going down, it tells the secondary to move into the active state. On the other hand, the secondary promotes itself if it notices that the primary is offline. The following events cause failovers:

➤ The primary firewall is turned off or the power supply fails.

➤ The primary firewall is rebooted.

➤ An interface on the active firewall goes down or the serial interface cable fails.

➤ The primary firewall experiences a block memory exhaustion condition.

When using the serial cable as the failover link between the firewalls, power off detection can take place. If the primary firewall's power is turned off, the secondary firewall starts to promote itself to active state within 15 seconds. If a LAN-based cable is used, the power failure cannot be detected.

The Four Interface Tests

The PIX firewall issues four tests to determine whether the active firewall is truly faulty before promoting the secondary to active. As stated previously,

for an interface (I believe)

hello messages are sent to detect interfaces on the opposite firewall. If two messages are missed, a series of tests is initiated to probe more deeply and help justify a failover. Table 11.3 explains the failover tests.

Table 11.3	Four Failover Tests
Test	**Function**
NIC status test	This tests the up/down status of the interface. If the link is down or unplugged, or the intermediate switch is turned off or plugged in to a switch-performing spanning tree, the interface is detected as a failure and the active firewall becomes the standby firewall. However, if the link is determined to be up, the test succeeds and the PIX searches more deeply during the second test to test for other possible problems that caused the missing hello messages.
Network activity	The PIX monitors the activity of the link for 5 seconds; if valid frames are detected, the failover testing is aborted. If no valid frames are detected, meaning the test failed, the PIX moves on to the third test.
ARP test	This test sends ARP requests to the last 10 IP addresses queued in the ARP table. If any response comes back, the testing is aborted and the firewall is considered operational. However, if no responses come back, the PIX moves to the fourth test.
Ping test	This is the last-chance test. A broadcast ping of 255.255.255.255 is sent, and if any device (host, router, and so on) replies, the test is considered a success and failover is aborted. However, if no requests come back, the failover to the standby takes place.

why?
should it be? The standby firewall be comes the active firewall ? or depends ?

according to Cisco press, the testing starts over again with the ARP test

should it be the standby firewall will become the active firewall.? or depends .?

During the testing, if any valid frames are received from the other PIX, the testing is aborted and the systems are deemed operational. The results of each test are passed back and forth between the primary and secondary firewalls to determine which firewall is operational. For example, the primary might determine that the secondary interfaces are down and thus not promote the secondary firewall to the active state.

The network activity test monitors for traffic for 5 seconds. If no traffic is found, the PIX moves to the next test, instead of to standby mode.

Failed State

When a firewall is deemed as failed, it disables all its network interfaces. However, every 15 seconds the failed PIX tries to test all the interfaces and automatically moves into the standby state. If problems still exist, it fails again.

if the problem is been fixed

To manually move the failed firewall back into the standby state, the `failover reset` command can be issued. For example, if Jack unplugs an interface, the PIX moves into the failed state. After Jack plugs the interface back in, the PIX automatically moves into the standby state in 15 seconds, as long as everything else is functioning correctly. Or Jack could issue the `failover reset` command if he doesn't want to wait 15 seconds. If a problem still exists after the command has been issued, the PIX again moves into the failed state.

Fail Back

After the secondary has been set to the active state, it will not fail back to the standby state until manually told to do so. For example, if Jack's primary firewall is turned off, the secondary moves to the active state. After Jack's primary comes back online, he will have to manually force the secondary to go into standby state, thus making the primary active again. This can be done from either unit. Table 11.4 lists the two commands used to force active or standby state.

Table 11.4   Failover Commands

Command	Description
failover active	You use this command on the primary firewall to set the primary to active mode. *from standby mode*
no failover active	You use this command on the secondary to force it back into standby mode. *from active mode*

If the firewalls are set up in a stateful configuration, stateful information is kept when the new active firewall takes over. Otherwise, the users will have to reconnect.

Failover Configuration

The failover configuration is actually quite simple. Only a handful of commands are necessary to fully configure failover, and cable-based failover takes even fewer commands than LAN-based. The following is an overview of some of the basic commands:

```
pixfirewall(config)# failover [active]          standby firewall
pixfirewall(config)# failover IP address <if_name> <IP_address>
pixfirewall(config)# failover link [stateful_if_name]
pixfirewall(config)# failover mac address <if_name>
<active_mac> <standby_mac>                      } optional
pixfirewall(config)# failover replicate http
```

for all interfaces

not a completed set of commands !!

Table 11.5 displays several of the configuration failover commands used to set up failover.

Table 11.5	Failover Configuration Commands
Command	**Description**
failover [active]	This enables failover. The **[active]** option manually forces the standby to be active.
failover ip address	This specifies the IP address of the standby firewall. When failover occurs, this is the IP address the firewall will be changed to.
failover link	This defines which FastEthernet interface is used for stateful failover.
failover mac address	This specifies the MAC addresses for the primary and standby firewalls. This is available in case you want to override the burned-in address (BIA) of the firewall.
failover replicate http	By default, HTTP connections are not replicated in stateful replication. This enables HTTP replication.

The commands listed in Table 11.5 are the basic commands needed to perform cable-based stateful failover capability. To support LAN-based failover, the following additional commands are necessary:

```
pixfirewall(config)# failover lan enable
pixfirewall(config)# failover lan unit primary|secondary
pixfirewall(config)# failover lan interface <if_name>
pixfirewall(config)# failover lan key <secret_key>
```

Table 11.6 displays a list of LAN-based commands used to configure the PIX firewall for failover.

Table 11.6	LAN-based Failover Commands
Command	**Description**
failover lan enable	Enables LAN-based failover instead of cable-based.
failover lan unit	Unlike the serial cable that helps define which firewall is the primary or secondary, the **lan unit** command specifies the function of the firewall.
failover lan interface	Defines which interface is used for LAN-based connections.
failover lan key	This gives you the ability to specify an encryption key to use for protected failover messages.

see p. 260 for e.g.

Configuring for Cable-based Failover

The following example demonstrates how to configure two PIX firewalls for serial cable-based failover. The first step attaches the serial cable, which has primary and secondary labels on its ends and is provided by Cisco. Be sure you install them in the correct order. Next, you configure a stateful failover system based on Figure 11.4.

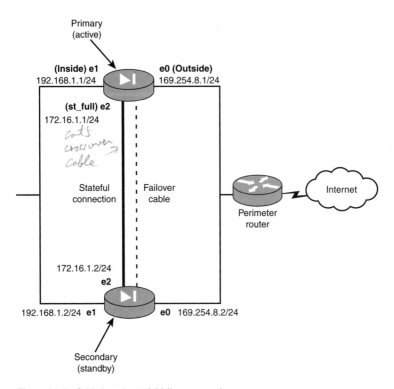

Figure 11.4   Cable-based stateful failover example.

Follow these steps, which are discussed in more detail in the following sections:

1. Configure the clock.

2. Configure the system addresses.

3. Enable failover.

4. Configure the failover addresses.

5. Enable stateful failover.

6. Finish the process.

Configuring the Clock

First, you must configure the clock on the primary firewall. The clock settings are replicated to the secondary firewall after the secondary firewall is enabled. The following is the command used to configure the clock's date and time values:

```
primaryfirewall(config)# clock set 16:00 August 31, 2003
```

Configuring the System Addresses

Now, you need to set the system addresses on the firewall. Be sure you force flow control and do not use autosensing. Listing 11.1 shows the commands needed to configure the system settings on the primary firewall.

Listing 11.1 Primary Firewall Cable-based Commands

```
primaryfirewall(config)# interface Ethernet0 100full
primaryfirewall(config)# interface Ethernet1 100full
primaryfirewall(config)# interface Ethernet2 100full

primaryfirewall(config)# nameif ethernet0 outside sec0
primaryfirewall(config)# nameif ethernet1 inside sec100
primaryfirewall(config)# nameif ethernet2 st_ful sec50

primaryfirewall(config)# IP address outside 169.254.8.1 255.255.255.0
primaryfirewall(config)# IP address inside 192.168.1.1 255.255.255.0
primaryfirewall(config)# IP address st_ful 172.16.1.1 255.255.255.0

primaryfirewall(config)# clear xlate
```

Now, you use the `show ip address` command to display the system and current address information, like so:

```
primaryfirewall(config)# show ip address
System IP Addresses:
     ip address outside 169.254.8.1 255.255.255.0
     ip address inside 192.168.1.1 255.255.255.0
     ip address st_ful 172.16.1.1 255.255.255.0
Current IP Addresses:
     ip address outside 169.254.8.1 255.255.255.0
     ip address inside 192.168.1.1 255.255.255.0
     ip address st_ful 172.16.1.1 255.255.255.0
```

When the primary is in active mode, it uses the system IP addresses and media access control (MAC) addresses. On the other hand, when the primary is in standby mode, it uses the failover IP addresses and the MAC addresses.

Enabling Failover

After the system addresses are configured, failover can be enabled. The following command enables failover on the primary:

```
primaryfirewall(config)# failover active
```
? can/we simply use failover ?

The command to enable failover can be used before you set the system addresses, but I like to do it just after to ensure that the addresses are configured prior to failover activation.

> Make sure you remember that the **failover active** command is used to enable failover on the PIX firewall.

Configuring the Failover Addresses

Configuring the failover addresses enables you to define what the secondary address will be and what the primary will become in the event of a failover. Listing 11.2 displays the commands needed on the primary firewall to define which secondary IP address will be used and which interface is the stateful interface.

Listing 11.2   Configuring Primary Cable-based Failover IP Addresses

```
primaryfirewall(config)# failover ip address outside 169.254.8.2
primaryfirewall(config)# failover ip address inside 192.168.1.2
primaryfirewall(config)# failover ip address st_ful 172.16.1.2
```

To verify the configuration, you can use the `show failover` command as shown here:

```
primaryfirewall(config)# show failover
Failover On
Cable status: Normal
Reconnect timeout 0:00:00
Poll frequency 15 seconds
    This host: primary - Active
                Active time: 240 (sec)
                Interface st_ful (172.16.1.1): Normal (Waiting)
                Interface outside (169.254.8.1): Normal (Waiting)
                Interface inside (192.168.1.1): Normal (Waiting)
    Other host: secondary - Standby
                Active time: 0 (sec)
                Interface st_ful (172.16.1.2): Unknown (Waiting)
                Interface outside (168.254.8.2): Unknown (Waiting)
                Interface inside (192.168.1.2): Unknown (Waiting)
```

The `other host` in the previous code is the secondary host. The status of `Unknown` is displayed if you have the secondary off, as I did in this case.

Enabling Stateful Failover

In this example, you are using stateful failover on the 172.16.1.1-to-172.16.1.2 link. The following command enables the stateful failover on the interface named st_ful. At this point, you must turn on the secondary firewall, using the following: *exact meaning ?*

```
primaryfirewall(config)# failover link st_ful
primaryfirewall(config)# show failover
Failover On
Cable status: Normal
Reconnect timeout 0:00:00
Poll frequency 15 seconds
    This host: primary - Active
                Active time: 251 (sec)
                Interface st_ful (172.16.1.1): Normal
                Interface outside (169.254.8.1): Normal
                Interface inside (192.168.1.1): Normal
    Other host: secondary - Standby
                Active time: 11 (sec)
                Interface st_ful (172.16.1.2): Normal
                Interface outside (168.254.8.2): Normal
                Interface inside (192.168.1.2): Normal

Stateful Failover Logical Update Statistics
    Link : failover
    Stateful Obj    xmit    xerr    rcv     rerr
    General         1201    0       0       0
    sys cmd         1130    0       0       0
    up time         0       0       0       0
    xlate           0       0       0       0
    tcp conn        0       0       0       0
    udp conn        0       0       0       0
    ARP tbl         0       0       0       0
    RIP Tbl         0       0       0       0

    Logical Update Queue Information

              Cur     Max     Total
    Recv Q: 0         0       0
    Xmit Q: 0         0       1201
```

Finishing Up

Now that the primary has been configured, the commands will be replicated to the secondary firewall when it is powered on or reloaded. The firewall will start with the sync started message; the sync completed message displays when the firewall replication has finished. After all the changes have been made on the primary and the secondary has been synchronized, use the write memory command on both firewalls to save the configuration to flash.

With cable-based topology, the primary firewall automatically replicates the configuration and setup information to the secondary unit. *see ⚹ in p.263*

Q: what about Lan-based case ?

Q: Do we have to do any configuration on Secondary PIX ?
A: see p.260 ⚹⚹

Configuring for LAN-based Failover

In the previous example, you configured a cable-based firewall that required a special 6-foot serial cable from Cisco. For this example, you will use the new LAN-based configuration to set up a failover system. The LAN-based failover uses dedicated Ethernet interfaces that interconnect the two firewalls. This interconnect must go through a dedicated hub, a switch, or a VLAN on a switch. In this example, you will use a switch, as shown in Figure 11.5. You will also use a stateful link to interconnect the firewalls for session state information replication. This connection can be a crossover cable, which is shown with a straight line in Figure 11.5. Be sure you don't cable them together until the last step.

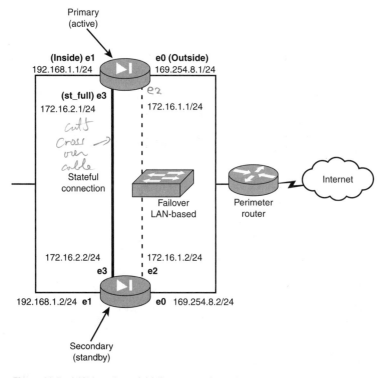

Figure 11.5 LAN-based stateful failover example.

The following steps, which are discussed in the following sections, are required to configure LAN-based failover:

1. Configure the clock.

2. Configure the primary system address.

3. Enable failover.

4. Configure the failover addresses.

5. Configure the primary LAN-based connections. *see p. 260*

6. Enable stateful failover.

7. Configure the standby firewall. *see p. 260**

8. Finish the process.

Configuring the Clock

You must first configure the clock on the primary firewall. The clock is replicated to the secondary firewall after it's enabled. Here's the code used to accomplish this:

```
primaryfirewall(config)# clock set 16:00 August 31, 2003
```

Configuring the Primary System Addresses

Now you have to set the system addresses on the primary firewall. Listing 11.3 shows the commands needed to configure the system settings on the primary firewall.

Listing 11.3 Primary Firewall LAN-based Commands

```
primaryfirewall(config)# interface Ethernet0 100full
primaryfirewall(config)# interface Ethernet1 100full
primaryfirewall(config)# interface Ethernet2 100full
primaryfirewall(config)# interface Ethernet3 100full

primaryfirewall(config)# nameif ethernet0 outside sec0
primaryfirewall(config)# nameif ethernet1 inside sec100
primaryfirewall(config)# nameif ethernet2 fl_ovr sec75
primaryfirewall(config)# nameif ethernet3 st_ful sec50

primaryfirewall(config)# IP address outside 169.254.8.1 255.255.255.0
primaryfirewall(config)# IP address inside 192.168.1.1 255.255.255.0
primaryfirewall(config)# IP address fl_ovr 172.16.1.1 255.255.255.0
primaryfirewall(config)# IP address st_ful 172.16.2.1 255.255.255.0

primaryfirewall(config)# clear xlate
```

Next, you use the `show ip address` command to display the system and current address information, like so:

```
primaryfirewall(config)# show ip address
System IP Addresses:
     ip address outside 169.254.8.1 255.255.255.0
     ip address inside 192.168.1.1 255.255.255.0
     ip address fl_ovr 172.16.1.1 255.255.255.0
     ip address st_ful 172.16.2.1 255.255.255.0
Current IP Addresses:
     ip address outside 169.254.8.1 255.255.255.0
     ip address inside 192.168.1.1 255.255.255.0
```

```
ip address fl_ovr 172.16.1.1 255.255.255.0
ip address st_ful 172.16.2.1 255.255.255.0
```

Enabling Failover

After the system addresses are configured, failover can be enabled using the following command:

```
primaryfirewall(config)# failover active
```

Configuring the Failover Addresses

Configuring the failover addresses enables you to define what the secondary address will be and what the primary will become in the event of a failover. Listing 11.4 shows a configuration example.

Listing 11.4   Configuring Primary LAN-based Failover IP Addresses

```
primaryfirewall(config)# failover ip address outside 169.254.8.2
primaryfirewall(config)# failover ip address inside 192.168.1.2
primaryfirewall(config)# failover ip address fl_ovr 172.16.1.2
primaryfirewall(config)# failover ip address st_ful 172.16.2.2
```

To verify the configuration, you can use the show failover command, as shown here:

```
primaryfirewall(config)# show failover
Failover On
Cable status: Normal
Reconnect timeout 0:00:00
Poll frequency 15 seconds
    This host: primary - Active
                    Active time: 250 (sec)
                    Interface outside (169.254.8.1): Normal (Waiting)
                    Interface inside (192.168.1.1): Normal (Waiting)
                    Interface fl_ovr (172.16.1.1): Normal (Waiting)
                    Interface st_ful (172.16.2.1): Normal (Waiting)
    Other host: secondary - Standby
                    Active time: 0 (sec)
                    Interface outside (168.254.8.2): Unknown (Waiting)
                    Interface inside (192.168.1.2): Unknown (Waiting)
                    Interface fl_ovr (172.16.1.2): Unknown (Waiting)
                    Interface st_ful (172.16.2.2): Unknown (Waiting)
```

Configuring LAN-based Connections

Because you are using a LAN-based configuration, the serial cable will not be used and you will have to tell the firewall that it is the primary unit. Listing 11.5 configures the primary firewall for LAN-based configuration.

Listing 11.5 Setting LAN-based Primary Firewall Commands

```
primaryfirewall(config)# no failover           ← why need those?
primaryfirewall(config)# failover lan unit primary
primaryfirewall(config)# failover lan interface fl_ovr
primaryfirewall(config)# failover lan key dog
primaryfirewall(config)# failover lan enable
primaryfirewall(config)# failover active
```

Listing 11.5 configures the firewall unit as the primary firewall, disables the failover, defines the failover link to fl_ovr, and uses the secret key (password) of dog when sending data. In a later step, you will configure the secondary with the same key (password).

Enabling Stateful Failover

In this example, you are using stateful failover on the st_ful interface (172.16.2.0/24). The command shown here enables the stateful failover on this link:

```
primaryfirewall(config)# failover link st_ful
```

Configuring the Standby Firewall

Now that you've configured the primary, the secondary needs to have basic LAN-based configuration set on it. Be sure the secondary has no configuration before you start the next three steps.

The first thing you must do is set the interface IP address so it can receive information from the primary. Listing 11.6 configures basic settings on the Ethernet interface on the firewall.

There is no need to configure e0, e1 d e3 !!

Listing 11.6 Secondary LAN-based Basic Configuration

```
secondaryfirewall(config)# interface Ethernet2 100full
secondaryfirewall(config)# nameif ethernet2 fl_ovr sec75
secondaryfirewall(config)# IP address fl_ovr 172.16.1.2 255.255.255.0
```

The second step is to configure the LAN-based settings. Listing 11.7 enables the firewall as a secondary unit. The last two code lines save the configuration to flash and reload the PIX.

Listing 11.7 Secondary LAN-based Configuration

```
secondaryfirewall(config)# failover IP address fl_ovr 172.16.1.2
secondaryfirewall(config)# failover lan unit secondary
secondaryfirewall(config)# failover lan interface fl_ovr
secondaryfirewall(config)# failover lan key dog
secondaryfirewall(config)# failover lan enable
secondaryfirewall(config)# failoversecondaryfirewall(config)# write memory
secondaryfirewall(config)# reload
```

Finishing Up

Now that the primary and secondary have been configured, make sure you have saved both configurations before cabling them together. Then use the show failover command to monitor their statuses.

Exam Prep Questions

Question 1

> When two PIX firewalls are configured for failover, what is sent across the seri-
> al cable?
>
> ○ A. The xlate table
> ○ B. The connection table
> Ö C. The RAM configuration
> ○ D. The flash configuration
> ○ E. Answers A and B

Answer C is correct. The serial cable connects two PIX firewalls to replicate RAM configuration and tests the power status of the other unit. Answers A, B, and E are incorrect because xlate and connection tables are not sent across the serial connection; they are sent across a dedicated Ethernet interface if stateful failover is configured. Answer D is incorrect because only the RAM configuration is sent across the link, not the flash configuration.

Question 2

> If a primary PIX firewall is the active unit, what happens to the current IP
> addresses if its interface fails?
>
> ○ A. The IP addresses on the primary and secondary are both set to the
>   standby IP addresses.
> ○ B. All IP addresses are removed, and the primary is put in a secondary
>   state.   *and MAC addresses*
> ○ C. The IP addresses become those of the standby PIX firewall.
> ○ D. The primary shuts down.

Answer C is correct. When the IP address interface fails on the primary active unit, the primary inherits the secondary IP addresses and the secondary inherits the primary unit's address and becomes the active unit. Answer A is incorrect because the secondary inherits the primary address and becomes active. Answer B is incorrect because the IP addresses change to that of the secondary. Answer D is incorrect because the unit does not shut down when it becomes a secondary unit; it just inherits the secondary unit's IP and MAC addresses.

Question 3

When designing a stateful failover topology, what is required? (Select two.)

- ☑ A. One interface interconnecting the firewalls
- ☑ B. A special PIX serial cable
- ☐ C. Token-Ring connections
- ☐ D. Four interfaces interconnecting the firewalls

for cable-based configuration

Answers A and B are correct. To establish stateful failover with the answers provided, a special serial interface cable is needed to link the primary and secondary units. This cable identifies which unit is the primary and which is the secondary. It also is used to detect power status and transfer configuration information between the firewalls. Next, each PIX needs a dedicated Fast Ethernet interface to interconnect them so stateful information can be passed. Answer C is incorrect because Token-Ring is not supported for failover. Answer D is incorrect because four interfaces are not needed to support stateful failover; only two are needed, at the most.

Question 4

If a serial-based failover topology is configured, how is the configuration set up on the secondary firewall?

- ☒ A. The primary unit is configured and replicated to the standby unit.
- ○ B. The standby unit is configured and replicated to the primary unit.
- ○ C. The primary unit sends the configuration after a failure is detected. → ?
- ○ D. The standby unit configuration is manually entered.

Answer A is correct. As changes are made on the primary unit, they are automatically replicated to the secondary unit, although they can also be forced ✗ with the `write standby` command. Answer B is incorrect because changes are never replicated from the secondary unit to the primary unit. Answer C is incorrect because the configuration is always replicated before a failover occurs. Answer D is incorrect because the secondary is configured from the primary and replicated across.

Question 5 ?

Configuration information is replicated automatically from the primary to the secondary PIX firewall. *Under what situation?*

- ○ A. True
- ○ B. False

Answer A is correct. When set up in failover mode, the primary unit automatically sends configuration settings to the secondary unit's RAM. Therefore, answer B is incorrect.

Question 6

What is required to make standard serial failover work? (Select two.)

- ☑ A. The same software on both
- ❏ B. Different software on both
- ❏ C. One primary model and one secondary hardware model
- ☑ D. The same hardware for both primary and secondary

Answers A and D are correct. For failover to work, several items need to be exactly the same between the two firewalls: RAM size, flash size, software versions, the number of interfaces, and the hardware model. Answer B is incorrect because software versions should be exactly the same for maximum compatibility. Answer C is incorrect because Cisco does not use different hardware for the primary and secondary units. Cisco uses licensing to unlock ? primary and secondary capabilities on the PIX firewalls.

Question 7 D

What happens to the active connections when firewalls are configured for non-stateful failover? *when a failover occurs*

- ○ A. Only TCP connections are dropped.
- ○ B. Only UDP connections are dropped.
- ○ C. All the connections are dropped.
- ○ D. Configuration is not replicated.

Answer C is correct. When configured for non-stateful failover, all the connections are dropped because the xlate and connection tables are not replicated across. Therefore, answers A, B, and D are incorrect.

Question 8

When using the special serial failover cable, what function does it provide? (Select three.)

- ❏ A. It sends stateful connection information.
- ☑ B. It checks the power status of the other firewall.
- ☑ C. It designates the units' identifications.
- ❏ D. It routes IP traffic when outside interfaces fail.
- ☑ E. It provides communication between the units.

Answers B, C, and E are correct. The special serial cable is labeled with primary and secondary to help identify which unit is designated for which purpose and to provide communication between the units. Answer A is incorrect because the serial cable does not send stateful information; the dedicated interface is used for that function. Answer D is incorrect because the serial cable does not route traffic.

Question 9

The Cisco PIX 506E supports failover capabilities.

- ○ A. True
- ⊘ B. False

Answer B is correct. Only the PIX 515, 525, and 535 support failover capabilities, not the PIX 506 or 501. Therefore, answer A is incorrect.

Question 10

Before using stateful failover what is required? (Select three.)

- ❏ A. A special Cisco serial cable
- ❏ B. Special failover IOS software
- ❏ C. Two dedicated Ethernet interfaces
- ❏ D. Unrestricted software licensing

For table-based configuration

primary : UR
secondary : UR or FO

Answers A, C, and D are correct. To support stateful failover, a special serial cable, two dedicated interfaces (one on each PIX), and unrestricted software licensing are all valid requirements. Answer C is correct because, in the case of LAN-based failover, two dedicated interfaces are needed. Answer B

serial-based failover

is incorrect because no software is needed; only the activation in licensing is necessary.

Question 11

When hello message packets are sent, how many can be missed before failover starts?

- A. 1
- B. 2
- C. 3
- D. 15

Answer B is correct. If two hello messages are missed, the sequence of failover starts. Hello messages, by default, are sent out every 15 seconds. So, in 30 seconds the secondary unit initiates the process of becoming active if two messages are missed. Therefore answers A, C, and D are incorrect.

Question 12

Which command enables failover?

- A. **failover active**
- B. **failover enable**
- C. **failover on**
- D. **active failover**

Answer A is correct. The command to enable failover is `failover active`. Answers B, C, and D are all invalid commands and are therefore incorrect.

Question 13

What happens during the network activity test? (Select two.)

- A. The PIX monitors for ARP requests for 5 seconds.
- B. The PIX monitors for valid frames for 5 seconds.
- C. If no activity is found, the PIX moves into standby mode.
- D. If no activity is found, the PIX moves on to the next test.

Answers B and D are correct. In the network activity test, the PIX monitors for any valid frame, not just ARP requests. *? really* If activity is found, the failover testing is aborted and the system goes back to normal. If the test fails, the PIX moves on to the next test, which is the ARP test. Therefore, answer C is incorrect. Answer A is incorrect because it states that only ARP requests are monitored, making it less correct than answer B.

Question 14

> When a failover to a standby PIX occurs, what needs to be done to client computers?
>
> *only applies to stateful failover*
>
> ○ A. Change their default gateway addresses.
>
> ○ B. Reboot to autodetect the new active firewall.
>
> ○ C. Receive new addresses from the DHCP server.
>
> ○ D. Nothing.

Answer D is correct. When the secondary firewall becomes active, it inherits the IP address and MAC addresses of the primary firewall. The clients are unaffected by this change, and no modifications are needed on their computers. Answers A, B, and C are therefore incorrect.

Question 15

> When configuring for stateful failover, what basic commands are required? (Select three.)
>
> ❑ A. failover active
>
> ❑ B. failover enable
>
> ❑ C. failover ip address inside 192.168.8.2
>
> ❑ D. failover stateful st_fal
>
> ❑ E. failover secondary ip address inside 192.168.8.2
>
> ❑ F. failover link st_fal
>
> *invalid commands*

Answers A, C, and F are correct. Only three of these commands are valid commands. The `failover active` command enables failover; the `failover ip address inside 192.168.8.2` command sets the secondary standby IP address; and the `failover link st_fal` command defines the interface named st_fal as the interface to be used for stateful replication. Therefore, answers B, D, and E are incorrect.

Need to Know More?

 Bastien, Greg and Christian Degu. *CCSP Cisco Secure PIX Firewall Advanced Exam Certification Guide.* Indianapolis, IN: Cisco Press, 2003.

 Chapman, David and Andy Fox. *Cisco Secure PIX Firewalls.* Indianapolis, IN: Cisco Press, 2002.

 See the Cisco PIX Firewall Command Reference, Version 6.2 at http://www.cisco.com/univercd/cc/td/doc/product/iaabu/pix/pix_sw/v_62/cmdref/index.htm.

 See the Cisco PIX Firewall Advanced Configuration at http://www.cisco.com/en/US/products/sw/secursw/ps2120/products_configuration_guide_chapter09186a008008996b.html#xtocid3.

 See How Failover Works on the Cisco Secure PIX Firewall at http://www.cisco.com/en/US/products/hw/vpndevc/ps2030/products_tech_note09186a0080094ea7.shtml#failovercable.

IPSec and Virtual Private Networks

Difficult

- -

Terms you'll need to understand:

& tedious !!

concept is M.C.C !!

✓ ISAKMP policies
✓ Internet Key Exchange (IKE)
✓ Internet Protocol Security (IPSec)
✓ Authentication header (AH)
✓ Encapsulation security payload (ESP)
✓ Transform sets
✓ Crypto maps
✓ IP local pool
✓ Security association

Techniques you'll need to master:

✓ Four steps to setting up IPSec
✓ ISAKMP policies
✓ Transform sets
✓ Crypto maps

Before the innovation of virtual private networks (VPNs), companies had no choice but to purchase expensive wide area network (WAN) connections to interlink sites or allow users access into their networks. These days, companies and home users alike can use VPNs to access network resources—not by traveling across dedicated WAN links, but by using public media such as the Internet. This chapter contains a high-level overview of VPN technology and discusses VPN functionality provided by the PIX firewall.

The Basics of VPN

The basic concept of a VPN is really quite simple: If a user wants to send traffic from one point to another, that data is placed inside another packet and sent to its destination. This process is known as *encapsulation*. For example, if Jack wants to send traffic from his computer to the headquarters office across the Internet, Jack first establishes a secure VPN tunnel with HQ. Then, all the traffic directed to HQ is broken up and placed into other packets being encapsulated, and perhaps even encrypted from prying eyes.

To give an analogy, VPNs are like having truck carry a payload of data for you. If you want to send data to another location, you place that data in the truck. Instead of an open, flatbed truck where everyone can see your data, the truck has a canopy enclosing (encrypting) the payload so other users cannot view your true data. Figure 12.1 displays Jack's traffic flowing through a remote access VPN tunnel to HQ. After the traffic reaches HQ, the data is taken out of the tunnel, reassembled, and sent along its way. As you can see, VPNs just perform a middleman action to carry data from one peer to another in a secure manner.

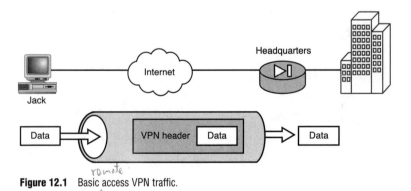

Figure 12.1 Basic access VPN traffic.

VPN Categories

VPNs can be divided into several categories to help define what type of connection you've created. The following is a list of the most common categories:

➤ *Access VPN*—These VPNs provide a means for remote users to access the network in a secure manner. For example, say Jack wants to connect from home temporarily to the office to check his email. Jack can set up a VPN to interlink his home PC to the office and send data securely. This is called an access VPN (refer to Figure 12.1)

➤ *Intranet VPN*—This allows a company to interconnect its remote networks. Intranet VPNs are commonly known as *site-to-site* VPNs and are used to link sites that are part of the same company. They don't just link a single user but whole networks. Figure 12.2 demonstrates a VPN across a site-to-site scenario.

➤ *Extranet VPN*—This is similar to the intranet VPN. However, this VPN solution is used when interlinking two different companies. For example, if company A wants to interconnect with company B, it can use the Internet as a backbone and set up a site-to-site VPN called an extranet VPN.

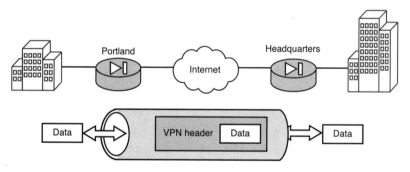

Figure 12.2   A site-to-site VPN.

The PIX firewall can perform all the functions of the previously mentioned categories, including linking site-to-site VPNs and remote user access VPNs. The PIX is capable of interlinking with other PIX firewalls, clients, routers, and even third-party firewalls, to name a few. Figure 12.3 shows various combinations using the PIX firewall.

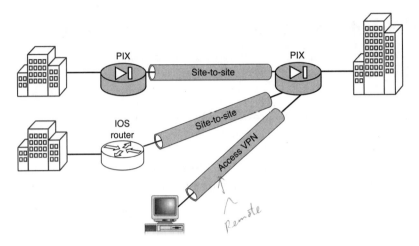

Figure 12.3 Using the PIX for VPNs.

Types of VPNs

The use of the term *VPN* makes it sound like a single thing, when actually it's just a technology with several types and flavors from which to choose. Several VPN types are available, but we will cover only the three main types used with the PIX: PPTP, L2TP, and IPSec.

PPTP

The Point-to-Point Tunneling Protocol (PPTP) VPN solution, primarily created by Microsoft, makes Point-to-Point (PPP) traffic routable. It provides for user authentication and uses Microsoft Point-to-Point Encryption (MPPE) to secure traffic. The PIX firewall supports PPTP for remote access; however, PPTP isn't supported by all vendors.

L2TP

Layer 2 Tunneling Protocol (L2TP) VPNs are an enhancement of the Cisco Layer 2 Forwarder (L2F) mechanism that works only at layer 2 to forward IP, IPX, and AppleTalk traffic. L2TP builds on L2F to make it routable across IP networks. This work was done by a combination of efforts from Cisco, Microsoft, Ascent, and 3Com to form RFC 2661. The L2TP VPN solution doesn't contain any encryption engine built in the way PPTP does. However, L2TP is typically implemented with IPSec to create what is called L2TP over IPSec, making L2TP very secure with the added benefit of user authentication. This tunneling protocol can authenticate on both user and machine levels, giving you more granularity over who can connect. Similar to PPTP, L2TP is typically used for remote access.

IPSec

IPSec VPN is an open standard defining a group of security protocols used together to form a secure connection between two peers. Basically, IPSec is a VPN tunnel that enables you to encrypt traffic or guarantee that it hasn't changed from one peer to another. The PIX firewall supports site-to-site and access VPN traffic with IPSec. Most products on the market that support VPNs also support IPSec for interoperability with other vendors.

Of the three types of VPNs covered here, IPSec is the main focus of this chapter and the following sections.

Defining Hashing, Encryption, and Keys

Before we dive into the deep dark depths of how IPSec VPNs work, let's take a moment to review hashing, encryption, and the keys used for everything throughout.

Hashing

Hashing is not encryption, but actually a result from an algorithm. When data, a key, and an algorithm are combined, a fixed result is generated. This result is a small, fixed-length piece of data, which you could call a fingerprint (message digest or hash) of the data and key. Every time the exact data and key are run through the algorithm, the exact same output value is produced. A modification of even 1 bit in the data or key produces an entirely different fingerprint. For example, if Jack wants to guarantee that his data doesn't change when he sends it to Peter, he could hash the data. After he has the hash result known as a *digital signature*, he can send this along with the data. When Peter receives the data and digital signature, he can use the same data, key, and hashing algorithm to generate a result himself. If this hash result is exactly the same as the signature Jack sent, the data is true and hasn't been modified.

Now for all of this to work, three things are needed: data, a key, and an algorithm. Both sides need all three to come up with the same result. Two algorithms commonly used in IPSec are Message Digest version 5 and Secure Hash Algorithm. Figure 12.4 displays an example of hashing data to get a single hashed value.

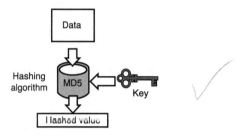

Figure 12.4 Hashing example.

Message Digest Version 5

Message Digest version 5 (MD5) is a hashing algorithm commonly used to authenticate data and ensure that data hasn't changed. It is a one-way hash that produces a fixed-length result called a *message digest*. MD5 feeds successive 512-bit blocks of data into the algorithm to eventually produce a 128-bit message digest.

Secure Hash Algorithm

Secure Hash Algorithm (SHA-1) is the second hashing algorithm that can be used by IPSec. It produces a 160-bit result and is considered more secure than MD5. Because SHA-1 is more secure, it also takes longer to perform its functions.

Encryption

Encryption is the process of taking data, a key, and an encryption algorithm and producing encrypted data known as *cipher text*. If the encrypted data needs to be extracted back to normal, a decryption key and algorithm are necessary. The following sections discuss the two main types of encryption used by IPSec: DES and 3DES.

Data Encryption Standard

Data Encryption Standard (DES) uses a 56-bit symmetric encryption key, meaning the 56-bit key used to encrypt the data is the same key used to decrypt the data. DES was published in 1977 and is considered a fast and reliable encryption engine that is commonly used to provide basic protection or in places outside the United States where the export of stronger encryption is not allowed.

 In 1998, the Electronic Frontier Foundation (EFF) built the first unclassified DES encryption cracker. This system took only three days to crack DES, proving it to be an insecure algorithm. Six months later, the Distributed.Net, a worldwide coalition of computer enthusiasts, networked 100,000 computers together to crack DES in only 22 hours. Needless to say, DES is considered to be unsuitable for highly secure environments. As of this writing, triple DES has not been cracked.

Triple DES

Triple DES (3DES) is a spin-off of DES itself. Basically, 3DES encrypts data, but it does it three times. 3DES iterates through the data three times with three different keys, dramatically increasing the protection level of the data. 3DES uses a 168-bit key and takes more time and processor power to run than normal DES does. Figure 12.5 shows an example of data encryption.

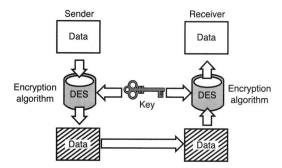

Figure 12.5 An encryption example.

 The Advanced Encryption Standard (AES) is a recent encryption algorithm standard sponsored by the National Institute of Standards and Technology. AES is gaining acceptance and is supported in most newer IPSec implementations in the place of 3DES. AES processing is faster and supports larger key sizes than 3DES does, making it a better choice based on speed and level of protection provided. This book mainly covers DES and 3DES because support for the older algorithms is widely used. See **http://www.nwfusion.com/links/Encyclopedia/A/597.html** for more information about the newer AES algorithm.

Keys

The two technologies, hashing and encryption, both require keys with their algorithms. Keys come in two main types—symmetric and asymmetric. You will see how these keys are used in several ways with different algorithms and technologies, but they all follow the same basic concepts.

Symmetric Keys

The *symmetric* key, also known as a *shared secret* key, is a single key used by both parties involved. This key is typically used to encrypt and decrypt data. For example, if Jack uses a key of x132w to encrypt his data, Peter will need to use the same x132w to decrypt that data. The hardest thing about using symmetric keys is getting the same key to the other side without anyone ever knowing what it is. Lastly, symmetric keys are generally used by very fast systems and are used to encrypt and decrypt bulk amounts of data.

Asymmetric Keys

The *asymmetric* key is actually two keys paired together. One is called the *public* key, and the other is called the *private* key. The public key is given out freely, whereas the private key never leaves the owner. When you encrypt something with the public key, it takes the corresponding private key to decrypt it, or vice versa. For example, if Jack has a copy of Peter's public key and uses that public key to encrypt some data, Peter could use his own matching private key to decrypt that data. Therefore, only Peter could decrypt the data. Asymmetric keys are considered slower and take more processor power; however, they are great for authentication and for use during the authentication phases of communication.

Internet Protocol Security

Internet Protocol Security (IPSec) is not really a protocol, as the name would suggest—it is actually a framework of many protocols and mechanisms working together to produce a secure connection between two peers. The heart of IPSec works at the Network layer of the OSI model. Some of the features this framework provides are as follows:

➤ *Data integrity*—A mechanism used to guarantee that data has not been changed. The MD5 or SHA-1 hashing algorithm is used to produce a message digest of the data that is then cross-checked at the destination for data integrity. IPSec uses the MD5 and SHA-1 hashing algorithms to perform this function.

➤ *Data origin authentication*—Authenticates the source of the data against the peer. For this to work, a data integrity feature is necessary.

➤ *Data confidentiality*—The technical form of saying the data is encrypted, meaning that confidential information is encrypted so no one else can make sense of it. IPSec uses symmetric key encryption algorithms (DES, 3DES, AES) for data confidentiality.

➤ *Anti-replay*—A feature that helps protect against hackers who want to cause harm by sending the same packet data repeatedly. Anti-replay helps guarantee that data is received only once.

IPSec Components

IPSec contains several separate components that all work together to make a secure connection between two peers. This section highlights these components; then we will link them all together to make an IPSec Security Association (SA).

According to this book, Data authentication = Data integrity + Data origin authentication.

Authentication Headers

The authentication header (AH) mode of IPSec provides data authentication and anti-replay protection. Data authentication is also known as data *integrity*, meaning that AH checks to ensure that the data has not been altered. AH also provides data origin authentication to ensure that the data is coming from the correct source. AH doesn't actually encrypt data. Also, if it's used alone, it does not provide data confidentiality. Figure 12.6 shows user data being placed in an AH-protected packet.

provides

AH = Data authentication

Hence

? ?

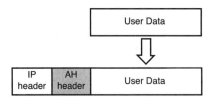

Figure 12.6   An AH example.

graphical representation?

Encapsulation Secure Payload

Encapsulation Secure Payload (ESP) performs what most people need, data confidentiality. ESP also performs data authentication and anti-replay protection. ESP encrypts the whole payload, which contains layer 4 headers and the data. ESP uses protocol port 50 and can either be used with AH or stand alone to provide data confidentiality. Figure 12.7 shows user data being encrypted and protected within ESP.

why?

why need both?

AH, which uses protocol port 51, helps protect against session hijacking, whereas ESP uses protocol port 50 and encrypts the data. Both AH and ESP can be used separately or together. When they are both used, ESP encryption is processed before the AH digest is created. Figure 12.8 shows data being encrypted by ESP and encapsulated by AH.

According to Sybex:
ESP has 4 components: 1. Confidentiality 2. Data origin authentication and connectionless integrity 3. Anti-replay service 4. Traffic flow

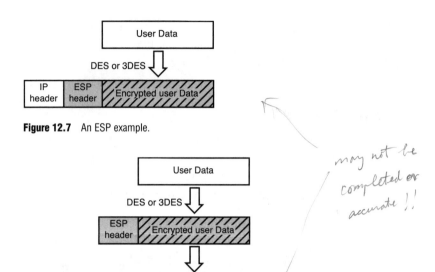

Figure 12.7 An ESP example.

may not be completed or accurate !!

Figure 12.8 ESP encapsulated in an AH.

Internet Key Exchange (IKE)

Internet Key Exchange (IKE) is a hybrid of several other protocols such as ISAKMP and the Oakley and Skeme key exchange. When two computers (peers) connect, they need to exchange policies and keys for hashing and encryption. IKE and ISAKMP perform these functions.

IKE is a hybrid protocol to exchange keys and uses UDP port number 500.

Diffie-Hellman

phase 1

The Diffie-Hellman (D-H) algorithm is actually part of the IKE process to exchange keys safely and securely. D-H uses a pair of asymmetric keys, and each peer's public key is exchanged with the other peer's. These public keys are then combined with the others' private keys to generate an identical symmetric key on both peers. This new shared secret (symmetric) key is used to provide encryption and decryption during the IKE establishment phases. The PIX is capable of using either 768-bit (group 1) or 1024-bit (group 2) D-H groups.

details?

Authentication

When two IPSec peers connect, they need to authenticate before secure data can be transmitted. This authentication can be done in several ways; the following list describes three methods that can be used to authenticate peers:

➤ *Pre-shared keys*—These are hard-coded values that are set on both peers. During authentication, if both values match, authentication succeeds. For example, if Jack codes the word "dog" and Peter also uses the word "dog," this would provide a positive authentication. This is by far the easiest to set up; however, if you had 100 VPN peers and wanted to change the key of "dog" to "cat," you have a lot of work to do.

➤ *RSA encrypted nonces*—This is a time-variant mechanism that uses asymmetric public and private keys that need to be manually created on each peer. Then the public keys must be shared with the peers that will be connecting. When VPN peers connect, each peer uses its own private key to create a digital signature, which is then sent across for authentication. Each peer uses the corresponding shared public key to verify the digital signature. RSA nonces are time-consuming to set up, and if they need to be changed, they take even more time and effort to change than pre-shared keys.

➤ *RSA signatures*—These are very similar to nonces and use asymmetric public and private key pairs. However, the use of a certificate authority (CA) is involved with certificate generation and authentication. During IKE phase 1, peers exchange each other's certificates. Then, they contact the respective CA to validate the received peer's certificate. This process enables you to change a peer's certificate; and all connecting peers don't need to be modified because the new certificate is sent down during the next connection. RSA signatures is a very scalable mechanism when supporting thousands of VPN peers.

 NOTE Diffie-Hellman is susceptible to man-in-the-middle attacks. To mitigate this problem, authentication is used during the D-H key agreement algorithm. The authentication methods used are preshared keys, nonces, and RSA signatures.

Security Association

The security association (SA) is similar to a session between TCP hosts. Whenever two peers make a successful transfer of data using IPSec, an SA is created in the background to maintain the connection. This SA identifies each peer by IP address, security protocols, and a security parameter index (SPI).

dynamically

Security associations can be created using IKE or a manual process. See Cisco for more details about manual security associations.

complicated
M C C

How IPSec Works

Now that we've reviewed hashing, keys, encryption, AH, and ESP, let's put them all together and see how the IPSec framework makes a secure connection between two peers. IPSec is similar to creating a TCP connection that uses a three-way handshake. The peers exchange several parameters to create a security association; then, after the security association has been established, data can be sent in a protected manner. This exchange is comprised of two main phases called phase 1 and phase 2.

Following are some of the steps needed to create an IPSec security association between two peers:

1. Connect to a peer.

2. IKE phase 1 starts, which involves the following:

   different from syblex's description

   2a. IKE exchange polices *i.e. ISAKMP policies*

   2b. Diffie-Hellman key agreements are set *? exact meaning ? !!*

   2c. Authentication

3. IKE phase 2 starts (this is the IPSec phase), causing the following actions:

   3a. Crypto maps are exchanged.

   3b. The SA lifetime is established.

4. When data that matches the crypto ACL is sent, it is protected.

To prepare you, phase 1 and phase 2 are where most of your parameters need to be configured between two peers. If they match, a successful security association can be made.

Phase 1 *complicated*

IKE controls phase 1 to create a management connection between the two peers. The management connection exchanges ISAKMP policies, keys, and authentication information. ISAKMP polices are negotiated parameter sets that each peer uses to communicate. Some of the parameters inside an ISAKMP policy include

➤ The encryption algorithm used is DES or 3DES.   *AES ?*

➤ The hashing algorithm used is MD5 or SHA-1.

➤ The Diffie-Hellman group used is group 1 or group 2. *see p. 278.*

➤ The authentication used is pre-shared keys, RSA nonces, or RSA signature with CAs.

➤ The lifetime of the management connection.

Peers can contain multiple policies; as peers connect, they iterate through the policies until a matching set is found on both sides. For example, say Jack's policy uses DES and MD5 and Peter's policy uses 3DES and MD5. Because these polices don't match, Jack and Peter will not be able to connect. However, if Peter's policy contains a second policy that matches Jack's, this phase will succeed and they can move on to the next step.

Phase 1 also uses Diffie-Hellman to generate symmetric keys for encryption or hashing. Finally, the authentication is completed between the two peers. When all this is completed, enough information exists to make a secure connection to send IPSec parameters in phase 2.

Phase 1 has two modes of operation: main and aggressive. Main mode takes three exchanges to complete and hides the peer's identity. Aggressive mode takes only two exchanges, making it faster, or more aggressive as it were. However, aggressive mode doesn't hide the peer's identity.

Phase 2   *complicated*

After phase 1 is completed, IKE starts phase 2. Phase 2 creates a user connection that negotiates IPSec parameters such as the transform sets. Transform sets are the modes or methods the two peers use to protect user data—for instance, AH, ESP, or both. Phase 2 also negotiates the encryption key, hash keys, and lifetime of how long the keys are valid before regeneration is necessary. When all these processes are complete, an SA is formed. The parameters contained on a crypto map that are sent between peers are as follows:

➤ The security protocol is AH, ESP, or both.   *: difference ?*

➤ The encryption algorithm for ESP is DES or 3DES.   *AES ?*

➤ The authentication method is AH, ESP, or both.

➤ The authentication hashing algorithm is MD5 or SHA-1.

➤ The ~~ESP mode~~ *transform set* is tunnel or transport. *mode*

➤ The lifetime *of the keys* is time in seconds, amount of data transmitted, or both.

After phase 2 is complete, peers start to send data securely. Figure 12.9 displays phase 1 and phase 2 checking for matching parameters before creating a security association and sending data.

Phase 2 has only one mode, which is called quick mode. Because it's already using a secure connection, phase 2 only needs to send parameters.

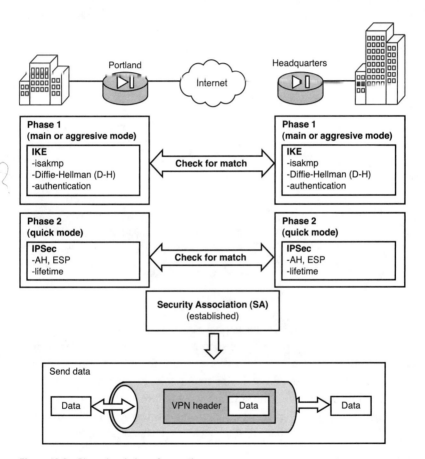

Figure 12.9 Phase 1 and phase 2 example.

Configuring an IPSec Site-to-Site Connection

Next, let's discuss configuring IPSec on a PIX firewall. This example shows you how to configure a site-to-site VPN using pre-shared keys. The four main tasks you perform when setting up the VPN connection are *(for site-to-site VPN)*

➤ *Preparing for IPSec*—Involves gathering IPSec parameter details.

➤ *Configure IKE*—Phase 1 parameters are configured.

➤ *Configure IPSec*—Phase 2 parameters are configured.

➤ *Testing and troubleshooting*—This is when configuration and current security associations are displayed.

The following sections discuss each task in detail.

Preparing for IPSec

In any implementation of IPSec, the preparation phase is a key element of a successful installation. This task enables you to document and plan all the settings that will be needed to configure IPSec. If any policies or transform sets don't match, your IPSec connection can fail. The steps needed to complete this task include the following:

1. Define the IKE phase 1 policies between peers. *peer IP address n hostnames*

2. Define the IKE phase 2 policies, transform sets, peer IP address or hostnames, and lifetime settings.

3. Verify the current PIX configuration for any previous access control list (ACL), ISAKMP policies, or crypto maps that might conflict with the new settings.

4. Perform a basic ping test to ensure you can actually reach the other peer before attempting to create a VPN.

5. Verify that perimeter routers will allow IPSec traffic using protocol 50, 51, and IKE UDP port 500 to pass through.

Your goal is to configure a site-to-site VPN from the Portland firewall to the Salem firewall. All traffic from the internal Portland LAN 192.168.1.0/24 will be protected by the VPN tunnel only if it's traveling to the Salem LAN of 10.0.0.0/8. Figure 12.10 shows an overview of the phase 1 settings. Note that these are just the parameters needed in phase 1 and loosely related to the actual commands you will use later to configure this phase.

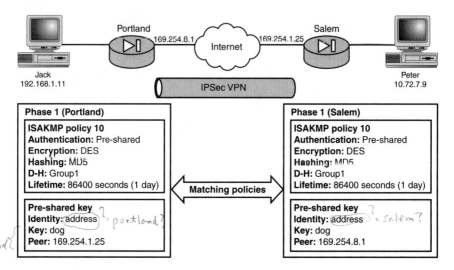

Figure 12.10 Phase 1 settings.

Figure 12.11 shows the phase 2 information for creating a crypto map called MapPtoS. The crypto map is a composite of access lists, global lifetimes, transform sets, and peers that are allowed to create a secure VPN connection. As you can see in Figure 12.11, the crypto maps take information for other areas and join them together. You'll use the actual command to create this in the step that configures IPSec.

Both of the diagrams in Figures 12.10 and 12.11 are referenced again in the following sections. They are basically your map to constructing a VPN between Portland and Salem.

Configuring IKE   *phase 1*

Now that you have prepared your firewall in the previous step, let's now begin the configuration stage. The basic steps to configuring IKE, which is also known by the CLI as ISAKMP, are as follows:

1. Enable IKE/ISAKMP.

2. Create an ISAKMP policy.

3. Configure the pre-shared key.

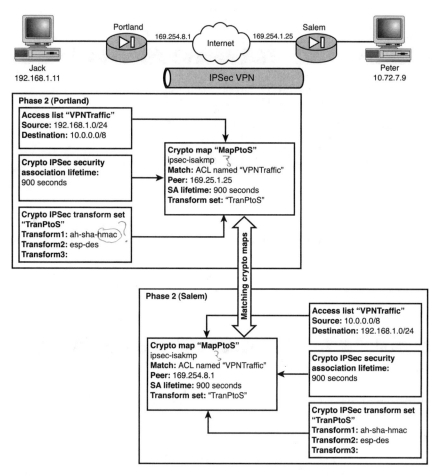

Figure 12.11 Phase 2 settings.

The commands needed to configure these steps are shown in Listings 12.1–12.3 and are described in the following sections. The command sequence you will need to configure your IKE configuration, as per Figure 12.6, is shown in Listing 12.1.

Listing 12.1   Portland Firewall

```
portland(config)# isakmp enable outside         (additional step as shown in fig 12.10)
portland(config)# isakmp policy 10 authentication pre-share
portland(config)# isakmp policy 10 encryption des
portland(config)# isakmp policy 10 hash md5
portland(config)# isakmp policy 10 group 1
portland(config)# isakmp policy 10 lifetime 86400
portland(config)# isakmp identity address
portland(config)# isakmp key dog address 169.254.1.25
                netmask 255.255.255.255
```

see p.287 for syntax

Salem's side

Listing 12.2 displays the Salem firewall settings for its ISAKMP policy.

Listing 12.2   Salem Firewall

```
salem(config)# isakmp enable outside
salem(config)# isakmp policy 10 authentication pre-share
salem(config)# isakmp policy 10 encryption des
salem(config)# isakmp policy 10 hash md5
salem(config)# isakmp policy 10 group 1
salem(config)# isakmp policy 10 lifetime 86400
salem(config)# isakmp identity address
salem(config)# isakmp key dog address 169.254.8.1 netmask 255.255.255.255
```

The isakmp enable Command

The first and most basic step is to enable IKE/ISAKMP. IKE can be enabled for all interfaces or on a per-interface basis. The command syntax is shown here:

```
pixfirewall(config)# isakmp enable <if_name>
```

Table 12.1 displays the isakmp enable options.

Table 12.1   isakmp enable Options

Option	Function
if_name	This enables you to specify which interfaces have ISAKMP enabled.

The isakmp policy Command

The isakmp policy command enables you to define a group of settings under one priority number. You can create several policies on the PIX firewall if needed; you simply give each group of settings a different priority number. When two peers connect, the lowest policy priority numbers are tried first. So, make your most desired policy the smallest number. The syntax of the isakmp policy command is shown in Listing 12.3.

Listing 12.3   The isakmp policy Command

```
pixfirewall(config)# isakmp policy <priority> authen <pre-share¦rsa-sig>
pixfirewall(config)# isakmp policy <priority> encrypt <des¦3des>
pixfirewall(config)# isakmp policy <priority> hash <md5¦sha>
pixfirewall(config)# isakmp policy <priority> group <1¦2>
pixfirewall(config)# isakmp policy <priority> lifetime <seconds>
```

Table 12.2 displays the available options for the isakmp policy command.

Q: Do both peers need to have same priority number to connect?

A:

Table 12.2	isakmp policy Options
Option	**Function**
priority	This uniquely identifies IKE policy settings to a single group/priority number. You can use numbers between 1 and 65,534.
authen	This defines where to use pre-shared keys or RSA signatures.
encrypt	This defines which encryption algorithm to use in the IKE policy (DES or 3DES).
hash	This defines which hashing algorithm should be used in the IKE policy (MD5 or SHA-1).
group	This defines which Diffie-Hellman group to use: group1 or group2.
lifetime	This specifies how many seconds each SA should exist before new keys are generated. Values are read in seconds and can be between 60 and 86,400 seconds (1 day).

The isakmp identity Command

When IKE does pre-shared authentication, it needs to associate a preshared key with an identity. The peers can identify themselves with either an IP address or a hostname. IP addresses work best in most cases; however, if your peer's address changes often, you should use a hostname instead. The command syntax is as follows:

```
pixfirewall(config)# isakmp identity <address¦hostname>
```

Keyword

from Cisco web site

As a general rule, set the PIX firewall and its peer's identities in the same way to avoid an IKE negotiation failure.

Table 12.3 displays the isakmp identity options available.

Table 12.3	isakmp identity Options
Option	**Function**
address	Indicates that the identity being used is an IP address
hostname	Indicates that the identity being used is a hostname

Q: When and how to use the hostname option?

The isakmp key Command

The isakmp key command creates a pre-shared key and links it to a specific identity. You can have different pre-shared keys per peer if you want by just adding them. If the key is "dog" on one side, it has to be "dog" on the other side because authentication will fail otherwise. The command syntax is shown here:

```
isakmp key <key-string> address <ip> [netmask <mask>]
```

Table 12.4 displays the `isakmp key` options.

Table 12.4	isakmp key Options
Option	**Function**
key-string	Specifies the pre-shared key used with an identity. It must match on both ends. The **key-string** can be up to 128 characters.
ip	Specifies the remote peer's IP address.
netmask	Specifies the remote peer's subnet mask.

Configuring IPSec *Phase 2*

Now that the management connection parameters are set (phase 1), you are ready to set phase 2 parameters. Phase 2 requires several settings combined to create a *crypto map*. This map, as shown in Figure 12.7, uses an ACL named "VPNTraffic", global SA lifetime settings (optional), and a transform set named "TranPtoS". These settings are bundled together and attached to an interface. When the two peers negotiate phase 2, they integrate through crypto maps looking for a matching set on both sides. If no match is found, IPSec communication fails. If a match is found, an SA is created and all traffic that matched the ACL in the crypto map is forwarded through the tunnel. The following is an overview of the required tasks:

1. Enable IPSec to enter the firewall.

2. Create a crypto access list. *access list name referenced by crypto map command*

3. Set the global SA lifetime.

4. Create a transform set. *transform set name referenced by crypto map command.*

5. Create a crypto map. *see p. 292*

6. Attach the crypto map to an interface. *see p. 293*

7. Enable traffic without being NAT translated.

The commands needed to configure Figure 12.11 are shown in Listing 12.4 and Listing 12.5.

Listing 12.4   Portland Firewall Crypto Map Settings

```
portland(config)# sysopt connection permit-ipsec        ①
portland(config)#
portland(config)# access-list VPNTraffic permit ip 192.168.1.0        ②
                255.255.255.0 10.0.0.0 255.0.0.0
portland(config)# crypto ipsec security-association lifetime seconds   ③
                28800 kilobytes 4608000
portland(config)# crypto ipsec transform-set TranPtoS ah-sha-hmac esp-des  ④
portland(config)# crypto map MapPtoS 20 ipsec-isakmp
```

need for error default

default

by default, I think? ⑤

Listing 12.4   Portland Firewall Crypto Map Settings *(continued)*

```
portland(config)# crypto map MapPtoS 20 match address VPNTraffic
portland(config)# crypto map MapPtoS 20 set peer 169.254.1.25
portland(config)# crypto map MapPtoS 20 set transform-set TranPtoS
portland(config)# crypto map MapPtoS interface outside
portland(config)# access-list NONAT permit IP 192.168.1.0
                255.255.255.0 10.0.0.0 255.0.0.0
portland(config)# nat (inside) 0 access-list NONAT
```

Listing 12.5   Salem Firewall Crypto Map Settings

```
salem(config)# sysopt connection permit-ipsec
salem(config)#
salem(config)# access-list VPNTraffic permit ip 10.0.0.0 255.0.0.0
                192.168.1.0 255.255.255.0
salem(config)# crypto ipsec security-association lifetime seconds
                28800 kilobytes 4608000
salem(config)# crypto ipsec transform-set TranPtoS ah-sha-hmac esp-des
salem(config)# crypto map MapPtoS 20 ipsec-isakmp
salem(config)# crypto map MapPtoS 20 match address VPNTraffic
salem(config)# crypto map MapPtoS 20 set peer 169.254.8.1
salem(config)# crypto map MapPtoS 20 set transform-set TranPtoS
salem(config)# crypto map MapPtoS interface outside
salem(config)# access-list NONAT permit IP 10.0.0.0 255.0.0.0
                192.168.1.0 255.255.255.0
salem(config)# nat (inside) 0 access-list NONAT
```

The sysopt connection permit-ipsec Command

To allow IPSec traffic into the firewall, you need to either create several ACL
entries permitting protocols 50–51 and port 500 (IKE) or use the sysopt command. The ACL option enables you to be granular in specifying which interface will allow IPSec traffic in. However, the sysopt connection permit-ipsec
command is easier to implement and allows IPSec and L2TP protocol connections on all interfaces. The command syntax is

```
pixfirewall(config)# sysopt connection permit-ipsec
```

The crypto access-list Command

Crypto ACL defines which IP traffic should or shouldn't be forwarded
through the tunnel. The crypto access-list command looks exactly like any
other access list but performs in a slightly different way. If traffic matches the
permit statement in the ACL, it's forwarded and protected by the tunnel.
Conversely, if the traffic doesn't match or is denied, the traffic is not dropped
but is allowed to travel outside the tunnel. Here is an example:

```
portland(config)# access-list VPNTraffic permit ip 192.168.1.0
                255.255.255.0 10.0.0.0 255.0.0.0
```

This access list states that any source traffic from 192.168.1.0/24 going to
destination 10.0.0.0/8 is permitted. Therefore, it is protected by the tunnel.

Note that the only difference between this and other ACLs is that it's used in the `crypto map` command's `match` parameter, making it a crypto ACL.

The `crypto ipsec security-association lifetime` Command

This command is used to set a global SA lifetime value for all crypto maps created. The lifetime value is used to define for how long hash and encryption keys are valid. When the lifetime is up, IPSec and IKE generate new keys. Although this is a global command, it can be overridden with a similar command within the `crypto map` commands. The following is the command syntax: *p.292 ✳*

```
pixfirewall(config)# crypto ipsec security-association lifetime seconds
            28800 kilobytes 4608000
```

Table 12.5 displays the command options for the `crypto   ipsec security-association` command.

Table 12.5	security-association lifetime Options
Option	**Function**
seconds	This defines the amount of time in seconds for which keys are valid. The default is 28,800 seconds (8 hours).
kilobytes	This defines the amount of data that can pass before the keys are regenerated. The default is 4,608,000KB (10Mbps).

 If two peers have different security association values, the lowest value is used. Also, to manually clear all current security associations, the **clear ipsec sa** command can be used.

The `transform-set` Command

Transform sets define how user data is protected with AH, ESP, or both. A set can contain a maximum of three transforms: one AH for authentication, one ESP for encryption, and one ESP authentication. The `transform-set` command also defines which mode to use—tunnel or transport mode. The command syntax is as follows:

```
pixfirewall(config)# crypto ipsec transform-set <trans-name> [ transform1 ]
            [ transform2 ] [ transform3 ]
pixfirewall(config)# crypto ipsec transform-set <trans-name> mode transport
```

[no] ⇒ tunnel mode (default)

Table 12.6 displays the command options for the `crypto ipsec transform-set` command.

Table 12.6	transform-set Options
Option	**Function**
trans-name	Defines the name of the transform set.
transform1	The first transform (see Table 12.7).
transform2	The second optional transform (see Table 12.7).
transform3	The third optional transform (see Table 12.7).
mode transport	Sets the transform set to transport mode. To make the set tunnel mode, just use the **[no]** option to turn off transport mode. By default, the mode transport is tunnel mode.

ESP authentication

Table 12.7 displays the possible transforms and their uses. *Q: what does hmac stand for?*

AH authentication

Table 12.7	Transform Options
Transform	**Description**
Ah-md5-hmac	Used for authentication
Ah-sha-hmac	Used for stronger authentication
Esp-md5-hmac	Used with ESP-DES or ESP-3DES for additional integrity
Esp-sha-hmac	Used with ESP-DES or ESP-3DES for additional integrity
Esp-des	Used to encrypt with DES (56 bit)
Esp-3des	Used to encrypt with 3DES (168 bit)

Q: what are all possible combinations?

ESP encryption

A: see Cisco press p.510

Following are two examples of using the `transform-set` command:

```
pixfirewall(config)# crypto ipsec transform-set TranData ah-sha-hmac
```

This example shows a transform set named TranData being created with two transforms, using AH with SHA-1 and no encryption.

Here's the second example:

```
pixfirewall(config)# crypto ipsec transform-set
        TranData2 ah-sha-hmac esp-des
```

possible combination !!

transform1   transform2

This example shows a transform set named TranData2 being created with two transforms, using AH with SHA-1 and ESP with DES encryption.

The **crypto ipsec transform-set** command can have only three transforms.

The crypto map Command

crypto map is the command that brings everything together for phase 2. Access lists, lifetimes, transform sets, and peers are all bundled together and given a name and sequence number in a crypto map. Then the map is attached to an interface or multiple interfaces. However, an interface can have only one crypto map assigned to it. Some of the functions the crypto map command performs are listed here:

> *[handwritten: Defines whether the IPSec SA is defined by IKE or (manually) meaning?]*

> Defines what traffic is to be protected by IPSec (crypto acl and match command)

> Designates where the protected traffic should be sent (the remote peer)

> Determines how traffic should be protected (transform set)

> Sets the IPSec security association lifetime (lifetime)

> Specifies the local interface to use for IPSec traffic *[handwritten: for what?]*

crypto map commands contain a sequence number that enables you to create multiple entries in a map, which are then iterated from lowest sequence number to highest. Listing 12.6 displays the crypto map commands.

Listing 12.6 crypto map Commands

```
pixfirewall(config)# crypto map <name> <seq_num> ipsec-isakmp¦ipsec-manual
pixfirewall(config)# crypto map <name> <seq_num>
                match address <access_list>
pixfirewall(config)# crypto map <name> <seq_num> set peer <IP_address>
pixfirewall(config)# crypto map <name> <seq_num>
                set transform-set <tran_name>
pixfirewall(config)# crypto map <name> <seq_num> set pfs [group1¦group2]
pixfirewall(config)# crypto map <name> <seq_num>
                set security-association lifetime
```

Table 12.8 displays the command options for the crypto map command.

Table 12.8 crypto map Command Options

Option	Function
name	This is the name of the crypto map you are creating.
seq_num	This is the sequence number of the option you are defining. The lowest number is tried first.
ipsec-isakmp I ipsec-manual	These define whether the IPSec SA is defined by IKE (isakmp) or manually (manual).
match address access_list	This specifies which addresses or crypto ACL address should be protected by the tunnel.

Table 12.8 crypto map Command Options *(continued)*	
Option	**Function**
peer <ip_address>	This defines the remote peer with which you generating an IPSec tunnel.
tran_name	This defines the transform set to use with the crypt map.
security-association lifetime	This specifies the lifetime for which the keys are valid, and it overrides the global command **crypto ipsec security-association lifetime.**

The crypto map interface Command

Now that you have created a crypto map for all your phase 2 IPSec parameters, you need to attach the map to an interface. The crypto map interface command can be used to accomplish this, and its syntax is as follows:

```
pixfirewall(config)# crypto map <name> interface <if_name>
```

Table 12.9 displays the options for the crypto map inteface command.

Table 12.9 crypto map interface Options	
Option	**Function**
name	This is the name of the crypto map you want to attach.
if_name	Is the name of the interface to which the crypto map is attached.

An interface can have only one crypto map assigned to it, but a crypto map can be used on several interfaces.

The nat 0 Command

Finally, the last command needed is the nat 0 command. This command enables traffic from the Portland internal site to travel to the Salem internal site without being NAT translated. The command shown here repeats what is shown in the original commands for the Portland configuration:

```
portland(config)# Access-list NONAT permit IP 192.168.1.0 255.255.255.0
               10.0.0.0 255.0.0.0
portland(config)# Nat (inside) 0 access-list NONAT
```

Testing and Troubleshooting IPSec

After IPSec has been up, the last task is to verify and monitor the connection and parameters. Table 12.10 displays a list of show commands used to verify configuration settings. Table 12.11 displays a list of show, clear, and debug commands used to monitor or clear IPSec settings.

Table 12.10 show Configuration Commands	
Command	Description
show isakmp	This displays the ISAKMP policy settings, similar to the **show running config** or **write terminal** command.
show isakmp policy	This displays the default and any other policies created.
show crypt map	This displays the crypto maps created.
show crypto ipsec transform-set	This displays the configured transform sets.
show crypt ipsec security-association lifetime	This displays the global IPSec SA lifetime values.

Table 12.11 displays a list of show, clear, and debug commands used to monitor or clear IPSec settings.

Table 12.11 show, clear, and debug IPSec Commands	
Command	Description
show isakmp sa	This displays a list of current statuses of IKE security associations.
show crypto ipsec sa	This displays very detailed information about crypto maps assigned to interfaces and traffic flowing across the maps.
clear crypto isakmp	This clears or resets the IKE security associations.
clear crypto ipsec sa	This clears or resets the IPSec security associations.
debug crypto isakmp	This command enables the debug feature of IKE communication between peers.
debug crypto ipsec	This command enables the debug feature between IPSec peers.

When a PIX firewall is configured to support a VPN tunnel, the VPN tunnel is not created until traffic needs to flow through it, which is similar to interesting traffic on a dial-on demand interface, in which the system does not dial until traffic actually needs to traverse across the line. In addition, several of the PIX firewalls contain VPN lights on their fronts, which show the status of a positive tunnel that has been created.

Configuring Remote Access Client VPNs

Remote access enables clients to access internal networks via VPN connections to the PIX firewall. You can use the Cisco VPN client software or even use Microsoft's VPN PPTP client to connect the PIX firewall.

When clients connect to the firewall, they must authenticate, and this can be done either locally or via a AAA server. After a client is authenticated, the firewall hands out an IP address, similar to a DHCP server issuing an IP address to the client. This address range is assigned using the `ip local pool` command. Additionally, the PPTP VPN tunnel parameters are set up using the `vpdn` command. This section briefly covers how to allow PPTP clients VPN access into the PIX firewall. Figure 12.12 displays a PPTP VPN client example.

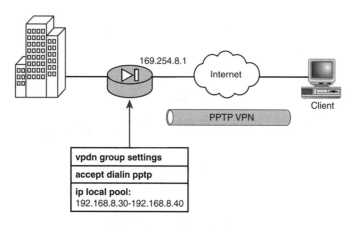

Figure 12.12   PPTP client example.

The following is a simple list of tasks you must perform:

➤ Allow PPTP traffic to enter the PIX.

➤ Create an IP address pool.

➤ Configure the VPDN group. ← a couple of steps

▷ Enable PPTP on the associated interface.

➤ Configure the usernames and passwords.

The commands in Listing 12.7 enable users to access the PIX firewall.

user defined

Listing 12.7 Remote Access Using PPTP

```
pixfirewall(config)# sysopt connection permit-pptp
pixfirewall(config)# ip local pool pptp-pool 192.168.8.30-192.168.8.40
pixfirewall(config)# vpdn group 1 accept dialin pptp
pixfirewall(config)# vpdn group 1 ppp authentication mschap
pixfirewall(config)# vpdn group 1 ppp encryption mppe 40
pixfirewall(config)# vpdn group 1 client configuration
                address local pptp-pool
pixfirewall(config)# vpdn group 1 client configuration dns 194.72.6.57
pixfirewall(config)# vpdn group 1 pptp echo 60
pixfirewall(config)# vpdn group 1 client authentication local
pixfirewall(config)# vpdn enable outside
pixfirewall(config)# vpdn username dnewman password 1234
```

The **sysopt connection permit-pptp** Command

One method of allowing PPTP traffic into the PIX firewall is to use a command similar to the one you used for IPSec. The sysopt connection permit-pptp allows PPTP traffic to bypass conduits and ACLs, thus allowing VPN connections into the PIX firewall.

The **ip local pool** Command

The ip local pool command enables you to create a pool of local addresses that are dynamically assigned to remote VPN clients. The following example creates a pool named pptp-pool that will allocate addresses from 192.168.8.30 to 192.168.8.40 for remote VPN clients:

```
pixfirewall(config)# ip local pool pptp-pool 192.168.8.30-192.168.8.40
```

The **ip local pool** command is used for remote access VPN clients.

The **vpdn group** Command

The vpdn group command is used to configure and enable L2TP and PPTP remote access VPNs. Table 12.11 describes several options of the vpdn group command for a PPTP connection. Listing 12.8 displays the vpdn group commands needed to set and configure a PIX firewall for PPTP remote access.

Listing 12.8   vpdn group Commands Needed for PPTP Remote Access

```
pixfirewall(config)# vpdn group 1 accept dialin pptp
pixfirewall(config)# vpdn group 1 ppp authentication mschap
pixfirewall(config)# vpdn group 1 ppp encryption mppe 40
pixfirewall(config)# vpdn group 1 client configuration
                address local pptp-pool
pixfirewall(config)# vpdn group 1 client configuration dns 194.72.6.57
pixfirewall(config)# vpdn group 1 pptp echo 60
pixfirewall(config)# vpdn group 1 client authentication local
pixfirewall(config)# vpdn enable outside
```

Table 12.11   vpdn group Options

Command	Description
accept dialin	This defines either L2TP or PPTP as a VPN protocol.
ppp authentication	This specifies the Point-to-Point authentications. The PIX supports PAP, CHAP, and MSCHAP.
ppp encryption _mppe_	This defines the allowable Microsoft Point-to-Point Encryption. The two types are 40 bit and 128 bit. _auto — to accommodate both_
client configuration address local	Specifies the local IP address pool for the VPDN group to use for remote clients.
client configuration dns	This specifies the DNS server IP address to hand out to VPN clients.
pptp echo	This specifies the keep-alive timeout value used to keep the VPN tunnel alive.
client authentication local	This specifies where the PIX firewall authentication will occur. AAA services and local databases can be used.
enable outside	This enables PPTP on a single interface.

The **vpdn username password** Command

The vpdn username password command enables you to create a local list of usernames and passwords for VPDN clients. The command shown here creates a user who can log in using a VPDN group:

```
pixfirewall(config)# vpdn username dnewman password 1234
```

Scaling VPN Tunnels   _MCC_

Using pre-shared keys works fine in small VPN environments such as the site-to-site configuration. Larger environments connecting several or even hundreds of VPN tunnels use certificate authorities to provide a more scalable solution than pre-shared keys.

When using CAs, each PIX generates its own public and private key pair. The private key stays privately secured on the PIX, whereas the public key eventually is used to create a digital certificate that is utilized during IKE phase 1 to perform authentication. The certificates are validated against the CA before authentication can succeed. This alleviates the need to manually reconfigure all the systems when the keys change, as in the case when using pre-shared keys. The four basic steps needed to configure CAs are as follows:

1. Generate RSA key pairs on the PIX.

difference? 2. Obtain the CA's certificate.

command? 3. Request a signed certificate from the CA with the RSA public key generated on the PIX.

command? 4. The CA verifies the request and sends the signed certificate back to be installed on the PIX.

Table 12.12 contains a general list of commands used in this process.

Table 12.12 ca Commands

Command	Description
ca generate rsa	This generates RSA key pairs, public keys, and private keys. The public key is sent to the CA.
show ca mypubkey rsa	This displays the public key generated.
ca identity <ca_name>	This command creates a name that identifies the IP address for the CA.
ca configure <ca_name>	This configures the CA identity parameters.
ca authenticate <ca_name>	This obtains the CA's certificate.
show ca certificate	This is used to view the CA's certificate.
ca enroll <ca_name>	This enrolls or sends a request to a CA for a certificate.
ca save all	This saves the certificates.

Details?

Exam Prep Questions

Question 1

> When using IPSec, AH and ESP can be used at the same time.
> - A. True
> - B. False

Answer A is correct. IPSec can be implemented with AH, ESP, or both AH and ESP enabled at the same time. Using both AH and ESP provides data confidentiality and header integrity. Therefore, answer B is incorrect.

Question 2

> How many transformations can you have in a transform set?
> - A. 1
> - B. 2
> - C. 3
> - D. 4

Answer C is correct. The `transform-set` command enables you to create a named set of transforms. The command supports up to three transforms: one AH, one ESP for authentication, and one for ESP data confidentiality. Therefore, answers A, B, and D are incorrect.

Question 3

> Which command enables you to give VPN clients addresses?
> - A. **ip dhcp pool**
> - B. **access-list**
> - C. **ip local pool**
> - D. **vpdn group pool**

Answer C is correct. The `ip local pool` command enables you to create a pool of addresses for VPN remote access clients. The `vpdn group` command can reference the IP local pool to issue IP addresses for connecting VPN clients. Answer A is an invalid command and is therefore incorrect. Answer B is used to create access lists but these are not used to hand out client addresses, so it is incorrect. The command in answer D, vpdn group pool, does not exist and is therefore incorrect.

Question 4   ✓ *read explanation*

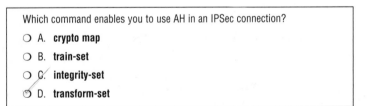

> What is the hybrid protocol used to exchange keys?
> ○ A. IPSec
> ◉ B. IKE
> ○ C. AH
> ○ D. DES

Answer B is correct. IKE stands for the Internet Key Exchange protocol. This hybrid protocol contains several other protocols that are used to create and establish a secure connection before passing IPSec parameters. Answer A is incorrect because IPSec is created after the key exchanges take place by IKE. Answer C is incorrect because AH is a method involving authentication headers that IPSec uses to guarantee data integrity. Answer D is incorrect because DES is an encryption algorithm and doesn't exchange keys.

Question 5

> Which command enables you to use AH in an IPSec connection?
> ○ A. **crypto map**
> ○ B. **train-set**
> ○ C. **integrity-set**
> ◉ D. **transform-set**

Answer D is correct. The transform-set command enables you to select up to a maximum of three transforms, one of which can be AH. This is later referenced inside a crypto map command. Answer A is incorrect because, although crypto map enables you to select a possible transform set that contains an AH setting, the transform-set command is the actual command used to specify AH. Answers B and C are invalid commands and are therefore incorrect.

Question 6

> To which interfaces should the **crypto map** command be applied?
>
> ○ A. Only the inside interface
> ○ B. Every interface
> ○ C. Only the outside interface
> ☑ D. Only to interfaces that have IPSec packets traversing them

Answer D is correct. The `crypto map` command should be applied to only the interfaces that IPSec packets will traverse. Answer A is incorrect because `crypto map` can be applied to more than just the inside interface. Answer B is incorrect because you should apply `crypto map` only to interfaces that have IPSec traveling across them. Answer C is incorrect because you need crypto maps on all interfaces that IPSec packets will traverse, not just the outside interface.

Question 7   *contradicts with A in p277!!*

> What does data authentication do? (Select two.)
>
> ☑ A. Data origin authentication
> ☐ B. Data confidentiality
> ☐ C. Data replay
> ☑ D. Data integrity

Answers A and D are correct. Data authentication is the ability to support data origin authentication and data integrity. This gives you the ability to authenticate the source of the IPSec packet. It does not, however, provide data confidentiality, which involves the encryption of user data. Therefore, answer B is incorrect. Answer C is incorrect because it does not provide data replay functionality.

Question 8

> Which security association lifetime timeout is used if two IPSec peers have different values?
>
> ○ A. The lowest one is used.
> ○ B. The difference between them is used.
> ○ C. The highest one is used.
> ○ D. The connection fails.

Answer A is correct. When two peers negotiate the security association lifetime value, the lowest value between the clients is used. Answers B and C are incorrect because the lowest value is used. Answer D is incorrect because the connection does not fail; the lowest value is used.

Question 9

> To delete all IPSec security associations, which command could you use?
>
> ○ A. **reset sa**
> ○ B. **reload security association**
> ○ C. **clear sa**
> ○ D. **clear ipsec sa**

Answer D is correct. The `clear ipsec sa` command is used to delete or clear all current security associations. Answers A, B, and C are all invalid commands.

Question 10

> When two IPSec peers connect, which transform set is selected if multiple sets are found?
>
> ○ A. The most secure one
> ○ B. The last one
> ○ C. The least secure one
> ○ D. The first one

Answer D is correct. When multiple transform sets are configured, the first matching transform set is used. The crypto map is used to create the order. Therefore, answers A, B, and C are incorrect. *The lowest sequence number is tried first?*

Question 11 *read answer key*

> In what way can security associations be established? (Select two.)
>
> ☑ A. IKE
> ☐ B. IPSec
> ☑ C. Manual
> ☐ D. Static

Answers A and C are correct. Security associations between two peers can be established dynamically using IKE or manually. Answer B is incorrect because IPSec does not actually create the SA; IKE does. Answer D is incorrect because static might be considered valid, but manual is more correct.

Question 12○ *Need answer key*

What does IKE provide? (Select three.)

❑ A. Peer authentication *— exact meaning ?*
❑ B. Security association negotiations
❑ C. User data encryption
❑ D. Key establishment

Not fully understood

Answers A, B, and D are correct. IKE provides a secure connection to exchange keys, authentication, and security associations between two peers. IKE has two main modes—main and aggressive—that are used to help exchange keys. Answer C is incorrect because IKE establishes an SA, whereas IPSec and ESP encrypt user data.

Question 13 ○ *Need answer key*

What does IPSec AH provide? (Select two.)

❑ A. Anti-replay protection
❑ B. User data encryption
❑ C. Data authentication
❑ D. IKE peer authentication

Answers A and C are correct. Authentication headers provide anti-replay protection and data authentication. Answer B is incorrect because user data is encrypted only when ESP is used. Answer D is incorrect because AH does not provide IKE; IKE authenticates peers and helps create an SA so IPSec AHs can be created.

Question 14

> IPSec provides security at which OSI layer?
>
> ○ A. 1
> ○ B. 2
> ○ C. 3
> ○ D. 7

Answer C is correct. IPSec provides protection at layer 3. If AH is used, all data from layer 3 and above is protected. If ESP is used, all information above layer 3 is encrypted. Answer A is incorrect because layer 1 is the physical layer and the data has already been encrypted by this point. Answer B in incorrect because the data has already been encrypted by this time. Answer D is incorrect because layer 7 is the Application layer and IPSec does not work at this level.

Need to Know More?

 Chapman, David and Andy Fox. *Cisco Secure PIX Firewalls.* Indianapolis, IN: Cisco Press, 2002.

 See the Cisco PIX Firewall Command Reference, Version 6.2 at http://www.cisco.com/univercd/cc/td/doc/product/iaabu/pix/pix_sw/ v_62/cmdref/index.htm.

PIX Device Manager

Terms you'll need to understand:

✓ PDM
✓ Unsupported commands
✓ Access Rules tab
✓ Translation Rules tab
✓ VPN tab
✓ Host/Network tab
✓ System Properties tab
✓ Monitoring tab

Techniques you'll need to master:

✓ Knowing which operating systems are supported
✓ Locating mroute
✓ Locating VPN settings
✓ Using the Startup Wizard
✓ Locating Java and ActiveX filters

Up to this point, you have been using the command-line interface to make changes and view information about the PIX firewall. The PIX Device Manager (PDM) is Cisco's Web-based interface, and it enables a graphical user interface (GUI) to configure the PIX via HTTPS. The interface enables you to view, configure, and monitor PIX functions and settings. This chapter covers system requirements and installation and an overview of the PDM interface.

PDM - single firewall
CSPM - multiple security
system at the
same time

PIX PDM Requirements

The PDM is just one of several GUI interface tools used to configure and monitor the PIX firewall. PDM is a Java Web-based interface that enables configuration of your firewall via a secure HTTPS connection. The tool is designed for a single firewall system. However, Cisco does have another GUI interface tool called the Cisco Secure Policy Manager (CSPM) that supports centralized management of several security systems simultaneously—PIX is one such security system.

PIX Device Requirements, Client Needs, and Limitations

The PIX PDM version 2.1 supports all models—501, 506/506E, 515/515E, 520, 525, and 535 models that run the PIX firewall software 6.2 or higher. The following is a list of all the requirements for these models:

➤ PIX software 6.2 or higher

➤ Minimum of 8MB of flash memory

➤ DES or 3DES activation keys

The encryption of DES or 3DES is required because of the HTTPS, Secure Socket Layer (SSL) connection needed to use the PDM interface. This SSL connection allows secure traffic to pass between the interface and Web browsers and typically used port 443.

The PDM software also supports the Cisco Firewall Service Module (FWSM) version 1.1 that can be installed in a Catalyst 6500 series switch.

Clients Using the PDM

The Java-based interface doesn't require a client installation; only an HTTPS connection to the firewall, which will download and execute the Java applets required to run the interface, is needed. Table 13.1 lists the client platforms that can run the interface.

Table 13.1	Supported Clients
Client	**Description**
Solaris	Version 2.6 or higher with a windows manager
Linux	Red Hat 7.0 or higher with KDE or GNOME as an X Window System manager
Windows	Windows 98, NT 4.0, 2000, XP, or Me

 To execute the PDM Java, the Web browser must support JavaScript and the Java Development Kit (JDK) version 1.1.4 or higher.

 The PDM is supported on Windows, Linux, and Sun Solaris operating systems.

but not all OS versions !!

PDM Limitations

The PDM can configure almost all commands necessary to make the PIX firewall work. However, several commands and features are not supported; the PDM might, in fact, prevent you from setting up certain configurations on the firewall with the GUI. When this happens, the only option you can use is the Monitoring tab, which we will look at later. Following is a list of *some* commands not supported on the PDM:

➤ The `alias` command

➤ The `aaa` command with the `match` option when other commands use the `include` and `exclude` options

➤ The `same access-lists` and `outbound` command linked to more than one interface

➤ The `established` command

See Cisco's Web site for other unsupported commands. Figure 13.1 displays the error message displayed when an unsupported command, such as the `alias` command, is found.

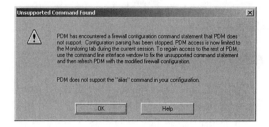

Figure 13.1 The unsupported commands alert box.

Unsupported commands on the PDM disable all configuration functionality on the interface. If unsupported commands are detected, the PDM locks out access to all tabs except the Monitoring tab.

Installing the PDM

The PDM is actually software stored on the PIX firewall itself and down-loaded to create the GUI after an HTTPS connection is made by a client. In addition, the PDM image can be acquired from Cisco. Before installing the PDM software, be sure the firewall meets the minimum requirements listed previously. The following are the basic steps needed to configure a new PIX firewall that has no current PDM or configuration:

1. Activate DES or 3DES.

2. Configure a basic IP address on the PIX.

3. Place the PDM software (image) on a TFTP server.

4. Upload the PDM image. copy tftp flash:pdm

Activating DES or 3DES

Encryption licensing can be obtained from Cisco. The DES activation key is free, whereas the 3DES key comes at a small cost. The show version command can display your current activation keys.

Configuring a Basic IP Address

To upload the PDM image, a basic IP address needs to be set on an interface. The command shown here demonstrates this:

```
pixfirewall(config)# ip address inside 192.168.1.1 255.255.255.255
```

PDM Software on a TFTP Server

After the PDM image/software is obtained from Cisco, save it on a basic TFTP server. A free TFTP server can be obtained from Cisco and be easily installed. After it's installed, make sure your TFTP server and the firewall can connect to each other.

Uploading the PDM Image

By now, everything should be ready to upload the image. The example shown here states that the TFTP server address is 192.168.1.2 and the image name is `pdm-211.bin`:

```
pixfirewall(config)# copy tftp flash:pdm
Address or name of remote host [127.0.0.1]? 192.168.1.2
Source file name [cdisk]? pdm-211.bin
copying tftp://192.168.1.2/pdm-211.bin to flash:pdm
[yes¦no¦again]? yes
Erasing current PDM file
Writing new PDM file
!!!!!!!!!!!!!!!!!!!!!!!!!!!!!!!!!!
PDM file installed.
```

The **copy tftp flash:pdm** command needs to have the **pdm** option; otherwise, you can overwrite the PIX operating system.

Configuring an HTTP Server

Now that the PDM is installed, let's see it in action. The PIX first must have the `http server enable` command set. This command enables the PIX to be a Web server and host PDM Web pages. The next step is to define which managed clients will be allowed HTTPS access to the PIX. This is very similar to the command for enabling Telnet users' access. The following commands are necessary to enable the Web server function and allow a single host access:

```
pixfirewall(config)# http server enable
pixfirewall(config)# http 192.168.1.2 255.255.255.255 inside
pixfirewall(config)# show http
http server enabled
192.168.1.2 255.255.255.255 inside
```

You can also allow an entire subnet access by using the following commands:

```
pixfirewall(config)# http 192.168.1.0 255.255.255.0 inside
pixfirewall(config)# show http
http server enabled
192.168.1.0 255.255.255.0 inside
192.168.1.2 255.255.255.255 inside
```

Connecting to the PDM

After the HTTP server functionality and managed clients have been configured, HTTPS clients can connect. To do so, open a Web browser on a supported operating system and browser, such as Microsoft Internet Explorer, and enter the PIX IP address on the HTTP server-enabled interface. Follow these steps to establish your first connection to the PDM:

1. Enter the PIX IP address in a Web browser. *must be in form of https://w.x.y.z*

2. Accept the certificate security alert.

3. Enter the password. *& username*

4. Accept the security warning.

5. Enter the PDM interface.

The following is the syntax for your 192.168.1.1 PIX inside interface:

```
https://192.168.1.1
```

When the browser connects to the PIX, HTTPS provides an SSL connection between the client and the PIX. The certificate dialog box is then displayed, warning you that this is an untrusted certificate. Figure 13.2 displays the first dialog box you will see.

Click Yes to proceed. Next, you are presented with the authentication dialog box. If you have configured AAA services, a username is required; otherwise, leave the Username field blank and enter the current enable password. Figure 13.3 shows the login dialog box.

may not be true, I think!

Figure 13.2 The security alert box.

Figure 13.3 The Login dialog box.

After the authentication succeeds, a security warning dialog box might be displayed requesting consent to install a publisher's certificate. Click Yes. Figure 13.4 shows this dialog box.

Figure 13.4 The security warning dialog box.

After it's installed, the PDM interface takes a few seconds to load. Figure 13.5 displays the window that appears during the loading stage.

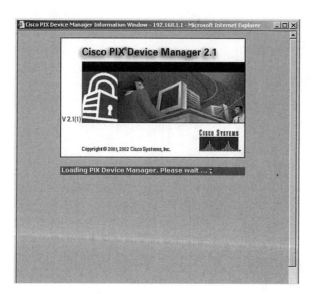

Figure 13.5 Loading the PDM.

After the PDM has loaded, you will see one of three possible screens.

The Startup Wizard is displayed if you don't have a configuration. The Startup Wizard automatically launches and walks you through several easy steps to configure the basic PIX system. Figure 13.6 displays this screen.

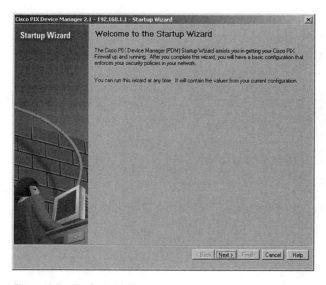

Figure 13.6 The Startup Wizard.

The Access Rules tab is displayed if you already have a configuration and all the commands in the configuration are supported. Figure 13.7 displays this screen.

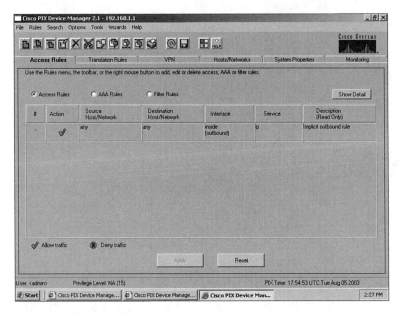

Figure 13.7 The Access Rules tab.

The Unsupported Commands dialog box is displayed if any unsupported commands are configured on the firewall. Figure 13.1, shown earlier in this chapter, displays this warning. After you click Yes, you are only able to monitor items on the firewall in the Monitoring tab. Figure 13.8 displays the only tab you will be able to access.

When your PIX has not been configured, the PDM Startup Wizard automatically is displayed.

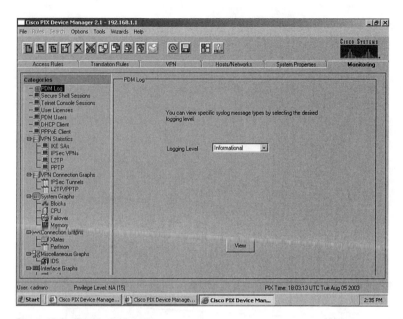

Figure 13.8 The Monitoring tab.

Using the PDM to Configure the PIX Firewall

The PDM can be used to edit almost all the commands supported on the PIX firewall. Most of the PDM functionality is broken up into six main tabs and wizards. This section provides an overview of the following wizards and main tabs:

➤ Access Rules

➤ Transition Rules

➤ VPN

➤ Host/Networks

➤ System Properties

➤ Monitoring

Make sure you know that the five main configuration areas are Access Rules, Translation Rules, VPN, Host/Networks, and System Properties.

The Access Rules Tab

The Access Rules tab enables configuration of which traffic is permitted or denied access through the firewall. Access lists, AAA rules, and URL filter rules can be configured on this tab (refer to Figure 13.7).

The Translation Rules Tab

The Translation Rules tab enables you to configure NAT pools and PAT configuration. On this screen you can manage pools of addresses by clicking the Manage Pools button. Figure 13.9 displays this screen.

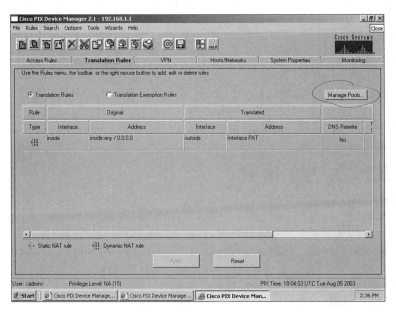

Figure 13.9 The Translation Rules tab.

The VPN Tab

The VPN tab is a very powerful screen that enables you to create VPN connections. This screen enables you to set the transform sets, IKE parameters, site-to-site settings, and even remote-access VPN settings, to name a few. Figure 13.10 displays this screen.

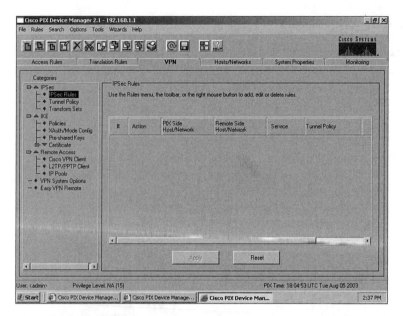

Figure 13.10 The VPN tab.

The Host/Network Tab

what purpose?

The Host/Network tab enables you to configure access list object groups for networks and hosts. The Host/Network section of the screen creates hosts and networks that can be used on the groups' commands on the right side of the screen. For example, you can create WWW, mail, and FTP server entries and then group them together in an object group using the Host and Network group section of the screen. Figure 13.11 displays this screen.

The System Properties Tab

The System Properties tab enables you to configure just about everything else, including interfaces, failover, routing, DHCP servers, logging, AAA services, intrusion detection, and multicast (see Figure 13.12).

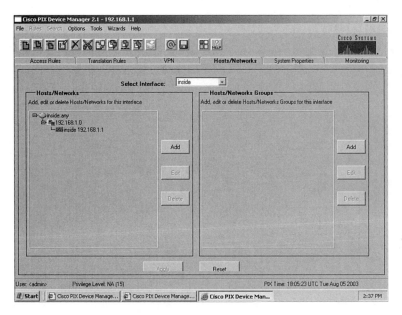

Figure 13.11   The Host/Network tab.

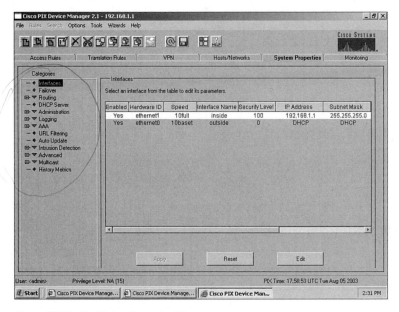

Figure 13.12   The System Properties tab.

The Monitoring Tab

The Monitoring tab, as its name suggests, is used to provide several monitoring features of the PIX firewall. The PIX provides a wealth of information that can be monitored via this screen, shown in Figure 13.13.

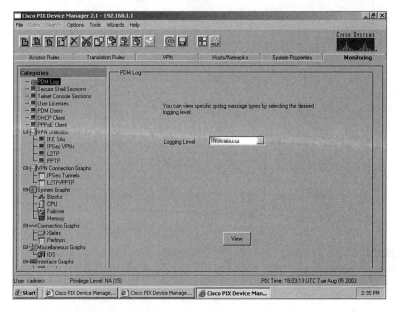

Figure 13.13 The Monitoring tab.

PDM Pull-down Menus

The pull-down menus also provide several configuration features and options. Figure 13.14 displays a snapshot of the PDM pull-down menu options.

The File Pull-down Menu

The File pull-down menu enables you to reset the firewall to the factory defaults, save the running configuration to flash or a TFTP server, or simply refresh the PDM interface. Figure 13.15 displays the options in the File menu.

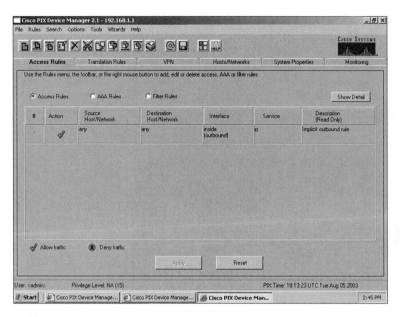

Figure 13.14   Pull-down menus.

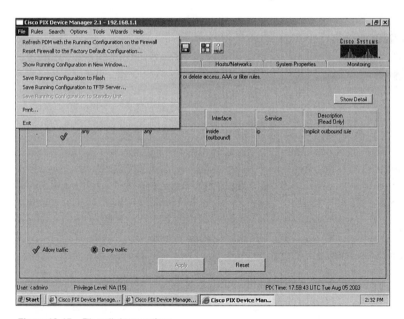

Figure 13.15   File pull-down options.

The Options Pull-down Menu

The Options pull-down menu enables you to select preferences and define three main settings: namely, preview commands, confirm before exiting, and display dialog about VPN wizards. The preview command preference is handy when you want to learn which commands the PDM is actually sending down to the firewall via the CLI. Figure 13.16 displays the preferences dialog box.

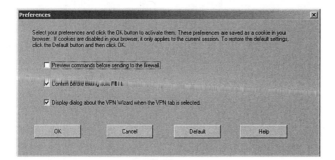

Figure 13.16   Preference options.

The Wizards Pull-down Menu

The Wizards pull-down menu contains two wizards that help you configure the PIX firewall (see Figure 13.17). The Setup Wizard enables you to configure a basic firewall by answering simple questions, whereas the VPN Wizard enables you to configure a VPN configuration for either site-to-site or remote access. Figure 13.18 displays the first screen of the VPN Wizard.

The PDM interface enables you to configure the PIX firewall using a Web-based interface. The PDM can be installed on almost all the PIX firewall products, and it provides several interface screens for PIX configuration. If commands are found that are not supported by the PDM, the interface warns you about them and sometimes even locks you out of all the configuration screens, thus limiting your monitoring ability. Lastly, the PDM contains two wizards that assist in the initial setup of the firewall's standard and VPN configurations.

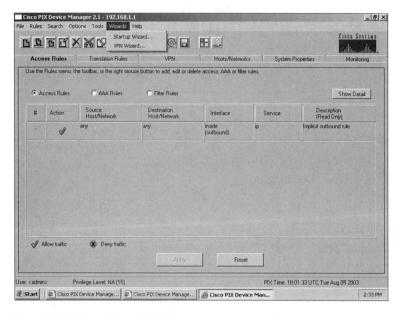

Figure 13.17 The available wizards.

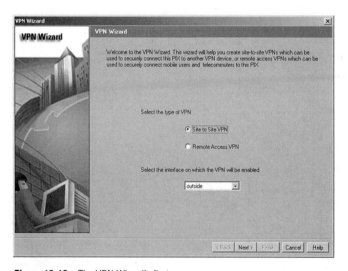

Figure 13.18 The VPN Wizard's first screen.

Exam Prep Questions

Question 1

> What are the major areas on the PDM interface? (Select five.)
> - ☐ A. Maintain
> - ☑ B. Access Rules
> - ☑ C. Host/Network
> - ☑ D. System Properties
> - ☑ E. VPN
> - ☐ F. Transform Ruloo
> - ☑ G. Translation Rules

Answers B, C, D, E, and G are correct. The five main tabs used to configure and set up the PIX firewall are Access Rules, Host/Network, System Properties, VPN and Translation Rules. The Monitoring tab is also available, but it's not used for configuration. Answers A and F are not main screens used to configure the PIX and are therefore incorrect.

Question 2

> On which operating systems is the PDM supported?
> - ⦿ A. Linux, Sun Solaris, Windows
> - ○ B. Sun Solaris, Windows, X Window System   *is not an OS !!*
> - ○ C. Windows, Macintosh, LInux
> - ○ D. Windows, Macintosh, Sun Solaris

Answer A is correct. The PDM is supported on Linux, Sun Solaris, and Windows. Although the PDM supports these vendor operating systems, not all OS versions are supported. Answer B is incorrect because not all versions of X Window System are supported, making this less correct than answer A; also X Window System in not an operating system. Answers C and D are incorrect because Macintosh is not supported, although the PDM might technically work on a Macintosh.

Question 3

> When you start the PDM interface, you are shown only the Monitoring tab. What is wrong?
>
> ○ A. You are using a Macintosh Web browser.
>
> ☒ B. Not all the commands in the PIX configuration are supported by the PDM.
>
> ○ C. The PIX firewall is a model 535, which is not fully supported by the PDM interface.
>
> ○ D. The PDM is being accessed via HTTP and not HTTPS.

Answer B is correct. Several commands are not supported by the PDM interface; the `alias` command is one such command. When unsupported commands are found, the PIX firewall allows only the Monitoring tab to be available. Answer A is incorrect because Macintosh Web browsers are not supported but do not prevent you from accessing the other interface tabs. Answer C is incorrect because the PDM is supported on the PIX 535. Answer D is incorrect because you cannot even access the PDM if you use HTTP; HTTPS is required.

Question 4

> When configuring Java and ActiveX filters and service groups for ACL, which tab do you use?
>
> ○ A. Monitoring
>
> ○ B. Translation Rules
>
> ○ C. Access Rules
>
> ○ D. Access List Rules

Answer C is correct. The Access Rules tab enables you to configure access rules, AAA rules, and filter rules. Filter rules enable you to configure Java and ActiveX filters, and AAA rules allow the configuration of AAA service rules. Answer A is incorrect because the Monitoring tab is used only to monitor information rather than to configure settings. Answer B is incorrect because the Translation Rules tab is used for creating NAT and PAT address pool configurations. Answer D is incorrect because this tab does not exist.

Question 5

> Which location enables you to delete global pools of IP addresses used for NAT?
>
> ○ A. Access Rules tab, Manage Pools button
> ○ B. System Properties tab, Manage Pools button
> ○ C. Translation Rules tab, Manage Pools button
> ○ D. Global Address tab, Manage Pools button

Answer C is correct. The Translation Rules tab contains a button called Manage Pools that enables you to add, delete, and view global pools used for NAT. Answer A is incorrect because the Access Rules tab is used to configure rules such as ACL, AAA, and filters. Further, the Manage Pools button doesn't exist on the Access Rules screen. Answer B is incorrect because, although the System Properties tab is used for several settings, NAT global pools is not one of them. Answer D is incorrect because the Global Address tab does not exist.

Question 6

> The PIX PDM VPN tab supports VPN and IPSec commands.
>
> ○ A. True
> ○ B. False

Answer A is correct. The VPN tab supports both VPN and IPSec commands. This tab contains a tree list of configurable options, such as IPSec, IKE, Remote Access, VPN system options, and Easy VPN Remote settings. Therefore, Answer B is incorrect.

Question 7

> To enable clients to connect to the PIX and use the PDM interface, which commands are needed? (Select two.)
>
> ❑ A. enable http server
> ❑ B. http server enable
> ❑ C. http 192.168.1.0 255.255.255.0 inside
> ❑ D. http (inside) 192.168.1.0 255.255.255.0

Answers B and C are correct. First, you must enable the HTTP server function of the PIX firewall, which is done with the `http server enable` command. Next, you must define which clients are allowed to access the HTTP server. The `http 192.168.1.0 255.255.255.0 inside` command allows anyone on the subnet of 192.168.1.0 access via the inside interface. Answers A and D are incorrect because they are invalid commands and syntax.

Question 8   Q

Which option is available on the System Properties tab? (Select four.)

☑ A. Multicast
☐ B. NAT   — *in Translation rules tab*
☐ C. Transform sets   — *in VPN tab*
☑ D. Failover
☑ E. Logging
☐ F. DHCP Server

Answers A, D, E, and F are correct. The System Properties tab allows for all the configuration setting not available on the other primary tabs. Answer B is incorrect because NAT is configured on the Translation Rules tab. Answer C is incorrect because transform sets are configured on the VPN tab.

Question 9   Q

Where do you configure Auto Update settings on the PDM?

○ A. Host/Network, Auto Update
◉ B. System Properties, Auto Update
○ C. Host/Network, Image Server
○ D. System Properties, Image Server

Answer B is correct. The auto update configuration settings are configured on the System Properties tab under the Auto Update link. This enables the firewall to be remotely managed by a server that supports the auto update specification, so that software updates can be sent from a centralized remote server such as a Cisco Secure Policy Manager (CSPM). Answers A, C, and D are incorrect because these options do not exist on these tabs.

see p. 308

Question 10

At which location would you configure the mroute options?

○ A. Host/Network, Multicast, IGMP

○ B. Translation Rules, Multicast

○ C. System Properties, Multicast

○ D. System Properties, Routing

Answer C is correct. The Multicast option on the System Properties tab enables you to configure the mroute options. The mroute command allows you to statically configure multicast routes. Answers A and B are incorrect because these locations do not exist. Answer D is incorrect because this location is where normal routing, not multicast routing, is configured.

Need to Know More?

 Chapman, , David and Andy Fox. *Cisco Secure PIX Firewalls.* Indianapolis, IN: Cisco Press, 2002.

 Deal, Richard A. *Cisco PIX Firewalls.* Berkeley, CA: McGraw-Hill/Osborne, 2002.

 See the Cisco PIX Firewall Command Reference, Version 6.2 at
`http://www.cisco.com/univercd/cc/td/doc/product/iaabu/pix/pix_sw/`
`v_62/cmdref/index.htm`.

Advance Management

Terms you'll need to understand:

✓ CiscoWorks VPN/Security Management Solution (VMS)
✓ CiscoWorks Management Center for Firewall (PIX MC)
✓ Cisco Firewall Services Module (FWSM)
✓ CiscoWorks Auto Update Server (AUS)
✓ Mandatory access rules
✓ Default access rules
✓ Device access rules
✓ PIX MC default groups
✓ PIX MC access rules

Techniques you'll need to master:

✓ Remembering CiscoWorks port numbers
✓ Knowing PIX MC management tabs
✓ Knowing the Auto Update Server process

Advanced Management

Cisco offers several advanced management tools that can help manage the PIX firewall from small- to large enterprise-sized companies. This chapter covers some of the possible modules, such as PIX Management Center (MC) and the Auto Update Server, which can be added to CiscoWorks products.

CiscoWorks

CiscoWorks is Cisco's flagship enterprise suite of integrated network management tools designed to simplify the administration and maintenance of small- to medium-sized business networks. The product line is quite extensive and could be a book in itself. However, a few modules are important to the PIX firewall, which we discuss here.

CiscoWorks VPN/Security Management Solution

The VPN/Security Management Solution (VMS) is a Web-based tool used for configuring, monitoring, and troubleshooting firewalls, VPNs, and intrusion detection systems (IDSs). The following is a list of the functions this product provides:

➤ Firewall management

➤ VPN monitoring

➤ Security monitoring

➤ Operation management

➤ VPN router management

➤ IDS management

This chapter focuses only on the firewall management section and not on VPNs or the IDS capabilities of CiscoWorks. Figure 14.1 displays the CiscoWorks screen that allows access to the PIX Management Center.

By default, CiscoWorks uses port 1741 on the Web server.

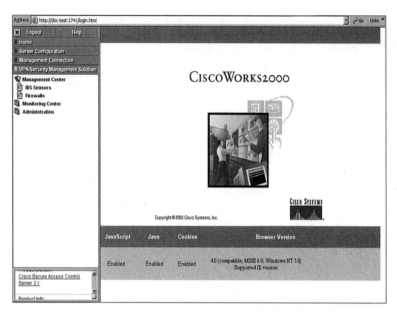

Figure 14.1 CiscoWorks VPN/Security screen.

abb.: PIX MC

CiscoWorks Management Center for Firewall

PIX MC vs PDM ?

VMS

The PIX MC is a Web-based interface tool used inside Cisco VPN/Security Management Solution within CiscoWorks. The tool is similar to the PIX Device Manager (PDM) that is used to manage a single PIX firewall. However, PIX MC offers centralized management of up to 1,000 firewalls at the same time.

The PIX MC enables you to configure new firewalls and import current firewall configurations. When paired with the PIX Auto Update Server, it can additionally download configurations, software upgrades, and PDM software to your PIX firewalls.

PIX MC works not only with the PIX firewalls, but also with the Firewall Service Modules (FWSM) that are used inside a 6500 Catalyst switch.

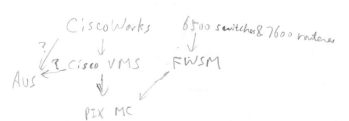

NOTE The Cisco Firewall Services Module is an integrated firewall module for Cisco Catalyst 6500 switches and Cisco 7600 Series routers. The FWSM provides fast firewall data throughput, based on the Cisco PIX firewall.

The following list displays some of the features PIX MC can provide:

➤ A Web-based interface for configuring and managing multiple firewall devices without requiring Command Line Interface (CLI) knowledge

➤ The importation of configurations from existing firewall devices

➤ A configuration hierarchy is used to configure rules and building blocks that are applied to groups, subgroups, and devices

➤ The configuration settings can be written to a file, directly to a firewall device, or to an AUS

➤ Support for firewall device operating systems 6.0, 6.1, and 6.2

➤ Multiple PIX MC user support

➤ Support for up to 1,000 devices

➤ A workflow and audit trail

Using the PIX MC

The PIX MC enables you to configure your PIX firewalls without the use of the command-line interface (CLI). The CiscoWorks Web interface requires you to log in to the system before you can access the PIX MC graphical user interface (GUI). Figure 14.2 displays the splash screen you will see when entering the PIX MC.

Table 14.1 lists the five main upper tabs—Devices, Configuration, Workflow, Reports, and Admin—and their submenu items.

Table 14.1	PIX MC Configuration Tabs
Tab	**Submenu Items**
Devices	Importing Devices
	Managing Devices
	Managing Groups
Configuration	Settings
	Access Rules
	Translation Rules
	Building Blocks
	View Config

Table 14.1	PIX MC Configuration Tabs *(continued)*
Tab	**Submenu Items**
Workflow	Activity Management
	Job Management
Reports	Activity
Admin	Workflow
	Maintenance
	Support

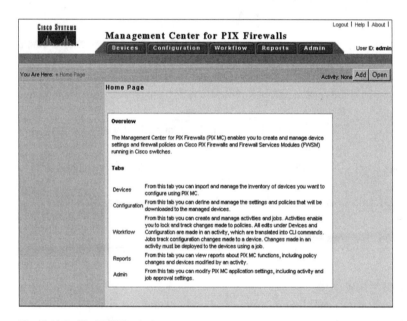

Figure 14.2   The PIX MC splash screen.

The Devices Tab

This tab is used to import and manage the PIX firewall device configuration settings. Table 14.2 contains this tab's three main submenu items with basic descriptions of what they do.

Table 14.2	PIX MC Devices Tab
Subitem	**Description**
Importing Devices	This enables you to import firewall configurations from a firewall or file.
Managing Devices	This enables you to move and place firewalls within groups created using the Managing Groups subitem.

Table 14.2   PIX MC Devices Tab *(continued)*

Subitem	Description
Managing Groups	This enables you to create groups of devices that contain similar attributes.

The Configuration Tab

This tab is used to define and manage settings that can be downloaded to the firewalls. Table 14.3 displays the Configuration tab's items and their descriptions.

Table 14.3   PIX MC Configuration Tab

Subitem	Description
Settings	This enables the use of wizards to configure firewalls based on group memberships.
Access Rules	This enables you to control traffic through the device. Access rules use ACLs to provide traffic control.
Translation Rules	This enables you to view and configure translation settings for NAT or PAT across your firewall.
Building Blocks	This enables you to create ACL **object-group** commands without using the CLI.
View Config	This enables you to view configuration files.

The Workflow Tab

The Workflow tab enables you to control and manage activity workflow and to create new activities that are used to control policy changes against a device (firewall). Table 14.4 displays the Workflow tab's subitems.

Table 14.4   PIX MC Workflow Tab

Subitem	Description
Activity Management	This tab is used to view, edit, and create activity tasks for your PIX firewalls. For example, if a firewall needs configuration, this tab is used to create an activity requesting some change that needs to take effect.
Job Management	This tab is used to manage jobs. A *job* represents a set of configurations that need to be deployed to a device, a configuration file, or an AUS.

The Reports Tab

This tab enables you to view reports about actions administrators have performed within an activity. Only one selection is available on this tab; it's called Activity. Table 14.5 displays the details of the activity report.

Table 14.5 PIX MC Reports Tab's Activity Report	
Report View	**Description**
Basic Information	Displays the activity name and any comments from the administrator
State Changes	Displays a history of the date and time the action occurred and who performed the action
Policy Changes	Displays which devices and groups were acted upon and identifies the policy changes made as part of that activity

The Admin Tab

The Admin tab configures the global settings for the PIX MC, such as enabling workflow and audit record retention. Table 14.6 describes the three submenu items available.

Table 14.6 PIX MC Admin Tab	
Report View	**Description**
Workflow	This option enables you to set whether workflow activities should require approval.
Maintenance	This option enables you to delete records and specify how long records should be retained.
Support	This option collects configuration and system information into a **.zip** file called **MDCSupportInformation.zip**. This file can be sent to tech support for assistance.

PIX MC Groups

The PIX MC provides the ability to place PIX firewall devices with similar attributes into groups. These groups enable you to configure these devices with similar settings. The default group, called Global, is the highest-level group; from here you can create subgroups. Devices are placed within these subgroups. Figure 14.3 displays three firewalls placed into the group called Corvallis Firewalls.

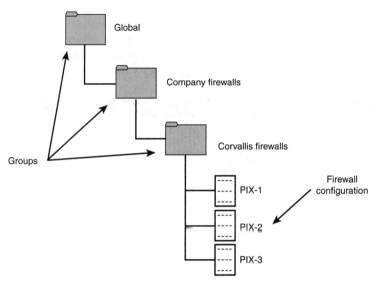

Figure 14.3 PIX MC Groups for attributes.

 The PIX MC provides the ability to group devices with similar attributes. By using the Devices tab, you can create more groups. However, the default group is called Global.

After groups are created, device (firewall) configurations can be imported into the group. Figure 14.3 shows three configurations currently imported: PIX-1, PIX-2, and PIX-3.

PIX MC Access Rules

The PIX MC enables you to define access rules, which are used to configure network security policies on your firewall. Access rules are grouped by interfaces that eventually are translated into access list (ACL) entries assigned to that interface. These rules are assigned to a group or subgroup and are merged to provide access control on the firewall.

The following shows the three types of access rules that can be created in the order of precedence:

1. Mandatory access rules

2. Device access rules

3. Default access rules

Mandatory access rules are the most important rules and take precedence over any other rules. This places them first in the ACL that is created. Device access rules are next. If no mandatory access rule opposes a device rule, the rule affects the PIX. Lastly are the default rules, which take effect only if no other rule overrides them.

Figure 14.4 displays access rules coming from each group and the device. The access rules from groups can be either mandatory or default. Access rules from a device are device rules applied only to that specific device. All these rules are combined and converted into the ACL for the device.

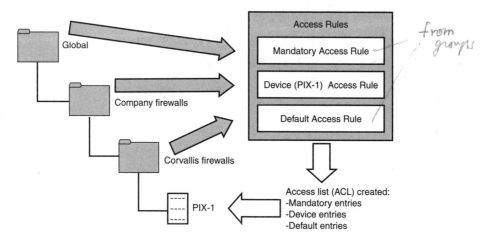

Figure 14.4 Access rules.

 Mandatory rules cannot be overridden, are applied at the group, and are ordered down to a device.

Default rules can be overridden and are ordered from the device up to the enclosing groups.

CiscoWorks Auto Update Server

The Auto Update Server provides a Web-based interface module inside CiscoWorks for upgrading device configuration files, software images, and PDM images. It is designed to interoperate with PIX MC to deploy the configuration files and to operate alone for updating PDM images.

AUS works off the principal of the devices (firewalls) periodically polling it for updates. If an update exists, the device requests to download the newer image or configuration file. Figure 14.5 displays the step-by-step flow of the PIX interacting with an AUS server.

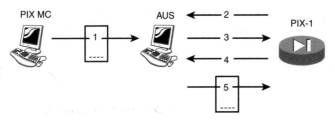

Figure 14.5 Auto Update Server updated process.

The following step numbers correspond to the numbers found on Figure 14.5:

1. The MC deploys the configuration file to the Auto Update Server.

2. The PIX periodically polls the AUS server for a list of updates.

3. The AUS sends the list of files to the PIX.

4. The PIX verifies it has the latest files; if it doesn't, it requests the latest version.

5. The newer configuration files are downloaded.

The Auto Update Server operates on port 443 (HTTPS).

Auto Update Server Configuration Tabs

The Web interface for the AUS is similar to PIX MC. It contains; Devices, Files (Images), Assignments, Reports, and Admin tabs are used to set up and configure the AUS system. Table 14.7 contains a brief description of each tab.

Table 14.7	CiscoWorks Auto Update Server Configuration Tab
Tab	**Description**
Devices	Provides summary information about devices.
Files (Images)	Provides details about configuration files, PIX firewall software images, and PDM images. It also enables you to add and delete images.
Assignments	Enables you to assign images to devices.
Reports	Displays reports.
Admin	Enables you to configure the AUS and change the database password.

In this chapter, we talked about CiscoWorks as the main enterprise software management product that can incorporate several modules to configure firewalls. The Cisco PIX MC is used to create groups of devices with similar attributes and provide configuration files. These configuration files can then be downloaded to the devices using the AUS feature of CiscoWorks.

Exam Prep Questions

Question 1

What is the default port CiscoWorks uses on the Web interface?

- A. 1741
- B. 80
- C. 4117
- D. 443

Answer A is correct. The default port for CiscoWorks is 1741. Answer B is incorrect because port 80 is the default port for a Web server, not the port for CiscoWorks' Web interface. Answer C is incorrect because this is an open port for any applications and it is not used for CiscoWorks. Answer D is incorrect because port 443 is the default for HTTPS secure communications.

Question 2

What is FWSM?

- A. A CiscoWorks software module for switches
- B. A CiscoWorks software backup utility
- C. A firewall hardware module for the Catalyst 6500 & 7600 routers
- D. A firewall hardware module for the Catalyst 1900

Answer C is correct. The Cisco Firewall Services Module (FWSM) is a PIX firewall-based module for the Catalyst 6500 Switch. Answers A and B are incorrect because FWSM is a hardware module—not a software module or a backup utility for CiscoWorks. Answer D is incorrect because it is a module for the Catalyst 6500, not the smaller 1900 series.

Question 3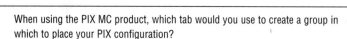

> When using the PIX MC product, which tab would you use to create a group in
> which to place your PIX configuration?
>
> ○ A. Admin tab
> ○ B. Clock tab
> ○ C. Devices tab
> ○ D. Group tab *← no such tab*

Answer C is correct. The Devices tab is used to create groups on the PIX
MC Web interface. The Devices tab is also used to add and delete devices in
the PIX MC system. Answer A is incorrect because the Admin tab is used to
enable workflow and general system configurations. Answers B and D are
incorrect because these tabs do not actually exist.

Question 4

> On the PIX MC, what does a mandatory access rule do?
>
> ○ A. Provides a conduit list for the firewall
> ○ B. Provides an access rule that will be used first
> ○ C. Provides a mandatory device to the system
> ○ D. Provides a mandatory permission for administrators

Answer B is correct. The mandatory access rules are attached to groups in
the PIX MC and are used as mandatory settings that all managed devices
receive. Therefore, it takes priority over the access rules, meaning it will be
used first. Answer A is incorrect because it is not used for conduit lists—
access rules are translated into access lists. Answer C is incorrect because
mandatory access rules are rules on devices in the system. Answer D is incorrect because mandatory access rules do not provide permissions to administrators; they are used to provide control to devices.

Question 5

Default access rules take precedence over mandatory access rules. (True or False)

○ A. True

○ B. False

Answer B is correct. Mandatory access rules always take priority over device or default access rules. Therefore, answer A is incorrect.

Question 6

What is the default port for the Cisco Auto Update Server?

○ A. 80

○ B. 1741

○ C. 443

○ D. 8080

Answer C is correct. The default port the Auto Update Server uses is port 443. Answers A and D are incorrect because they are just normal Web server ports, not the AUS port. Answer B is incorrect because port 1741 is the default port used by CiscoWorks, not the AUS.

Question 7

Which of the following is a type of access rule used in the PIX MC product? (Select two.)

❑ A. Global

❑ B. Mandatory

❑ C. Firewall

❑ D. Default

Answers B and D are correct. The three types of access rules on the PIX MC product are mandatory, default, and device access rules. Answers A and C are incorrect because they are not access rules that can be used on the PIX MC product.

Question 8

Which of the following can be downloaded using the Auto Update Server? (Select three.)

❑ A. Configuration files

❑ B. Software images

❑ C. PDM images

❑ D. VPN configuration and activation keys only

Answers A, B, and C are correct. The AUS can download three types of files: configuration files, software images, and PDM images. Answer D is incorrect because the AUS does not download only VPN configuration settings or activation keys. It downloads the show configuration file.

Question 9

Which default group is installed on the PIX MC?

○ A. Device group

○ B. Firewall group

◉ C. Global group

○ D. Office group

Answer C is correct. By default, a group called Global is created as the highest-level group. All other subgroups are created below this group. Remember that groups enable you to place devices with similar attributes together. Answers A, B, and D are incorrect because these groups are not created by default and must be manually created.

Question 10

Does PIX MC provide auto updated services for the PIX series firewalls? (True or False.)

○ A. True

◉ B. False

Answer B is correct. The CiscoWorks Management Center for Firewall (PIX MC) provides configuration creation files for firewalls but does not provide auto updated features. The CiscoWorks Auto Update Server (AUS) product provides auto update features. Answer A is incorrect because B is the correct answer.

Need to Know More?

 Visit the CiscoWorks VPN/Security Management Solution at
http://www.cisco.com/en/US/products/sw/cscowork/ps2330/index.html

 See the Bootstrapping Managed Devices at http://www.cisco.com/
en/US/products/sw/cscowork/ps3993/products_user_guide_
chapter09186a0080143342.html.

 Visit the CiscoWorks Management Center for Firewalls at
http://www.cisco.com/en/US/products/sw/cscowork/ps3992/index.html

 See the Using Management Center for PIX Firewalls 1.1 at http://
www.cisco.com/univercd/cc/td/doc/product/rtrmgmt/cw2000/mgt_pix/
pix1_1/use_man/index.htm.

 Visit the CiscoWorks Management Center for Firewalls Sample
Network Scenarios at http://www.cisco.com/en/US/products/sw/cscowork/
ps3992/products_user_guide_chapter09186a00800e7215.html#xtocid0.

 See the CiscoWorks Auto Update Server Software Getting Started
with AUS at http://www.cisco.com/en/US/products/sw/cscowork/ps3993/
products_user_guide09186a008019b14c.html#wp1040441.

 See the CiscoWorks Auto Update Server Software Introduction at
http://www.cisco.com/en/US/products/sw/cscowork/ps3993/products_
user_guide_chapter09186a008014333f.html#wp1021195.

 See the Cisco Catalyst 6500 Series Firewall Services Module at
http://www.cisco.com/en/US/products/hw/modules/ps2706/ps4452/index.
html.

Sample Test 1

In this chapter, I provide pointers to help you develop a successful test-taking strategy, including how to choose proper answers, how to decode ambiguity, how to work within the Cisco testing framework, how to decide what you need to memorize, and how to prepare for the test. At the end of the chapter, I include 55 questions on subject matter pertinent to the Cisco CSPFA 642-521 exam. In Chapter 16, "Answer Key 1," you'll find the answer key to this test. Good luck!

Questions, Questions, Questions

There should be no doubt in your mind that you are facing a test full of specific and pointed questions. If the version of the exam you take is fixed-length, it will include 55–65 questions, and you will be allotted 75 minutes to complete the exam. If it's an adaptive test (the software should tell you this as you begin the exam), it might consist of a different number of questions and be alloted a different amount of time. Whichever type of test you take, exam questions will belong to one of five basic types:

➤ Multiple-choice with a single answer

➤ Multiple-choice with multiple answers

➤ Multipart with a single answer

➤ Multipart with multiple answers

➤ Simulations, in which you click a GUI screen capture to simulate using the Cisco IOS interface

You should always take the time to read a question at least twice before selecting an answer, and you should always look for an Exhibit button as you examine each question. *Exhibits* include graphic information related to a question. An exhibit is usually a screen capture of program output or GUI information you must examine to analyze the question's contents and formulate an answer. The Exhibit button displays graphics and charts used to help explain a question, provide additional data, or illustrate page layout or program behavior.

Not every question has only one answer; many questions require multiple answers. Therefore, you should read each question carefully, determine how many answers are necessary or possible, and look for additional hints or instructions when selecting answers. Such instructions often appear in brackets immediately following the question itself (for multiple-answer questions).

Picking Proper Answers

Obviously, the only way to pass any exam is to select enough of the right answers to obtain a passing score. However, Cisco's exams are not standardized like the SAT and GRE exams are; they are far more diabolical and convoluted. In some cases, questions are strangely worded, and deciphering them can be a real challenge. In those cases, you might need to rely on answer-elimination skills. Almost always, at least one answer out of the possible choices for a question can be eliminated immediately because it matches one of these conditions:

➤ The answer does not apply to the situation.

➤ The answer describes a nonexistent issue, an invalid option, or an imaginary state.

➤ The answer can be eliminated because of information in the question itself.

After you eliminate all answers that are obviously wrong, you can apply your retained knowledge to eliminate further answers. Look for items that sound correct but refer to actions, commands, or features that are not present or not available in the situation the question describes.

If you're still faced with a blind guess among two or more potentially correct answers, reread the question. Try to picture how each of the possible remaining answers would alter the situation. *Be especially sensitive to terminology*; sometimes the choice of words ("remove" instead of "disable") can make the difference between a right answer and a wrong one.

Only when you've exhausted your ability to eliminate answers but remain unclear about which of the remaining possibilities is correct should you guess at an answer. An unanswered question offers you no points, but guessing gives you at least some chance of getting a question right; just don't be too hasty when making a blind guess.

 If you're taking a fixed-length test, you can wait until the last round of reviewing marked questions (just as you're about to run out of time or out of unanswered questions) before you start making guesses. If you're taking an adaptive test, you'll have to guess to move on to the next question (if you can't figure out an answer some other way). Either way, guessing should be a last resort.

Decoding Ambiguity

Cisco exams have a reputation for including questions that can be difficult to interpret, confusing, or ambiguous. In my experience with numerous exams, I consider this reputation to be completely justified. The Cisco exams are tough, and they're deliberately made that way.

The only way to beat Cisco at its own game is to be prepared. You'll discover that many exam questions test your knowledge of things that are not directly related to the issue raised by a question. This means the answers you must choose from, even incorrect ones, are just as much a part of the skill assessment as the question itself. If you don't know something about most aspects of the Cisco IOS, you might not be able to eliminate answers that are wrong because they relate to an area of the IOS other than the one that's addressed by the question at hand. In other words, the more you know about the IOS and the hardware environment, the easier it will be for you to tell right from wrong.

Questions often give away their answers, but you have to be Sherlock Holmes to see the clues. Often, subtle hints appear in the question text in such a way that they seem almost irrelevant to the situation. You must realize that each question is a test unto itself and that you need to inspect and successfully navigate each question to pass the exam. Look for small clues, such as the mention of command mode, IP ranges, and configuration settings. Little things such as these can point to the right answer if they're properly understood; if missed, they can leave you facing a blind guess.

Another common difficulty with certification exams is vocabulary. Cisco has an uncanny knack for naming some utilities and features entirely obviously in some cases and completely inanely in other instances. Be sure to brush up on the key terms presented at the beginning of each chapter of this book. You also might want to read the glossary at the end of this book the day before you take the test.

Working Within the Framework

The test questions appear in random order, and many elements or issues mentioned in one question can also crop up in other questions. It's not uncommon to find that an incorrect answer to one question is the correct answer to another question, or vice versa. Take the time to read every answer to each question, even if you recognize the correct answer to a question immediately. That extra reading can spark a memory or remind you about an IOS feature or function that helps you on another question elsewhere in the exam.

If you're taking a fixed-length test, you can revisit any question as many times as you like. If you're uncertain of the answer to a question, check the box that's provided to mark it for easy return later. You should also mark questions you think might offer information you can use to answer other questions. On fixed-length tests, I usually mark somewhere between 25% and 50% of the questions. The testing software is designed to let you mark every question if you choose; use this framework to your advantage. Everything you'll want to see again should be marked; the testing software can then help you return to marked questions quickly and easily.

If you're taking an adaptive test and see something in a question or in one of the answers that jogs your memory on a topic, or that you feel you should record if the topic appears in another question, write it down on your piece of paper. Just because you can't go back to a question in an adaptive test doesn't mean you can't take notes on what you see early in the test, in hopes that it might help you later in the test.

For adaptive tests, don't be afraid to take notes on what you see in various questions. Sometimes, what you record from one question can help you on other questions later, especially if it's not as familiar as it should be or reminds you of the name or use of some utility or interface details.

Deciding What to Memorize

The amount of memorization you must undertake for an exam depends on how well you remember what you've read and how well you know the software. If you're a visual thinker and can see the command line in your head, you won't need to memorize as much as someone who's less visually oriented. However, the exam will stretch your abilities to memorize product features and functions, interface details, and proper configuration, as well as how they all relate to the Cisco IOS.

At a minimum, you'll want to memorize the following types of information:

➤ PIX firewall models, services modules, and licensing

➤ ASA security levels

➤ Firewall, syslog, and DHCP server configuration

➤ PPPoE

➤ Transport protocols, DNS support configuration, NAT, and PAT

➤ ACLS and converting conduits to ACLS

➤ Object groups and nested object groups

➤ Advanced protocols and multimedia support

➤ Attack guards, intrusion detection, and shunning

➤ AAA and using CSACS and downloadable ACLS

➤ Failover types and configuration

➤ VPN configuration, IKE, and IPSec

➤ Remote access and authorization for maintenance

➤ Using the PDM for configuration

➤ Enterprise firewall configuration, administration, and maintenance

➤ Using AUS settings, devices, images, and assignments

➤ FWSM

If you work your way through this book while sitting at an appropriate PIX device with the 6.x IOS installed and try to manipulate this environment's features and functions as they're discussed throughout, you should have little or no difficulty mastering this material. Also, don't forget that the Cram Sheet at the front of the book is designed to capture the material that's most important to memorize; use this to guide your studies as well.

Preparing for the Test

The best way to prepare for the test—after you've studied—is to take at least one practice exam. I've included one in this chapter for that reason; the test questions are located in the pages that follow. (Unlike the questions in the preceding chapters in this book, the answers don't follow the questions immediately; you'll have to turn to Chapter 16 to review the answers separately.)

Give yourself 90 minutes to take the exam, and keep yourself on the honor system—don't look at earlier text in the book or jump ahead to the answer key. When your time is up or you've finished the questions, you can check your work in Chapter 16. Pay special attention to the explanations for the incorrect answers; these can also help reinforce your knowledge of the material. Knowing how to recognize correct answers is good, but understanding why incorrect answers are wrong can be equally valuable.

Taking the Test

Relax. When you're sitting in front of the testing computer, there's nothing more you can do to increase your knowledge or preparation. Take a deep breath, stretch, and start reading that first question.

You don't need to rush, either. You have plenty of time to complete each question, and if you're taking a fixed-length test, you'll have time to return to the questions you skipped or marked for return. On a fixed-length test, if you read a question twice and you remain clueless, you can mark it; if you're taking an adaptive test, you'll have to guess and move on. Both easy and difficult questions are intermixed throughout the test in random order. If you're taking a fixed-length test, don't cheat yourself by spending too much time on a hard question early in the test, thereby depriving yourself of the time you need to answer the questions at the end of the test. If you're taking an adaptive test, don't spend more than 5 minutes on any single question—if it takes you that long to get nowhere, it's time to guess and move on.

On a fixed-length test, you can read through the entire test, and, before returning to marked questions for a second visit, you can figure out how much time you have per question. As you answer each question, remove its mark. Continue to review the remaining marked questions until you run out of time or complete the test.

On an adaptive test, set a maximum time limit for questions and watch your time on long or complex questions. If you reach your limit, it's time to guess and move on. Don't deprive yourself of the opportunity to see more questions by taking too long to puzzle over questions, unless you think you can figure out the answer. Otherwise, you're limiting your opportunities to pass.

That's it for pointers. Here are some questions for you to practice on. Good luck!

Question 1

What can an access list on the PIX use to permit or deny traffic? (Select all that apply.)

- ❑ A. Protocol number
- ❑ B. IP address (source or destination)
- ❑ C. Port number (source or destination)
- ❑ D. IPX address (source or destination)

Question 2

Which command is used to save the configuration on a PIX firewall?

- ○ A. **save**
- ○ B. **write terminal**
- ○ C. **sync**
- ○ D. **write memory**
- ○ E. None of the above

Question 3

The **nameif** command does which of the following? (Select all that apply.)

- ❑ A. Assigns a name to PIX network interface
- ❑ B. Specifies the interface's security level
- ❑ C. Configures the interface type and speed
- ❑ D. Allows the **security-level** command to be used

Question 4

Which is the correct command to reboot the PIX?

- ○ A. **cycle**
- ○ B. **reload**
- ○ C. **init 1**
- ○ D. **init 5**
- ○ E. **restart**

Question 5

How many syslog messages can be stored on the PIX if all the syslog servers are unavailable?

○ A. Zero.

○ B. 100.

○ C. 250.

○ D. 500.

○ E. This is limited only by the physical memory of the PIX platform.

Question 6

IP phones might be required to get their configuration files from a TFTP server. Which command enables the PIX to distribute the IP address of a TFTP server?

○ A. **dhcpd option 66**

○ B. **dhcpd option ip-phone tftp**

○ C. **tftp <ip address> ip-phone**

○ D. **tftp ip-phone send**

○ E. **dhcpd ip phone <ip address>**

Question 7

Which of the following statements is true? (Select all that apply.)

❑ A. Translations are at the Transport layer.

❑ B. Translations are a subset of connections.

❑ C. Connections are at the Transport layer.

❑ D. Connections are at the Network layer.

❑ E. Translations are at the Network layer.

Question 8

What is the purpose of the DNS option used in a **nat** or **static** command?

○ A. It allows DNS doctoring (by the PIX) of DNS responses to hosts.

○ B. It uses the **alias** command to perform DNS doctoring.

○ C. It filters from any internal host.

○ D. It restricts internal users establishing outside connections.

Question 9

Which of the following commands implements the Turbo ACL feature for all ACLs?

○ A. **access-list turbo all**

○ B. **access-list turbo compiled all**

○ C. **access-list compiled**

○ D. No command is needed; the Turbo ACL feature is on by default.

○ E. **turbo-acl compile all**

Question 10

Which of the following is correct regarding nesting of object groups? (Select all that apply.)

❏ A. An object group can be a member of another object group.

❏ B. A group object can be a member of another group object.

❏ C. You can nest object groups of different types.

❏ D. You can nest only object groups that are of the same type.

❏ E. Object groups cannot be nested.

Question 11

Why is there a need for advanced protocol handling with some popular protocols and applications to allow them to work with a firewall? (Select all that apply.)

- ❏ A. Source ports can be dynamically assigned.
- ❏ B. Destination ports can be dynamically assigned.
- ❏ C. IP addresses can be dynamically assigned.
- ❏ D. Source ports can be embedded in upper layers.
- ❏ E. IP addresses can be embedded above the Network layer.

Question 12

Which statement is true regarding the PIX's IDS feature? (Select all that apply.)

- ❏ A. It uses a subset of the full signature set available on the IDS appliances.
- ❏ B. It uses the full signature set available on the IDS appliances.
- ❏ C. It uses a DoS class signature type.
- ❏ D. It uses an attack class signature type.
- ❏ E. It uses an access class signature type.

Question 13

Which IP address goes into the Access Server IP Address field during the installation of ACS on a Windows 2000 computer?

- ○ A. The computer from which you will be accessing the ACS server
- ○ B. The PIX firewall that will be the client of the ACS server
- ○ C. The computer that is running the ACS software
- ○ D. None of the above

Question 14

Which of the following is a valid PIX firewall model? (Select all that apply.)

- ❏ A. 626
- ❏ B. 506E
- ❏ C. 535
- ❏ D. 511
- ❏ E. 501

Question 15

Which license type is available for select firewall models? (Select all that apply.)

❑ A. Restricted

❑ B. Unlimited

❑ C. Unrestricted

❑ D. Failover

Question 16

The capabilities of the clock command include which of the following? (Select all that apply.)

❑ A. It specifies the time.

❑ B. It specifies the year.

❑ C. It is retained by the battery.

❑ D. It sets the PIX firewall clock.

Question 17

If two interfaces are set to the same security level, what is the result?

○ A. This is not a possible configuration, and it would not be allowed.

○ B. Traffic configured on the lowest-numbered interface would be considered more trusted than the other interface, and traffic would flow from the low number to the high number (for example, E2 traffic would flow to E3).

○ C. Traffic configured on the highest-numbered interface would be considered more trusted than the other interface, and traffic would flow from the high number to the low number (for example, E3 traffic would flow to E2).

○ D. Traffic would not flow between these two interfaces if the security level was the same on each.

Question 18

Customers on the outside need to access a Web server on a DMZ interface. A static has been configured, but customers still can't access the Web server. What needs to be added to make the server accessible from the outside?

- ○ A. NAT 0
- ○ B. Alias
- ○ C. Access list
- ○ D. Global

Question 19

Which applies to the ASA security level 100?

- ○ A. It's the lowest level for the outside interface of the PIX.
- ○ B. It is usually used for your Internet connection.
- ○ C. It's a default that can be changed.
- ○ D. It's the most trusted interface security level.
- ○ E. It's assignable to perimeter interfaces.

Question 20

When the multicast source is on the inside, what are the required commands that allow the PIX to forward multicast traffic to the outside? (Select all that apply.)

- ❑ A. **igmp forward**
- ❑ B. **mroute**
- ❑ C. **multicast routing**
- ❑ D. **multicast interface**
- ❑ E. No command is required. By default, the PIX forwards traffic from high security interfaces to low security interfaces.

Question 21

Which command, when used with the **global** command, allows IP address translation?

○ A. **nat command**

○ B. **ip address command**

○ C. **ip_ addr command**

○ D. **nameif command**

○ E. None of the above

Question 22

The PIX firewall can send Syslog messages to document events related to which of the following?

○ A. Security

○ B. Resources

○ C. System

○ D. Accounting

○ E. All of the above

Question 23

The PIX operating system version 6.x is based on which of the following?

○ A. BSD Unix

○ B. ATT Unix

○ C. The Hardened NT kernel

○ D. Cisco IOS

○ E. The Proprietary Finesse operating system

Question 24

Users need to authenticate with the PIX so they can use their email applications through the PIX. Which service should be configured on the PIX?

- ○ A. Virtual SMTP.
- ○ B. Virtual HTTP.
- ○ C. Virtual Telnet.
- ○ D. SMTP fixup, which is on by default, will allow the traffic.

Question 25

Configuration replication between the active PIX and the standby PIX configured for standard failover occurs over which of the following?

- ○ A. Over any active interface
- ○ B. Over the inside interface
- ○ C. Over the outside interface only if the failure occurred on the inside interface
- ○ D. Over the stateful failover cable
- ○ E. Over the failover cable

Question 26

Which two commands work together to perform network address translation?

- ○ A. **ip address pppoe** and **nameif** commands
- ○ B. **dhcpd dns** and **dhcpd wins** commands
- ○ C. **ip address** and **nameif** commands
- ○ D. **nat** and **global** commands

Question 27

Which statement is true about security levels?

- ○ A. Interfaces with lower security levels can access interfaces with higher security levels.
- ○ B. Interfaces with higher security levels can access interfaces with lower security levels.
- ○ C. Both higher and lower security levels have access to each other with an unrestricted license.
- ○ D. None of the above.

Question 28

How does the PIX firewall manage the TCP and UDP protocols? (Select all that apply.)

- ❑ A. It uses a stateful database for tracking sessions.
- ❑ B. It uses a connection table for TCP and UDP sessions.
- ❑ C. It uses a translation table for NAT sessions.
- ❑ D. It uses a stateless database for TCP and UDP sessions.

Question 29

The PIX 535 firewall can be configured with up to how many interfaces?

- ○ A. 4
- ○ B. 6
- ○ C. 8
- ○ D. 10
- ○ E. 12

Question 30

Which of the following is not true regarding ACLs?

- ○ A. ACLs improve performance for matching packets.
- ○ B. ACLs enable you to determine which systems can establish connections through your PIX.
- ○ C. Cisco recommends migration from conduits to ACLs if you're using the PIX MC.
- ○ D. Turbo ACLs improve search times for large ACLs.

Question 31

The PIX, in combination with which of the following, allows only specific user traffic through the firewall?

- ○ A. Cisco Secure ACS
- ○ B. Traffic Director
- ○ C. Management Center
- ○ D. Cisco Secure Policy Manager

Question 32

What is the correct command to delete a saved RSA key from flash memory?

- ○ A. **write erase**
- ○ B. **ca zeroize rsa**
- ○ C. **no rsa key**
- ○ D. **clear key rsa**

Question 33

Which of the following is true about the MailGuard feature on the PIX? (Select all that apply.)

- ❑ A. The MailGuard feature is enabled by default.
- ❑ B. The MailGuard feature is available only on PIX firewalls with at least 32MB of memory.
- ❑ C. The MailGuard feature protects against spam.
- ❑ D. The MailGuard feature allows only the RFC 821 legal SMTP commands through the PIX.

Question 34

What is the function of the **object-group** command? (Select all that apply.)

- ❑ A. It names the object group.
- ❑ B. It allows grouping of AAA users.
- ❑ C. It enables a sub-command mode for the type of object specified.
- ❑ D. It removes all defined object groups not being used.

Question 35

Which is true concerning RIP version 2?

- ○ A. The PIX firewall advertises learned RIP multicast updates when RIP is in aggressive mode.
- ○ B. The PIX firewall transmits default route updates if configured for RIP version 2 using the default keyword.
- ○ C. The IP destination is 224.0.0.100.
- ○ D. None of the above.

Question 36

Which command allows you to change the enable password to **secret**?

- ○ A. **enable secret secret**
- ○ B. **enable password secret**
- ○ C. **passwd secret**
- ○ D. **set enable secret**

Question 37

Which statement regarding PAT on the PIX is true?

- ○ A. It provides for address expansion.
- ○ B. It maps port numbers to a single IP address.
- ○ C. The PAT address can be different from the outside interface address.
- ○ D. All of the above.

Question 38

What does DNS Guard do? (Select all that apply.)

❑ A. It controls which DNS servers clients can access.

❑ B. It tears down the UDP return patch after the first response from a given DNS server is seen.

❑ C. It helps prevent UDP session hijacking.

❑ D. Answers A and B are both correct.

Question 39

Which command should be used to allow IKE on the outside interface?

○ A. **crypto isakmp enable outside**

○ B. **crypto isakmp enable e0**

○ C. **isakmp enable outside**

○ D. **isakmp enable e0**

Question 40

What is the correct command to set the Telnet password?

○ A. **password**

○ B. **enable password**

○ C. **telnet password**

○ D. **passwd**

Question 41

What is required to initiate SSH connections from the PIX to another device?

○ A. The Telnet password must be set on the PIX.

○ B. It must have a 3DES license on the PIX.

○ C. It must have either a DES or 3DES license on the PIX.

○ D. None of the above. PIX does not support outbound SSH sessions.

Question 42

Which command is used to assign a name to an interface?

○ A. **name**

○ B. **nameif**

○ C. **hostname**

○ D. **ifName**

Question 43

Which option allows the PIX to reload without user confirmation when using the **reload** command?

○ A. **noconfirm**

○ B. **justdoit**

○ C. **confirm**

○ D. There is no option for this; user confirmation is required before a reload occurs.

Question 44

Which command should be used to set the speed and duplex on a PIX interface?

○ A. **speed**

○ B. **100full**

○ C. **nameif**

○ D. **interface**

○ E. None of the above

Question 45

Which of the following is true concerning the PIX firewall and AAA services? (Select all that apply.)

❑ A. TACACS+ or RADIUS can be used for authorization.

❑ B. TACACS+ or RADIUS can be used for authentication.

❑ C. RADIUS authorization is not supported on the PIX.

❑ D. TACACS+ can be used with downloadable ACLs.

Question 46

Which command specifies a variable IP address that will be used during a new NAT?

○ A. **nat**

○ B. **static**

○ C. **global**

○ D. **local**

Question 47

What is the correct command for the PIX to use a default route of 172.168.1.1?

○ A. **route outside 0.0.0.0 0.0.0.0 172.168.1.1 1**

○ B. **route outside default 172.168.1.1 1**

○ C. **route 172.168.1.1 default**

○ D. **route default outside 172.168.1.1 1**

Question 48

Which is a valid translation type on the PIX? (Select all that apply.)

❑ A. **dynamic inside nat**

❑ B. **static inside nat**

❑ C. **dynamic outside nat**

❑ D. **static outside nat**

Question 49

Which syntax would allow any host on the 10.2.0.0 / 16 network to reach a Web server on the 30.0.0.0 / 8 network?

- ○ A. **access-list ACL1 permit tcp 10.2.0.0 0.0.255.255 30.0.0. 0 0.255.255.255 eq 80**

- ○ B. **access-list ACL1 permit tcp 10.2.0.0 255.255.0.0 30.0.0. 0 255.0.0.0 eq 80**

- ○ C. **access-list ACL1 permit tcp 30.0.0.0 0.255.255.255 10.2.0. 0 0.0.255.255 eq 80**

- ○ D. **access-list ACL1 permit tcp 30.0.0.0 255.0.0.0 10.2.0. 0 255.255.0.0 eq 80**

Question 50

Which command is used to apply an access list to an interface?

- ○ A. **interface**
- ○ B. **access-list**
- ○ C. **name-if**
- ○ D. **access-group**

Question 51

Which traffic should be allowed through the PIX outside interface to support IPSec? (Select all that apply.)

- ❑ A. Protocol 50
- ❑ B. TCP port 23
- ❑ C. UDP port 500
- ❑ D. All of the above

Question 52

Which is the best definition of AAA Flood Guard?

- ○ A. It prevents synflood attacks against AAA servers.
- ○ B. It reclaims authorization given to users if attacks are sourced from their AAA-derived IP address.
- ○ C. It reclaims overused AAA resources to help prevent DoS attacks on AAA services.
- ○ D. It is disabled by default.

Question 53

Which option is available for the PIX in response to a detected attack? (Select all that apply.)

- ❏ A. Send an alarm to a syslog server.
- ❏ B. Implement a shun statement to stop future attacks.
- ❏ C. Drop the offending packet.
- ❏ D. Send a TCP reset if the signature match is TCP based.

Question 54

In the PIX MC, valid options for importing a device include all except which of the following?

- ○ A. Import the configuration from a device.
- ○ B. Import the configuration file for a device.
- ○ C. Import the configuration files for multiple devices.
- ○ D. Import the configuration from Cisco Secure Policy Manager.

Question 55

Which of the statements is true regarding access rules in the PIX MC? (Select all that apply.)

- ❏ A. Rules are recognized as either mandatory or default.
- ❏ B. Rules can be applied only at a group level or individual device.
- ❏ C. Default rules can be overridden.
- ❏ D. Rules can be applied at the global level.

Answer Key 1

1. A, B, C	**20.** B, D	**39.** C
2. D	**21.** A	**40.** D
3. A, B	**22.** E	**41.** D
4. B	**23.** E	**42.** B
5. B	**24.** C	**43.** A
6. A	**25.** E	**44.** D
7. C, E	**26.** D	**45.** B, C
8. A	**27.** B	**46.** C
9. C	**28.** A, B, C	**47.** A
10. A, D	**29.** D	**48.** A, B, C, D
11. A, B, C, D, E	**30.** A	**49.** B
12. A, D	**31.** A	**50.** D
13. B	**32.** B	**51.** A, C
14. B, C, E	**33.** A, D	**52.** C
15. A, C, D	**34.** A, C	**53.** A, C, D
16. A, B, C, D	**35.** B	**54.** D
17. D	**36.** B	**55.** A, C, D
18. C	**37.** D	
19. D	**38.** B, C	

Question 1

Answers A, B, and C are correct. An access list on the PIX can filter on source and destination IP addresses as well as the source and destination port number. The protocol number can also be used for a match within the access list. Answer D is incorrect because the PIX does not support IPX.

Question 2

Answer D is correct. The write memory command saves the configuration on the PIX to persistent memory (flash) on the PIX. Answers A and C are not valid PIX commands and are therefore incorrect. Answer B is incorrect because the write terminal command shows the configuration on the terminal but does not save it to flash.

Question 3

Answers A and B are correct. The nameif command assigns a name to each perimeter interface on the PIX firewall and specifies its security level. Answer C is incorrect because the interface command enables an interface and configures its type and speed. There is no security-level command on the PIX, so answer D is incorrect.

Question 4

Answer B is correct. The reload command reboots the PIX and loads the configuration saved to flash memory upon bootup. The init commands—cycle, init, and restart—are not native commands on the PIX operating system for performing a reboot of the PIX, so answers A, C, D, and E are incorrect. When issuing the reload command and confirming the reboot, any unsaved commands in the configuration will be not be present upon bootup.

Question 5

Answer B is correct. Normally, syslog messages are sent to the syslog specified in the configuration of the PIX. In the event that a configured syslog server cannot be reached, 100 messages are buffered, which makes answers

A, C, D, and E incorrect. Any additional messages overwrite the previous messages, beginning with the oldest in a first in first out (FIFO) manner.

Question 6

Answer A is correct. One of the options an IP phone can use is the address of a TFTP server. The phone can then use the TFTP server information to download configuration information the phone needs for correct operation. You use option 66 to forward a single TFTP IP address or option 150 to forward a list of TFTP server IP addresses. This information is useful only to the DHCP clients who need the TFTP information, such as IP telephones. Answers B, C, D, and E are not the correct syntax and are therefore incorrect.

Question 7

Answers C and E are correct. Translations occur at the Network layer. A host going through NAT would have a layer 3 translation from the inside local to the inside global. The same computer can have multiple connections to servers using the same translation but multiple connections. One TCP session could be to `www.site1.com`, whereas another could be to `www.site2.com` and another to `ftp.site3.com`. Connections occur at the Transport layer. One translated IP address can support multiple connections to these servers. Connections are a subset of translations. Answers A, B, and D are therefore incorrect.

Question 8

Answer A is correct. If a client on an inside network requests DNS resolution of an inside resource from an external or outside DNS, the DNS A-Record is translated by the PIX correctly before it is forwarded to the inside client. This enables the inside client to receive the inside IP address for the server and correctly reach that resource. The `dns` option in the `nat` or `static` command replaces the need to use an `alias` command, which makes answer B incorrect. The `alias` command, in earlier versions of the PIX operating system, performed the same function as the new `dns` option on the `nat` or `static` command and does not filter or restrict, which makes answers C and D incorrect.

Question 9

Answer C is correct. Globally enabling Turbo access lists is a simple configuration. You use the `access-list compiled` command to configure Turbo ACLs, which makes answer D incorrect. This command causes the Turbo ACL process to scan through all existing ACLs. You can also use Turbo ACLs on a specific access list, as opposed to enabling them globally. Answers A, B, and E are not the correct syntax and are therefore incorrect.

Question 10

Answers A and D are correct. For object groups to be nested, they must be of the same type. You can group two or more network object groups together, but you cannot nest different group types together, such as a protocol group and a network group. Therefore, answers C and E are incorrect. Nesting an object group within another object group is possible using the command-line interface, but no group object exists, so answer B is incorrect.

Question 11

Answers A, B, C, D, and E are correct. A good firewall inspects packets above the Network layer and securely opens and closes negotiated ports or IP addresses for legitimate connections through the PIX. This is important, especially in multimedia applications where ports are assigned on-the-fly and manual configuration for each application is reasonably accomplished in a busy network. The stateful nature of the PIX dynamically compensates for advanced protocols, such as h.323.

Question 12

Answers A and D are correct. The PIX can detect two signature types: informational and attack. Therefore, answers C and E are incorrect. Information class signatures are triggered by normal network activity, whereas attack signatures are triggered by an activity known to be, or that could lead to, unauthorized data retrieval, system access, or privileged escalation. Because A is correct, B is incorrect.

Question 13

Answer B is correct. The access server IP address is the IP address of the PIX firewall that will be using the ACS services. From the ACS server perspective, any devices that will be requesting AAA services via TACACS+ or RADIUS from the ACS server are considered clients. During installation, the access server IP address is requested. This access server is the PIX that will be the AAA client, and the PIX IP address should be supplied. Therefore, answers A, C, and D are incorrect.

Question 14

Answers B, C, and E are correct. The 501, 506E, 515E, 525, and 535 models are all valid firewall models. Answers A and D are incorrect because these models do not exist.

Question 15

Answers A, C, and D are correct. Restricted, unrestricted, and failover are the types of licenses for PIX firewall models 515E, 525, and 535. Answer B is incorrect because the unlimited license does not exist.

Question 16

Answers A, B, C, and D are correct. The clock command sets the Pix firewall clock and enables you to specify the time, month, date, and year. It is retained in memory by a battery on the motherboard.

Question 17

Answer D is correct. If two interfaces, such as E2 and E3, were both set to a security level of 50, no packets would be capable of flowing directly between the two interfaces. This is a valid configuration, such as when a provider has two servers that should never communicate directly. Therefore, answer A is incorrect. Answers B and C are incorrect because the physical number of the interface has nothing to do with the logical security levels the PIX uses to identify higher or lower security interfaces.

Question 18

Answer C is correct. Traffic that needs to go from a lower security interface to a higher needs to have permission to do so. The application of an access list could provide this permission. Answers A, B, and D are incorrect because they do not provide the permissions from lower to higher security levels.

Question 19

Answer D is correct. Security level 100 is the most trusted interface security level. Answers A and B are incorrect because they apply to security level 0. Answer C is incorrect because security level 100 is the default and cannot be changed. Answer E is incorrect because it correlates to security levels 1–99.

Question 20

Answers B and D are correct. The `multicast interface` command on each interface enables multicast forwarding, and the `mroute` command creates a static route from the transmission source to the next-hop router; therefore, answer E is incorrect. The `igmp forward` command could allow clients on the inside to receive a multicast stream from the outside, so answer A is incorrect. `multicast routing` is an IOS command, but it is not a valid command on the PIX, so answer C is incorrect.

Question 21

Answer A is correct. The `nat` command, when used with the `global` command, can enable translation for a single host or a range of hosts. Answers B and D are incorrect because they aren't the commands to configure translation. Answer C is incorrect because this command does not exist.

Question 22

Answer E is correct. Answers A, B, C, and D are all events that syslog is used to document.

Question 23

Answer E is correct. The PIX operating system is Cisco proprietary and is called Finesse. Answers A, B, C, and D are incorrect because the OS is not based on any flavor of Unix nor NT.

Question 24

Answer C is correct. The only options for authentication with the PIX are HTTP, FTP, and Telnet. By using virtual Telnet, users could Telnet to the PIX, authenticate, and then use their email applications through the PIX. Answer A is incorrect because it is not a valid option on the PIX. Answer B is incorrect because virtual HTTP does not provide a user interface for authentication to the PIX. Answer D is incorrect because the SMTP fixup protocol doesn't provide the authentication needed by the users.

Question 25

Answer E is correct. Configuration replication occurs over the serial failover cable from the primary/active PIX firewall to the secondary/standby PIX firewall. Therefore, answers A, B, C, and D are incorrect.

Question 26

Answer D is correct. The nat command's companion is the global command. Both are used together to translate IP addresses. Answers A, B, and C are incorrect commands for this task.

Question 27

Answer B is correct. By default, only interfaces with higher security levels can access interfaces with lower security levels, which makes answers A, C, and D incorrect.

Question 28

Answers A, B, and C are correct. A connection table is used for TCP and UDP sessions, and a translation table is used for NAT sessions. A stateful database is used for tracking sessions, so answer D is incorrect.

Question 29

Answer D is correct. The PIX 535 firewall can be configured with up to 10 interfaces, making answers A, B, C, and E incorrect.

Question 30

Answer A is correct. ACLs do not improve performance for matching packets; rather they slow down the processor. Answers B, C, and D are all correct concerning ACLs.

Question 31

Answer A is correct. The Cisco Secure ACS allows specific user traffic through the PIX while denying packets from unknown users. Traffic Director, Management Center, and Cisco Secure Policy Manager don't provide per-user access control, which makes answers B, C, and D incorrect.

Question 32

Answer B is correct. The `ca zeroize rsa` command is used to delete a saved RSA key from flash memory. Answer A is incorrect because this command erases the configuration but not the RSA key(s). Answers C and D are not valid PIX commands and are therefore incorrect.

Question 33

Answers A and D are correct. The MailGuard feature is enabled by default and allows only the RFC 821 legal SMTP commands through the PIX. The IDS feature can protect against spam, so answer C is incorrect. The MailGuard feature is part of the PIX OS and is not limited to PIX firewalls that have at least 32MB of RAM, making answer B incorrect.

Question 34

Answers A and C are correct. the `object-group` command names your object group and enables a subcommand mode for the type of object you specify. Answer B is completely false regarding the command, and answer D is incorrect because the `clear object-group` command removes all defined object groups.

Question 35

Answer B is correct. The PIX firewall transmits default route updates using an IP destination of 224.0.0.9. if configured for RIP version 2 with the keyword `default`. Answer A is incorrect because RIP version 2 does not have an aggressive mode. Answer C is incorrect because the IP destination is 224.0.0.9. Answer D is incorrect because the question *does* have a correct answer.

Question 36

Answer B is correct. The command to change the enable password is `enable password`. The PIX has no `enable secret` command, so answer A is incorrect. The `passwd` command sets the Telnet password, making answer C incorrect. The `set` command shown in answer D is not a valid option and is therefore incorrect.

Question 37

Answer D is correct. PAT provides for address expansion, it maps port numbers to a single IP address, and the PAT address can be different from the outside interface address. Answers A, B, and C are all correct statements regarding PAT.

Question 38

Answers B and C are correct. DNS Guard tears down the UDP return path after the first response from a given DNS server is seen, which helps prevent UDP session hijacking. Answers A and D are incorrect because DNS Guard does not control which DNS servers the clients can access.

Question 39

Answer C is correct. The `isakmp enable outside` command enables IKE on the PIX firewall's outside interface. Answers A and B are incorrect because the `crypto` command is not used for enabling IKE on an interface. Answer D is incorrect because the physical interface is being used instead of the name of the interface.

Question 40

Answer D is correct. The `passwd` command sets the password for Telnet access to the PIX, making answers A and C incorrect. The `enable password` command sets the enable password, making answer B incorrect.

Question 41

Answer D is correct. The PIX firewall SSH implementation functions only as a server, which means that the PIX can't initiate SSH outbound connections. Thus, answers A, B, and C are incorrect.

Question 42

Answer B is correct. The `nameif` command assigns a name to an interface. The `name` command enables you to configure a list of name-to-IP address mappings, making answer A incorrect. `hostname` enables you to change the hostname on the PIX, so answer C is incorrect. `ifName` is not a valid command on the PIX, making answer D incorrect.

Question 43

Answer A is correct. The noconfirm option permits the PIX to reload without user confirmation, which makes answer D incorrect. Answers B and C are incorrect because they are not options for the reload command.

Question 44

Answer D is correct. The interface command enables an interface and configures its type and speed, making answer E incorrect. Answer A is not a valid PIX command and is therefore incorrect. Answer B is an option that can be used with the interface command and is not a correct answer. nameif is used to set the name and security level of an interface, so answer C is incorrect.

Question 45

Answers B and C are correct. RADIUS and TACACS+ are methods used by a PIX to communicate with an AAA server, such as ACS. Downloadable ACLs are supported with RADIUS only. The downloadable ACLs are a function of AAA authentication and require RADIUS, so answer D is incorrect. Authorization, a separate function, is available only between the PIX and the ACS if TACACS+ is used; therefore, answer A is incorrect.

Question 46

Answer C is correct. The global command specifies the IP addresses that will be used with dynamic NAT for a new translation. Answer D is incorrect because it is not a valid PIX command. Answer A is incorrect because it specifies which devices are allowed to be translated. Answer B is incorrect because the static command causes the same IP address to be used every time.

Question 47

Answer A is correct. route outside 0.0.0.0 0.0.0.0 172.168.1.1 1 is the correct syntax for the PIX to use a default route of 172.168.1.1. Answers B, C, and D are incorrect because they're incorrect syntax.

Question 48

Answers A, B, C, and D are correct. Dynamic and static inside and outside NAT are all valid options.

Question 49

Answer B is correct. `access-list ACL1 permit tcp 10.2.0.0 255.255.0.0 30.0.0.0 255.0.0.0 eq 80`, within an applied access list, would allow any host on the 10.2.0.0 / 16 network to reach a Web server on the 30.0.0.0 / 8 network, which makes answers A, C, and D incorrect.

Question 50

Answer D is correct. The command used to apply an access list to an interface is `access-group`. `interface`, `access-list`, and `nameif`, though valid commands, are incorrect for this task. Therefore, answers A, B, and C are incorrect.

Question 51

Answers A and C are correct. IPSec uses UDP port 500 for IKE phase 1 and protocol 50 (ESP) for encrypted traffic. TCP port 23 is not required, so answers B and D are incorrect.

Question 52

Answer C is correct. AAA Flood Guard reclaims overused AAA resources to help prevent DoS attacks on AAA services and is enabled by default, which makes answer D incorrect. It does not protect against synflood attacks against AAA servers, which means answer A is incorrect. It also does not take back authorization from users, meaning answer B is incorrect.

Question 53

Answers A, C, and D are correct. When the PIX detects an attack, it can be configured either to send an alarm to a syslog server and drop the offending packet or drop the packet and send a TCP reset to close the TCP session. The PIX can't, on its own power, apply a shun statement to block the attacker from future access, which makes answer B incorrect. To dynamically implement a shun requires an IDS appliance or a similar external resource.

Question 54

Answer D is correct. Answers A, B, and C are all valid options for importing a device in the PIX MC. The MC does not have an import menu option to pull a configuration from CSPM.

Question 55

Answers A, C, and D are correct. Rules are recognized as mandatory or default and can be applied at the global level, at a group level, or to an individual device. Thus, answer B is incorrect. In addition, default rules can be overridden.

Sample Test 2

Question 1

Which of the following statements are true regarding proxy servers? (Select all that apply.)

- ❑ A. They examine packets at higher layers of the OSI model.
- ❑ B. They limit packets going into a network based on static packet header information.
- ❑ C. They have high performance under stress.
- ❑ D. They provide fault tolerance using a single proxy.
- ❑ E. They have a single point of failure.

Question 2

Which of the following statements is true regarding stateful packet filtering? (Select all that apply.)

- ❑ A. It has slower performance than a proxy firewall.
- ❑ B. It has better performance than a proxy server.
- ❑ C. It maintains complete session state.
- ❑ D. It records data only for connection-oriented communications.
- ❑ E. Packets are compared against the stateless database.

Question 3

Which of the following statements is true about a connection logged in a stateful session flow table?

- ○ A. It's for inbound TCP connections only.
- ○ B. It's for outbound TCP connections only.
- ○ C. It's used each time a TCP connection is established inbound or outbound.
- ○ D. It's used only when a TCP connection is established from a lower security level to higher level.

Question 4

Where should configuration be applied in a fault-tolerant scenario?

○ A. On the primary firewall only

○ B. On the secondary firewall only

○ C. On the active firewall only

○ D. On the standby firewall only

Question 5

In which bus should a quad Ethernet card or a VPN Accelerator card be installed on a PIX 535?

○ A. Bus 0

○ B. Bus 1

○ C. Bus 2

○ D. Bus 3

○ E. Bus 4

Question 6

Which of the following is correct regarding PIX license keys?

○ A. The key is specific to the hardware platform.

○ B. The key is not specific to the software version.

○ C. The key is specific to the serial number on the box.

○ D. The key is specific to the show system serial number.

○ E. The key is specific to the software version.

Question 7

Which administrative access modes does a PIX firewall support? (Select all that apply.)

❏ A. Configuration

❏ B. User

❏ C. Privileged

❏ D. Monitor

❏ E. Object-group

Question 8

Which of the following best describes the options in privileged mode?

○ A. Change current settings

○ B. Change system configurations

○ C. Modify IPX network parameters

○ D. Recover passwords

○ E. View future features

Question 9

What are the two ways in which to configure the PIX firewall through interactive prompts? (Select all that apply.)

❏ A. Use the **setup** command.

❏ B. Use the **init 0** command.

❏ C. Use the **init 6** command.

❏ D. Reboot the PIX.

❏ E. Erase the saved configuration and reboot the PIX.

Question 10

To obtain a software feature upgrade, what information is needed?

○ A. Serial number displayed by the **write terminal** command

○ B. The serial number on the chassis

○ C. The serial number displayed by the **show version** command

○ D. Either the serial number on the chassis or the serial number displayed by the **show version** command

○ E. Either the serial number on the chassis or the serial number displayed by the **write terminal** command

Question 11

Which of the following characterizes the PIX's Adaptive Security Algorithm? (Select all that apply.)

❑ A. It randomizes initial TCP sequence numbers.

❑ B. It randomizes all TCP sequence numbers.

❑ C. It tracks source and destination ports.

❑ D. It tracks TCP flags.

❑ E. It randomizes TCP flags.

Question 12

Which of the following is true regarding the ASA?

○ A. Allows one-way outbound connections without explicit configuration for each internal system application

○ B. Allows one-way outbound connections with explicit configuration for each internal system and application

○ C. Allows two-way outbound connections without explicit configuration for each internal system and application

○ D. Allows two-way outbound connections with explicit configuration for each internal system and application

○ E. Allows two-way inbound connections without explicit configuration for each internal system and application

Question 13

What are the correct commands to specify the security level and duplex for an interface? (Select all that apply.)

- ❑ A. **interface**
- ❑ B. **nameif**
- ❑ C. **ip address**
- ❑ D. **security-level**
- ❑ E. **global**

Question 14

Which PIX syslog events are considered system events? (Select all that apply.)

- ❑ A. Dropped UDP packets
- ❑ B. Translation slot deletion
- ❑ C. Bytes transferred by connection
- ❑ D. PIX reboot
- ❑ E. Console logouts

Question 15

Which command is used to specify the DHCP pool used by the PIX firewall to support DHCP clients?

- ○ A. **dhcp address**
- ○ B. **dhcp pool**
- ○ C. **dhcpd address**
- ○ D. **dhcpd ip pool**
- ○ E. **dhcpd pool**

Question 16

You have configured the PIX to obtain its outside IP address via DHCP. You want the PIX to forward configuration parameters received from the DHCP server on the outside interface to inside DHCP client hosts. What command should you use?

○ A. **dhcpd auto_config**

○ B. **dhcpd outside inside**

○ C. **dhcpd configure inside**

○ D. **dhcpd pass inside**

○ E. **dhcpd enable inside**

Question 17

How many DNS servers can a DHCP client acquire from a PIX DHCP server?

○ A. 1

○ B. 2

○ C. 4

○ D. 6

Question 18

What is the command to start the DHCP server service on a PIX firewall?

○ A. **dhcp enable**

○ B. **service dhcp**

○ C. **dhcp service**

○ D. **dhcpd enable**

○ E. None of the above

Question 19

Which of the following statements is true regarding the PIX and PPPoE?

- ○ A. PPPoE increases reliability exponentially.
- ○ B. PPPoE is used with broadband connections.
- ○ C. The PIX's PPPoE client is compatible with failover.
- ○ D. The PIX's PPPoE client is compatible with L2TP.
- ○ E. The PIX's PPPoE client is compatible with PPTP.

Question 20

Which option is used when configuring PPPoE on the PIX?

- ○ A. Crypto maps
- ○ B. Transform sets
- ○ C. VPDN groups and usernames
- ○ D. Digital certificates

Question 21

Why is UDP difficult to inspect properly? (Select all that apply.)

- ❏ A. It has no sequencing or handshaking.
- ❏ B. It has no clear beginning.
- ❏ C. It uses unknown layer 4 attributes.
- ❏ D. It has no clear flow state.

Question 22

What is the minimum number of **nat** and **global** statements to allow dmz hosts and inside hosts to reach servers on the outside?

- ○ A. One **global**, one **nat**
- ○ B. One **global**, two **nat**
- ○ C. Two **global**, one **nat**
- ○ D. Two **global**, two **nat**

Question 23

What happens when a **global** command and **static** command compete to use the same IP address?

- ○ A. The first one appearing in the configuration uses the IP address.
- ○ B. The first one that actually uses the IP address is given exclusive use of it.
- ○ C. The **global** command, being systemwide, always takes precedence over a **static** command.
- ○ D. The **static** command takes precedence over the nat and **global** pairs.

Question 24

What would be an ideal reason to use dynamic outside NAT?

- ○ A. To improve the performance of the ASA
- ○ B. To simplify router configuration on internal or perimeter networks
- ○ C. To contain hidden codes that can destroy data on the internal network
- ○ D. To promptly secure packets after failover

Question 25

What technique is used to allow an inside host to have the same local and global inside address?

- ○ A. NAT-T Nat Traversal
- ○ B. Alias
- ○ C. Identity NAT (or NAT 0)
- ○ D. None of the above

Question 26

Which of the following statements is correct regarding PAT? (Select all that apply.)

- ❑ A. It can use the outside interface address as the PAT address.
- ❑ B. It can use the DMZ interface address as the PAT address.
- ❑ C. The PAT address must be the outside interface IP address.
- ❑ D. PAT and NAT can be used together.
- ❑ E. The PAT address can be received via DHCP.

Question 27

You have only one publicly routable IP address available, and this is the PAT
address. Which command will enable an outside host to connect to specific
servers on the inside interface for a specific service?

- ○ A. **alias**
- ○ B. **conduit**
- ○ C. **global**
- ○ D. **nat**
- ○ E. **static**

Question 28

You want to apply an access list named DMZ to the inside interface. What is the
correct command?

- ○ A. **access-list DMZ apply inside**
- ○ B. **access-group DMZ out inside**
- ○ C. **access-group DMZ in interface inside**
- ○ D. **access-group DMZ interface inside out**
- ○ E. **access-group DMZ out interface inside**

Question 29

Which of the following is true regarding Turbo ACLs? (Select all that apply.)

- ❏ A. Turbo ACLs improve the average search time for all ACLs containing a
  large number of entries.
- ❏ B. Turbo ACLs improve the average search time for all ACLs containing
  any number of entries.
- ❏ C. Turbo ACLs improve the average search time only for ACLs containing
  a small number of entries.
- ❏ D. Turbo ACLs require a significant amount of memory.
- ❏ E. Turbo ACLs do not require a significant amount of memory.

Question 30

Why can ActiveX controls create security problems on your network? (Select all that apply.)

❑ A. ActiveX controls can be inserted into Web pages.

❑ B. ActiveX controls can be used to attack servers.

❑ C. ActiveX controls can be used to reroute packets on an IOS router.

❑ D. ActiveX controls can be inserted into applications.

❑ E. ACLs are used to block ActiveX controls.

Question 31

What is the purpose of object groups?

○ A. To easily apply specific security policies to specific groups

○ B. To ease the configuration of security policies

○ C. To reduce the number of ACL entries required to implement complex security policies

○ D. To speed the configuration of complex security policies

○ E. To ease troubleshooting issues when implementing security policies

Question 32

After issuing the **object-group protocol MYPROTO** command, which prompt does the PIX display?

○ A. **pix(config-if)#**

○ B. **pix(config-protocol)#**

○ C. **pix(object-config)#**

○ D. **pix(network-config)#**

○ E. **pix(config-object)#**

Question 33

Which elements of an access list can be replaced using an object group? (Select all that apply.)

- ❏ A. The source IP address
- ❏ B. The port number
- ❏ C. The configuration sequence number
- ❏ D. The access list name
- ❏ E. The ICMP type

Question 34

You want to enable RIP version 2 on the inside interface of the PIX. You do not want the PIX to broadcast a default route. What is the correct command to accomplish this?

- ○ A. **rip version 2 default inside**
- ○ B. **rip version 2 passive inside**
- ○ C. **rip version 2 inside**
- ○ D. **rip inside version 2 passive**
- ○ E. **rip inside passive version 2**

Question 35

What is the required command(s) to allow the PIX to forward multicast traffic if the multicast source is on a higher security level interface? (Select all that apply.)

- ❏ A. **mroute**
- ❏ B. **multicast interface**
- ❏ C. **igmp forward**
- ❏ D. **multicast routing**
- ❏ E. No command is required. By default, the PIX forwards traffic from high security interfaces to low security interfaces.

Question 36

What is the required command(s) to allow hosts on the inside to receive multi-cast traffic from a server on the outside of the PIX? (Select all that apply.)

- ❑ A. **mroute**
- ❑ B. **multicast interface**
- ❑ C. **igmp join**
- ❑ D. **igmp forward**
- ❑ E. **multicast routing**

Question 37

Which of the following is correct regarding the **fixup** protocol for FTP? (Select all that apply.)

- ❑ A. You must manually enable this command for standard FTP port inspection.
- ❑ B. It is enabled by default for standard FTP port inspection.
- ❑ C. It causes the PIX to perform NAT or PAT in the payloads of packets.
- ❑ D. You must manually configure the **fixup** protocol **ftp** command to perform NAT or PAT for packet payloads.
- ❑ E. It automatically logs **ftp** commands.

Question 38

Which advanced protocol enables call handling sessions—particularly two-party audio conferences?

- ○ A. SCCP
- ○ B. H.323
- ○ C. RTSP
- ○ D. SIP

Question 39

The Mail Guard feature inspects port 25 by default. Which of the following is correct for the **fixup** protocol for SMTP? (Select all that apply.)

❑ A. If it's disabled, no SMTP traffic is allowed through the PIX.

❑ B. If it's disabled, all SMTP traffic is allowed through the PIX.

❑ C. It allows only RFC-compliant commands through the PIX.

❑ D. It's enabled by default.

❑ E. It must be manually enabled.

Question 40

Which of the following is true when using the DNS Guard feature? (Select all that apply.)

❑ A. DNS Guard always remains on.

❑ B. The DNS server response is recognized by the PIX firewall.

❑ C. After a DNS request, UDP packets are allowed to return from the DNS server.

❑ D. DNS Guard recognizes an inbound query to port 51.

❑ E. DNS Guard tears down the UDP conduit after the first DNS response is received.

Question 41

Which statement is true regarding the PIX's TCP Intercept feature for OS versions 5.2 and higher? (Select all that apply.)

❑ A. It's on by default when you optionally configure an embryonic limit.

❑ B. It must be explicitly configured.

❑ C. When the embryonic limit is reached, the PIX intercepts SYN packets.

❑ D. When the embryonic limit is reached, the PIX drops new SYN packets.

❑ E. The PIX can respond to a SYN with a SYN/ACK packet after the embryonic limit is reached.

Question 42

Which command is used to enable intrusion detection on the PIX?

○ A. **ip audit**

○ B. **ip ids**

○ C. **ip info**

○ D. **ip attack**

○ E. **ip access**

Question 43

Which command is used to apply an IDS policy named **DETECT** to the outside interface?

○ A. **ip audit outside DETECT**

○ B. **ip audit in interface outside DETECT**

○ C. **ip audit outside DETECT**

○ D. **ip audit interface outside DETECT**

○ E. **ip audit DETECT interface outside**

Question 44

Which of the following applies when considering the PIX firewall's shunning capabilities? (Select all that apply.)

❑ A. The **shun** command's blocking capability is applied only when the specified connection is currently active.

❑ B. The **shun** command is designed primarily for use by a Cisco IDS appliance.

❑ C. The blocking function can be removed manually or automatically by the IDS appliance.

❑ D. Packets are dropped if they contain the IP source address of the attacking host.

Question 45

When authenticating to the PIX via FTP, with AAA enabled, what is the correct way to enter your username if the authentication database differs from the username configured on the remote FTP server you are trying to access?

○ A. **aaa_username**

○ B. **remote_username**

○ C. **remote_username@aaa_username**

○ D. **aaa_username@remote_username**

○ E. Both usernames must be the same to authenticate.

Question 46

What is the purpose of the **aaa group** tag?

○ A. To specify RADIUS-only server groups

○ B. To enable identical groups of TACACS+ servers

○ C. To access servers one at a time for a close, examined startup

○ D. To direct authentication, authorization, or accounting traffic to the appropriate AAA server

Question 47

Which protocol can be used with AAA authentication prompts? (Select all that apply.)

❏ A. FTP

❏ B. HTTP

❏ C. Kerberos

❏ D. SIP

❏ E. Telnet

Question 48

Which statement is true regarding Virtual Telnet? (Select all that apply.)

- ❑ A. It provides a mechanism for users to authenticate with the PIX.
- ❑ B. The IP address must be an unused global address to authenticate inbound and outbound clients.
- ❑ C. The IP address must be an unused global address to authenticate outbound clients only.
- ❑ D. After authentication, the PIX firewall forwards a Web request to the intended Web server.

Question 49

Which of the following statements is true regarding Telnet? (Select all that apply.)

- ❑ A. The default password for Telnet is **in-default**.
- ❑ B. The PIX requires the generation of RSA keys to support Telnet.
- ❑ C. The PIX allows a maximum of five simultaneous Telnet sessions.
- ❑ D. Telnet is available on the outside interface with or without IPSec.
- ❑ E. Telnet is available on the outside interface if it's used with IPSec.

Question 50

Which is true regarding the PIX firewall and AAA services? (Select all that apply.)

- ❑ A. TACACS+ or RADIUS can be used for authentication.
- ❑ B. TACACS+ or RADIUS can be used for authorization.
- ❑ C. TACACS+ can be used with downloadable ACLs.
- ❑ D. RADIUS authorization is not supported on the PIX.

Question 51

When using the PIX's downloadable named ACL feature, where can the ACLs that will be downloaded into the PIX reside?

○ A. RADIUS server

○ B. TACACS+ server

○ C. Router

○ D. TFTP server

○ E. FTP server

Question 52

When the primary PIX fails, which IP addresses and MAC addresses will the primary PIX use?

○ A. The system IP addresses and system MAC addresses

○ B. The failover IP addresses and MAC addresses

○ C. The primary IP addresses and primary MAC addresses

○ D. The virtual IP addresses and virtual MAC addresses

○ E. The virtual IP addresses and primary MAC addresses

Question 53

For a PIX to successfully fail over, which of the following parameters must be the same on all the PIXs configured for fallover? (Select all that apply.)

❑ A. Same model number

❑ B. Same software versions

❑ C. Same manufacture date

❑ D. Same amount of flash

❑ E. Same amount of RAM

Question 54

When are commands replicated from the active PIX to the standby PIX? (Select all that apply.)

- ❑ A. When changes are made to the standby.
- ❑ B. As commands are entered on the active PIX.
- ❑ C. The standby PIX must be manually configured.
- ❑ D. When the standby PIX firewall completes its initial bootup.
- ❑ E. When the **write standby** command is used.

Question 55

Which of the following is correct regarding the failover interface testing process? (Select all that apply.)

- ❑ A. The purpose of the tests is to determine which PIX firewall has failed.
- ❑ B. After 30 seconds of no response on an interface, the PIX uses the backup interface.
- ❑ C. One test sends out a broadcast ping request.
- ❑ D. The Link Up/Down test tests the NIC.

Question 56

How does configuration replication occur between the active PIX firewall and the standby PIX firewall configured for standard failover?

- ○ A. Over any active interface
- ○ B. Over the inside interface
- ○ C. Over the outside interface only if the failure occurred on the inside interface
- ○ D. Over the failover cable
- ○ E. Over the stateful failover cable

Question 57

Which of the following is a characteristic of LAN-based failover? (Select all that apply.)

- ❑ A. It incorporates the ACL packets in flow tables.
- ❑ B. It can use message encryption and authentication to secure failover transmissions.
- ❑ C. It requires a dedicated switch, hub, or VLAN.
- ❑ D. It uses an Ethernet cable rather than the serial failover cable.

Question 58

Which of the following describes IKE? (Select all that apply.)

- ❑ A. It is a variant of DES.
- ❑ B. It provides authentication of the IPSec peers.
- ❑ C. It is synonymous with ISAKMP.
- ❑ D. It is a hybrid protocol.

Question 59

The IKE policy parameters include which of the following? (Select all that apply.)

- ❑ A. The peer authentication method
- ❑ B. The message encryption algorithm
- ❑ C. RSA key pair generation parameters
- ❑ D. The message integrity algorithm
- ❑ E. The ISAKMP-established security association's lifetime

Question 60

Which command allows you to enable ISAKMP on **e0**?

- ○ A. **no isakmp enable outside**
- ○ B. **isakmp enable outside**
- ○ C. **no isakmp enable**
- ○ D. **enable IKE outside**

Question 61

What is the purpose of crypto ACLs?

- ○ A. To define interesting traffic
- ○ B. To encrypt traffic
- ○ C. To decrypt traffic
- ○ D. To prevent traffic from using the IPSec tunnel
- ○ E. To authenticate IPSec peers

Question 62

What is the maximum number of transforms that can belong to a transform set?

- ○ A. 1
- ○ B. 2
- ○ C. 3
- ○ D. 4

Question 63

What is the command **ip local pool** used for?

- ○ A. DHCP pools
- ○ B. DHCPD pools
- ○ C. IPSec pools
- ○ D. VPDN pools

Question 64

Which configuration item is vital for a VPN software client successfully connecting to a PIX using IPSec?

- ○ A. The VPN group IP address matches the address in the VPN client.
- ○ B. The VPN group ACL count matches the count in the VPN client.
- ○ C. The VPN group password matches the password in the VPN client.
- ○ D. None of the above.

Question 65

Which of the following statements is true regarding SSH?

○ A. The PIX supports only SSH version 1.

○ B. The PIX supports only SSH version 2.

○ C. The PIX supports either SSH version 1 or 2.

○ D. The PIX must have a 3DES activation key to support SSH.

○ E. SSH passwords are configured with the **ssh passwd** command.

Question 66

What is the correct command to associate privilege level 10 with the password of **supersecret**?

○ A. **enable supersecret 10**

○ B. **privilege 10 password supersecret**

○ C. **privilege 10 supersecret**

○ D. **enable password supersecret level 10**

○ E. **enable password supersecret 10**

Question 67

What is required for password recovery on a PIX? (Select all that apply.)

❑ A. Privilege level 15 password

❑ B. A TFTP server

❑ C. Files from Cisco designed for password recovery

❑ D. Privilege level 1 password

Question 68

In PDM, how do you allow the previewing of commands before sending them to the PIX firewall?

○ A. The GUI prevents the viewing of the actual CLI commands.

○ B. Use the View menu and select the CLI commands at any time.

○ C. Select Options, Preview Commands Before Sending to PIX.

○ D. Select Tools, Preview Task Dialog Before Sending to PIX.

Question 69

Which of the following transforms is predefined by PDM? (Select all that apply.)

❏ A. ESP-DES-SHA

❏ B. ESP-3DES-SHA

❏ C. ESP-3DES-AH

❏ D. ESP-DES-AH

Question 70

What does PDM do when it reads a crypto map from a configuration, if the map is not applied to any interfaces?

○ A. PDM logs it in a stateful flow table.

○ B. PDM applies it to the required interface based on deduction.

○ C. PDM prompts you to run setup.

○ D. PDM parses and ignores it.

Question 71

Which of the following statements is true regarding the PIX Management Center? (Select all that apply.)

❏ A. It provides a workflow and audit trail.

❏ B. It allows Web-based management of multiple PIX firewalls.

❏ C. It uses SSL to ensure secure remote connectivity between the browser and server.

❏ D. It supports a maximum of 100 PIX firewalls.

Question 72

What is the name of the conversion tool to convert conduits to access lists?

○ A. **makeACL**

○ B. **conv**

○ C. **con2acl**

○ D. **mcfixup**

Question 73

From a browser, what is the correct port used to launch the PIX MC?

○ A. 443

○ B. 1812

○ C. 1741

○ D. 80

○ E. 1742

Question 74

How often does a PIX firewall check with the AUS for updates?

○ A. Every 720 minutes

○ B. Every 800 minutes

○ C. Every 1440 minutes

○ D. Every 1460 minutes

Question 75

What does AUS allow you to manage? (Select all that apply.)

❑ A. PIX firewall software images

❑ B. Bug tracking information

❑ C. PDM images

❑ D. IOS firewall feature sets

❑ E. PIX firewall configuration files

Answer Key 2

. . . .

1. A, E	**20.** C	**39.** B, C, D	**58.** B, C, D
2. B, C	**21.** A, B, D	**40.** A, B, C, E	**59.** A, B, D, E
3. C	**22.** B	**41.** A, C, E	**60.** B
4. C	**23.** D	**42.** A	**61.** A
5. C	**24.** B	**43.** D	**62.** C
6. B	**25.** C	**44.** B, C, D	**63.** C
7. A, C, D	**26.** A, B, D, E	**45.** D	**64.** C
8. A	**27.** E	**46.** D	**65.** A
9. A, E	**28.** C	**47.** A, B, E	**66.** D
10. C	**29.** A, D	**48.** A, B	**67.** B, C
11. A, C, D	**30.** A, B, D	**49.** C, E	**68.** C
12. A	**31.** C	**50.** A, D	**69.** A, B
13. A, B	**32.** B	**51.** A	**70.** D
14. D, E	**33.** A, B, D, E	**52.** B	**71.** A, B, C
15. C	**34.** E	**53.** A, B, D, E	**72.** B
16. A	**35.** A, B	**54.** B, D, E	**73.** C
17. B	**36.** B, D	**55.** A, C, D	**74.** A
18. D	**37.** B, C, E	**56.** D	**75.** A, C, E
19. B	**38.** D	**57.** B, C, D	

Question 1

Answers A and E are correct. One firewall technology is a proxy server. Proxy servers request connections between a client on the internal network and the external network. A client on the inside network establishes a connection to the proxy server, and the proxy server establishes a connection to the outside resource. All data flowing between the client to the outside server is processed at the higher layers by the intermediate proxy server; because of this layer 7 capability, answer B is incorrect. Proxy servers do not deliver high performance compared to other firewall options, so answer C is incorrect. One disadvantage of a single proxy server that processes each packet from inside hosts to outside servers is that it is also a single point of failure for the network, which makes answer D incorrect.

Question 2

Answers B and C are correct. The PIX uses stateful packet filtering and maintains a table for every connection or connectionless transaction. Packets are compared against a connection object, which determines which return packets are allowed from the outside network into the higher security inside network. A stateful packet-filtering device provides better performance over a proxy server because it does not have to analyze each packet at the upper layers of the OSI model, which makes answer A incorrect. Stateful packet filtering devices approximate connectionless protocols such as UDP, which makes answer D incorrect. The firewall uses a stateful, not stateless, database, which makes answer E incorrect.

Question 3

Answer C is correct. Each time a TCP connection is established for inbound or outbound connections through the PIX firewall, the information about the connection is logged in a stateful session flow table, which makes answers A, B, and D incorrect.

Question 4

Answer C is correct. This is a tricky question. When failover is configured, configuration changes should be made only on the active firewall. Normally, the primary firewall is the active one. However, in a failed condition, the active firewall is in standby mode, the secondary PIX is active, and configurations should be applied to the active PIX, which makes answer C the best answer and answers A, B, and D incorrect.

Question 5

Answer C is correct. The PIX-4FE and PIX-VPN-ACCEL cards can be installed only in the 32-bit, 33MHz bus, or bus 2, and they must never be installed in the 64-bit, 66MHz bus. Installing either of these cards in the faster bus can cause the system to hang, which make answers A and B incorrect. Buses 3 and 4 do not exist on the PIX 535; therefore, answers D and E are incorrect.

Question 6

Answer B is correct. License keys are not specific to a particular PIX software version, so answer E is incorrect. The same license key can be applied to the same physical PIX and is not tied to the physical serial number on the chassis nor the model type; therefore, answers A and C are incorrect. Answer D is incorrect, because there is no `show system` command on the PIX.

Question 7

Answers A, C, and D are correct. Configuration mode, privileged mode, monitor mode, and unprivileged mode are the four PIX firewall administrative access codes. The IOS familiar user mode is termed unprivileged mode on the PIX firewall. Answer B is incorrect because, on the PIX, the > prompt is referred to as unprivileged mode, not user mode. Answer E is incorrect because object group is considered a sub-command mode.

Question 8

Answer A is correct. Privileged mode allows you to change the current settings on the PIX. Any unprivileged command works in privileged mode. Changing system configurations requires configuration mode. Configuration changes are made from configuration mode, which makes answer B incorrect. The PIX does not support native IPX, which makes answer C incorrect. Password recovery is performed from monitor mode, which makes answer D incorrect. Answer E was a simple attempt at humor, which also means it is incorrect.

Question 9

Answers A and E are correct. The interactive prompts are designed to minimally configure the PIX for use with PDM. Setup is invoked when you type in the command setup or when you boot a PIX that has no configuration. If you erase the configuration stored in flash and reboot the PIX, you are prompted to run the interactive setup script. The init commands are not valid on a PIX, which makes answers B and C incorrect. Rebooting a PIX that has a configuration saved does not invoke the setup, which makes answer D incorrect.

Question 10

Answer C is correct. The serial number is listed with the show version command on PIX versions 5.3 and higher. This is the number that must be used to upgrade the PIX image. The write terminal command doesn't show the serial number; therefore, answer A is incorrect. The serial number on the physical chassis is not part of the critical information required; therefore, answers B, D, and E are incorrect.

Question 11

Answers A, C, and D are correct. The ASA is the heart of the PIX and tracks source and destination IP addresses, ports, and TCP flags. The reason the Adaptive Security Algorithm is adaptive is that is dynamically tracks outbound sessions and adapts the security policy to allow the correct return traffic for the outbound initiated sessions on an application-by-application basis. The PIX doesn't randomize all sequence numbers, nor does it randomize TCP flags; therefore, answers B and E are incorrect.

Question 12

Answer A is correct. ASA allows one-way outbound connections without explicit configuration for each internal system application, which makes answers B and D incorrect. An outbound connection is a connection originating from a host on a higher security level interface to a lower security level interface. Answers C and E are incorrect because the two-way inbound and two-way outbound options are invalid options.

Question 13

Answers A and B are correct. The `nameif` command assigns a name to each perimeter interface on the PIX firewall and specifies its security level. The `interface` command enables an interface and configures its type and speed. By default, the `E0` interface is given the name of `outside`, with a security level of `0`. Also by default, the `E1` interface is given the name of `inside` with a security level of `100`. Because the `ip address` and `global` commands do not specify security level nor duplex, answers C and E are incorrect. There is no `security-level` command on the PIX, so answer D is incorrect.

Question 14

Answers D and E are correct. The PIX firewall categorizes syslog events. A PIX reboot and console logouts are classified as system events. Answers A, B, and C are incorrect because dropped UDP packets, translation slot deletion, and bytes transferred are not classified as system events.

Question 15

Answer C is correct. The `dhcpd` command is used for virtually all the DHCP server functions on the PIX firewall. `dhcp address`, `dhcp pool`, `dhcpd ip pool`, and `dhcpd pool` are invalid commands on the PIX, so answers A, B, D, and E are incorrect. The `dhcpd address` command specifies the range of IP addresses for the server to distribute. This pool of addresses should be planned in such a way that it will not conflict with existing configured addresses on the client network.

Question 16

Answer A is correct. The dhcpd auto_config command enables the PIX to automatically configure DNS, WINS, and domain names received from an outside DHCP server to internal DHCP clients. dhcpd enable inside enables the service but does not in itself forward configuration parameters learned from a DHCP server, which makes answer E incorrect. Answers B, C, and D are invalid options and are therefore incorrect answers.

Question 17

Answer B is correct. The dhcpd dns command specifies the IP address of the DNS server for the DHCP clients. Up to two DNS servers can be specified with this command. Because 2 is the correct answer, answers A, C, and D are incorrect.

Question 18

Answer D is correct. Configuring the IP pools and options for DHCP clients is a large part of the PIX DHCP configuration. It is also critical that the service, once configured, is also enabled on the PIX. Enabling the DHCP daemon within the PIX firewall enables you to listen for DHCP client requests on the enabled interface. Enabling DHCP on the PIX is done by executing the dhcpd enable command. The commands shown in answers A, B, and C are incorrect. Answer E is incorrect because the question *does* have a correct answer.

Question 19

Answer B is correct. The PIX has tools available that make it a viable solution in a wide variety of scenarios. If a customer has an ISP that is delivering IP addresses and connectivity to the Internet via PPPoE, the PIX firewall is compatible with broadband offerings that require PPPoE usage. The PPPoE is not compatible with failover, L2TP, or PPTP, so answers C, D, and E are incorrect. Reliability is not increased exponentially with PPPoE, so answer A is incorrect.

Question 20

Answer C is correct. The vpdn family of commands configures a VPDN group and user information for PPPoE. Crypto maps, transform sets, and digital certificates are associated with IPSec configurations on the PIX firewall, so answers A, B, and D are incorrect.

Question 21

Answers A, B, and D are correct. Applications using UDP are difficult to secure properly because no handshaking or sequencing is involved. Maintaining the state of session is difficult because it has no clear beginning, flow state, or end. Because of the difficult nature in tracking UDP, it is not as trusted as TCP through the PIX firewall. The PIX approximates UDP sessions and, by default, has a shorter timeout for UDP flows through the PIX. UDP has well-known layer 4 attributes, making answer C incorrect.

Question 22

Answer B is correct. One global and two nat statements is the minimum configuration based on the listed requirement because one nat command would be needed for each higher security interface (the DMZ and inside) and one global statement would be needed for the outside interface. Because you need one global and two nat statements, answers A, C, and D, which show different required nat(s) and global(s), are incorrect. If we changed the scenario and added the requirement for the inside to talk to the DMZ interface as well, you would need to add another global statement to specify the addresses to use when translating from the inside to the DMZ network.

Question 23

Answer D is correct. Careful planning should be used to avoid overlapping IP addresses between static and nat/global pairs. Use static translations when you want an inside host to always appear with a fixed address on the PIX firewall's global network. Answers A, B, and C are incorrect because static translations always take precedence over nat and global command pairs regardless of where they appear in the configuration.

Question 24

Answer B is correct. Dynamic outside NAT is useful for simplifying router configurations on your internal or perimeter networks by controlling the addresses that appear on these networks. Dozens of outside networks could be made to appear as a few or even one network to the inside hosts. Performance would not improve as a result, so answer A is incorrect. Answers C and D are incorrect because dynamic outside NAT is not used to contain hidden codes or secure packets after failover.

Question 25

Answer C is correct. The nat 0 command lets you disable address translation so that inside IP addresses are visible on the outside without address translation. This is also referred to as identity NAT. With nat 0, the IP address you configure on an inside resource is the same IP address that is used by clients on the outside, as a destination address, to reach the inside resource. NAT-T is an industry standard for transparently using IPSec, which makes answer A incorrect. The alias command is used to help internal clients reach DNS resolved servers, which makes answer B incorrect. Answer D is incorrect because there *is* a correct answer.

Question 26

Answers A, B, D, and E are correct. PAT is a many-to-one translation. The outside interface can receive its IP address via DHCP, and this address can be the PAT address as well (although it's not required). For translation from an inside network to the DMZ, the DMZ interface could be used as the PAT address. This is a feature that helps conserve IP addresses because no separate IP address—other than the interface IP—is required in this configuration. The PAT address does not need to be the outside address, so answer C is incorrect.

Question 27

Answer E is correct. PIX versions 6.0 and higher support port redirection, which enables outside users to connect to a specific server/application on a higher security level interface. The static command was modified to accommodate port redirection. The benefit is that you can have a single IP address on the outside (the outside interface address) and through port redirection, depending on the requested service or port (such as HTTP port 80 or FTP port 21), the PIX can forward that request to the specific physical server on the inside via port redirection. In addition to the port redirection, you would also need to have the appropriate permissions (ACLs or conduits) in place to allow traffic from the lower security interface to a higher security interface. Answers A, B, C, and D are incorrect because the alias, conduit, global, and nat commands are all valid on the PIX but do not provide port redirection.

Question 28

Answer C is correct. The access-group command binds an ACL to an interface. The ACL compares the traffic inbound (and only inbound) to an interface. Only one ACL at a time can be bound to an interface using the access-group command. Answers A, B, D, and E are incorrect for applying the access list as required. If an access list is applied to an interface and the configuration commands to apply a new access list to the same interface are used, the new access list will replace the existing access list on the interface.

Question 29

Answers A and D are correct. By causing the PIX firewall to compile tables for ACLs, Turbo ACLs improve the average search time for ACLs containing a large number of entries; therefore, answer B and C are incorrect. The Turbo ACL feature is most appropriate for high-end PIX firewall models because it requires significant amounts of memory, making answer E incorrect.

Question 30

Answers A, B, and D are correct. ActiveX controls can provide significant functionality in current applications. Unfortunately, ActiveX controls create a potential security problem because they can provide a way for someone to attack servers. Because of this potential security problem, you can use the PIX firewall to block all ActiveX controls. You can specify that ActiveX controls are not allowed globally, as well as use a configuration that specifies which addresses (source and destination) require ActiveX filtering. Java filtering uses similar syntax and provides the same type of filtering for Java. IOS routers do not process ActiveX controls, so answer C is incorrect. ACLs are not used to identify and block ActiveX, which makes answer E incorrect.

Question 31

Answer C is correct. Access lists can have hundreds of individual lines in them. Object groups simplify the creation of access lists. Using object groups does not improve the performance of an access list, but it does simplify the implementation by the engineer. A complex security policy that normally requires 3,300 ACL entries manually entered might require only 40 ACL entries by using object groups. Turbo ACLs could be used to improve the performance when the resulting ACL entries are longer than 19 lines. Answers A, B, D, and E are incorrect because the serious planning, configuration, implementation, and troubleshooting of a complex security policy are still required even when using object groups.

Question 32

Answer B is correct. The `pix(config-protocol)#` prompt is the prompt the PIX firewall displays after naming and creating a protocol object group. The prompt changes to reflect the type of object group you are creating. In this example, a protocol object group was created. Answers A, C, D, and E are incorrect because each is an invalid prompt on the PIX.

Question 33

Answers A, B, D, and E are correct. The source IP address, port number, access list name, and icmp type are valid elements of object groups that can be used in an access list. The main benefit of using object groups is the simplification of ACL creating. By creating the object groups first and then replacing the traditional elements of the ACLs with object groups, implementation of the actual ACL entries can be simplified. The configuration sequence number is not an element identified by an object group, so answer C is incorrect.

Question 34

Answer E is correct. The `rip inside passive version 2` command allows you to enable the RIP version 2 on the inside interface without broadcasting a default route. The syntax shown in answers A, B, C, and D are not the correct syntax for accomplishing this task and are therefore incorrect.

Question 35

Answers A and B are correct. The `multicast interface` command on each interface enables multicast forwarding, and the `mroute` command creates a static route from the transmission source to the next-hop router. Therefore, answer E is incorrect. This would be the case if you had a multicast server on the DMZ network and you had clients on the outside who needed to receive the multicast stream from the server. The `igmp forward` command could allow clients on the inside to receive a multicast stream from the outside, so answer C is incorrect. `multicast routing` is not a valid command on the PIX, so answer D is incorrect.

Question 36

Answers B and D are correct. The PIX does not function as a full-multicast router; however, the PIX does support stub multicast routing (SMR). By using the `multicast interface` and `igmp forward` commands, you could allow clients on the inside to receive a multicast stream from a server on a lower security interface, such as the outside, without using GRE tunnels to pass multicast traffic through the PIX. The `mroute` command is not required for this scenario so answer A is incorrect. Answers C and E are IOS commands and are not found on the PIX, making them incorrect.

Question 37

Answers B, C, and E are correct. The `ftp fixup` protocol causes the PIX firewall to perform NAT or PAT in packet payload, create conduits for the FTP data connections, and log FTP commands when syslog is enabled. `ftp fixup`, which is enabled by default, allows standard (active) FTP to function through the PIX, so answers A and D are incorrect.

Question 38

Answer D is correct. Session Initiation Protocol enables call handling sessions—particularly calls or two-party audio conferences. SIP provides the ability to integrate traditional voice services with Web-based data services, including self-based provisioning, instant messaging, presence, and mobility services. The fixup protocol for SIP allows the PIX to securely manage SIP traffic through the PIX. Answers A, B, and C are all valid protocols the PIX can work with, but they do not match the description and are therefore incorrect.

Question 39

Answers B, C, and D are correct. If you're using a nonstandard SMTP port, you use the fixup protocol smtp command to enable the Mail Guard feature on the nonstandard port. The Mail Guard feature is on by default on port 25, so answer E is incorrect. If Mail Guard fixup is disabled, SMTP traffic, with the appropriate ACLs configured, goes through the PIX but is not inspected for malicious or nonstandard SMTP commands, making answer A incorrect.

Question 40

Answers A, B, C, and E are correct. The DNS Guard is always on and recognizes only outbound DNS queries. UDP packets can return due to the ASA allowing the reply from the DNS server back to the inside client. DNS Guard does not wait for the default UDP timer to close the session but instead closes it after the first DNS response is received from a specific DNS server. If two requests were sent from a client, to two different DNS servers, the PIX allows the first request from each server to return to the client and then closes the return path from the DNS server to the client immediately and independently after each response is returned. DNS Guard does not look for port 51, so answer D is incorrect.

Question 41

Answers A, C, and E are correct. Prior to PIX version 5.2, after the embryonic limit was reached for a particular server, the PIX would drop any new

SYN packets destined for the same server. The current version, by default, intercepts new TCP connections until the number of half-formed sessions drops below the embryonic limit, meaning answers B and D are incorrect.

Question 42

Answer A is correct. Intrusion detection is enabled with the PIX firewall `ip audit` commands, which makes answers B, C, D, and E incorrect. After a policy is created, it can be applied to any PIX firewall interface. When a policy for a given signature class is created and applied to an interface, all supported signatures of that class are monitored unless disabled with the `ip audit signature disable` command.

Question 43

Answer D is correct. `ip audit interface outside DETECT` is the correct syntax to apply an IDS policy named `DETECT` to the outside interface on the PIX, which makes answers A, B, C, and E incorrect. All supported signatures, except those disabled or excluded by the `ip audit signature` command, become part of the policy by default.

Question 44

Answers B, C, and D are correct. The `shun` command, intended for use by a Cisco IDS appliance, applies a blocking function to an interface receiving an attack. Packets containing the IP source address of the attacking host are dropped and logged until the blocking function is removed manually or by the Cisco IDS master unit, which makes answer A incorrect. No traffic from the IP source address is allowed to traverse the PIX firewall.

Question 45

Answer D is correct. `aaa_username@remote_username` is the correct format, making answers A, B, C, and E incorrect. The PIX firewall sends the `aaa_username` and `aaa_password` to the AAA server; if the authentication is successful, the `remote_username` and `remote_password` are passed to the destination FTP server.

Question 46

Answer D is correct. The `aaa group` tag is used to direct authentication, authorization, or accounting traffic to the appropriate AAA server, so answers B and C are incorrect. The PIX firewall enables you to define separate groups of TACACS+ and RADIUS servers for specifying different types of traffic, making answer A incorrect.

Question 47

Answers A, B, and F are correct. The PIX firewall interacts with only Telnet, FTP, and HTTP to display the prompts for logging in, so answers C and D are incorrect. You can specify that only a single service be authenticated, but this must agree with the AAA server to ensure that both the firewall and the server agree.

Question 48

Answers A and B are correct. When using virtual Telnet to authenticate inbound clients, the IP address must be an unused global address. When using virtual Telnet to authenticate outbound clients, the IP address must be an unused global address routed directly to the PIX firewall. Inbound and outbound are supported, making answer C incorrect. Virtual Telnet does not provide HTTP forwarding, making answer D incorrect.

Question 49

Answers C and E are correct. Telnet access to the PIX firewall console is available from any internal interface as well as from any outside interface with IPSec configured. The maximum number of simultaneous connections via Telnet is five. Telnet is allowed only on the outside interface when IPSec is used to protect the data stream, so answer D is incorrect. Telnet does not encrypt the packets, and without IPSec protection, it could be susceptible to an eavesdropping attack. Answers A and B are incorrect because the default password is not `in-default` and RSA keys are not required for Telnet.

Question 50

Answers A and D are correct. RADIUS and TACACS+ are both methods a PIX can use to communicate with an AAA server such as ACS. Downloadable ACLs are supported with RADIUS only. The downloadable ACLs are a function of AAA authentication and require RADIUS, so answer C is incorrect. Authorization, a separate function, is available between the PIX and the ACS only if TACACS+ is used; therefore, answer B is incorrect.

Question 51

Answer A is correct. During authentication, the PIX firewall builds a RADIUS request with the user identification and password and sends it to the AAA server. The AAA server then authenticates the user and retrieves from its configuration database the ACL name associated with the user. The AAA server then builds a RADIUS response packet containing the ACL name and sends it to the PIX firewall. The ACL is stored on the ACS server and is available to the PIX only when using the RADIUS protocol; therefore, answers B, C, D, and E are incorrect.

Question 52

Answer B is correct. When actively functioning, the primary PIX uses system IP addresses and MAC addresses. The secondary PIX uses failover IP addresses and MAC addresses when on standby. If the primary PIX fails, it then uses the failover IP and MAC addresses, while the secondary PIX goes active and uses the system addresses. Therefore, answers A, C, D, and E incorrect.

Question 53

Answers A, B, D, and E are correct. Failover is not successful unless the OS versions, flash, model, and RAM are the same on the PIX firewalls. For failover to work, both firewalls must have the same software version, activation key type, flash memory, and RAM. The manufacture date does not have to be identical on both PIX firewalls, so answer C is incorrect.

Question 54

Answers B, D, and E are correct. When the standby PIX firewall completes its initial bootup, the active firewall replicates its entire configuration to the standby firewall. Commands are entered on the active PIX firewall, making answer A incorrect; they are also sent across the failover cable to the standby firewall. Entering the `write standby` command on the active PIX firewall forces the entire configuration to be sent to the standby firewall. Because the standby learns configuration from the active PIX, answer C is incorrect.

Question 55

Answers A, C, and D are correct. The link up/down test does test the NIC. The network activity test tests the received network activity, the ARP test reads the firewall's ARP cache for the 10 most recently acquired entries, and the broadcast ping test sends out a broadcast ping request. The purpose of the tests is to generate network traffic to determine which, if either, PIX firewall has failed. Before each test, the PIX firewall clears its received packet count for its interfaces. The PIX does not use a backup interface after 30 seconds, so answer B is incorrect.

Question 56

Answer D is correct. Configuration replication occurs over the serial failover cable from the primary/active PIX firewall to the secondary/standby PIX firewall, meaning answers A, B, C, and E are incorrect. The configuration is done exclusively on the primary, and the replication happens automatically when the secondary PIX—with the serial failover cable attached—is booted.

Question 57

Answers B, C, and D are correct. LAN-based failover provides long-distance failover functionality; uses an Ethernet cable; requires a dedicated LAN interface; requires a dedicated switch, hub, or VLAN; and uses message encryption and authentication to secure failover transmissions. Using a crossover Ethernet cable between the two PIX firewalls with LAN-based failover is not supported. The ACL packets answer is not real, so answer A is incorrect.

Question 58

Answers B, C, and D are correct. IKE is a hybrid protocol that provides utility services for IPSec, including authentication of the IPSec peers, negotiation of IKE and IPSec security associations (SAs), and establishment of keys for encryption algorithms used by IPSec. IKE is synonymous with ISAKMP in PIX firewall configuration. IKE is not a variant of DES, so answer A is incorrect.

Question 59

Answers A, B, D, and E are correct. The IKE policy parameters are the message encryption algorithm, message integrity algorithm, peer authentication method, key exchange parameters, and ISAKMP-established security association's lifetime. Both IPSec peers need to negotiate a compatible IKE phase 1 policy before an SA can be established between the two devices. RSA key pair generation parameters are not part of IKE policies, so answer C is incorrect.

Question 60

Answer B is correct. The command for enabling the IKE outside interface is `isakmp enable outside`. The default name for `e0` is `OUTSIDE`. If ISAKMP is not enabled on a given interface, the PIX is not capable of using that interface to successfully negotiate an IKE phase 1 policy with an IPSec peer. Answers A, C, and D are not the correct commands, so those answers are incorrect.

Question 61

Answer A is correct. Crypto ACLs define which traffic is interesting and therefore are protected by IPSec when included in an active crypto map. Answers B, C, D, and E address items included with IPSec but do not answer the question, so they are incorrect. When a crypto access list is configured and applied via a crypto map, the IPSec device expects any traffic coming into the interface of the PIX that inversely matches the crypto access list to be encrypted traffic. The crypto access lists on two IPSec peers needs to be symmetrical.

Question 62

Answer C is correct. Three transforms can belong to a transform set, making answers A, B, and D incorrect. One of the transforms can specify AH, another can specify ESP encryption, and a third can specify ESP authentication using MD5 or SHA1.

Question 63

Answer C is correct. The `ip local pool` command is used to assign a group of addresses that will dynamically be assigned to the VPN clients, which makes answers A, B, and D incorrect. This pool will be used during IKE phase 1 to hand out local (private) IP addresses to VPN clients. The VPN clients will use these addresses as source addresses when they communicate over the VPN tunnel with corporate resources.

Question 64

Answer C is correct. The VPN group name of TRAINING and password match the group name and password in the VPN client. This password is effectively the preshared key used during IKE phase 1 authentication. Answers A and B are incorrect because they are not valid parameters that need to match. Answer D is incorrect because there *is* a correct answer.

Question 65

Answer A is correct. The PIX firewall needs to have either a DES or 3DES license to support SSH, which makes answer D incorrect. SSH sessions use the configured Telnet password, which makes answer E incorrect. A maximum of five simultaneous sessions is supported on the PIX. Answers B and C are incorrect because the PIX supports only SSH version 1.

Question 66

Answer D is correct. You can create privilege levels and secure them by using the `enable password` command, as shown in answer D, which makes answers A, B, C, and E incorrect. You can then gain access to a particular privilege level from the > prompt by entering the `enable` command with a privilege level designation and entering the password for that level when prompted.

Question 67

Answers B and C are correct. The password recovery for the PIX firewall requires a TFTP server, and files are needed for password recovery. The process involves rebooting the PIX, avoiding a normal startup, going into monitor mode, using the `monitor` commands to connect to a TFTP server, and using Cisco-provided files for the password recovery. Answers A and D are incorrect because monitor mode is used and privilege level 15 and 1 are not part of that scenario.

Question 68

Answer C is correct. Selecting Options, Preview Commands Before Sending to PIX enables you to preview any commands generated by any panel before they are sent to the PIX firewall; therefore, answers A and D are incorrect. This is a convenient tool to allow the engineer to see the exact CLI commands that will be issued on the PIX before they are applied. Answer B is incorrect because you can't use the View menu and select the CLI commands at any time.

Question 69

Answers A and B are correct. ESP-DES-SHA and ESP-3DES-SHA, along with their MD5 counterparts, are predefined by PDM. By using the predefined transforms, along with the VPN Wizard built in to the PIX Device Manager, the creation of VPN configurations can be done without using the command-line interface. Answers C and D are incorrect because those transforms are not predefined by PDM.

Question 70

Answer D is correct. PDM does not support crypto maps that are not applied to any interface. If such a map exists in the configuration, PDM parses and ignores it. Therefore, answers A, B, and C are incorrect. By understanding this, you will avoid the loss of an unapplied crypto map. A quick solution is to apply the crypto map to the appropriate interface before PDM parses the configuration. Within PDM, the concept of a crypto map is hidden, even though the end result of the VPN Wizard applies a crypto map to the actual configuration.

Question 71

Answers A, B, and C are correct. The PIX Management Center (MC) provides a workflow and audit trail, allows Web-based management of multiple PIX firewalls, and uses SSL to ensure secure remote connectivity between the browser and server. The MC can support 1,000 PIX firewalls, making answer D incorrect. This enterprise tool enables centralized management and change control in the management of PIX firewalls.

Question 72

Answer B is correct. The PIX MC does not support the use of conduits for access in the PIX firewall. To assist customers who need to migrate their conduits to ACLs so they can use the MC, Cisco has provided a tool named conv. The conv conversion tool uses a command-line interface to convert conduits to their equivalent access lists. Answers A, C, and D are incorrect because they are not PIX-related applications.

Question 73

Answer C is correct. 1741 is the correct port used to launch the PIX MC. Any other port will not be the default port, which is why answers A, B, D, and E are incorrect. To access the management center, a user must open a browser window and type in the URL for the MC server, followed by a colon and the port number of 1741.

Question 74

Answer A is correct. The default poll period is 720 minutes. Every 720 minutes (or 12 hours), a PIX firewall checks with the Automatic Update Server (AUS) to see whether there are any updates, which makes answers B, C, and D incorrect. The AUS can contain updated software images, PDM images, and PIX firewall configuration files.

Question 75

Answers A, C, and E are correct. The Auto Update Server is a tool used to upgrade device configuration files and software images. The main advantage of AUS is that it primarily manages devices that obtain their addresses through DHCP, although it can be used to manage any device that uses the auto update feature. The AUS enables you to manage PIX firewall software images, PDM images, and PIX firewall configuration files. Answers B and D are incorrect because AUS doesn't allow you to manage bug tracking information or IOS firewall feature sets.

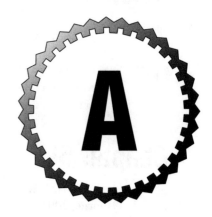

Resources

Chapter 2

 Chapman, David and Andy Fox. *Cisco Secure PIX Firewalls.* Indianapolis, IN: Cisco Press, 2002.

 Visit the Computer Security Institute Web site at `http://www.gocsi.com`.

 See the Cisco Secure Encyclopedia at `http://www.cisco.com/pcgi-bin/front.x/csec/csecHome.pl`.

Chapter 3

 Khan, Umer, Vitaly Osipov, Mike Sweeney, and Woody Weaver. *Cisco Security Specialist's Guide to PIX Firewall.* Rockland, MA: Syngress Media Inc., 2002.

 Read about the Cisco PIX 500 Series Firewalls at `http://www.cisco.com/en/US/products/hw/vpndevc/ps2030/prod_models_home.html`.

 Read the Cisco PIX 500 Series Firewalls Data Sheets at `http://www.cisco.com/en/US/products/hw/vpndevc/ps2030/products_data_sheets_list.html`.

Chapter 4

 See the Cisco PIX Firewall Command Reference, Version 6.2 at `http://www.cisco.com/univercd/cc/td/doc/product/iaabu/pix/pix_sw/v_62/cmdref/index.htm`.

See the Password Recovery and AAA Configuration Recovery Procedure for the PIX at `http://www.cisco.com/warp/public/110/34.shtml`.

Chapter 5

 Deal, Richard A. *Cisco PIX Firewalls*. Berkeley, CA: McGraw-Hill/Osborne, 2002.

Chapter 6

 See Using and Configuring PIX Object Groups at `http://www.cisco.com/en/US/products/hw/vpndevc/ps2030/products_tech_note09186a00800d641d.shtml`.

 Read the commands reference, M through R, at `http://www.cisco.com/en/US/products/sw/secursw/ps2120/products_command_reference_chapter09186a008010423e.html#1038172`.

 Read "Handling ICMP Pings with the PIX Firewall" at `http://www.cisco.com/en/US/products/hw/vpndevc/ps2030/products_tech_note09186a0080094e8a.shtml`.

 Find out about the turbo ACL Commands, A through B, at `http://www.cisco.com/en/US/products/sw/secursw/ps2120/products_command_reference_chapter09186a0080104239.html#1054473`.

Chapter 7

 See the Cisco PIX Firewall Command Reference, Version 6.2 at `http://www.cisco.com/univercd/cc/td/doc/product/iaabu/pix/pix_sw/v_62/cmdref/`.

Chapter 8

 Chapman, David and Andy Fox. *Cisco Secure PIX Firewalls*. Indianapolis, IN: Cisco Press, 2002.

 Deal, Richard A. *Cisco PIX Firewalls*. Berkeley, CA: McGraw-Hill/Osborne, 2002.

See the Cisco PIX Firewall Command Reference, Version 6.2 at
http://www.cisco.com/univercd/cc/td/doc/product/iaabu/pix/pix_sw/
v_62/cmdref/index.htm.

Chapter 9

 See Security Considerations for IP Fragment Filtering at http://
www.ietf.org/rfc/rfc1858.txt.

 See Cisco PIX Firewall System Log Messages, Version 6.2 at http://
www.cisco.com/en/US/products/sw/secursw/ps2120/products_system_
message_guide_book09186a008014638a.html.

Chapter 10

 See the Cisco Secure Access Control Server for Windows at http://
www.cisco.com/en/US/products/sw/secursw/ps2086/index.html.

 See the Cisco Secure Access Control Server for Windows at http://
www.cisco.com/en/US/products/sw/secursw/ps2086/index.html.

 See the Cisco Secure Access Control Server for UNIX at http://www.
cisco.com/en/US/products/sw/secursw/ps4911/index.html.

 See the Cisco Secure Access Control Server Solution Engine at
http://www.cisco.com/en/US/products/sw/secursw/ps5338/index.html.

Chapter 11

 Bastien, Greg and Christian Degu. *CCSP Cisco Secure PIX Firewall
Advanced Exam Certification Guide.* Indianapolis, IN: Cisco Press,
2003.

 See Cisco PIX Firewall Advanced Configuration at http://www.
cisco.com/en/US/products/sw/secursw/ps2120/products_configuration_
guide_chapter09186a008008996b.html#xtocid3.

 See How Failover Works on the Cisco Secure PIX Firewall at
http://www.cisco.com/en/US/products/hw/vpndevc/ps2030/products_
tech_note09186a0080094ea7.shtml#failovercable.

Chapter 12

 Chapman, David and Andy Fox. *Cisco Secure PIX Firewalls.* Indianapolis, IN: Cisco Press, 2002.

 See the Cisco PIX Firewall Command Reference, Version 6.2 at `http://www.cisco.com/univercd/cc/td/doc/product/iaabu/pix/pix_sw/ v_62/cmdref/index.htm`.

Chapter 13

 Chapman, David and Andy Fox. *Cisco Secure PIX Firewalls.* Indianapolis, IN: Cisco Press, 2002.

 Deal, Richard A. *Cisco PIX Firewalls.* Berkeley, CA: McGraw-Hill/ Osborne, 2002.

 See the Cisco PIX Firewall Command Reference, Version 6.2 at `http://www.cisco.com/univercd/cc/td/doc/product/iaabu/pix/pix_sw/ v_62/cmdref/index.htm`.

Chapter 14

 Visit the CiscoWorks VPN/Security Management Solution at `http://www.cisco.com/en/US/products/sw/cscowork/ps2330/index.html`.

 See the Bootstrapping Managed Devices at `http://www.cisco. com/en/US/products/sw/cscowork/ps3993/products_user_guide_ chapter09186a0080143342.html`.

 Visit the CiscoWorks Management Center for Firewalls at `http:// www.cisco.com/en/US/products/sw/cscowork/ps3992/index.html`.

 Read about the Using Management Center for PIX Firewalls 1.1 at `http://www.cisco.com/univercd/cc/td/doc/product/rtrmgmt/cw2000/ mgt_pix/pix1_1/use_man/index.htm`.

 Visit the CiscoWorks Management Center for Firewalls Sample Network Scenarios at `http://www.cisco.com/en/US/products/sw/ cscowork/ps3992/products_user_guide_chapter09186a00800e7215. html#xtocid0`.

 See the CiscoWorks Auto Update Server Software Getting Started with AUS at `http://www.cisco.com/en/US/products/sw/cscowork/ps3993/ products_user_guide09186a008019b14c.html#wp1040441`.

Read about the CiscoWorks Auto Update Server Software Introduction at `http://www.cisco.com/en/US/products/sw/cscowork/ps3993/products_user_guide_chapter09186a008014333f.html#wp1021195`.

 See the Cisco Catalyst 6500 Series Firewall Services Module at `http://www.cisco.com/en/US/products/hw/modules/ps2706/ps4452/index.html`.

Other Resources

 Visit InformIT.com for IT-related books and information, at `http://www.informit.com`.

 Visit the SANS Information Security Reading Room at `http://rr.sans.org/index.php`.

What's on the CD-ROM

This appendix provides a brief summary of what you'll find on the CD-ROM that accompanies this book. For a more detailed description of the PrepLogic Practice Exams, Preview Edition exam simulation software, see Appendix C, "Using the PrepLogic Practice Exams, Preview Edition Software." In addition to the PrepLogic Practice Exams, Preview Edition software, the CD-ROM includes an electronic version of the book—in Portable Document Format (PDF)—and the source code used in the book.

The PrepLogic Practice Exams, Preview Edition Software

PrepLogic is a leading provider of certification training tools. Trusted by certification students worldwide, PrepLogic is the best practice exam software available. In addition to providing a means of evaluating your knowledge of this book's material, PrepLogic Practice Exams, Preview Edition features several innovations that help you improve your mastery of the subject matter.

For example, the practice tests allow you to check your score by exam area or domain to determine which topics you need to study further. Another feature enables you to obtain immediate feedback on your responses in the form of explanations for the correct and incorrect answers.

PrepLogic Practice Tests, Preview Edition exhibits all the full-test simulation functionality of the Premium Edition but offers only a fraction of the total questions. To get the complete set of practice questions, visit www.preplogic.com and order the Premium Edition for this and other challenging exam training guides.

For a more detailed description of the features of the PrepLogic Practice Exams, Preview Edition software, see Appendix C.

An Exclusive Electronic Version of the Text

As mentioned previously, the CD-ROM that accompanies this book also contains an electronic PDF version of this book. This electronic version comes complete with all the figures as they appear in the book. You can use Acrobat's handy search capability for study and review purposes.

Using the PrepLogic Practice Exams, Preview Edition Software

This book includes a special version of the PrepLogic Practice Exams software, a revolutionary test engine designed to give you the best in certification exam preparation. PrepLogic offers sample and practice exams for many of today's most in-demand and challenging technical certifications. A special Preview Edition of the PrepLogic Practice Exams software is included with this book as a tool to use in assessing your knowledge of the training guide material while also providing you with the experience of taking an electronic exam.

This appendix describes in detail what PrepLogic Practice Exams, Preview Edition is, how it works, and what it can do to help you prepare for the exam. Note that although the Preview Edition includes all the test simulation functions of the complete retail version, it contains only a single practice test. The Premium Edition, available at www.preplogic.com, contains a complete set of challenging practice exams designed to optimize your learning experience.

The Exam Simulation

One of the main functions of PrepLogic Practice Exams, Preview Edition is exam simulation. To prepare you to take the actual vendor certification exam, PrepLogic is designed to offer the most effective exam simulation available.

Question Quality

The questions provided in PrepLogic Practice Exams, Preview Edition are written to the highest standards of technical accuracy. The questions tap the content of this book's chapters and help you review and assess your knowledge before you take the actual exam.

The Interface Design

The PrepLogic Practice Exams, Preview Edition exam simulation interface provides the experience of taking an electronic exam, enabling you to effectively prepare to take the actual exam by making the test experience familiar. Using this test simulation can help eliminate the sense of surprise or anxiety you might experience in the testing center because you will already be acquainted with computerized testing.

The Effective Learning Environment

The PrepLogic Practice Exams, Preview Edition interface provides a learning environment that not only tests you through the computer, but also teaches the material you need to know to pass the certification exam. Each question includes a detailed explanation of the correct answer, and most of these explanations provide reasons as to why the other answers are incorrect. This information helps to reinforce the knowledge you already have and also provides practical information you can use on the job.

Software Requirements

PrepLogic Practice Exams requires a computer with the following:

➤ Microsoft Windows 98, Windows Me, Windows NT 4.0, Windows 2000, or Windows XP

➤ A 166MHz or faster processor

➤ A minimum of 32MB of RAM

➤ 10MB of hard drive space

As with any Windows application, the more memory, the better the performance.

Installing PrepLogic Practice Exams, Preview Edition

You install PrepLogic Practice Exams, Preview Edition by following these steps:

1. Insert the CD-ROM that accompanies this book into your CD-ROM drive. The Autorun feature of Windows should launch the software. If you have Autorun disabled, select Start, Run. Go to the root directory of the CD-ROM and select `setup.exe`. Click Open, and then click OK.

2. The Installation Wizard copies the PrepLogic Practice Exams, Preview Edition files to your hard drive. It then adds PrepLogic Practice Exams, Preview Edition to your desktop and the Program menu. Finally, it installs the test engine components to the appropriate system folders.

Removing PrepLogic Practice Exams, Preview Edition from Your Computer

If you elect to remove the PrepLogic Practice Exams, Preview Edition, you can use the included uninstallation process to ensure that it is removed from your system safely and completely. Follow these instructions to remove PrepLogic Practice Exams, Preview Edition from your computer:

1. Select Start, Settings, Control Panel.

2. Double-click the Add/Remove Programs icon. You are presented with a list of software installed on your computer.

3. Select the PrepLogic Practice Exams, Preview Edition title you want to remove. Click the Add/Remove button. The software is removed from your computer.

How to Use the Software

PrepLogic is designed to be user friendly and intuitive. Because the software has a smooth learning curve, your time is maximized because you start practicing with it almost immediately. PrepLogic Practice Exams, Preview Edition has two major modes of study: Practice Exam and Flash Review.

Using Practice Exam mode, you can develop your test-taking abilities as well as your knowledge through the use of the Show Answer option. While you are taking the test, you can expose the answers along with detailed explanations of why answers are right or wrong. This helps you better understand the material presented.

Flash Review mode is designed to reinforce exam topics rather than quiz you. In this mode, you are shown a series of questions but no answer choices. You can click a button that reveals the correct answer to each question and a full explanation for that answer.

Starting a Practice Exam Mode Session

Practice Exam mode enables you to control the exam experience in ways that actual certification exams do not allow. To begin studying in Practice Exam mode, select the Practice Exam radio button from the main exam customization screen. This enables the following options:

➤ *Enable Show Answer Button*—Clicking this button activates the Show Answer button, which allows you to view the correct answer(s) and full explanation(s) for each question during the exam. When this option is not enabled, you must wait until after your exam has been graded to view the correct answer(s) and explanation(s) for each question.

➤ *Enable Item Review Button*—Clicking this button activates the Item Review button, which allows you to view your answer choices. This option also facilitates navigation between questions.

➤ *Randomize Choices*—You can randomize answer choices from one exam session to the next. This makes memorizing question choices more difficult, thereby keeping questions fresh and challenging longer.

On the left side of the main exam customization screen, you are presented with the option of selecting the preconfigured practice test or creating your own custom test. The preconfigured test has a fixed time limit and number of questions. Custom tests, on the other hand, enable you to configure the time limit and number of questions in your exam.

The Preview Edition on this book's CD-ROM includes a single preconfigured practice test. You can get the compete set of challenging PrepLogic Practice Exams at www.preplogic.com to ensure you're ready for the big exam.

Click the Begin Exam button to begin your exam.

Starting a Flash Review Mode Session

Flash Review mode provides an easy way to reinforce topics covered in the practice questions. To begin studying in Flash Review mode, select the Flash Review radio button from the main exam customization screen. Then, select either the preconfigured practice test or the option to create your own custom test.

Click the Begin Exam button to begin a Flash Review mode session.

Standard PrepLogic Practice Exams, Preview Edition Options

The following list describes the function of each of the buttons you see across the bottom of the screen:

Depending on the options, some of the buttons will be grayed out and inaccessible—or they might be missing completely. Buttons that are appropriate are active.

➤ *Exhibit*—This button is visible if an exhibit is provided to support the question. An *exhibit* is an image that provides supplemental information that is necessary to answer a question.

➤ *Item Review*—This button leaves the question window and opens the Item Review screen, from which you can see all the questions, your answers, and your marked items. You can also see the correct answers listed here, when appropriate.

➤ *Show Answer*—This option displays the correct answer with an explanation about why it is correct. If you select this option, the current question is not scored.

➤ *Mark Item*—You can check this box to flag a question you need to review further. You can view and navigate your marked items by clicking the Item Review button (if it is enabled). When your exam is being graded, you are notified if you have any marked items remaining.

> *Previous Item*—You use this option to view the previous question.

> *Next Item*—You use this option to view the next question.

> *Grade Exam*—When you have completed your exam, you can click Grade Exam to end your exam and view your detailed score report. If you have unanswered or marked items remaining, you are asked whether you want to continue taking your exam or view the exam report.

Seeing Time Remaining

If your practice test is timed, the time remaining is displayed in the upper-right corner of the application screen. It counts down the minutes and seconds remaining to complete the test. If you run out of time, you are asked whether you want to continue taking the test or end your exam.

Getting Your Examination Score Report

The Examination Score Report screen appears when the Practice Exam mode ends—as a result of time expiration, completion of all questions, or your decision to terminate early.

This screen provides a graphical display of your test score, with a breakdown of scores by topic domain. The graphical display at the top of the screen compares your overall score with the PrepLogic Exam Competency Score. The *PrepLogic Exam Competency Score* reflects the level of subject competency required to pass the particular vendor's exam. Although this score does not directly translate to a passing score, consistently matching or exceeding this score does suggest that you possess the knowledge necessary to pass the actual vendor exam.

Reviewing Your Exam

From the Your Score Report screen, you can review the exam you just completed by clicking the View Items button. You can navigate through the items, viewing the questions, your answers, the correct answers, and the explanations for those questions. You can return to your score report by clicking the View Items button.

Contacting PrepLogic

If you would like to contact PrepLogic for any reason, including to get information about its extensive line of certification practice tests, you can do so online at www.preplogic.com.

Customer Service

If you have a damaged product and need to contact customer service, please call the following number:

800-858-7674

Product Suggestions and Comments

PrepLogic values your input! Please email your suggestions and comments to feedback@preplogic.com.

License Agreement

YOU MUST AGREE TO THE TERMS AND CONDITIONS OUT-LINED IN THE END USER LICENSE AGREEMENT ("EULA") PRESENTED TO YOU DURING THE INSTALLATION PROCESS. IF YOU DO NOT AGREE TO THESE TERMS, DO NOT INSTALL THE SOFTWARE.

Glossary

3DES

3DES is a symmetric encryption algorithm based on DES that uses three separate 56-bit keys that aggregate to a 168-bit encryption key.

AAA

This stands for authentication, authorization, and accounting. Cisco equipment uses AAA services to provide a method of authenticating, authorizing, and accounting services for traffic traveling across or access into the PIX.

AAA Floodguard

An attack guard is used to protect the PIX firewall against excessive AAA requests that can result in a denial-of-service attack.

access attack

An attack that involves exploiting vulnerabilities in the network or systems to gain access to secure information.

access control list (ACL)

A filter list mechanism used to identify hosts, ports, or networks on a device.

access-group

A command used to attach an access list to an interface.

activation keys

The PIX firewall uses activation keys to enable features in the software.

Adaptive Security Algorithm (ASA)

It controls all traffic flow through the PIX firewall, performing stateful inspection of packets, and creates remembered entries in connections and translations to allow return traffic to pass through the firewall to the requested host.

Advanced Encryption Standard (AES)

AES is a new Federal Information Processing Standard encryption method that enables encryption for IPSec with a cipher block chaining mode.

antireplay

Provides protection against replay attacks with AH and ESP.

appliance

A dedicated device used to perform a single function, such as a PIX firewall that is dedicated for firewall capabilities.

asymmetric keys

A pair of keys consisting of a public key and a private key. The public key is given to others and the private key is kept secret. Data encrypted with the public key can be decrypted only by the private key, and data encrypted with the private key can be decrypted only with the corresponding public key.

attack guards

Attack guards allow the PIX firewall to monitor and reject requests or messages sent to commonly used applications or protocols that hackers commonly attack.

authentication headers (AHs)

A component of IPSec used to provide data integrity, authentication, and antireplay features. AH does not provide any data confidentiality functions; the IPSec ESP component provides this function.

bastion hosts

Bastion hosts are systems that are typically within the demilitarized zone (DMZ). These hosts are typically hardened with lock-down procedures and all possible service packs to help keep them as secure as possible.

cable-based failover

This is the PIX firewall configuration that requires a special serial cable from Cisco to interconnect the firewalls and allow stateful or non-stateful failover. However, the serial cable replicates only configuration information and not stateful information. Cable-based does provide a means of power outage detection of the other device, whereas LAN-based failover does not.

certificate

Can also be known as a digital certificate and is used to bind an entity to a public key providing a mechanism to help authenticate and identify a user or device. Certificates typically come from issuing CA systems.

certification authority (CA)

A system that can issue, distribute, and maintain information about digital certificates. Clients request certificates from a CA, which validates the information given and in return issues a certificate that can be distributed to requesting clients.

Challenge Handshake Authentication Protocol (CHAP)

A commonly used authentication method that sends a hashed form of a user's password to the access server that uses a three-way handshake. CHAP is an improvement over PAP authentication, which sends passwords as clear text.

Cisco Secure Access Control Server (CSACS)

Used to manage AAA services with RADIUS and TACACS+ security protocols. CSACS can use its own internal user database or connect to an external database using the RADIUS or TACACS+ security protocol.

Cisco Secure Scanner

A Cisco tool used to test and identify security holes. This tool can be used to support the monitoring component of the Cisco Security Wheel.

Cisco Security Wheel

A graphic representation of the continuously evolving process of updating a security policy. The wheel contains five main parts: the security policy, securing the network, monitoring, testing, and improving.

command-line interface (CLI)

A text-based interface used to configure and display settings in the PIX firewall. You can use the console port, Telnet, or SSH to connect to the firewall and access the CLI interface.

conduit

This command makes an exception in the ASA to permit or deny specific traffic from lower security level interfaces to pass to higher security level interfaces. This command is being replaced by the `access-list` command.

configuration mode

The mode in the CLI that allows access to configure interfaces, VPNs, DHCP servers, hostnames, settings, and so on.

connection table

A table that contains layer 4 TCP or UDP sessions between internal and external hosts.

crypto maps

A collection of parameters used in phase 2 of an IKE/IPSec connection to establish a command security association with a peer.

cut-through proxy

This enables you to control HTTP, FTP, and Telnet services through the PIX firewall. It requires a username and password before allowing access.

DDoS attack

A distributed denial-of-service attack involves several systems all attacking a single network or host in an effort to slow or disable the service.

demilitarized zone (DMZ)

A portion of the network containing hosts that need to be accessed from untrusted areas. For example, a Web server in the DMZ, known as a bastion host, can be accessed by people on the Internet.

DES

The Data Encryption Standard (DES) was originally developed by IBM as an encryption algorithm. It requires the sender and receiver to use the same key for encryption and decryption and is commonly used in IPSec. DES provides 56-bit encryption.

Diffie-Hellman (D-H)

A process that uses asymmetric public and private keys to generate a secret key in IKE Phase 1 process.

DNSGuard

A protection mechanism that prevents DoS attacks and UDP session hijacking by closing the UDP port after the first received DNS response. This guard cannot be turned off.

domain name system (DNS)

A hierarchal naming structure that maps or associates hostnames to IP addresses, or vice versa.

DoS attack

A denial-of-service attack involves sending useless, malformed, or malicious data to a network or computer port in an effort to slow down or disable a system. For example, embryonic half-open connections waste resources on a computer by causing it to wait for a response that never occurs. Flooding a computer with ping requests can slow it down or even disable it, which is another form of DoS.

dynamic mapping

Dynamic mapping is the process that network address translation (NAT) and NAT overloading (PAT) use to dynamically map an internal address to an outside or external address.

embryonic connection

A half-open TCP three-way handshake connection that could be left open intentionally by a hacker to create a DoS attack.

Encapsulating Security Payload (ESP)

One of two protocols that can be used with IPSec. It provides data authentication, antireplay, and data confidentiality (encryption) functionality.

external threats

Threats originating from individuals who are operating outside an organization's internal network.

File Transfer Protocol (FTP)

A commonly used protocol for transferring files from one host to another. In addition, it uses TCP to guarantee delivery of the data. FTP can be configured to operate in either active or passive mode.

fixups

A set of features that performs what is known as *application inspection* on a limited number of advanced protocols. Fixups try to make connections as secure as possible by dynamically opening only the ports needed to support protocols such a FTP, SMTP, and multimedia applications.

Fragmentation Guard (FragGuard)

A monitoring mechanism used to track the number of fragments. Hackers might send hundreds or thousands of fragmented packets in an effort to disguise an attack or just cause a DoS. FragGuard places a limit on the number of fragments the PIX accepts.

H.323

A complicated hybrid protocol that can be used for VoIP, video, and data. The protocol is actually a suite of other protocols put together to make the desired connections. Programs such as Cisco Multimedia Conference Manager, Microsoft NetMeeting, CU-SeeMe Meeting Point and Pro, Intel Video Phone, VocalTec Internet Phone, and Gatekeeper use H.323. This protocol requires application inspection using the PIX fixup protocol to operate correctly.

hash value

When data, a key, and an algorithm are combined, a fixed result is generated; this is called a hash value.

Hashes are typically used for data integrity checks.

hashing

The process of placing data and a key into a mathematical algorithm to produce a fixed-length value called a hash.

internal threats

Threats that typically come from users who have legitimate access to the computers or networks they want to harm.

Internet Control Message Protocol (ICMP)

A protocol used to send control and error messages between devices. Two utilities that use ICMP are ping and trace route. The PIX firewall has an object group ACL type specifically used for ICMP.

Internet Key Exchange (IKE)

IKE is a hybrid protocol used to authenticate end points and create a secure connection to exchange security keys and establish a security association for IPSec.

Internet Protocol Security (IPSec)

An open VPN standard defining a group of security protocols used together to form a secure connection between two peers.

Internet service provider (ISP)

A company that provides connectivity to the Internet.

intrusion detection system (IDS)

The process of monitoring networks for traffic patterns or traffic signatures that might be causing harm to a network. They can be integrated with the PIX firewall to shun potential attackers.

ISAKMP policies

The Internet Security Association and Key Management Protocol (ISAKMP) is synonymous with IKE in the Cisco world. ISAKMP policies are those parameters that are used to negotiate security associations.

LAN-based failover

Enables the use of a dedicated Ethernet interface to perform the same functions as the serial cable-based failover without the 6-foot distance limitation. However, LAN-based failover cannot detect power outages of the other device as cable-based configuration can.

Layer Two Tunneling Protocol (L2TP)

VPN is an enhancement of the Cisco Layer 2 Forwarder (L2F) mechanism that works only at layer 2 to forward IP, IPX, and AppleTalk traffic. L2TP builds on L2F to make it routable across IP networks. IPSec is used with L2TP to make it secure.

MAC address

A physical burned-in address that cannot be changed on a device. This address helps identify the device for layer two protocols in the OSI model.

Mail Guard (also called MailGuard)

A fixup protocol is used to protect Simple Mail Transfer Protocol (SMTP) servers from known, potentially harmful security problems. Mail Guard inspects SMTP traffic and allows only the seven commands defined in RFC 821 section 4.5.1 to pass. These commands are DATA, HELO, MAIL, NOOP, QUIT, RCPT, and RSET. All other commands result in a 500 command unrecognized response to the client, and the packet is discarded before the SMTP server ever receives it.

Message Digest 5 (MD5)

A hashing algorithm commonly used to authenticate or validate that data has not been modified in transit. It is known as a one-way hashing alogrithm that produces a fixed-length result called a message digest. MD5 uses 512-bit blocks as inputs to produce a 128-bit message digest.

Microsoft Challenge Handshake Authentication Protocol (MS-CHAP)

A protocol that is similar to CHAP but does not need the reversible encrypted password requirement that CHAP does. Microsoft has created MS-CHAP version 1 and version 2, which is more secure.

monitor mode

This special mode allows the PIX to perform maintenance features that are sometimes not available during normal operation. When in this mode, images for an operating system and PDM software can be uploaded to flash memory.

multicasting

The process of using one source to send information to several destinations without sending the data more than once. It is used to send data to subnets of IP networks and not just a single host.

NAT overloading

The process of translating many internal IP addresses to one external (global) IP address by using port numbers to uniquely identify each internal address. NAT overloading is sometimes called port address translation (PAT) and performs a many-to-one mapping.

Network Address Translation (NAT)

The process of translating one IP address to a different IP address, creating a one-to-one mapping of the two addresses. NAT overloading (PAT) performs many-to-one address mappings by uniquely identifying internal addresses by modifying the port numbers.

Network Time Protocol (NTP)

NTP works off a hierarchy wherein one master clock server dictates the time settings and sends them down to several NTP servers, which synchronize with the master server. Devices such as the PIX firewall can synchronize their clocks to a common time server.

non-stateful failover

Non-stateful failover is a basic solution that allows for a secondary standby firewall to take over if the primary firewall fails. The non-stateful dictates that only configuration information is maintained and not xlate or connection table information, causing all connections inside the primary to be lost when the secondary takes over.

one-time passwords (OTP)

A system that helps to protect against passive attacks that capture passwords. OTP systems change passwords on every login, helping prevent captured passwords from being used to log in.

packet filters

A basic filtering mechanism that inspects layer 3 and 4 information. These filters allow traffic to pass through provided that the source and destination information match the configured rule.

Password Authentication Protocol (PAP)

An authentication protocol that uses a two-way clear-text handshake to pass usernames and passwords.

PIX Device Manager (PDM)

A Java Web-based interface that enables you to configure the single PIX firewall via a secure HTTPS connection.

Point-to-Point Protocol (PPP)

A standard method of encapsulating Network layer protocol information over point-to-point links. PPP is capable of supporting multiple layer 3 protocols.

Point-to-Point Protocol over Ethernet (PPPoE)

A layer 2 protocol based on PPP, it's typically used on digital subscriber lines. PPPoE allows ISPs to authenticate users connecting via Ethernet for Internet service.

port redirection

The process of redirecting incoming traffic on PAT-enabled devices to a specific internal port number to create access via an outside device.

private addresses

Address that have been reserved from use on the Internet. These addresses are intended for use in the private sector to help conserve public addresses. The address ranges are 10.0.0.0–10.255.255.255, 172.16.0.0–172.31.255.255, and 192.168.0.0–192.168.255.255. Private addresses are not routable on the public Internet.

private key

One of two keys used in an asymmetric algorithm that is kept by the host and used to encrypt and decrypt data. The private key has a corresponding public key that is shared with other users.

privileged mode

Also known as EXEC mode or enable mode. Privileged mode gives you the full set of available commands that can be used to view restricted settings and enable you to enter configuration mode to configure the PIX firewall.

proxy filters

Also known as application proxy servers, these sit between the client and the destination working as middlemen between the two communicating parties. They extend beyond the reach of packet filters by examining information from layer 4 to layer 7. However, they can be quite slow.

public key

One of two keys used in an asymmetric algorithm, it is sent by the host to a peer and used to encrypt and decrypt data. The public key has a corresponding private key that is maintained on the owner's system only.

Real Time Streaming Protocol (RTSP)

A real-time audio and video protocol used by several multimedia applications, such as RealPlayer, Cisco IP/TV, QuickTime 4, Netshow, and VDO Live. The PIX firewall requires application inspection using fixup protocols to enable these protocols to work across the device.

reconnaissance attack

An attack that involves probing a network or system in an effort to discover what exists. Port scanners and network sniffers are tools that could be used to help discover a network or system.

Remote Authentication Dial-in User Services (RADIUS)

The RADIUS protocol was originally developed by Livingston Enterprises, Inc., as an access protocol. RADIUS provides authentication and accounting services using the connectionless UDP protocol.

Remote Shell (RSH)

Originally created for Unix systems as an easy-to-use remote console that doesn't need a login, as Telnet does. RSH is inherently insecure and is being phased out; therefore, it should be avoided.

ROBO

Stands for remote-office-branch-office locations. The PIX 506 has been designed specifically to meet the needs of the ROBO environments.

Routing Information Protocol (RIP)

A common distance vector protocol used by routers to periodically exchange routing table information. RIP uses a hop count metric to determine the best possible path through the network. Although the PIX does not forward routing updates, it can be configured to forward its default route or update its local routing table with routes received from routers using RIP.

RSA

An asymmetric public-key encryption technology developed by RSA Data Security, Inc. The acronym stands for Rivest, Shamir, and Adelman, the inventors of the technique, which uses varying key lengths depending on the required encryption levels.

script kiddies

Hackers who don't make their own tools but use prebuilt tools, programs, or scripts readily available on the Internet.

Secure Hash Algorithm 1 (SHA-1)

A hashing algorithm that creates a 160-bit hash value output. It's commonly used on IPSec for data integrity.

Secure Shell (SSH)

A secure virtual terminal similar to Telnet, it provides protected data transfer over a public media. Because Telnet cannot be used to access the PIX from the outside interface, SSH is often used to overcome this and provide a secure channel.

Secure Sockets Layer (SSL)

A method for protecting Web traffic, it was developed by Netscape. The SSL security protocol provides data encryption, message integrity, and server authentication for application layer protocols such as HTTP.

security association (SA)

A result of a successful IKE and IPSec negotiation that defines all security parameters used to provide data integrity, confidentiality, and a secure connection.

security policy

A core document or set of procedures used to describe how an organization's information, data, and services will be protected.

Session Initiation Protocol (SIP)

A VoIP protocol that allows connections between audio devices using IP. The caller contacts a VoIP gateway that locates the destination phone and the caller and helps the two connect. This advanced protocol requires PIX fixup protocols to allow traffic to pass through the firewall device.

shunning

The process of blocking addresses from entering the firewall, it's typically done dynamically by an IDS.

Simple Mail Transport Protocol (SMTP)

A mail messaging system used between devices to deliver mail.

Simple Network Management Protocol (SNMP)

An Application layer protocol that is used to exchange management information between network devices. Network devices are called *agents* and can either be polled for information or sent to what is called a network management station. Although the PIX supports

SNMP versions 1 and 2, its built-in security feature allows SNMP to read and monitor the PIX.

Skinny Client Control Protocol (SCCP)

Typically it's just called Skinny, and it was created by Cisco. Cisco uses this simplified protocol for its VoIP phones and CallManager servers. This advanced protocol requires PIX fixup protocols to allow traffic to pass through the firewall device.

SOHO

Stands for small-office-home-office locations. The PIX 501 model is most suitable for SOHO environments.

spoofing

A method used to gain unauthorized access to computers, in which the hacker sends packets to a computer with a source IP address, indicating that the message is coming from a trusted host.

SQL*Net Protocol

A protocol used to query SQL databases by Oracle clients and servers. This advanced protocol requires PIX fixup protocols to allow traffic to pass through the firewall device.

stateful failover

Stateful failover behaves in a similar way to non-stateful failover when a failover occurs. However, xlate and connection table information is maintained continually across a second, dedicated Ethernet connection between the firewalls. This helps users by not requiring reestablishment of the connection after a failover.

stateful packet filters

These monitor traffic similar to packet filters, but they record the traffic into a connection and xlate table and allow only requested traffic back into the system. The PIX uses stateful packet filters.

static mapping

Creates a binding or permanent mapping from an internal address to a global address when using NAT.

structured threats

Structured threats are threats done by skilled attackers who have the ability and skills to develop their own new methods of attack against unknown vendor vulnerabilities.

symmetric key

Also known as a shared secret key. This symmetric key is used by two peers for encrypting and decrypting data or to produce a result in a hash.

SYN Floodguard

A PIX guard used to protect hosts from half-open TCP SYN attacks by limiting the number of half-open connections allowed. The PIX also protects against flooding DoS attacks by ensuring that AAA services are still available during times of high traffic.

Syslog server

Typically the primary location to log data. These servers can store and log messages to disk for later review.

TCP intercepts

Work with embryonic connections to intercept TCP three-way handshakes to determine whether they are valid requests before forwarding them to the actual host. The PIX performs the three-way handshake with the external host in an attempt to determine whether the external host's intentions are genuine.

Telnet

A standard protocol and application used to provide a virtual terminal from a remote device.

Terminal Access Controller Access Control System Plus (TACACS+)

The TACACS+ protocol is used to provide a reliable TCP connection between the client and the server for AAA service requests. These requests are more secure than RADIUS because the body of the transaction is always encrypted and more reliable than RADIUS, which employs UDP.

transform sets

The modes or methods the two peers use to protect user data—for instance, AH, ESP, or both when using IPSec.

translation table

A table used for IP address-to-IP address mapping as IP packets traverse the firewall. This table is commonly known as the xlate table.

Transmission Control Protocol (TCP)

A layer 4 connection-oriented protocol that guarantees delivery of data by using acknowledgements and windowing.

Trivial File Transfer Protocol (TFTP)

A protocol that allows transferring of data using the User Datagram Protocol (UDP). However, it does not provide any security features. It is often used by servers to boot diskless workstations or upload and download images and configurations to routers and firewalls. TFTP is typically used on trusted parts of a network.

trojan horse

A destructive program disguised as a normal, safe application. Trojan horses do not usually replicate themselves like viruses do; however, they can be just as destructive.

tunnel mode

Tunnel mode transports packets between two networks by encapsulating that data. Tunnel mode refers to encapsulating data from one point to another. IPSec can use either tunnel mode or transport mode. Tunnel mode is commonly used for site-to-site VPNs, whereas transport mode is typically used for remote access.

Turbo ACLs

Turbo ACLs decrease the time it takes to scan through large access lists by compiling them and creating an index of the list. Turbo ACLs are not supported on the PIX 501 because of their memory requirement.

unprivileged mode

This is the first access mode you come to when entering the CLI, and it allows only a very small subset of the available commands.

unstructured threats

Unstructured threats caused by individuals commonly known as *script kiddies*. These are people who are not skilled in hacking but who can do damage by using prebuilt tools, programs, or scripts readily available on the Internet to launch attacks.

URL filtering

An integrated feature that allows the PIX firewall to work with content filtering services. These services allow the capturing of World Wide Web requests to support the enforcement of policies or monitoring of user traffic.

User Datagram Protocol (UDP)

UDP is a connectionless layer 4 transport protocol. This protocol does not use acknowledgments or sessions like TCP does and lacks guaranteed delivery of data. However, UDP is fast and commonly used by multimedia applications.

Virtual HTTP

Allows browser and Web server authentication to work correctly with the PIX when authentication with the cut-through proxy is problematic.

virtual private network (VPN)

A method of encapsulating traffic to traverse a common media in a secure manner. Several types of VPNs exist, including IPSec, PPTP, and L2TP, to name a few.

virtual Telnet

Allows users to preauthenticate using a virtual Telnet session before executing the application that needs to pass through the PIX. Typically, it's used when nonstandard port access is needed. HTTP, FTP, and Telnet are the standard ports.

virus

A piece of code or program that has been loaded on a computer that runs against your will, possibly causing damage.

Voice of IP (VoIP)

A method of using hardware and software to enable communication, such as telephone calls, across IP networks.

VPN accelerator card (VAC)

The Cisco PIX firewall is a hardware-based accelerator designed to provide higher-performance tunneling and encryption for DES and 3DES by offloading the encryption processing to the VPN accelerator card.

well-known ports

A set of ports ranging from 1 to 1,023 that are reserved for specific TCP/IP protocols and services.

wide area network (WAN)

This connects two sites by using the layer 2 protocol to transmit data.

Index

Symbols

3DES (Triple Data Encryption Standard) activation keys, PDM installations, 310

A

AAA (authentication, authorization, and accounting) services, 216

accounting

  component, 217

  configuring, 229

additional resources, 239

administrator management features, 216

authentication

  component, 217

  configuring, 224-225

  cut-through proxy, 226-228

  prompts, 233

  timeouts, 233

authorization

  component, 217

  configuring, 225-226

  cut-through proxy, 228

commands

  clear aaa, 232

  clear uauth, 232

  show aaa, 232

  show aaa-server, 232

  show uauth, 232

configuring usernames, 221-223

exam prep questions, 234-238

group tags, location configuration, 223-224

protocols

  RADIUS, 217-218

  TACACS+, 217-219

support servers, Cisco Secure Access Control Server (CSACS), 219-221

aaa-authentication command, 224-225

aaa-server command, location options, 223-224

AAA Floodguard, authentication request flooding, 204-205

absolute timeouts, 233

access attacks, 12

  denial-of-service (DoS), 13

  distributed denial-of-service (DDoS), 13

Q - R

How can we make this index more useful? Email us at indexes@quepublishing.com

What if Que

joined forces to deliver the best technology books in a common digital reference platform?

We have. Introducing
InformIT Online Books
powered by Safari.

POWERED BY
InformIT
Online Books Safari

- **Specific answers to specific questions.**
InformIT Online Books' powerful search engine gives you relevance-ranked results in a matter of seconds.

- **Immediate results.**
With InformIt Online Books, you can select the book you want and view the chapter or section you need immediately.

- **Cut, paste, and annotate.**
Paste code to save time and eliminate typographical errors. Make notes on the material you find useful and choose whether or not to share them with your workgroup.

- **Customized for your enterprise.**
Customize a library for you, your department, or your entire organization. You pay only for what you need.

As an InformIT partner, Que has shared the knowledge and hands-on advice of our authors with you online. Visit InformIT.com to see what you are missing.

informit.com/onlinebooks

Get your first 14 days FREE!

InformIT Online Books is offering its members a 10-book subscription risk free for 14 days.
Visit **http://www.informit.com/onlinebooks** for details.

inform**IT**

www.informit.com

Your Guide to Information Technology Training and Reference

Que has partnered with **InformIT.com** to bring technical information to your desktop. Drawing on Que authors and reviewers to provide additional information on topics you're interested in, **InformIT.com** has free, in-depth information you won't find anywhere else.

Articles

Keep your edge with thousands of free articles, in-depth features, interviews, and information technology reference recommendations – all written by experts you know and trust.

Online Books

Answers in an instant from **InformIT Online Books'** 600+ fully searchable online books. Sign up now and get your first 14 days **free**.

Catalog

Review online sample chapters and author biographies to choose exactly the right book from a selection of more than 5,000 titles.

As an **InformIT** partner, **Que** has shared the knowledge and hands-on advice of our authors with you online. Visit **InformIT.com** to see what you are missing.

www.quepublishing.com

Get Certified!

You have the experience and the training — now demonstrate your expertise and get the recognition your skills deserve. An IT certification increases your credibility in the marketplace and is tangible evidence that you have the know-how to provide top-notch support to your employer.

Why Test with VUE?

Using the speed and reliability of the Internet, the most advanced technology and our commitment to unparalleled service, VUE provides a quick, flexible way to meet your testing needs.

Three easy ways to register for your next exam, all in real time:

- Register online at www.vue.com
- Contact your local VUE testing center. There are over 3000 quality VUE testing centers in more than 130 countries. Visit www.vue.com for the location of a center near you.
- Call a VUE call center. In North America, call toll-free 800-TEST-NOW (800-837-8734). For a complete listing of worldwide call center telephone numbers, visit www.vue.com.

Call your local VUE testing center and ask about TESTNOW!™ same-day exam registration!

The VUE testing system is built with the best technology and backed by even better service. Your exam will be ready when you expect it and your results will be quickly and accurately transmitted to the testing sponsor. Test with confidence!

Visit www.vue.com for a complete listing of IT certification exams offered by VUE

When IT really matters... Test with VUE!

CramSession

– the difference between Pass ... or Fail

"On top of everything else, I find the best deals on training products and services for our CramSession members".

Jami Costin,
Product Specialist

CramSession.com is #1 for IT Certification on the 'Net.

There's no better way to prepare for success in the IT Industry. Find the best IT certification study materials and technical information at CramSession. Find a community of hundreds of thousands of IT Pros just like you who help each other pass exams, solve real-world problems, and discover friends and peers across the globe.

CramSession – #1 Rated Certification Site!

- *#1 by TechRepublic.com*
- *#1 by TechTarget.com*
- *#1 by CertMag's Guide to Web Resources.*

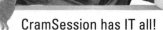

CramSession has IT all!

- **The #1 study guides on the 'Net.** With over 250 study guides for IT certification exams, we are the web site every techie visits before passing an IT certification exam.

- **Practice questions.** Get the answers and explanations with our CramChallenge practice questions delivered to you daily.

- **The most popular IT Forums.** Cramsession has over 400 discussion boards loaded with certification infomation where our subscribers study hard, work hard, and play harder.

- **e-Newsletters.** Our IT e-Newsletters are written by techs for techs: IT certification, technology, humor, career and more.

- **Technical Papers and Product Reviews.** Find thousands of technical articles and whitepapers written by industry leaders, trainers, and IT veterans.

- **Exam reviews.** Get the inside scoop before you take that expensive certification exam.

- **And so much more!**

Visit Cramsession.com today!
...and take advantage of the best IT learning resources.

CramSession
Prepare for Success!

www.cramsession.com